A Future for Capitalism

A Future for Capitalism

Classical, Neoclassical and Keynesian Perspectives

Peter Flaschel
Professor of Economics
Bielefeld University, Germany

Alfred Greiner
Professor of Economics
Bielefeld University, Germany

Edward Elgar
Cheltenham, UK • Northampton, MA, USA

Published by
Edward Elgar Publishing Limited
The Lypiatts
15 Lansdown Road
Cheltenham
Glos GL50 2JA
UK

Edward Elgar Publishing, Inc.
William Pratt House
9 Dewey Court
Northampton
Massachusetts 01060
USA

A catalogue record for this book
is available from the British Library

Library of Congress Control Number: 2011924195

ISBN 978 1 84980 855 2

Printed and bound by MPG Books Group, UK

Contents

Notations

Steady state or trend values are indicated by a sub(super)script 'o' or superscript $*$. When no confusion arises, letters F, G, H define certain functional expressions in a specific context. Moreover there is some 'local' notation which only applies to certain chapters of the book. A dot over a variable $x = x(t)$ denotes the time derivative, a caret its growth rate; $\dot{x} = dx/dt$, $\hat{x} = \dot{x}/x$.

As far as possible, the notation tries to follow the logic of using capital letters for level variables and lower case letters for variables in intensive form, or for constant (steady state) ratios. Greek letters are most often constant coefficients in behavioral equations (with, however, the notable exceptions being the π's, and ω).

B	outstanding government fixed-price bonds (priced at $p_b = 1$)
C	real private consumption (demand is generally realized)
E	number of equities
F	neoclassical production function
	otherwise generic symbol for functions defined in a local context
G	real government expenditure (demand is always realized)
I	real net investment of fixed capital (demand is always realized)
$\mathcal{I}$	desired real inventory investment
J	Jacobian matrix in the mathematical analysis
K	stock of fixed capital
L^d	employment, i.e., total working hours per year (labor demand is always realized)
L^w	employed workforce, i.e., number of employed people
L	labor supply, i.e., supply of total working hours per year
M	stock of money supply
N	inventories of finished goods
N^d	desired stock of inventories

S_f	real saving of firms
S_g	real government saving
S_p	real saving of private households
S	total real saving; $S = S_f + S_g + S_h$
T	total real tax collections
$T_w(t_w)$	real taxes of workers (per unit of capital)
$T_c(t_c)$	real taxes of asset holders (per unit of capital)
W	real wealth of private households
Y	real output
Y^p	potential real output
Y^f	full employment real output
Y^d	real aggregate demand
Y^e	expected real aggregate demand
c	marginal propensity to consume
e	employment rate
$U = 1 - e$	unemployment rate
$f_x = f_1$ *etc.*	partial derivative
i	nominal rate of interest on government bonds
m	real balances relative to the capital stock; $m = M/pK$
ν	inventory–capital ratio; $n = N/K$
p	price level
p_e	price of equities
q	return differential; $q = r - (i - \pi^c)$ or Tobin's q r rate of return on fixed capital, specified as $r = (pY - wL - \delta pK)/pK$
s_c	propensity to save out of capital income on the part of asset owners
$s = s_w$	workers' propensity to save out of their income
u	rate of capacity utilization; $u = Y/Y^n = y/y^n$
v	wage share (in gross product); $v = wL/pY$
w	nominal wage rate per hour
y	output–capital ratio; $y = Y/K$;
	except in Chapter 8.3 and Chapter 10.3, where y denotes the output gap
y^d	ratio of aggregate demand to capital stock; $y^d = Y^d/K$
y^e	ratio of expected demand to capital stock; $y^e = Y^e/K$
y^n	normal output–capital ratio (a constant; no recourse to a neoclassical production function)
l	labor intensity (in efficiency units)
k	capital intensity K/L

z or x	labor productivity, i.e., output per worker; $z = Y/L^d$
β_x	generically, reaction coefficient in an equation determining x, $\dot{x}$ or $\hat{x}$
β_y	adjustment speed in adaptive sales expectations
β_{π^c}	general adjustment speed in revisions of the inflation climate
β_{xy}	generically, reaction coefficient related to the determination of variable x, $\dot{x}$ or $\hat{x}$ with respect to changes in the exogenous variable y
α_x	responsiveness of investment (capital growth rate) to changes in x
α_{n^d}	desired ratio of inventories over expected sales
β_{pu}	reaction coefficient of u in price Phillips curve
β_{pv}	reaction coefficient of $(1+\mu)v - 1$ in price Phillips curve
β_{we}	reaction coefficient of e in wage Phillips curve
β_{wv}	reaction coefficient of $(v - v^o)/v^o$ in wage Phillips curve
γ	government expenditures per unit of fixed capital; $\gamma = G/K$ (a constant)
τ	lump sum taxes per unit of fixed capital; $\tau = T/K$ (a constant)
δ	rate of depreciation of fixed capital (a constant)
$\eta_{m,i}$	interest elasticity of money demand (expressed as a positive number)
κ	coefficient in reduced-form wage–price equations; $\kappa = 1/(1 - \kappa_p\kappa_w)$
κ_p	parameter weighting $\hat{w}$ vs. π^c in price Phillips curve
κ_w	parameter weighting $\hat{p}$ vs. π^c in wage Phillips curve
$A = 1 + a$	actual markup rate
π^c	general inflation climate;
$\tau_c = T_c/K$	tax parameter for T^c (net of interest and per unit of capital); $T^c - iB/p$
τ_w	tax rate on wages
ω	real wage rate w/p

General Introduction

This book builds on the M(arx)–K(eynes)–S(chumpeter) approach to the understanding and further evolution of capitalism, the foundations of which we have laid in Flaschel and Greiner (2011a). It does so in a self-contained way by now focusing on current approaches to the study of macrodynamical systems in the tradition of the classical, the neoclassical and the Keynesian interpretation of the working of modern capitalist economies and the societies that are built on them. Instead of trying to combine important elements of the theories of Marx (1954), Keynes (1936) and Schumpeter (1942) into a coherent whole we now focus on different paradigms of economic theorizing in their applicability to an understanding of primarily labor market problems and their cure in the context of growing economies. These approaches have their formal point of departure in the tradition of Goodwin (1967) type models of classical growth, Solow (1956) type models of neoclassical growth and Harrod (1939)–Domar (1946) type models of Keynesian growth.

In the first tradition we study (in Part II) forms of the Marxian reserve army mechanism, the creation of mass unemployment when the profitability of capitalist economies is endangered by a profit squeeze. We do this first against the background of the Ricardian theory of capital accumulation, by showing the limitations of this approach as compared to the classical growth cycle model of Richard Goodwin (1967). On this basis we then develop a distributive cycle approach with recurrent phases of mass unemployment, basic elements of social security, minimum wages as well as basic income guarantees, where the employment decision of the firms is characterized by complete flexibility in the sense of free hiring and firing of employees. We then study in this context the occurrence of low income work (atypical employment) and, thus, situations of segmented labor markets and their consequences for the well-being of the workers at the lower end of the labor market hierarchy when there is no protection by means of minimum wages for them.

In a next step such minimum wages as well as basic income guarantees are again introduced and shown to be beneficial for the working of the economy after some temporary adjustment processes. This situation is extended by allowing for a neoclassical production function with smooth factor substitution – in place of the so far used fixed proportions in production – and shown to be valid also in such a case, where neoclassical economists would claim that factor substitution would work to the disadvantage of the low income workers and their employment situation in the case of minimum wages.

In sum, our classical approach in Part II of the book demonstrates that classical supply side dynamics need not bring about the economic consequences asserted by most academic writers and politicians in the public discussion of a general minimum wage legislation. The future of capitalism is not endangered by these basic changes in the social structure of accumulation, but – as this part shows – in fact improved by it, both from the economic as well as from the social point of view.

With respect to the second tradition, in Part III we analyze neoclassical models of endogenous growth where particular attention is paid to unemployment and welfare issues of public policies. To do so we consider three different prototype models of endogenous growth where we allow for unemployment. In the first model, we assume that ongoing growth results from positive externalities of investment that prevent the marginal product of capital from declining as capital grows. We first study the structure of this model, and then analyze how taxation and different degrees of flexibility on the labor market affect the economy.

In the second model, sustained growth results from investment in human capital where we allow for heterogenous agents with one type of individuals acquiring skills through higher education whereas the second type of individuals remains low-skilled. Both types of individuals may be subject to unemployment and receive unemployment benefits in case they lose their jobs. Higher education is financed by the government that hires teachers and uses additional spending for the education of students. Growth and welfare effects of different fiscal policies are analyzed for that model type and we derive effects of different degrees of labor market flexibility.

The last model, finally, posits that investment in a public capital stock generates endogenous growth where the government may finance its expenditures by taxes or by issuing government bonds. Again, labor may become unemployed and the government pays unemployment subsidies. The analysis studies different policy rules where special attention is paid to debt policy. In particular the outcome of a balanced budget scenario is compared to that where the government runs permanent deficits.

Finally, working in the third (Keynesian) tradition in fact means that both the classical as well as the neoclassical perspective on economic growth and the business fluctuations which are surrounding it are or can be augmented in an important way, simply by introducing the Keynesian concept of effective goods demand into their supply side orientation and also by embedding into the demand side extension the working of financial markets in the form of a Tobin (1982) portfolio approach as the necessary extension of the Keynesian theory of liquidity preference. The Keynesian approach is therefore in its nature more an (important) extension of the other ones than an alternative to them in line with what is claimed in the title of Keynes's (1936) book.

In Part IV of the book we are laying the foundations for the ideal Keynesian approach to flexi(ble-sec)curity capitalism. We present and analyze the baseline model of a supply-driven flexicurity economy against the background of a Goodwin Kalecki welfare economy (and its breakdown after the prosperity phase following World War II). We show the stability and the sustainability of such an institutional framework, with first and second (but not segmented) labor markets, by including pension fund accumulation as well as credit supply out of such funds. This situation is then extended towards the treatment of neoclassical smooth factor substitution implying that the possibility to substitute labor through capital does not change this framework very much. In place of the segmented labor markets of Part II of the book we also study here the interrelationships between labor markets for skilled and high-skilled employees and the educational system on which such a distinction is based.

The first three chapters of Part IV consider from various outlooks the problems caused by Keynesian demand rationing, yet do so in a way that does not fully integrate the financial markets of a general Keynesian approach as we have investigated it in the introductory Chapter 1, in order to provide a baseline model of unleashed capitalism and its various destabilizing feedback chains within and between the real and the financial markets. It is the task of the final chapter of the book to integrate the approach to a flexicurity system of Part IV into such a framework in order to provide a full employment scenario also in a fully-fledged model of Keynesian real financial market interactions. In this chapter we therefore add significant labor market reforms to the welfare measures of Part II and to the reformulations of monetary and fiscal policy measures of Chapter 1, which are also further discussed in this final chapter.

In this book the Keynesian approach is therefore used on two levels. In Part I of the book we use it to study the basic stabilizing and destabilizing forces of the current form of an unleashed capitalism as well as basic possibilities of fiscal, monetary and labor market policies appropriate to tame the in general dominant destabilizing features of this unleashed form of capitalism. In the final chapter of the book we then go on from this discussion to the implementation of the far-reaching labor market reforms we have been suggesting and analyzed in the first three chapters of Part IV.

The final chapter, therefore, shows that the construction of a full-employment economy by suitable labor market reforms is a viable strategy in the context of a complete Keynesian model of the real financial market interaction and can make such an economy not only a stable one (also by suitably chosen monetary and fiscal policy rules), but also one where the distributive cycle that we have investigated in detail in Part II can be controlled through the establishment of a corporatist regime between capital and labor, founded on labor market institutions and employment decisions that are not only flexible, but also offer employment guarantees (not job guarantees) on the basis of the principle of an employer of first resort (EFR). While Part I may be describing the status quo of current capitalist economies, the final chapter is therefore providing the ideal of a full employment market economy with a full interaction of financial, goods and labor markets as described in Keynes's (1936) General Theory and in Chapter 1. Reform proposals for actual economies are then always a compromise between what we have studied in Chapter 1 and have proposed as alternatives in Chapter 11 of the book. Summing up, the book provides an important and new approach for the study of the future of capitalism, a topic that has never been more urgent than in the current times after World War II. The scope of the book is aimed at providing an alternative to the often very narrow discussions of current forms of capitalism which focus too much on the current status quo of such economies instead of providing an ideal scenario on the basis of which compromises between the status quo and the ideal can only be discussed in a meaningful way.

The book therefore represents a novel approach to the macroeconomics of capitalist societies, an approach which we believe is urgently needed in the present situation of a new classical/New Keynesian macroeconomic consensus theory that is exclusively focussed on representative economic agents in place of principal agent relationships, market-clearing in place of the study of gradual adjustment processes to such equilibrium positions and, above all, purely forward-looking and extremely perfect 'rational expectations' in place of agents with different (heterogenous) expectations formation (also of the animal spirit type).

The modeling approaches chosen in this book are, on the one hand, certainly of an advanced type, which are fully usable at the post-graduate level of economic teaching, in particular when compared with the New Keynesian ones. The chapters of the book are fairly self-contained and therefore can by and large be used as teaching material and read independently of each other. They represent a unique approach to macrodynamic theorizing, rooted in the initially discussed MKS tradition of the understanding of the growth dynamics of capitalist economies. The material of the book is, on the other hand, not only clearly related to current macroeconomic research which goes beyond the New Consensus macroeconomics but can also be related to the discussion between practitioners and politicians on the reform of the financial as well as the labor markets. This holds true in particular within the European community where the future of capitalism is more clearly related to significant labor market reforms than is the case in the USA and the rest of the world.

A number of professional colleagues, too numerous to name here, have contributed to the present project through stimulating discussions on various aspects of the subject matter of this book as well as on related research projects. We are also grateful for comments and criticisms we have received from participants at presentations of aspects of the material of this book at numerous international conferences and research seminars. Of course, we alone are responsible for the remaining errors in this work. We also wish to thank Uwe Köller for his excellent editorial work. Finally we would like to thank Matthew Pitman of Edward Elgar for all he has done to make the publication process go as smoothly as it has.

Bielefeld, February 2010

Peter Flaschel
Alfred Greiner

PART I

Stabilizing an Unstable Economy: The Challenge in Place

1. Real–Financial Market Interactions and the Choice of Policy Measures

> *As we approach the last decade of the twentieth century, our economic world is in apparent disarray. After two secure decades of tranquil progress following World War II, in the late 1960s the order of the day became turbulence – both domestic and international. Bursts of accelerating inflation, higher chronic and higher cyclical unemployment, bankruptcies, crunching interest rates, and crises in energy, transportation, food supply, welfare, the cities, and banking were mixed with periods of troubled expansions. The economic and social policy synthesis that served us so well after World War II broke down in the mid-1960s. What is needed now is a new approach, a policy synthesis fundamentally different from the mix that results when today's accepted theory is applied to today's economic system.* (Minsky 1982, p.3)

1.1 Introduction

The impact of a financial market crisis on the real side of the economy has been studied for many years.[1] Extensive work has been undertaken to understand the Asian currency and financial crises in the years 1997/98 as well as the stock market meltdown after the burst of the IT asset price bubble. Yet, the current financial crisis is less well understood. It seems to be neither a financial crisis triggered by a currency run, nor by the burst of a technology bubble, but rather a crisis originating in the financial market in one of the most advanced countries of the world economy, the USA. It appears to have resulted from two driving forces: macroeconomic changes (low interest rates, high liquidity, easy credit, and external imbalance) and the use of new financial innovations which substantially contributed to increase leveraging and drive up asset prices. Yet, conclusive studies on the recent financial market meltdown are still missing.[2]

The financial crisis, that started in the US subprime sector, has spread worldwide as a great recession. A hyperactive monetary and fiscal policy since the end of 2007 has aimed at preventing a further financial meltdown in the advanced countries. Some observers maintain that a slow recovery appears to be on the horizon. Nevertheless, it is worthwhile exploring the fragility and potentially destabilizing feedbacks of advanced macroeconomies in the context of Keynesian macro models. Further macroeconomic work is needed. As the history of macroeconomic dynamics and business cycles – which recently have been developed as boom–bust cycles – has taught us, fragilities and destabilizing feedbacks are known to be potential features of all markets – the product markets, the labor market, and the financial markets.

In this chapter we will focus on the financial market. We use a Tobin type of macroeconomic portfolio approach, coupled with the interaction of heterogeneous agents on the financial market, to characterize the potentials for financial market instability. Though the study of the latter has been undertaken in many partial models, we focus here on the interconnectedness of all three markets. Furthermore, we study what potentials labor market, fiscal and monetary policies can have in stabilizing unstable macroeconomies. It was Hyman Minsky (1982) in particular who put forward many ideas on how to to stabilize an unstable economy. Besides other stabilizing policies we propose in particular a countercyclical monetary policy that sells assets in the boom and purchases assets in recessions. Modern dynamic and stability analyses are brought to bear to demonstrate the stabilizing effects of those suggested policies.

The chapter provides a starting point for the proper design of a macrodynamic framework and labor market, fiscal and monetary policies in a framework which allows in general for large swings in financial and real economic activities. It builds on baseline models of the dynamic interaction of labor market, product market and financial markets with risky assets. We revive a framework of a macroeconomic portfolio approach that Tobin (1969, 1980) has suggested, but that also builds on recent work on the interaction of heterogeneous agents in the financial market.[3] We allow for heterogeneity in share and goods price expectations and study the financial, nominal and real cumulative feedback chains that may give rise to the potential of an unstable economy. The work connects to traditional Keynesian business cycle analysis as Tobin, Minsky and Akerlof have suggested.

The remainder is organized as follows. Sections 1.2 and 1.3 provide the modules of a portfolio approach to Keynesian business cycle theory. Though the portfolio approach can be stabilizing if gross substitution of assets is allowed for, it can generate fragile dynamics and destabilizing potentials through expected asset price dynamics. This is briefly moooted in Section 1.4 and illustrated from the numerical perspective in Section 1.5. Section 1.6 studies labor market and fiscal policies that give rise to stabilizing feedbacks channels powerful enough to stabilize an unstable private sector of the economy. Section 1.7 shows the same for monetary policies. It proposes a new form of monetary policy that is not concerned with interest rates, but with countercyclical selling and buying of financial assets, a policy that the US Fed in fact has undertaken and which is, in spirit, close to Minsky's (1982) ideas. Section 1.8 concludes.

1.2 Keynesian Business Cycles: A Portfolio Approach

In the tradition of Tobin (1969, 1980) we will depart from standard theory and provide the structural form of a growth model using a portfolio approach and building in heterogeneous agents' behavior on asset markets.[4] In order to discuss details we split the model into appropriate modules that refer to the sectors of the economy, namely households, firms, and the government (fiscal and monetary authority). Besides presenting a detailed structure of the asset market, we also represent the wage–price interactions, and connect the financial market to the labor and product market dynamics.

Households

In the following we solely use the aggregate $M_2 = M + B$ of money supply M and short-term bond supply B and postpone the discussion of its composition M, B to the section on the proper choice of monetary policy.

As discussed in the introduction we disaggregate the sector of households into worker households and asset holder households. We begin with the description of the behavior of workers:

Worker households:

$$\omega = w/p, \tag{1.1}$$
$$C_w = (1-\tau_w)\omega L^d, \tag{1.2}$$
$$S_w = 0, \tag{1.3}$$
$$\hat{L} = n = \text{ const.} \tag{1.4}$$

Equation (1.1) gives the definition of the real wage ω before taxation, where w denotes the nominal wage and p the actual price level. We operate in a Keynesian framework with sluggish wage and price adjustment processes. We follow the Keynesian framework by assuming that the labor demand of firms can always be satisfied out of the given labor supply.[5] Then, according to (1.2), real income of workers equals the product of real wages times labor demand, which net of taxes $\tau_w\omega L^d$, equals workers' consumption, since we do not allow for savings of the workers as postulated in (1.3).[6] No savings implies that the wealth of workers is zero at every point in time. This in particular means that the workers do not hold any assets and that they consume instantaneously their disposable income. As is standard in theories of economic growth, we finally assume in equation (1.4) a constant growth rate n of the labor force L based on the assumption that labor is supplied inelastically at each moment in time. The parameter n can be easily reinterpreted to be the growth rate of the working population plus the growth rate of labor augmenting technical progress.

The income, consumption and wealth of the asset holders are described by the following set of equations:

Asset–holder households:

$$r_k^e = (Y^e - \delta K - \omega L^d)/K, \tag{1.5}$$
$$C_c = (1-s_c)[r_k^e K + iB/p - T_c], \quad 0 < s_c < 1, \tag{1.6}$$
$$S_p = s_c[r_k^e K + iB/p - T_c] \tag{1.7}$$
$$= (\dot{M} + \dot{B} + p_e\dot{E})/p, \tag{1.8}$$
$$W_c = (M + B + p_e E)/p, \quad W_c^n = pW_c. \tag{1.9}$$

The first equation (1.5) of this module of the model defines the expected rate of return on real capital r_k^e to be the ratio of the currently expected real cash flow and the real stock of business fixed capital K. The expected cash flow is given by expected real revenues from sales Y^e

diminished by real depreciation of capital δK and the real wage sum ωL^d. We assume that firms pay out all expected cash flow in the form of dividends to the asset holders. These dividend payments are one source of income for asset holders. The second source is given by real interest payments on short-term bonds (iB/p) where i is the nominal interest rate and B the stock of such bonds. Summing up these types of interest incomes and taking account of lump sum taxes T_c in the case of asset holders (for reasons of simplicity) we obtain the disposable income of asset holders given by the terms in the square brackets of equation (1.6), which together with a postulated fixed propensity to consume $(1 - s_c)$ out of this income gives us the real consumption of asset holders.

Real savings of pure asset owners is real disposable income minus their consumption as exposed in equation (1.7). The asset owners can allocate the real savings in the form of money $\dot{M}$, or buy other financial assets, namely short-term bonds $\dot{B}$ or equities $\dot{E}$ at the price p_e, the only financial instruments that we allow for in the present reformulation of the Keynes–Metzler–Goodwin (KMG) growth model. Hence, the savings of asset holders must be distributed to these assets as stated in equation (1.8). Real wealth of pure asset holders is thus defined in equation (1.9) as the sum of the real cash balance, real short-term bond holdings and real equity holdings of asset holders. Note that the short-term bonds are assumed to be fixed price bonds with a price of one, $p_b = 1$, and a flexible interest rate i.

Next we introduce portfolio holdings to be described as follows. Following the general equilibrium approach of Tobin (1969) we can express the demand equations of asset-owning households for financial assets as:

$$M^d = f_m(i, r_e^e)W_c^n, \tag{1.10}$$

$$B^d = f_b(i, r_e^e)W_c^n, \tag{1.11}$$

$$p_e E^d = f_e(i, r_e^e)W_c^n, \tag{1.12}$$

$$W_c^n = M^d + B^d + p_e E^d. \tag{1.13}$$

The demand for money balances of asset holders M^d is determined by a function $f_m(i, r_e^e)$ which depends on the interest rate on short-run bonds i and the expected rate of return on equities r_e^e. The value of this function times the nominal wealth W^n gives the nominal demand for money M^d, so that f_m describes the portion of nominal wealth that is allocated to pure money holdings. Note that this formulation of money demand is not based on a transaction motive, since the holding of transaction balances will be the job of firms.

We do not assume that the financial assets of the economy are perfect substitutes, but make the assumption that financial assets are imperfect substitutes. This is implicit in the approach that underlies the above block of equations. But what is the motive for asset holders to hold a fraction of their wealth in form of money, when there is a riskless interest bearing asset? In our view it is reasonable to employ a speculative motive: asset holders want to hold money in order to be able to buy other assets or goods with zero or very low transaction costs. This of course assumes that there are (implicitly given) transaction costs when fixed price bonds are turned into money.[7]

The nominal demand for bonds is determined by $f_b(i, r_e^e)$ and the nominal demand for equities by $f_e(i, r_e^e)$, which again are functions that describe the fractions that are allocated to these forms of financial wealth. From equation (1.9) we know that actual nominal wealth equals the stocks of financial assets held by the asset holders. We assume, as is usual in portfolio approaches, that the asset holders demand assets of an amount that equals in sum their nominal wealth as stated in equation (1.9). In other words, they just reallocate their wealth in view of new information on the rates of returns on their assets and take account of their wealth constraint.

What remains to be modeled in the household sector is the expected rate of return on equities r_e^e which, as usual, consists of real dividends per unit of equity $(r_k^e pK/p_e E)$, and expected capital gains, π_e, the latter being nothing other than the expected growth rate of equity prices. Thus we can write

$$r_e^e = \frac{r_k^e pK}{p_e E} + \pi_e. \tag{1.14}$$

In order to complete the modeling of asset-holders' behavior, we need to describe the evolution of π_e. In the tradition of recent work on heterogeneous agents in asset markets, we here assume that there are two types of asset holders, who differ with respect to their expectation formation of equity prices.[8] There are behavioral traders, called 'chartists' who in principle employ an adaptive expectations mechanism

$$\dot{\pi}_{ec} = \beta_{\pi_{ec}}(\hat{p}_e - \pi_{ec}), \tag{1.15}$$

where $\beta_{\pi_{ec}}$ is the adjustment speed towards the actual growth rate of equity prices. The other asset holders, the fundamentalists, employ a forward looking expectation formation mechanism

$$\dot{\pi}_{ef} = \beta_{\pi_{ef}}(\eta - \pi_{ef}), \tag{1.16}$$

where η is the fundamentalists' expected long-run growth rate of share prices. Assuming that the aggregate expected rate of share price increase is a weighted average of the two expected rates, where the weights are determined according to the size of the groups, we postulate

$$\pi_e = \alpha_{\pi_{ec}}\pi_{ec} + (1 - \alpha_{\pi_{ec}})\pi_{ef}. \tag{1.17}$$

Here $\alpha_{\pi_{ec}} \in (0, 1)$ is the ratio of chartists to all asset holders.

Firms

We consider the behavior of firms by means of two submodules. The first describes the production framework and their investment in business fixed capital and the second introduces the Metzlerian approach of inventory dynamics concerning expected sales, actual sales and the output of firms

Firms: production and investment

$$r_k^e = (pY^e - wL^d - p\delta K)/(pK), \tag{1.18}$$
$$Y^p = y^p K, \tag{1.19}$$
$$u = Y/Y^p, \tag{1.20}$$
$$L^d = Y/x, \tag{1.21}$$
$$e = L^d/L = Y/(xL), \tag{1.22}$$
$$q = p_e E/(pK), \tag{1.23}$$
$$I = i_q(q - 1)K + i_u(u - \bar{u})K + nK, \tag{1.24}$$
$$\hat{K} = I/K, \tag{1.25}$$
$$p_e \dot{E} = pI + p(\dot{N} - \mathcal{I}). \tag{1.26}$$

Firms are assumed to pay out dividends according to expected profits (expected sales net of depreciation and minus the wage sum), see the above module of the asset-owning households. The rate of expected profits r_k^e is expected real profits per unit of capital as stated in equation (1.18). Firms produce output utilizing a production technology that transforms demanded labor L^d combined with business fixed capital K into output. For convenience we assume that the production takes place with a fixed proportion technology[9]. According to (1.19) potential output Y^p is given at each moment of time by a fixed coefficient y^p times the existing stock of physical capital. Accordingly, the utilization of productive capacities is given by the ratio u of actual production Y and the potential output Y^p. The fixed proportions in production give rise to a constant output–labor coefficient x, by means of which we can deduce labor demand from goods market determined output as in equation (1.21). The ratio L^d/L thus defines the rate of employment in the model.

The economic behavior of firms must include their investment decision with regard to business fixed capital, which is determined independently of the savings decision of households. We here model investment decisions per unit of capital as a function of the deviation of Tobin's q, see Tobin (1969), from its long-run value 1,[10] and the deviation of actual capacity utilization from a normal rate of capital utilization. We add an exogenously given trend term, here given by the natural growth rate n in order to allow this rate to determine the growth path of the economy in the usual way. We employ here Tobin's average q which is defined in equation (1.23). It is the ratio of the nominal value of equities and the reproduction costs for the existing stock of capital. Investment in business fixed capital is reinforced when q exceeds one, and is reduced when q is smaller than one. This influence is represented by the term $i_q(q-1)$ in equation (1.24).

The term $i_u(u-\bar{u})$ models the component of investment which is due to the deviation of utilization rate of physical capital from its non-accelerating inflation value $\bar{u}$. The last component, nK, takes account of the natural growth rate n which is necessary for steady state analysis if natural growth is considered as exogenously given. Equation (1.26) is the budget constraint of the firms. Investment in business fixed capital and unintended changes in the inventory stock $p(\dot{N}-\mathcal{I})$ must be financed by issuing equities, since equities are the only financial instrument of firms in this chapter. Capital stock growth finally is given by net investment per unit of capital I/K in this demand-determined model of the short-run equilibrium position of the economy.

Next we model the inventory dynamics following Metzler (1941) and Franke (1996). This approach is a very useful concept for describing the goods market disequilibrium dynamics with all of its implications.

Firms' output adjustment:

$$N^d = \alpha_{n^d} Y^e, \tag{1.27}$$
$$\mathcal{I} = nN^d + \beta_n(N^d - N), \tag{1.28}$$
$$Y = Y^e + \mathcal{I}, \tag{1.29}$$
$$Y^d = C + I + \delta K + G, \tag{1.30}$$
$$\dot{Y}^e = nY^e + \beta_{y^e}(Y^d - Y^e), \tag{1.31}$$
$$\dot{N} = Y - Y^d, \tag{1.32}$$
$$S_f = Y - Y^e = \mathcal{I}, \tag{1.33}$$

where $\alpha_{n^d}, \beta_n, \beta_{y^e} \geq 0$.

Equation (1.27) states that the desired stock of physical inventories, denoted by N^d, is assumed to be a fixed proportion of the expected sales. The planned investments $\mathcal{I}$ in inventories follow a sluggish adjustment process toward the desired stock N^d according to equation (1.28). Taking account of this additional demand for goods, equation (1.29) writes the production Y as equal to the expected sales of firms plus $\mathcal{I}$. To explain the expectation formation for goods demand, we need the actual total demand for goods which in (1.30) is given by consumption (of private households and the government) and gross investment by firms.

From a knowledge of the actual demand Y^d, which is always satisfied, the dynamics of expected sales is given in equation (1.31). It models these expectations to be the outcome of an error correction process, that also incorporates the natural growth rate n in order take account of the fact that this process operates in a growing economy. The adjustment of sales expectations is driven by the prediction error $Y^d - Y^e$, with an adjustment speed that is given by β_{y^e}. Actual changes in the stock of inventories are given in (1.32) by the deviation of production from goods demanded.

The savings of the firms S_f is as usual defined by income minus consumption. Because firms are assumed to not consume anything, their income equals their savings and is given by the excess of production over expected sales, $Y - Y^e$. According to the production account in Table 1.1 the gross accounting profit of firms finally is $r_k^e pK + p\mathcal{I} = pC + pI + p\delta K + p\dot{N} + pG$. Substituting in the definition of r_k^e from equation (1.18), we compute that $pY^e + p\mathcal{I} = pY^d + p\dot{N}$ or equivalently $(Y - Y^e) = \mathcal{I}$ as stated in equation (1.33).

Table 1.1: The four activity accounts of the firms

Uses	Resources
Production Account of Firms:	
depreciation $p\delta K$	private consumption pC
wages wL^d	gross investment $pI + p\delta K$
gross accounting profits $\Pi = r_k^e pK + p\mathcal{I}$	inventory investment $p\dot{N}$
	public consumption pG
Income Account of Firms:	
dividends $r_k^e p_y K$	gross accounting profits Π
savings $p\mathcal{I}$	
Accumulation Account of Firms:	
gross investment $pI + p\delta K$	depreciation $p\delta K$
inventory investment $p\dot{N}$	Savings $p\mathcal{I}$
	financial deficit FD
Financial Account of Firms:	
financial deficit FD	equity financing $p_e\dot{E}$

Fiscal and Monetary Authorities

The role of the government in this chapter is to provide the economy with public (non–productive) services within the limits of its budget constraint. Public purchases (and interest payments) are financed through taxes, through newly printed money, or newly issued fixed-price bonds ($p_b = 1$). The budget constraint gives rise to some repercussion effects between the public and the private sector[11].

$$T = \tau_w \omega L^d + T_c, \tag{1.34}$$

$$T_c - iB/p = t_c K, \qquad t_c = \text{const.} \tag{1.35}$$

$$G = gK, \qquad g = \text{const.} \tag{1.36}$$

$$S_g = T - iB/p - G, \tag{1.37}$$

$$\hat{M} = \mu, \tag{1.38}$$

$$\dot{B} = pG + iB - pT - \dot{M}. \tag{1.39}$$

We model the tax income consisting of taxes on wage income and lump sum taxes on capital income T_c. With regard to the real purchases of the government for the provision of government services we assume, again as in Sargent (1987), that these are a fixed proportion g of real capital, which taken together allows us to represent fiscal policy by means of simple parameters in the intensive form representation of the model and in the steady state considerations to be discussed later on. The real savings of the government, which is a deficit if it has a negative sign, is defined in equation (1.37) by real taxes minus real interest payments minus real public services. For reasons of simplicity the growth rate of money is given by a constant μ. Equation (1.38) is the monetary policy rule of the central bank and shows that money is assumed to enter the economy via open market operations of the central bank, which buys short-term bonds from the asset holders when issuing new money. Then, the changes in the short-term bonds supplied by the government are given residually in equation (1.39), which is the budget constraint of the governmental sector. This representation of the behavior of the monetary and the fiscal authority clearly shows that the treatment of policy questions is not a central part of the chapter.[12]

Wage–Price Interactions

We now turn to a module of our model that can be the source of significant centrifugal forces within the complete model. These are the three laws of motion of the wage–price spiral. Picking up the approach of Rose (1967) of two short-run Phillips curves[13], i) the wage Phillips curve and ii) the price Phillips curve, the relevant dynamic equations can be written as

$$\hat{w} = \beta_w(e - \bar{e}) + \kappa_w\hat{p} + (1 - \kappa_w)\pi^c, \tag{1.40}$$
$$\hat{p} = \beta_p(u - \bar{u}) + \kappa_p\hat{w} + (1 - \kappa_p)\pi^c, \tag{1.41}$$
$$\dot{\pi^c} = \beta_{\pi^c}(\alpha\hat{p} + (1 - \alpha)(\mu - n) - \pi^c). \tag{1.42}$$

where $\beta_w, \beta_p, \beta_{\pi^c} \geq 0$, $0 \leq \alpha \leq 1$, and $0 \leq \kappa_w, \kappa_p \leq 1$. This approach makes use of the assumption that relative changes in money wages are influenced by demand pressure in the market for labor and price inflation (cost–pressure) terms. Price inflation in turn depends on demand pressure in the market for goods and on money wage (cost–pressure) terms. Wage inflation therefore is described in equation (1.40) on the one hand by means of a demand pull term $\beta_w(e-\bar{e})$, which states that relative changes in wages depends positively on the gap between actual employment e and its NAIRU value $\bar{e}$. On the other hand, the cost push elements in wage inflation is the weighted average of short-run (perfectly anticipated) price inflation $\hat{p}$ and medium-run expected overall inflation π^c, where the weights are given by κ_w and $1 - \kappa_w$. The price Phillips curve is quite similar, it also displays a demand pull and a cost push component. The demand pull term is given by the gap between capital utilization and its NAIRU value, $(u - \bar{u})$, and the cost push element is the κ_p and $1 - \kappa_p$ weighted average of short-run wage inflation $\hat{w}$ and expected medium-run overall inflation π^c.

What is left to model is the expected medium-run inflation rate π^c. We postulate in equation (1.42) that changes in expected medium-run inflation are due to an adjustment process towards a weighted average of the current inflation rate and steady state inflation. Thus we introduce here a simple kind of forward looking expectations into the economy. This adjustment is driven by an adjustment velocity β_{π^c}.

The economy described here is detailed on the real, nominal and financial side. Yet, with respect to the government sector it is still rudimentary. This can be justified at the present stage of analysis by observing that many of the typical macrodynamic models have similar features.[14]

1.3 Capital Markets

The Stable Core Dynamics on the Financial Markets

We have not yet discussed the determination of the nominal rate of interest i and the price of equities p_e and thus have not yet formulated how capital markets are organized. Following Tobin's (1969) portfolio approach, and also Franke and Semmler (1999), we here simply postulate that the following equilibrium conditions

$$M = M^d = f_m(i, r_e^e)W_c^n, \tag{1.43}$$

$$B = B^d = f_b(i, r_e^e)W_c^n, \tag{1.44}$$

$$p_eE = p_eE^d = f_e(i, r_e^e)W_c^n, \tag{1.45}$$

$$\text{with} \quad W_c^n = M + B + p_eE,$$

$$\text{and} \quad r_e^e = \frac{pY^e - wL^d - p\delta K}{p_eE} + \pi_e^e = \rho/q + \pi_e^e$$

always hold (with ρ the rate of profit of firms) and thus determine the above two prices for bonds and equities as statically endogenous variables of the model. Note here that all asset supplies are given magnitudes at each moment in time and recall from (1.14) that r_e^e is given by $\frac{r_k^e pK}{p_e E} + \pi_e$ and thus varies at each point in time here solely due to variations in the share price p_e. Our model thus supports the view that the secondary market is the market where the prices or interest rates for the financial assets are determined such that these markets are cleared at all moments in time. This implies that newly issued assets do not impact significantly on these prices.

The trade between the asset holders induces a process that makes asset prices fall or rise in order to equilibrate demands and supplies. In the short run (in continuous time) the structure of wealth of asset holders, W_c^n, is disregarding changes in the share price p_e, given to them and for the model. This implies that the functions $f_m(\cdot)$, $f_b(\cdot)$ and $f_e(\cdot)$, introduced in equations (1.10) to (1.12), must satisfy the well known conditions

$$f_m(i, r_e^e) + f_b(i, r_e^e) + f_e(i, r_e^e) = 1, \tag{1.46}$$

$$\frac{\partial f_m(i, r_e^e)}{\partial z} + \frac{\partial f_b(i, r_e^e)}{\partial z} + \frac{\partial f_e(i, r_e^e)}{\partial z} = 0, \quad \forall z \in \{i, r_e^e\}. \tag{1.47}$$

These conditions guarantee that the number of independent equations is equal to the number of statically endogenous variables (i, p_e) that the asset markets are assumed to determine at each moment in time.

We postulate that the financial assets display the gross substitution property

$$f_{b1} = \frac{\partial f_b(i, r_e^e)}{\partial i} > 0, \quad f_{m1} = \frac{\partial f_m(i, r_e^e)}{\partial i} < 0, \quad f_{e1} = \frac{\partial f_e(i, r_e^e)}{\partial i} < 0,$$
$$f_{e2} = \frac{\partial f_e(i, r_e^e)}{\partial r_e^e} > 0, \quad f_{m2} = \frac{\partial f_m(i, r_e^e)}{\partial r_e^e} < 0, \quad f_{b2} = \frac{\partial f_b(i, r_e^e)}{\partial r_e^e} < 0,$$

which originally – in the real markets – stated that the demand for all other assets increases whenever the price of one asset rises.[15] The above discussion, however, concentrates on financial asset demands and their rates of return and the impact of these rates on asset prices.

Assuming that bonds and equities (and money) are temporarily given magnitudes (denoted by a bar over them in the following) and assuming that the above gross substitutes conditions (whereby assets depend positively on their own rate of return and negatively on the other ones) are holding, we get the following proposition for the stability of the asset markets when capital gain expectations are still static.

Proposition 1: Stable Financial Markets Interaction *Assume that capital gain expectations are static. Then: The ultra short-run dynamics for asset prices p_e and the rate of return i on short-term bonds*

$$\frac{dp_e}{dt} = \beta_e[f_e(i, r_e^e)W_c^n - p_e\bar{E}], \tag{1.48}$$

$$\frac{di}{dt} = -\beta_b[f_b(i, r_e^e)W_c^n - \bar{B}] \tag{1.49}$$

converges to the current equilibrium state of the asset markets for all adjustment speeds β_e, β_b of asset 'prices' p_e, i.

Proof: We assume for the time being that share prices are equal to Tobin's q by setting $E/(pK)$ equal to one. The matrix of partial derivatives of the considered two laws of motion is then given by:

$$J = \begin{pmatrix} \beta_e[f_{e2}(\cdot)(-\rho/q^2)W_c^n + (f_e - 1)\bar{E}] & \beta_e f_{e1}(\cdot)W_c^n \\ -\beta_b[f_{b2}(\cdot)(-\rho/q^2)W_c^n + f_b\bar{E}] & -\beta_b f_{b1}(\cdot)W_c^n \end{pmatrix}.$$

The trace of this matrix is obviously negative and for the determinant of the Jacobian J at the given temporary equilibrium state of the asset markets we get the following expression:

$$|J| = -\beta_e\beta_b \begin{vmatrix} -f_{e2}(\cdot)\rho/q^2W_c^n + (f_e - 1)\bar{E} & f_{e1}(\cdot)W_c^n \\ -f_{b2}(\cdot)\rho/q^2W_c^n + f_b\bar{E} & f_{b1}(\cdot)W_c^n \end{vmatrix}.$$

We have due to the gross substitutes assumption

$$-(f_{e2} + f_{b2})(\cdot)\rho/q^2W_c^n + (f_e + f_b - 1)\bar{E} = f_{m2}(\cdot)\rho/q^2W_c^n - f_m\bar{E} < 0$$

and

$$(f_{e1}(\cdot) + f_{b1}(\cdot))W_c^n = -f_{m1}(\cdot)W_c^n > 0$$

and thus get that the entries in the diagonal dominate the entries in the off-diagonal in their absolute amounts. This implies that the shown determinant must be negative and the determinant of J therefore positive and thus proves the validity of the Routh–Hurwitz stability conditions for the considered planar dynamical system. □

We thus get the result that the adjustment processes on the financial market are stable as long as expectations do not disturb them too much. This provides a fairly tranquil starting point for our subsequent discussion of the accelerating processes that may destabilize the functioning of the financial sector of our economy.

Expectations: Fundamentalists, Chartists and Asset Price Dynamics

Next we consider again, as final closure of our portfolio approach to the business cycle suggested here, the potentially stabilizing and destabilizing capital gains expectations of fundamentalists and chartists. The addition of such expectations may be treated in two steps, first the fairly tranquil fundamentalists' expectations and then the chartists' expectations coming from the behavioral traders that tend to be destabilizing if they adjust with sufficient strength. This last feature of the model, the by and large formation of capital gains expectations, is the most demanding aspect (as far as stability analysis is concerned) of the dynamical system that we are considering and is mainly left to future research as far as exact stability proofs are concerned.[16]

The laws of motion governing the expectations about the equity prices are not changed by the transformation to intensive form and thus continue to read as

$$\dot{\pi}_{ef} = \beta_{\pi_{ef}}(\eta - \pi_{ef}), \tag{1.50}$$
$$\dot{\pi}_{ec} = \beta_{\pi_{ec}}(\hat{p}_e - \pi_{ec}). \tag{1.51}$$

In the following only the value of aggregate capital gains expectations is needed, but its computation requires the historical values of the actual appreciation of equity prices $\hat{p}_e$. However we lack a law of motion for this latter quality, because the general equilibrium portfolio approach only provides us with $\hat{p}_e$ by taking the time derivative of the equilibrium conditions. This leads to very complicated expressions for equity price appreciation that are here only considered implicitly. Assuming instead the working of the considered disequilibrium adjustment processes on the financial markets can therefore indeed simplify the mathematical complexity of the sector of financial markets, since it avoids the use of integral equations for the adaptive adjustment processes (see Sargent 1987, ch.5), by allowing for a uniform representation in terms of differential equations (though increased by two such equations then).

In concluding this section we stress that chartists' and fundamentalists' behavior are here described in very simple terms in order to allow a mathematical treatment of the dynamics of financial markets in the following. When one makes use of numerical simulations instead, the assumed adaptive and regressive processes are, however, easily replaced by much more advanced ones as they are discussed in the literature on adaptive learning and theory guided expectations formation. The above two differential equations – describing heterogenous expectation formation – are therefore only surrogates for the situation that there is both backward- and forward-looking behavior on the financial markets of actual economies.

1.4 The Feedback Structure of the Model

Before we come to the potentially destabilizing role of chartist-type capital gains expectations, we discuss the full structure of our model by means of what is shown in Figure 1.1.

This figure highlights the destabilizing role of the wage–price spiral, where now – due to the assumed investment behavior – we always have a positive impact of real wages on aggregate demand and thus the result that wage flexibility will be destabilizing (if not counteracted by its effects on expected profits and their effect on financial markets and Tobin's q). We have already indicated that financial markets adjust towards their equilibrium in a stable manner as long as we disregard the expectations dynamics on the financial market.

Monetary policy, whether money supply oriented and thus of type $i(M, p)$ or of a Taylor type $M(i, \hat{p})$, should – via the gross substitution effects – also contribute to the stability of financial markets. Fiscal policy impacts on the goods and the financial markets and may be of an orthodox type or of a Keynesian countercyclical kind. Due to the very intertwined, dynamical structure that we are now facing, it is, however, not clear how fiscal policy in detail might contribute to the shaping of the business cycle, a topic that here will be left to future research.

There remains the discussion of the self-reference within the asset markets (that is the closed loop structure between capital gains expectations and actual capital gains) which is the most difficult part of the considered dynamical system, when processes of boundedness for these spirals are to be designed.

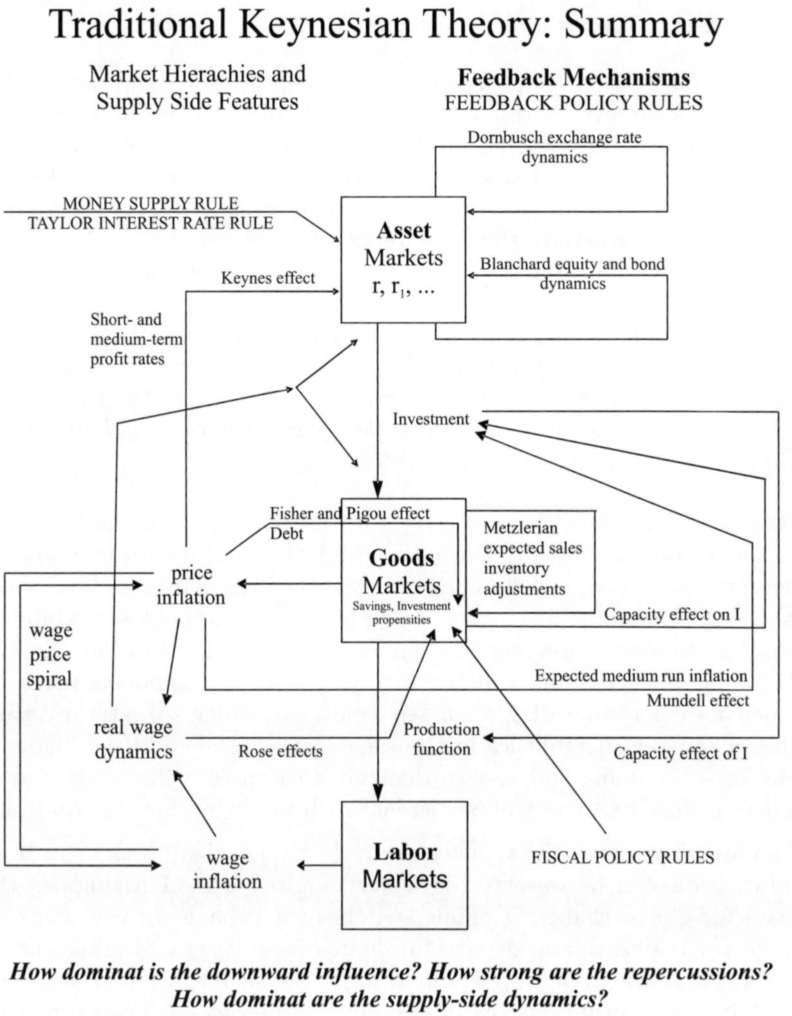

Fig. 1.1: Keynes' causal downward nexus (from self-contained financial markets dynamics to economic activity), repercussive feedback chains (from economic activity to expected returns on equities), supply side dynamics (the wage–price spiral) and policy rules in a Keynesian model with portfolio dynamics

1.5 Basic Sources of Instability

We do not study the considered KMG portfolio dynamics at its intensive form level in this introductory chapter and will also skip the derivation of its unique interior steady state position (see Chapter 11 in this respect). The reader is referred to Asada, Chiarella, Flaschel and Franke (2010) for the details of such an investigation of the model. Next we want to study the potential sources of instability. We hereby will use eigenvalue analysis as well as simulation studies.

Lemma 1 *The steady state of the considered dynamical system loses its stability by way of a Hopf bifurcation, that is in particular, in a cyclical fashion. Such Hopf bifurcations occur when the parameters we assume in the next section as being sufficiently small are made sufficiently large.*

Remark: The proof basically rests on the fact that the determinant of the Jacobian of steady state of the full dynamical system is always negative, so that eigenvalues have to cross the imaginary axis (excluding zero) when stability gets lost. With respect to the actual loss of stability one has to study, however, the minors of order 1, 2 and more of the Jacobian of the dynamics at the steady state or use numerical methods (such as eigenvalue diagrams, see below) in order to get the result that significant flexibilities in the wage–price spiral or in the financial markets (including high money demand elasticities) will indeed lead to a loss of stability by way of persistent or explosive business fluctuations.

As numerical simulations have shown, the range where such local Hopf bifurcation can be observed is a very limited one. This implies the need for global changes (regime switches) in behavior if the economy is locally explosive and departs too much from its steady state. There is indeed at least one important example for such a behavioral switch that in many situations (as far as the real markets are concerned) is sufficient to restrict the trajectories of the dynamics to an economically meaningful domain of their whole phase space. This nonlinearity concerns the fact, already observed by Keynes (1936), that money wages may be flexible in an upward direction, but are rigid (or at least considerably less flexible) in the downward direction.

Let us assert without proof that the normal or adverse Rose effect of changing real wages leads to changing aggregate demand and thereby to further changes in money wages, the price level and the real wage. This holds for the baseline model, with no explicit financial market,[17] but will also be present in the currently considered model with portfolio choice and heterogeneous agents on the asset market. Either wage or price flexibility will, through their effects on the expected rate of return on capital, and from there on asset markets, be destabilizing and lead to Hopf bifurcations, limit cycles or (locally) purely explosive behavior eventually. The Mundell or real rate of interest effect is not so obviously present in the considered dynamics as there is no long real rate of interest involved in investment (or consumption) behavior. Increasing expected price inflation does not directly increase aggregate demand, economic activity and thus the actual rate of price inflation. This surely implies that the model needs to be extended in order to take account of the role that is generally played by the real rate of interest in macrodynamic models. There are finally two accelerator effects involved in the dynamics, the Metzlerian inventory accelerator mechanism and the Harrodian fixed business investment accelerator. We therefore expect that increasing the parameters β_n and i_u will also be destabilizing and also lead to Hopf bifurcations and other complex dynamic behavior.

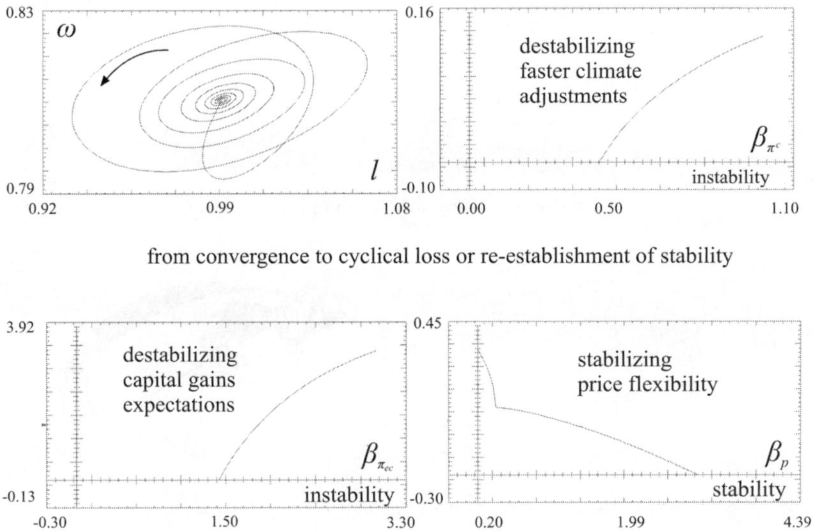

Fig. 1.2: Damped oscillations (top left) and the loss of local stability via Hopf bifurcations with respect to β_{π^c}, $\beta_{\pi_{ec}}$ and β_p

We finally provide two numerical examples, concerning damped oscillations, loss of stability via Hopf bifurcation, the generation of limit cycles as business cycle fluctuations from the global perspective by the addition of downward money wage rigidity to the money wage Phillips curve and finally – through this kinked wage Phillips curve – the generation of complex dynamics if increases in certain adjustment speeds make the steady state strongly repelling. We refer the reader to Chiarella and Flaschel (2000a) for more detailed numerical studies of the implications of kinked money wage Phillips curves.

The simulations in the top left of Figure 1.2 show damped oscillations when the parameter choices of our stability propositions are applied. The other three figures show eigenvalue diagrams that plot the maximum real part of eigenvalues against crucial parameters of the dynamical system under consideration namely β_{π^c}, $\beta_{\pi_{ec}}$ and β_p. These show the expected results that increasing speeds of adjustments in the movements of the inflationary climate and the capital gain expectations of chartists will be destabilizing, while price flexibility is stabilizing (and correspondingly: wage flexibility is destabilizing).

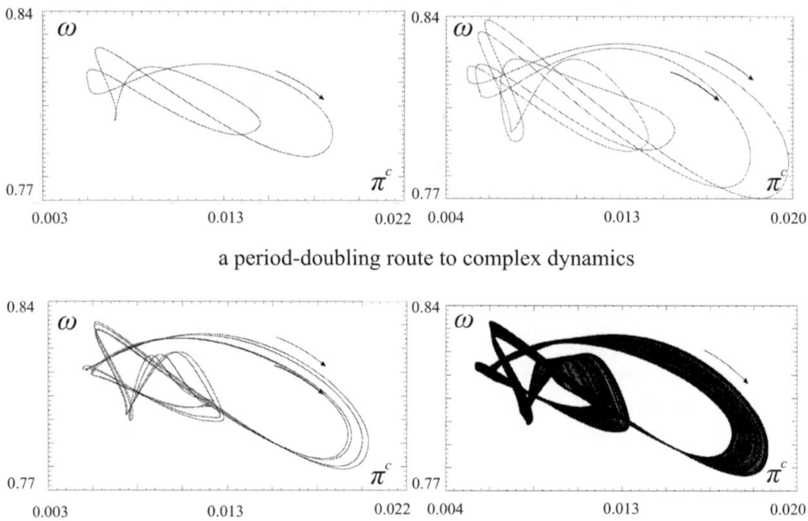

Fig. 1.3: A period-doubling route to complex dynamics through an accelerating wage–price spiral, augmented by downward money wage rigidity (with financial market accelerators still tranquil)

In Figure 1.3 we show an example of a period (cycle) doubling route to complex dynamics (but not chaos) from the economic point of view, since the cycles that are generated are fairly similar to each other. We increase the speed of adjustment of money wages from $\beta_w = 1.4$ to

$\beta_w = 2.0$ and from there to $\beta_w = 2.82$ and then to $\beta_w = 3.0$. The first thing to note is that the dynamics remain viable over such a broad range of adjustment speeds for money wages, due to the kink in the money wage Phillips curve and despite a strong local instability around the steady state described above. To the right of the shown attractors the trajectories are of a fairly smooth type, yet top left they are going through some turbulence which makes the attractor more and more complex with the increasing adjustment speed of money wages.

We do not go into the details of such simulations any further here, but only present them as evidence that the considered model type is capable of producing various dynamic outcomes and is thus a very open one with respect to possible business cycle implications. We might also need some empirical estimation of parameter values in order to get more specific results from our instability analysis. Yet overall we could demonstrate that the high dimension dynamics may have many sources of instability.

1.6 Dampened Business Cycles: Labor Market and Fiscal Policies

Next we want to raise the question of what might stabilize our macroeconomic dynamics. Let us first suppose that the there is a unique interior steady state position of the considered dynamics; see Asada, Chiarella, Flaschel and Franke (2010) in this regard. What is left to analyze then is the dynamical behavior of the system, when it is displaced from its steady state position but still remains in a neighborhood of the steady state. In the following we provide propositions, which in sum imply that there must be a locally stable steady state, if some sufficient conditions are met that are very plausible from a Keynesian perspective.

We begin with an appropriate subsystem of the full dynamics for which the Routh–Hurwitz conditions can be shown to hold. Setting $\beta_p = \beta_w = \beta_{\pi_{ef}} = \beta_{\pi_{ec}} = \beta_n = \beta_{\pi^c} = 0$, $\beta_{y^e} > 0$, and keeping $\pi^c, \pi_e, \omega = w/p, \nu = N/K$ thereby at their steady state values we get an isolated subdynamics in state variables $m = M/pK$, $b = B/pK$ and $y^e = Y^e/K$ which are then independent of the rest of the system.

Theorem 1 *The steady state of the system of differential equations of the state variables* $m = M/pK$, $b = B/pK$ *and* $y^e = Y^e/K$ *is locally asymptotically stable if* β_{y^e} *is sufficiently large, the investment adjustment speed* i_u *concerning deviations of capital utilization from the* *normal capital utilization is sufficiently small and the partial derivatives of desired cash balances with respect to the interest rate* $\partial f_m/\partial i$ *and the rate of return on equities* $\partial f_m/\partial r_e^e$ *are sufficiently small. Moreover the equity market must be in a sufficiently tranquil state, that is the partial derivative* $\partial f_e/\partial r_e^e$ *must also be sufficiently small.*

Proof: See Asada, Chiarella, Flaschel and Franke (2010), also with respect to the following propositions of this section. □

The proposition asserts that local asymptotic stability at the steady state of the considered subdynamics holds when: the demand for cash is not very much influenced by the rates of return on the financial asset markets,[18] the accelerating effect of capacity utilization on the investment behavior is sufficiently small, and the adjustment speed of expected sales towards actual demand is fast enough. Moreover, and this is an important condition, the stock markets must be sufficiently tranquil in the reaction to changes in the rate of return on equities, that is they are in particular not close to a liquidity trap.

In order to show how policy can enforce the validity of this situation we need some preliminary observations first. In the given structure of financial markets it is natural to assume that even $\partial f_m/\partial r_e^e = 0$ and $\partial f_e/\partial i = 0$ holds true, since fixprice bonds are equivalent to saving deposits and thus form together with money M just what is named M_2 in the literature. The internal structure of M_2 is, however, just a matter of proper cash management and should therefore imply that the rate of return r_e^e on equities does not matter for it. The latter only concerns the demand for equities versus the demand for the aggregate M_2 which both solely then depend on the rate of return for equities, since the dependence on the rate of interest cancel when M_2 is formed.

Moreover, since the transaction costs for reallocations within M_2 can be assumed as being fairly small and the speed of adjustment of the dynamic multiplier (which is infinite if IS equilibrium is assumed) may be assumed to be large, we have only one critical parameter left in the above proposition which may be crucial for the stability of the considered subsystem of the dynamics, the investment parameter i_u, potentially representing an accelerator of the Harrodian type. This suggests that fiscal policy should be used to counteract the working of this accelerator mechanism which leads from higher capacity utilization to higher investment to higher goods demand and thus again to higher capacity utilization.

The following theorem formulates how fiscal policy should be designed in order to create damped oscillations around the balanced growth path of the model (if they are not yet present).

Theorem 2 *Assume an independent fiscal authority solely responsible for the control of business cycle fluctuations (acting independently from the business cycle neutral fiscal policy of the government) which implements the following two rules for its activity oriented expenditures and their funding:*

$$g^u = -g_u(u - \bar{u}), \quad t^u = g_u(u - \bar{u})$$

The budget of this authority is always balanced and we assume that the tributes t^u are paid by asset-holding households. The stability condition on i_u is now extended to the consideration of the parameter $i_u - g_u$. Then: An anti-cyclical policy g^u that is chosen in a sufficiently active way will enforce damped oscillations in the considered subdynamics if the savings rate s_c of asset holders is sufficiently close to one, if β_{y^e} is sufficiently large and if the asset markets are sufficiently tranquil.

Note that neither the steady state nor the laws of motions are changed through this introduction of a self-regulating business cycle authority, if $s_c = 1$ holds true, which we assume to hold true in the following for reasons of simplicity.

Next we consider the same system but allow β_p to become positive, though only small in amount. This means that $\omega = w/p$ which had previously entered the m, b, y^e subsystem only through its steady state value now becomes a dynamic variable, which gives rise to a 4D dynamical system.

Theorem 3 *The interior steady state of the dynamical system m, b, y^e, ω is locally asymptotically stable if the conditions in Proposition 1 are met and β_p is sufficiently small.*

Note here that the implication of this new condition for the considered subdynamics is also obtained by the assumption $\kappa_w = 1$, that is workers and their representatives should always demand for a full indexation of their nominal wages to the rate of price inflation. This implies:

Theorem 4 *Assume that the cost push term in the money wage adjustment rule is given by the current rate of price inflation (which is perfectly foreseen). Then: the considered 4D subdynamics implies damped oscillations around the given steady state position of the economy.*

This type of a scala mobile thus implies stability instead of - as might be expected - instability, since it simplifies the real wage channel of the model considerably. It needs, however, the following theorem in addition in order to really tame the wage–price spiral of the model.

Enlarging the just considered system by letting β_w become positive we get that the previous subsystem of the full dynamics is now augmented by the state variable $l = L/K$. For this enlarged system there holds:

Theorem 5 *The steady state of the dynamical system* m, b, y^e, ω, l *is locally asymptotically stable if the conditions in Proposition 3 are met and* β_w *is sufficiently small.*

Theorem 6 *We assume that the economy is a consensus based one, that is labor and capital reach agreement with respect to the scala mobile principle in the dynamic of money wages. Assume that they also agree on this background that additional money wage increases should be small in the boom* $(u - \bar{u})$ *and vice versa in the recession. This makes the steady state of the considered 5D subdynamics asymptotically stable.*

Given the described consensus between capital and labor, both parts can benefit from it (also with respect to a simplification of negotiations about the general level of money wages).

We now enlarge the system further by letting β_n become positive which adds the state variable $\nu = N/K$ to it.

Theorem 7 *The steady state of the dynamical system* $m, b, y^e, \omega, l, \nu$ *is locally asymptotically stable if the conditions in Proposition 5 are met and* β_n *is sufficiently small.*

Theorem 8 *The Metzlerian feedback between expected sales and output per unit of capital is given by*

$$y = (1 + \alpha_{n^d}(n + \beta_n))y^e - \beta_n \nu.$$

This static relationship implies that lean production α_{n^d} *or cautious inventory adjustment* β_n *(or both) can tame the Metzlerian output accelerator.*

We do not introduce any regulation of this Metzlerian sales–inventory adjustment process, but simply assume that this inventory accelerator process is of a secondary nature in the business cycle fluctuations generated by the dynamics, in particular if the control of the Harrodian goods market accelerator is working properly.

We now let β_{π^c} become positive so that we then are back at the differential equation system $m, b, y^e, \omega, l, \nu, \pi^c$.

Theorem 9 *The steady state of the dynamic system $m, b, y^e, \omega, l, \nu, \pi^c$ is locally asymptotically stable if the conditions in Proposition 7 are met and β_π^c is sufficiently small.*

Theorem 10 *Assume that the business cycle is controlled in the way we have described it so far and that this implies that the fundamentalists' expectations of inflation become dominant in the adjustment rule for the inflationary climate:*

$$\dot{\pi^c} = \beta_{\pi^c}(\alpha\hat{p} + (1-\alpha)(\mu - n) - \pi^c).$$

Choosing α sufficiently small guarantees the applicability of the preceding proposition.

The economy will thus exhibit damped fluctuations if in the parameter α in the law of motion the inflationary climate expression π^c is chosen sufficiently small, which is a reasonable possibility if the business cycle is damped and actual inflation, here only generated by the market for goods:

$$\hat{p} \sim \beta_p(u - \bar{u})/(1 - \kappa_p) + \pi^c$$

is moderate. A stronger orientation of the change in the inflation climate on a return to the steady state rate of inflation thus helps to stabilize the economy.

Note that the consideration of expectation formation on financial markets are still ignored (assumed as static). It is, however, obvious that an enlargement of the dynamics by these expectations does not destroy the stability properties if only fundamentalists are active, since this enlarges the Jacobian by a negative entry in its diagonal solely. Continuity then implies that a portion of chartists that is relatively small as compared to fundamentalists will also admit to preserve the damped fluctuations we have shown to exist in the above sequence of propositions.

Theorem 11 *The steady state of the full dynamic system is locally asymptotically stable if the parameter α_{π_e} is sufficiently small.*

In order to get this result enforced by policy action, independently of the size of the chartist population, we introduce the following type of a Tobin tax on the capitals gains of equities:

$$\dot{\pi}_{ef} = \beta_{\pi_{ef}}(\eta - \pi_{ef}), \tag{1.52}$$
$$\dot{\pi}_{ec} = \beta_{\pi_{ec}}(\tau_e \hat{p}_e - \pi_{ec}). \tag{1.53}$$

Such a tax may be monitored through a corresponding tax declaration scheme which not only taxes capital gains, but also subsidizes capital losses (and thus is not entirely to the disadvantage of the asset holders of the model).

Theorem 12 *The Tobin tax parameter τ_e implies that damped business cycle fluctuations remain damped for all tax rates chosen sufficiently large (below 100 percent).*

The financial market accelerator can therefore be tamed through the introduction of an appropriate level of a Tobinian capital gain taxation rule.

Note, however, that this rule introduces a new sector to the economy which accumulates or reduce reserve funds R according to the rule

$$\dot{R} = \tau_e \dot{p}_e E.$$

In order to keep again the laws of motion of the economy unchanged (to allow the application of the above stability propositions) we thus assume that this sector is independent from the other public institutions. For the steady state value ρ^o of these funds of this new sector we get, when expressed per value unit of capital pK:

$$\rho^o = (R/pK)^o = \tau_e(\mu - n)/\mu < 1.$$

This easily follows from the law of motion

$$\hat{\rho} = \hat{R} - \hat{p} - \hat{K} = \frac{\dot{R}}{R}\frac{R}{pK} - \hat{p} - \hat{K},$$

since $\hat{p} - \hat{K} = \mu$ holds and $\hat{E} = n, q = 1, \hat{p}_e = \hat{p}$ in steady state. It is assumed that the reserves of this institution are sufficiently large so that they will not become exhausted during the damped business cycle fluctuations generated by the model.

The stability results of the propositions are intuitively very appealing in view of what we know about Keynesian feedback structures and from what has been discussed in the preceding sections, since it basically states that the wage–price spiral must be fairly damped, the Keynesian dynamic multiplier be stable and not distorted too much by the emergence of Metzlerian inventory cycles, that the Harrodian knife-edge growth accelerator is weak, and that inflationary and capital gains expectations are fundamentalist in orientation and money demand subject to small transaction costs and fairly unresponsive to rate of return changes on financial assets (that is money demand is not close to a liquidity trap). Such assumptions represent indeed fairly natural conditions from a Keynesian perspective.

On this basis we then obtained in the above theorems the result that independently conducted countercyclical fiscal policy can limit the fluctuations on the goods market, that an appropriate consensus between capital and labor can tame the wage–price spiral and that a Tobin tax can tame the financial market accelerator. Metzlerian inventory dynamics and fluctuations in the inflationary climate that is surrounding the economy may then also be weak and thus does not endanger asymptotic stability. But what about monetary policy?

1.7 Dampened Business Cycles: Monetary Policy

So far we have presumed that in the baseline model traditional monetary policy, as money supply and interest rate policy, is ineffective in the control of the economy between the short and the medium run. As it is set up it only effects the cash management process of asset holders, but leaves $M_2 = M + B$ invariant. But note that such a monetary policy can be dangerous in the case of the liquidity trap, since this model allows equity owners to sell their equities against the fully liquid assets M, B. This would imply – as in the current financial crisis – that the public could end up sitting on the bad assets.

The alternative is to suggest that the Central Bank buys the bad assets and drives up asset prices again. This is a demanding policy option that must be investigated and discussed in more detail. Yet this policy seems to have been pursued in the current financial market meltdown and this variant of monetary policy has recently come to the forefront in the discussion. Details may be beyond the scope of the present chapter but we might make some important observations about this policy.

The fiscal authority, the US Treasury, has extensively purchased equity, for example by taking over Fannie Mae and Freddie Mac, and taking over shares of automobile companies. The Fed has purchased, in order to clean up banks' balance sheets, a large amount of complex securities, MBSs (Mortgage Backed Securities) and CDOs (Collateralized Debt Obligations) to avoid fire sales of bad assets and a downward spiral of asset prices. It also undertook extensive lending to the private sector by accepting bad assets as collaterals. This extensive purchase, or acceptance, of equity assets was a new policy variant coming to the forefront as the financial meltdown evolved in the years 2008/9. This attempt to rescue the financial and banking sectors, through the purchase of securities, was widely viewed as a step to prevent a system-wide breakdown. Next we want to build into our macro model some elements of this new policy.

In our baseline portfolio approach to Keynesian macrodynamics we so far have first formulated a really tranquil monetary policy as far as the long-run is concerned, that is we assumed a constant growth rate of the money supply $\mu > n$. This policy was oriented towards the long-run and implied in our model a positive inflation rate in the steady state. This rate should be chosen high enough in order to allow for avoiding deflationary situations where the compromise between capital and labor described above may break down – since labor may be very opposed to money wage reductions (as Keynes (1936) already noted as a behavioral rule, a fact ignored by those economists who disregard the psychology of workers).

We take this as a starting point for our result that a monetary policy only oriented towards the short-term rate of interest is ineffective in our type of portfolio model, as we have presented it here – unless it impacts capital gain expectations on the stock market. This holds for money supply steering as well as for the now fashionable interest rate policy rules, since such policy only affects the cash management process within the given stock of money $M_2 = M + B$. This result is a limit case of what Keynes already observed in the General Theory, where he wrote:

> Where, however, (as in the United States, 1933–1934) open-market operations have been limited to the purchase of very short-dated securities, the effect may, of course, be mainly confined to the very short-term rate of interest and have but little reaction on the much more important long-term rates of interest. (Keynes 1936, p.197)

We do not yet have long-term bonds present in our model type, and also no debt of firms, but only equities as means of financing their investment.[19] Therefore, the following proposal of Keynes must be applied to the stock market in order to discuss its implications.

> If the monetary authority were prepared to deal both ways on specified terms in debts of all maturities, and even more so if it were

> prepared to deal in debts of varying degrees of risk, the relationship between the complex of rates of interest and the quantity of money would be direct. (Keynes 1936, p.205)

We do this in addition to the above monetary policy that concerns the long-run by assuming in extension of the rule $\dot{M} = \mu M,\ \mu = const.$ as integration of the long- as well as short- and medium-run orientation of monetary policy as follows:[20]

$$\hat{M} = \mu - \beta_{mq}(q - q^o), \tag{1.54}$$

$$\text{with} \quad \mu M = \dot{B}_c, \dot{M} - \mu M = -\beta_{mq}(q - q^o)M = p_e\dot{E}_c. \tag{1.55}$$

This additional policy of the Central Bank takes the state of the stock market as measured by the gap between Tobin's q and its steady state value $q^o = 1$ as a reference point in order to increase money supply above its long-run rate in the bust, by purchasing equities, by selling stock and decreasing therewith money supply below its long-run trend value in the boom. The opposite policy should be pursued in a recession.

This is clearly a monetary policy that attempts to control the fluctuations in equity assets and security prices since it buys stocks when the stock market is weak and sells stocks in the opposite case, for example. We stress that this policy is meant to be applied under normal conditions on financial markets and may not be so easily available in the cases where a liquidity trap is in operation.

Transferred to the intensive form level this rule, which we call a Tobin rule in the following, now gives rise to the law of motion for real balances per value unit of capital:

$$\hat{m} = \mu - \beta_{mq}(q - q^o) - (\hat{p} + \hat{K}), \quad m = M/pK. \tag{1.56}$$

We already know that the trend increase in money supply by the Central Bank through open market operations in short-term bonds simply implies that part of government debt is purchased by the Central Bank such that the change in government debt is exactly given by the actual change in M_2. In addition to holding government bonds it is now also assumed that the Central Bank holds equities in a sufficient amount in order to pursue its short-run-oriented stock market policy. This policy is sustainable in the long-run, since the Central Bank buys stock when cheap and sells it when expensive. It gives as a new law of motion for real balances the differential equation

$$\dot{m} = \mu m - \beta_{mq}(q(m+b, r_k^e + \pi_e) - 1) - \\ (\kappa[\beta_p(u-\bar{u}) + \kappa_p\beta_w(e-\bar{e})] + \pi^c + i(\cdot))m.$$

It thus implies a significant change in the complexity of the dynamics to be investigated. We therefore only conjecture that the above propositions and theorems can again be formulated and proved and will show that such a policy adds to the stability of the steady state of the dynamics:

Theorem 13 *The initially considered, now augmented 3D sub-dynamics in the state variables m, b, y^e of the full 9D dynamics can be additionally stabilized (by increasing the parameter range where damped oscillations are established and by making the originally given damped oscillations even less volatile) by an increasing parameter value β_{mq} of the new term $-\beta_{mq}(q-q^o)m$ in the law of motion for real balances, if anticyclical fiscal policy is sufficiently active to make the dynamic multiplier process a stable one (by neutralizing the Harrodian investment accelerator) and if the savings rate s_c of asset holders is sufficiently close to one (which allows us to ignore the effects from taxation on the consumption of asset holders).*

The important means to stabilize the economy or to make it at least less volatile are therefore given here by Keynesian anticyclical demand management, consensus-based wage management, Tobin type management of the financial market accelerating processes and – hopefully – also by the above willingness of the Central Bank to trade not only in bonds, but also in equities. We stress here briefly that this extension is based on the following stock–flow relationships:

$$\begin{aligned}
\dot{B} &= pG + iB - pT - \mu M, \\
\dot{E} &= \dot{E}_f - \dot{E}_c, \\
p_e\dot{E}_c &= -\beta_{mq}(q-q^o)M = \dot{M}_q, \\
\dot{M} &= \mu M + \dot{M}_q, \\
\dot{\Pi}_c &= r_k^e pKp_eE_c/(p_eE + p_eE_c) + \dot{p}_eE_c, \\
\dot{B}_c &= \mu M.
\end{aligned}$$

Note that we now have to use 'f' for firms and 'c' for central bank as indices in order to distinguish their stock–flow contributions from the one of asset holders where we continue to use no index at all. Note also that interest payments on B_c are assumed to be transferred back to the government so that part of the government deficit is just money financed. Note also that equity prices are determined by current stocks solely and thus independent of the inflow of new assets. Note finally that the Central Bank accumulates (or sells) government bonds B_c, equities E_c and dividend payments.

1.8 Conclusions

To summarize, we have derived in this chapter the following propositions and as a result the following policy implications with respect to the Keynes–Metzler–Goodwin–Tobin (KMGT) model of this chapter.

KMGTobin Stability Proposition:

Eight Dimensional Attracting Balanced Growth holds in the considered model if:

- Harrod/Metzler accelerators are sufficiently small
- Money Demand is sufficiently inelastic
- Equity Market is sufficiently tranquil
- Wage–Price Spiral is of Scala Mobile type
- Inflationary Climate Update is sufficiently sluggish
- Fundamentalists dominate Chartists

KMGTobin Policy Theorem:

Eight Dimensional Attracting Balanced Growth holds in the considered model for:

- A Strong Tax Financed Countercyclical Fiscal Policy
- An Implementation of a Scala Mobile situation
- A Secondary Role of Metzler Inventory Accelerator
- A Sufficiently Slow Inflationary Climate Adjustment
- A Sufficiently Large Tobin Tax on Capital Gains

- A Constant long-run Money Supply Growth
- An anticyclical stock-market-oriented Open Market Policy

Thus, it is not the individual behavior of economic agents (firms, households, institutions), but rather the interconnectedness of agents and sectors that produces the stabilizing or destabilizing feedback effects. Left to itself, the macroeconomy has experienced large boom–bust cycles, with extensive externalities when the bubble bursts. In the context of our proposed model we might argue that boom bust cycles could be dampened. More specifically, in terms of policy of institutions, we have shown that countercyclical labor market and fiscal policies, with a tranquilized wage–price spiral, a Tobin tax on capital gains and the implementation of a Tobin rule in place of a Taylor rule could be – taken together – powerful means to make the business cycle not only less volatile, but damped and maybe also converging to some balanced growth path of the economy. Besides demand management by a fiscal authority, wage management through cooperation between capital and labor, we must have monetary policies that concentrate on financial markets in order to dampen business cycles on the macro level by means of new policies of buying and selling equity and securities.

In the next part of the book we will focus exclusively on the labor market and this primarily in a supply–driven framework. We will consider means whereby the overshooting cycle mechanism of the baseline model of this part can be reduced in its amplitudes and can be made a socially acceptable one. This also holds for economies with a low wage income sector and a large segment of atypical work demanded and supplied. We will return to Keynesian effective demand problems (in the Metzlerian guise of this chapter) in Part IV of the book. In the models of flexicurity capitalism considered there we will finally again make use of the present KMG portfolio approach and extend it by suitable labor market reforms into a KMGT prototype model of the flexicurity variety.

Notes

[1] An important framework for studying the history of financial crisis can be found in Minsky (1982).

[2] There seems to be some truth to the view that Greenspan has expressed: That the Fed can take down short-term interest rates, but has no power over long-term rates and, consequently, the yield curve, which also impacted the mortgage rates. In fact, the yield curve, in recent years, had

become rather flat or even downward sloping as the USA had become a safe haven and had become a magnet for capital and attracted savings from the rest of the world; this kept the interest rate on the long end rather low.

[3] In recent work on behavioral finance the interaction of the fundamentalist and behavioral traders is seen as central in creating bubbles and bursts, see Brunnermeier (2009).

[4] Flow–oriented equations for the prices of the assets were used in Chiarella et al. (2000).

[5] We do not allow for regime switches as they are discussed in Chiarella et al. (2000, ch.5)

[6] See Chiarella et al. (2000) for the inclusion of workers' savings into a KMG framework.

[7] Köper (2003), in his ch. 7 , modifies this framework by assuming that money holdings equal M_2 and that bonds are flexprice or long-term bonds which give rise to capital gains or losses just as the equities of the present chapter.

[8] Brunnermeier (2009) calls them behavioral and fundamentalist traders.

[9] See Chiarella et al. (2000, ch.4) for the treatment of a production function with smooth factor substitution and a discussion as to why this assumption is not as restrictive as might be believed by many economists.

[10] This holds if there is no adjustment cost of capital.

[11] See, for example, Sargent (1987, p.18) for the introduction of net of interest taxation rules.

[12] See Köper (2003) for an explicit treatment of government interest payments.

[13] See also Rose (1990).

[14] See also the basic model by Sargent (1987).

[15] For a formal definition see, for example, MasCollel et al. (1995).

[16] Brunnermeier (2009) shows that instabilities, bubbles and crashes are overwhelmingly due to the fact that there are heterogeneous agents in the asset market, giving rise to heterogeneous information, heterogeneous beliefs and limits to arbitrage, see also Abreu and Brunnermeier (2003).

[17] See Chiarella and Flaschel (2000a) and Chiarella et al. (2000).

[18] This would correspond to a strong Keynes effect in the corresponding working model of Chiarella and Flaschel (2000a).

[19] To include debt issuance of firms would amplify the bubbles and bursts, since the interaction of asset price movements and leveraging is rather destabilizing

[20] Which makes Central Bank money now endogenous in a pronounced way. Note, however, that we do not yet consider commercial banks and the endogenous money supply that they are creating.

PART II

Classical Unbalanced Growth and Social Evolution

2. Income Security within the Bounds of the Reserve Army Mechanism

In this chapter we start from Marx's (1954) analysis of the role of the reserve army mechanism, that is mass unemployment, in a capitalistic economy in *Capital*, Vol. I. We analyze the necessity of such mass unemployment for the proper working of capitalism from a very basic perspective where we focus on Goodwin's (1967) modeling of the interaction between (un-)employment and income distribution. However, his model of a distributive growth cycle is only one aspect of the conflict between capital and labor, concerning the distribution of the income between these two types of economic agents. We show that the phases of the distributive cycle and the pronounced reserve army mechanism underlying it can be moderated in amplitude – at least in theory – significantly, if both labor and capital can reach an appropriate consensus with respect to maximum real wages in the prosperity phase and with respect to minimum real wages in the stagnant phase.

2.1 The Classical Theory of Capital Accumulation

The central propositions of Ricardo's *Principles of Political Economy*[1] and the classical theory of income distribution and accumulation are the assertions that (real) profits and (real) wages must fall in the long-run to their minimum values, while the rent of landlords will increase in the course of this process. The classical authors then concluded that the economy will in general be approaching the stationary state, since commercial crises – which interrupt this process – are only temporary phenomena and since technological change will be too weak (in the agrarian sector) to reverse this tendency towards stationarity.[2]

To provide a clear-cut picture of the above assertions of the classical authors, we follow Samuelson's (1978) version of the classical model, since Marx's critique of the classical theory of capital accumulation can be reformulated with regard to this model in a particularly simple and illuminating way. Samuelson's model makes use of the following technological and economic assumptions:

1. Capital K and labor L are applied in fixed proportions: $K/L = z/y$, a magnitude which – due to the absence of technological change – will be set equal to one by an appropriate choice of units in the following. In difference to the preceding chapter, we here consider the agrarian sector of the economy (as being representative of the whole economy). Capital and labor inputs are thus subject to the classical law of diminishing returns which is here formulated as follows:
$$Y = f(\min\{K, L\}), \quad f' > 0, f'' < 0, \tag{2.1}$$
where Y stands for (real) output.
2. For the competitive equilibrium which is assumed to prevail at each moment of time it is assumed that both factors K, L^s are always fully employed ($L = L^s$) and that the real rates of wages ω and of profits r are uniform. Due to (2.1) we must have $f'(K) = f'(L) \geq \omega + r$ on the marginal (or worst) land that is used for production, since the price for renting it cannot become negative. Competition with the best unused land (which due to our technological assumptions has 'nearly' the same productivity) then in addition implies $f'(K) = f'(L) = \omega + r$, namely no (absolute)rent (following Richard) on the worst land that is in use.[3] Total rent is then – because of diminishing returns to extensive agrarian production – given by
$$R = f(K) - f'(K)K \tag{2.2}$$
and positive.[4]
3. Economic evolution is driven in the classical model by the following two dynamic relationships:
$$\widehat{K} = \dot{K}/K = \alpha(r - \overline{r}), \quad \alpha(0) = 0, \quad \alpha' > 0, \tag{2.3}$$
where $\overline{r}$ is the exogenously given minimum rate of profit where capital accumulation comes to an end, and:
$$\widehat{L} = \dot{L}/L = \beta(\omega - \overline{\omega}), \quad \beta(0) = 0, \quad \beta' > 0, \tag{2.4}$$
where $\overline{\omega}$ is the so-called subsistence wage at which population growth (or decline) becomes stationary. Equation (2.3) is a special

formulation of the classical investment (and savings) function, which is based on the simple version of Say's Law (only direct investment). Equation (2.4) is the so-called population law of classical economics.

We have assumed – following Samuelson – that the labor market is in permanent equilibrium (or that it exhibits a constant rate of employment as time evolves), that is

$$\alpha(r - \overline{r}) = \alpha(f'(K) - \omega - \overline{r}) = \beta(\omega - \overline{\omega}), \tag{2.5}$$

which defines a functional relationship $\omega(K)$ with $w'(K) < 0$ by the implicit function theorem. This function characterizes real wage/capital stock combinations ω, K which guarantee the persistence of full employment in the course of time. According to Samuelson (1978, p.1421) the background of this function is given by the following characterization of 'ruthless competition':

$$L^s > K : \omega = 0, \quad K > L^s : r = 0,$$

where $\omega + r = f'(\min\{K, L^s\}), L^s \geqq K$. Surplus supply is thus acting in an extreme way on the remunerations of the productive factors (and their laws of growth).

The above function $\omega(K)$ now implies that the dynamics of this economy is subject to a single law of motion which is given by

$$\widehat{K} = \alpha(f'(K) - \omega(K) - \overline{r}) = \beta(\omega(K) - \overline{\omega}).$$

Since the function on the right-hand side of this equation is strictly decreasing ($w'(K) < 0$!), we thus know that the stationary state [$f'(K^\star) = \overline{\omega} + \overline{r}$!] must be globally asymptotically stable.

Graphically, the above approach to capital accumulation can be summarized as shown in Figure 2.1.[5]

This figure shows that the temporary equilibrium at K (with its determination of the distribution of income: $\omega L + rK + R = Y$) will indeed evolve toward the stationary level $K^\star$ (where we have $\overline{\omega} L^\star + \overline{r} K^\star + R^\star = Y^\star$). In the course of this process, real wages fall from ω to $\omega^\star = \overline{\omega}$, due to the $\omega(K)$ relationship, and the rate of profit $r = f'(K) - \omega(K)$ decreases too, since the right-hand side of (2.5) is falling with the increase in K.

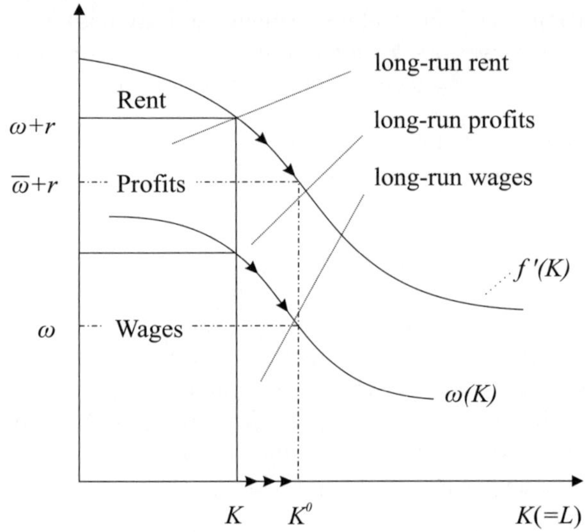

Fig. 2.1: The classical theory of accumulation

Due to the above equilibrium condition for the market for labor we know that the wage rate and the rate of profit will 'reach' their minimum levels simultaneously. Finally R, on the other hand, must increase, since $R'(K)$ is equal to $f'(K) - f'(K) - f''(K)K = -f''(K)K > 0$.

The above model therefore provides a good illustration of central classical hypothesis on the consequences of the process of capital accumulation.

Taken literally, it is to be expected that the subsistence wage of the assumed population law must be fairly low. In a developing capitalist economy, we may therefore expect that there will exist many voices which recommend that actual real wages should not fall to this level, but should be limited from below by a historically determined minimum wage $\widetilde{\omega}$ (resulting from legislation, at the time of Richard: the so-called 'poor laws'). Yet, the establishment of such a floor to the real wage (above $\overline{\omega}$) only has destructive consequences: Population growth will continue in such a case, but capital accumulation will nevertheless come to a halt – due to the law of diminishing returns. Unemployment and misery must therefore be the consequence of such a policy. In the words of Ricardo, see Sraffa (1970, p.105), the following conclusion results:

> These then are the laws by which wages are regulated, and by which the happiness of far the greatest part of every community is governed. Like all other contracts, wages should be left to the fair and free competition of the market, and should never be controlled by the interference of the legislature. The clear and direct tendency of the poor laws is in direct opposition to these obvious principles: it is not, as the legislature benevolently intended, to amend the condition of the poor, but to deteriorate the conditions of both poor and rich.

It is thus the 'natural' wage rate $\overline{\omega}$ which should govern the evolution of wages over time!

2.2 Marx's Critique of the Classical Accumulation Theory

Marx's (1954, p. 597) comment on the results of the preceding section was this: 'A beautiful mode of motion'. The battle between capital and labor is instead analyzed by him in the following way:

> a rise in the price of labor resulting from accumulation of capital implies the following alternative: Either ... Or, on the other hand, accumulation slackens in consequence of the rise in the price of labor, because the stimulus of gain is blunted. The rate of accumulation lessens; but with its lessening, the primary cause of that lessening vanishes, that is the disproportion between capital and exploitable labor-power. The mechanism of the process of capitalist production removes the very obstacles that it temporarily creates. The price of labor falls again to a level corresponding with the needs of the self-expansion of capital, whether the level be below, the same as, or above the one which was normal before the rise of wages took place. We see thus: In the first case, it is not the diminished rate either of the absolute, or of the proportional, increase in labor-power, or laboring population, which causes capital to be in excess, but conversely, the excess of capital that makes exploitable labor-power insufficient. In the second case, it is not the increased rate either of the absolute, or of the proportional, increase in labor-power, or laboring population, that makes capital insufficient, but, conversely, the relative diminution of capital that causes the exploitable labor-power, or rather its price, to be an excess. It is these absolute movements of the accumulation of capital which are reflected as relative movements of the mass of exploitable labor-power, and therefore seem produced by the latter's own independent movement. (Marx 1954, pp. 580–581)

Instead of the monotonic laws derived in the preceding section Marx here develops the picture of an 'industrial cycle' as the consequence of the growth of capital 'on the lot of the laboring class'. Growth will – according to the above quotation[6] – consequently be accompanied by fluctuations in economic activity which originate from changing labor market conditions and their effect on the distribution of income between capital and labor. Furthermore, this cyclical process is not viewed by Marx as something that describes forces which are active near a steady state. Instead, this cycle is the basic mechanism which guarantees the viability of the capitalistic system in the long-run, in Marx's (1954, p.582) words:

> The rise of wages therefore is confined within limits that not only leave intact the foundations of the capitalistic system, but also secure its reproduction on a progressive scale.

Since the population law is at the heart of Marx's critique of classical accumulation theory we want to model this critique at first by removing only this law from the model of the preceding section – replacing it by the Marxian hypothesis of the effect of the reserve army on the evolution of wages. Our procedure here is therefore similar to the one we have used for a critique of the classical model.

Instead of eq. (2.4) we therefore make use of the following type of a real-wage Phillips curve

$$\widehat{\omega} = h(e) = h(L/L^s), \quad h' > 0, \tag{2.6}$$

where we assume in addition that there is some level $e^\star$ of the rate of employment e between 0 and 1 where $h(e^\star) = 0$ holds true. This percentage $e^\star$ describes in the present model (by means of $1 - e^\star = U^\star$) the (least) percentage amount of reserve army (of unemployed) that is necessary to keep wages from rising.[7]

Since the model now distinguishes between employment $L(= K!)$ and labor supply L^s, the $\omega(K)$ curve of the preceding section – which synchronized capital and labor growth – no longer has any meaning here. The model that results now exhibits two dynamical laws instead of only one:

$$\widehat{K} = \alpha(f'(K) - \omega - \overline{r}), \tag{2.7}$$

$$\widehat{\omega} = h(K/L^s). \tag{2.8}$$

The stationary state of this model is given by $K^\star = e^\star L^s$ and $\omega^\star = f'(K^\star) - \overline{r}$. We assume that this state lies below (to the left of) the stationary state of the classical model, that is the labor supply L^s –

which is presently considered as given – is not (yet) at a level which would bring the economy within the reach of the Malthusian biological subsistence limit as far as the production conditions which presently prevail are concerned: $\omega^\star = f'(K^\star) - \overline{r} > \overline{\omega}$.

The Jacobian of the right-hand side of the above dynamical system is given by

$$J = \begin{pmatrix} \alpha' f'' & -\alpha' \\ h'/L^s & 0 \end{pmatrix},$$

i.e. it fulfills tr(ace) $J < 0$, $\det J > 0$ and $J_{21}, J_{12} \neq 0$ throughout the positive orthant $\mathbb{R}^2_+$ of $\mathbb{R}^2$ – which, according to Figure 2.2, implies that the equilibrium point $z^\star = (K^\star, \omega^\star)'$ is a local sink.[8]

By an appropriate version of Olech's theorem,[9] we can therefore conclude that the above dynamical system is globally asymptotically stable in $\mathbb{R}^2_+$ with regard to its unique stationary state $(K^\star, \omega^\star)$. And by means of local stability analysis we can furthermore investigate the conditions under which the response of this system to disturbances will be of a cyclical nature.

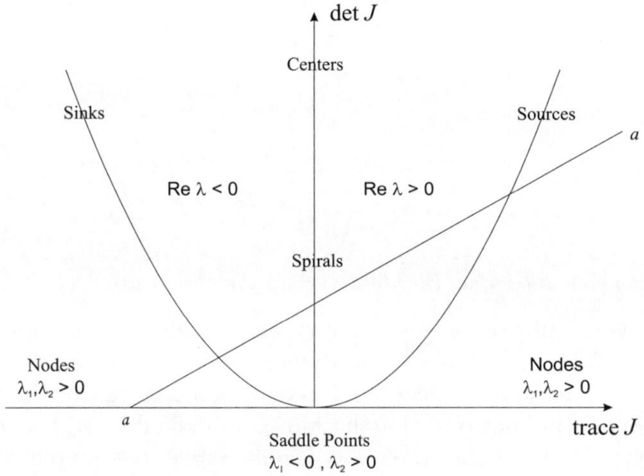

Fig. 2.2: Determinant/trace-stability characterizations

Due to the fact that the characteristic polynomial of the matrix J is given by $\lambda^2 - \text{tr } J \cdot \lambda + \det J$ in the two-dimensional case, the fundamental eigenvalue characterizations of the local dynamics of systems of dimension 2 can easily be translated into a $\operatorname{tr} J/\det J$ diagram as shown in Figure 2.2:[10]

We already know that the equilibrium of the system must be a sink. In order to have that it will be a spiral in addition we must according to Figure 2.2 furthermore establish that $4\det J = 4\alpha' h'(\omega^\star K^\star/L^s) > (\alpha' f'' K^\star)^2 = (\operatorname{tr} J)^2$ holds true at the stationary state.[11] This expression immediately reveals that, for example, a sufficiently steep Phillips curve or sufficiently slowly decreasing marginal product will give rise to cyclical movements in the adjustment toward equilibrium. In place of Figure 2.1 we thus get the picture shown in Figure 2.3. As in Section 1.3 a single new behavioral relationship is therefore capable of producing quite a different outlook for the economic mechanism that is at work.

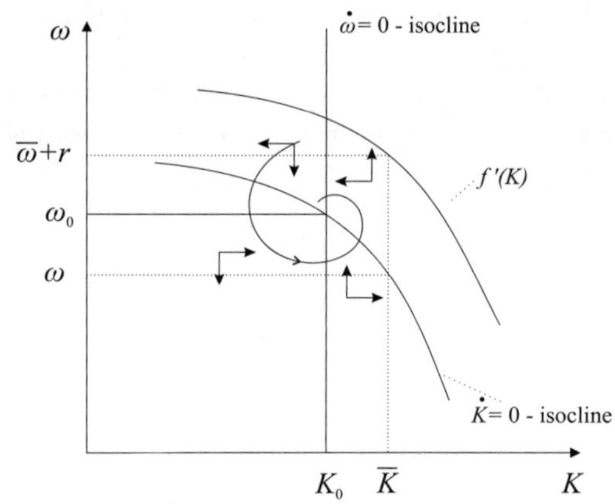

Fig. 2.3: A new type of ω/K-interaction in the classical model

The above result represents, nevertheless, only a first step in the direction of Marx's view on the dynamics of a capitalistic economy, since the above approach still requires exogenous shocks for the creation of economic fluctuations. Furthermore, a defender of the classical approach may object that the above is only a medium-run picture of the economy, and that the population law will exercise its influence in the very long-run. While Marx may therefore have been right in asserting that the 'industrial cycle' is not determined by variations in the absolute number of the working population, but by the varying proportions in which the working class is divided into active and reserve army (p.596), this statement may nevertheless only be true for a limited amount of time, while classical forces will again come into being once population pressure and capital accumulation have moved the system sufficiently close to the classical stationary state.

A simple attempt to formalize this view is given by the following modification of the above model, which reintroduces the population law into it (yet, now in combination with Marx's reserve army mechanism) and which in addition assumes that accumulation has pushed the system to a point where the marginal product of land has become so low that it is close to the minimum requirement $\overline{\omega} + \overline{r}$ for the factors which are applied to this land. In such a case wage increases are fairly limited and we may expect the Phillips curve to be flat.

Adding again equation (2.4)[12] – but not (2.5)! – to the dynamics (2.7), (2.8) makes this system a three-dimensional one with $\overline{\omega}, \overline{K}, L^s = \overline{K}/e^\star > \overline{L} = \overline{K}$ as the new stationary state. The Jacobian of this extended dynamics is

$$J = \begin{pmatrix} \alpha' f'' \cdot K & -\alpha' \cdot K & 0 \\ h' \cdot \omega / L^s & 0 & -h' \cdot \omega K/(L^s)^2 \\ 0 & \beta' \cdot L^s & 0 \end{pmatrix}.$$

The characteristic polynomial is in this case given by

$$\lambda^3 - \text{ tr } J \cdot \lambda^2 + a_2 \lambda - \det J,$$

where a_2 is determined by

$$\alpha' h' \cdot (\omega K/L^s) + \beta' h' \cdot \omega K/L^s), \quad \text{and where}$$

$$\text{tr } J = \alpha' f'' \cdot K; \quad \det J = h' \alpha' \beta' f'' \cdot \omega K^2 / L^s.$$

Applying the necessary and sufficient conditions for local asymptotic stability we immediately see that all coefficients a_1, a_2, a_3 of the above polynomial are indeed positive ($a_0 = 1$). And for the final condition $a_1 a_2 - a_3 > 0$ we get from the above

$$\begin{aligned} -\alpha' f'' \cdot (\alpha' h' + \beta' h') \cdot \omega K^2 / L^s + h' \alpha' \beta' f'' \cdot \omega K^2 / L^s \\ = -\alpha' f'' \cdot \alpha' h' \cdot \omega K^2 / L^s > 0. \end{aligned}$$

We simply assert here that the classical stationary state – just proved to be asymptotically stable – will be approached monotonically if wage reactions to unemployment are slow (of course, β' can be safely assumed to be small as well).

Marx's claim that the process of capitalistic accumulation is essentially independent from the labor supply and its rate of change thus still rests on shaky grounds, since the classical laws of accumulation will still succeed in the end here and remove thereby any scope for the working of the reserve army mechanism.

There is, however, one further basic assumption in Marx's (1954, ch. XX, section 1) approach, which overcomes this critique. This is the assumption of a given 'organic composition of capital'[13] which in modern terms is represented by the assumption of a constant capital coefficient v (or of a constant capital productivity y) already made in Section 1.2. This (standard) assumption will replace the – for industrial societies – implausible agrarian law of diminishing returns (2.1). It will be used in the following section to obtain Goodwin's (1967) version of the Marxian growth cycle.

2.3 Goodwin's Distributive Growth Cycle Model

Replacing the pessimistic view on technology of the classics by Marx's assumption of constant capital productivity (but still neglecting technological change) gives rise to the following dynamic model:

$$K/Y = v = 1/y, \quad (K = L), \tag{2.9}$$
$$\widehat{\omega} = h(K/L^s), \quad h' > 0, h(e^\star) = 0, \tag{2.10}$$
$$r = (yK - \omega L)/K = y - \omega, \tag{2.11}$$
$$\widehat{K} = \alpha(r - \overline{r}), \quad \alpha' > 0, \alpha(0) = 0, \tag{2.12}$$
$$\widehat{L}^s = \beta(\omega - \overline{\omega}), \quad \beta' > 0, \beta(0) = 0. \tag{2.13}$$

There is no longer any rent R; in fact the model now considers the manufacturing sector as being representative and does not pay any attention to agrarian production.

This model can be reduced to an autonomous system of differential equations of dimension 2 in the following way ($e = L/L^s = K/L^s$):

$$\widehat{\omega} = h(e),$$
$$\widehat{e} = \widehat{K} - \widehat{L}^s = \alpha(y - \omega - \overline{r}) - \beta(\omega - \overline{\omega}).$$

The steady state of this system is determined by $e = e^\star$ and

$$\widehat{K} = \alpha(y - \omega - \overline{r}) = \beta(\omega - \overline{\omega}) = \widehat{L}^s.$$

For a capitalist economy it is natural to assume that $y = Y/K$ is larger than $\overline{\omega} + \overline{r}$, that is the minimum rate of profit allows for a wage $\omega_y = y - \overline{r}$ that is larger than the subsistence level $\overline{\omega}$. We then have the situation shown in Figure 2.4.

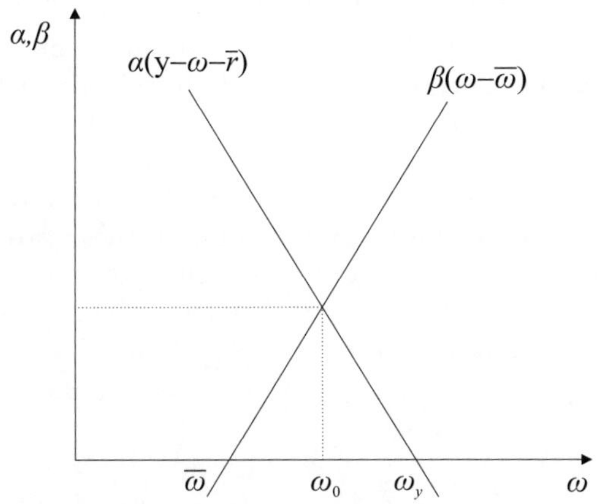

Fig. 2.4: Reformulating the classical model

This assumes that the positions of these two curves are such that they will intersect indeed. Turning to the dynamics of the above system it is easy to establish the phase diagram in Figure 2.5 for it (which already suggests the existence of cyclical movements!):

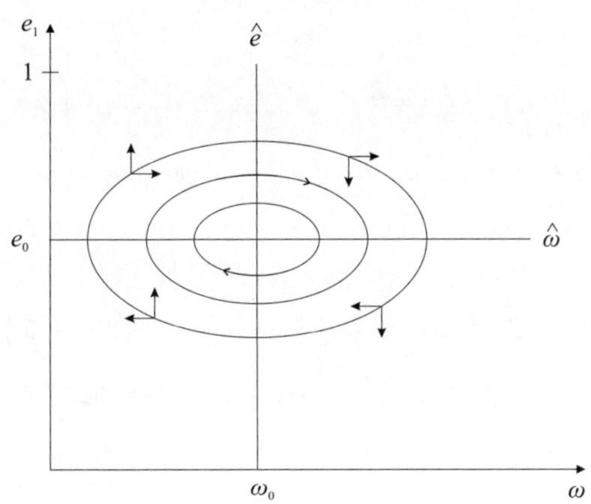

Fig. 2.5: The Goodwin growth cycle model

This diagram furthermore suggests the final conclusion that can be established for this model (not by graphics, but by means of the following calculations), namely that all orbits of the given dynamical system will be closed curves, that is its cycles are neither damped nor explosive and every solution to it is of this simple cyclical type.

To prove this assertion we shall construct a Liapunov function for this system and then apply Theorem 1 in Hirsch and Smale (1974, p.193) on the stability implications of such a construction. Let us denote by J and I the primitives (integrals) of the functions $h(e)/e$ and $-(\alpha(y-\omega-\overline{r})-\beta(\omega-\overline{\omega}))/\omega$ for positive e and ω which in addition fulfill $J(e^\star)=I(\omega^\star)=0$. We denote by H the 'sum' of these two functions, i.e. $H:\mathbb{R}^2_+\mapsto\mathbb{R}$, $\quad H(\omega,e)=I(\omega)+J(e)$. Obviously $H(\omega^\star,e^\star)=0$. Furthermore $H(\omega,e)>0$ if $(\omega,e)\neq(\omega^\star,e^\star)$, since the functions H and I must both be of the following type:

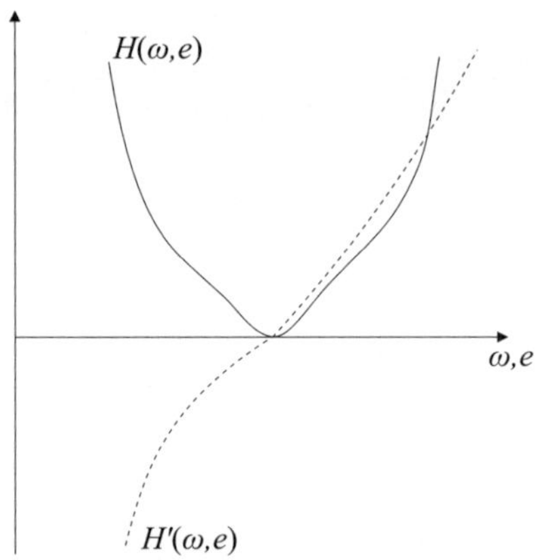

Fig. 2.6: Building a Liapunov function for the above dynamics

With regard to the above dynamical system and this function H we finally have[14]

$$\dot{H}=L_e\dot{e}+L_\omega\dot{\omega}=h(e)\widehat{e}-(\alpha(y-\omega-\overline{r})-\beta(\omega-\overline{\omega}))\widehat{\omega}$$

$$=h(e)(\alpha(y-\omega-\overline{r})-\beta(\omega-\overline{\omega}))-(\alpha(y-\omega-\overline{r})-\beta(\omega-\overline{\omega}))h(e)\equiv 0.$$

This function is therefore constant along the trajectories of the considered dynamics. This implies that the equilibrium $(\omega^\star,e^\star)$ is Liapunov-stable, see again Hirsch and Smale (1974, p.193). Furthermore, in the simple situation we are facing, it is not difficult to see that the function H must be of a form as it is depicted in the following Figure 2.7,[15] which implies that the orbits of the considered dynamics – which are the projections of the level curves of the function H into the phase plane – must all be closed curves as shown for one case in the following picture.

This wage rate/employment rate dynamics is therefore always strictly periodic – with phase length and amplitude of the cycles being determined by initial conditions.

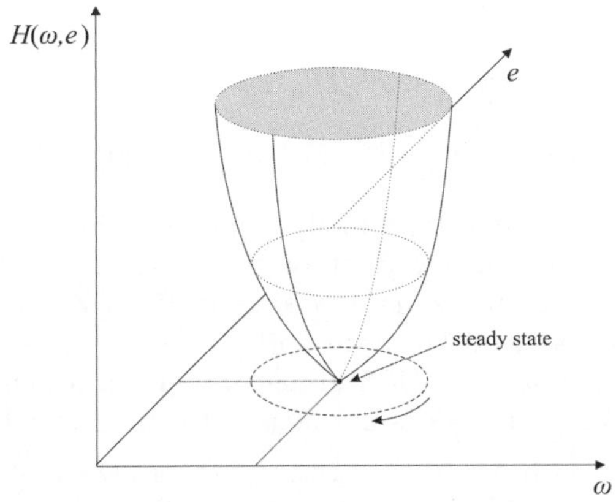

Fig. 2.7: The Liapunov function and the implied center dynamics

An important consequence of this new approach to Marx's reserve army mechanism is that the population law (2.13) is now deprived of its classical consequences. A constant capital-output ratio is sufficient to establish this result (without any help from assumptions about technological change). The labor force will grow – in the steady state – with the rate $n = \beta(\omega^\star - \overline{\omega})$, but so will the capital stock $n = \alpha(r - \overline{r})$, due to the fact that $\omega^\star$ and $r^\star$ are both larger than their minimum values $\overline{\omega}, \overline{r}$. Two basic modifications of the classical approach are consequently in the end sufficient to overthrow its classical content and make it a Marxian model of cyclical growth.[16]

It is now very simple to modify the above model once again so that Goodwin's (1967) meanwhile well-known growth cycle model will be established. It is first of all not sensible to make use of the Malthusian population law in the analysis of steady states of developed capitalist economies. Population growth is instead often considered as being exogenously given and constant, that is the above endogenously determined n is turned into an exogenous magnitude right from the start. Furthermore, instead of the Ricardian investment function (2.12) it is now assumed in this model that all profits are accumulated, while all wages are consumed. Instead of (2.12) this gives

$$\begin{aligned}\widehat{K} &= \dot{K}/K = rK/K = r = (yK - \omega K)/K \\ &= y - \omega = y(1 - \omega/y) = y(1 - v),\end{aligned}$$

where v is the share of wages in national income ($\widehat{v} = \widehat{\omega}$ in the present context!). The above dynamical system thereby becomes

$$\widehat{v} = h(e), \quad \widehat{e} = y(1 - v) - n \quad (= g(v)), \tag{2.14}$$

which establishes the same type of dynamic behavior as the former model.[17] This is Goodwin's variant of the Marxian growth cycle[18] (which in general also assumes that labor productivity Y/L grows at the constant rate m to be deducted from both of the above two equations then in order to integrate this Harrod-neutral type of technical change into this model. Again, this does not modify the models behavior).

It is no exaggeration to state that the Goodwin growth cycle model represents just as important a prototype model as the Solow growth model. Robert Solow himself has recently expressed his admiration for this compact model, see Solow (1990) where he discusses its background, its strength and its weaknesses as well as its empirical importance. Yet, despite its importance, Goodwin's model has been largely neglected in mainstream economics and the textbook literature.

2.4 Hiring and Firing, Social Security and Restricted Reserve Army Fluctuations

We assume – referring to the extension of the Goodwin model in Section 2.5 – the prevalence of a balance between a consensus and a dissent driven economy, that is the limit case $\eta = 1$, which is in fact the only case we have considered so far, namely the closed orbit structure of the original Goodwin (1967) growth cycle model. The question then is whether such an economy (where there is significant overshooting in unemployment and income distribution) can be further improved by allowing for unemployment compensations and also for minimum wages (and later on also for maximum wages), viewed as expressing certain compromises in the interaction between capital and labor.

Human Rights: Basic Income and Minimum Wages

> 1 Everyone has the right to work, to free choice of employment, to just and favorable conditions of work and to protection against unemployment.
>
> 2 Everyone, without any discrimination, has the right to equal pay for equal work.
>
> 3 Everyone who works has the right to just and favorable remuneration ensuring for himself and his family an existence worthy of human dignity, and supplemented, if necessary, by other means of social protection.
>
> 4 Everyone has the right to form and to join trade unions for the protection of his interests.
>
> United Nations (1998, article 23): Universal Declaration of Human Rights, 1948 (http://www.un.org/Overview/rights.html)

In this section we want to show that the quoted article 23 from the United Nations' declaration of human rights does not only represent a normative statement, but can also be justified from the economic point of view in the context of our supply side analysis of the process of capital accumulation. We believe that capitalism is a very robust system of resource allocation and income distribution that can adjust to many social restrictions if these restrictions are justified from a societal point of view. For more detailed discussions of such an approach, the reader is referred to Bowles, Gordon and Weisskopf's (1983) work *Beyond the Waste Land* and in particular to their chapter on 'an economic bill of rights'.

We now augment the analysis of the working of the reserve army mechanism in a capitalist economy of the preceding section by two fundamental human rights: the right for basic (real) income when unemployed and the right that the wages of the employed should not fall below a certain real minimum level. Of course, there are also obligations connected with the formulations of these rights which concern the need of skill preservation when unemployed and the provision of adequate social services for the considered society. In this chapter our focus is, however, on the macroeconomic sustainability of these minimum restrictions on the working of a capitalist economy and not on the detailed analysis on how such a system can work on the micro level. We here argue that the social costs of reproduction mechanisms as they are shown in Figure 2.5 are much higher than what will be the result under the above minimum restrictions on the working of a capitalist economy in a democratic society, and that it is the duty of capital as well as labor to provide the necessary behavior such that these restrictions can be realized not only theoretically, but also – at least – in actual (advanced) capitalist democracies.

Capital's and Labor's Responsibility: Minimum Wages and Basic Income Needs

The dynamical system underlying for the time being this section reads:

$$\hat{v} = \beta_w(e - \bar{e}), \tag{2.15}$$
$$\hat{e} = \bar{y}(1 - v) - n. \tag{2.16}$$

We now modify this system by way of assuming that a fraction measured by τ of the wage income of the employed must be provided as means for unemployment insurance and the restriction that the real wage of the employed can at most fall to the level ω_{min}. The basic income of the unemployed is then derived by assuming that their 'real wage' is a certain fraction of this minimum real wage and given by $\bar{\omega}$. The supply of labor of the unemployed is $(1-e)L$ and is assumed to go into activities that concern skill preservation or social services. Since labor productivity z is a given magnitude the above assumptions can of course be equally represented by constraints $v_{min}, \bar{v}$.

We thus assume for the above dynamics that $\bar{v} < v_{min} < v^\star$ and that $v_{min} \leq v$ holds true at all points in time (since minimum wages must of course lie below the steady state value). The only modification that this implies for the above dynamics is that they are now augmented by $\hat{v} = 0$ in the cases where $v = v_{min}$ applies in the original Goodwin growth cycle dynamics.

We consider the viability of the assumed transfer payments structure first. Reserves for unemployment benefits (a physical stock in this model[19]) are represented by the symbol R. Their rate of change is on the basis of the above assumptions given by

$$\dot{R} = \tau\omega eL - \bar{\omega}(1 - e)L,$$

where L is the total labor supply. Transferred to intensive form magnitudes this gives

$$\dot{R}/K = \tau\omega\bar{y}/\bar{z} - \bar{\omega}(l - \bar{y}/\bar{z}) = \tau v\bar{y} - \bar{v}(\bar{z}l - \bar{y}).$$

For the dynamic of the intensive form variable $r = R/K$ we get from these equations:

$$\hat{r} = \hat{R} - \hat{K} = \frac{\dot{R}}{K}/r - \hat{K}, \quad i.e. \tag{2.17}$$

$$\dot{r} = \tau v\bar{y} - \bar{v}(\bar{z}l - \bar{y}) - (\bar{y}(1-v))r. \tag{2.18}$$

For the steady state value of r this gives

$$r^\star = \frac{\tau v^\star \bar{y} - \bar{v}(\bar{z}l^\star - \bar{y})}{n} = \frac{\bar{y}[\tau v^\star - \bar{v}(1/\bar{e} - 1)]}{n}, \quad i.e.$$

$$\left(\frac{R}{L}\right)^\star = \frac{r^\star}{l^\star} = \frac{(\tau\omega^\star + \bar{\omega})e - \bar{\omega}}{n}.$$

Assuming, for example, the parameter values $n = 0.02, \tau = 0.15, \bar{\omega} = 0.5\omega^\star$, and as minimum for the actual employment rate $e = 0.8$ gives for $(\frac{R}{L})^\star$ the value $\bar{\omega}$ which means that the steady state reserves for unemployment benefits per worker – at an unemployment rate of 20% – are just equal to the basic income wage, while steady state employment is $\bar{e}$ and steady state real wages are given by $\omega^\star = (1 - \frac{n}{\bar{y}})\bar{z}$. At least for the steady state we therefore have that the economy is reproducible at base income wages $0.5\omega^\star$, with no role to play for the minimum wage $\omega_{min} \in (\bar{\omega}, \omega^\star)$ in this case.

The question now, however, is how the dynamics of the original Goodwin model are modified in the large through the assumption of a minimum wage rate for the employed workers. Figure 2.8 shows what is happening in the growth cycle dynamics if a minimum wage restriction is added to the model. We stress with respect to this figure that the base income real wage does not matter for it, since it only concerns the redistribution of income between employed and unemployed workers (who both have a propensity to spend equal to one).

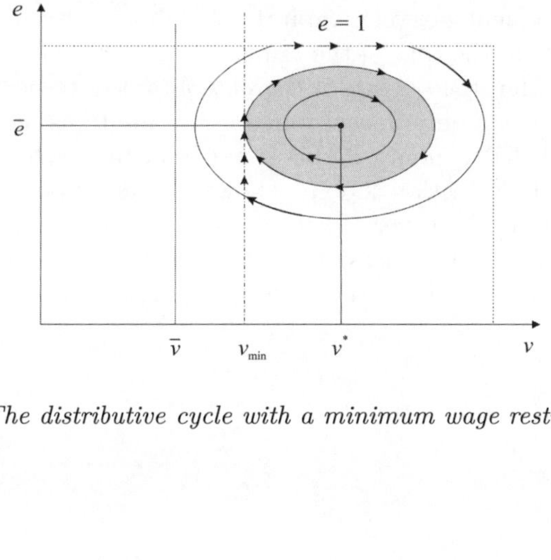

Fig. 2.8: The distributive cycle with a minimum wage restriction

The smallest cycle in the figure first of all shows that nothing is changed if the minimum real wage is less than the lowest real wage along this cycle. The minimum wage restriction then simply is not a binding one. If, however, as shown by the largest cycle the minimum wage bound is hit, the economy will move along this boundary upwards (since profitability is above the steady state profit rate) until the NAIRU rate of employment is reached. From there on real wages are rising again along the cycle that is just tangent to the minimum wage restriction. The result therefore is that all larger cycles will be dampened towards this boundary case (around the grey area in Figure 2.8). Minimum real wages therefore make the fluctuations the economy is subject to less severe, reduce stagflationary periods among others, and diminish the volatility in the employment rate in the longer run.

This is clearly an economically more desirable situation, since excessive fluctuations of the employment rate are now avoided, and this positive judgment is further strengthened, since the social consequences of unemployment are also avoided through the transfer payments underlying this tamed operation of the classical reserve army mechanism. Moreover, increasing minimum real wages moderately will improve this situation further, while a return to a cold turkey strategy of no minimum wages at all may be the faster solution to end the depression, but one that reintroduces severe fluctuations in the employment rate and in income distribution with all their social consequences. We note that this latter case also characterizes the case of combined wages, see the digression below.

We conclude that minimum real wages contribute significantly to an improvement of the classical growth cycle in the cases where convergence to the steady state is not given originally. It may, however, well be that such an additional restriction to falling real wages – when based on an agreement between capital and labor – also modifies the behavior of agents in the case of the unrestricted wage–price dynamics. If convergence to the steady state is thereby obtained, to be considered in Section 2.5, this can only be welcomed as an additional contribution to the stability of the economy. If this is not happening, the arguments in the case $\eta > 1$ of Section 2.5 can, however, again be applied and imply as before that the severe fluctuations in employment and wage income of the unrestricted classical growth cycle are dampened to a degree that is acceptable from the societal point of view.

Digression: Combined Wages in Place of Minimum Wages

In the case where combined wage payments replace the minimum wage barrier as a type of 'government' subsidy of minimum wage payments to workers (which frees firms from this social obligation) we get the following law of motion for the evolution of the funds out of which unemployment benefits and the excesses of the minimum wage over the actual wage (in depressions) are paid:

$$\dot{R} = \tau\omega eL - \bar{\omega}(1-e)L - \phi(1-\tau)(\omega_{min} - \omega)eL,$$

where ϕ is 0 for $\omega_{min} \leq \omega$ and 1 otherwise. Whereas minimum wages represent a change in collective bargaining policies, this rule of workers' funds accumulation does not intervene in the labor market, but leaves wage negotiations to the social partners on the labor market. From this law of motion we now get for the evolution of $r = R/K$:

$$\hat{r} = \hat{R} - \hat{K} = \frac{\dot{R}}{K}/r - \hat{K}, \quad i.e.$$

$$\dot{r} = \tau v\bar{y} - \bar{v}\bar{y}\frac{1-e}{e} - (\bar{y}(1-v))r - \phi(1-\tau)\bar{y}(v_{min} - v), \quad v = \omega/\bar{z}$$

$$= \bar{y}\left(\tau v - \bar{v}\frac{1-e}{e} - (1-v)r - \phi(1-\tau)(v_{min} - v)\right).$$

The steady state value of the state variable r is the same as before, since of course v_{min} is assumed to lie left of its steady state value. And for the dynamics of r we must restrict its investigation to growth cycle magnitudes that do not lead to values of the state variables v, e that imply $\dot{r} < 0$. This is a matter of choosing the right parameter sizes or of choosing an appropriate modification of the model such that $r > 0$ is ensured endogenously.

There is, however, one central implication of the combined wage approach that makes it clearly inferior to the approach we considered previously. This implication is given by the fact that the original Goodwin growth cycle is reestablished through the combined wage scenario, since profits of firms are not modified through this institutional regulation. The Goodwin overshooting mechanism here remains fully effective and leads us back to the large recurrent distributive cycle we have considered above. By contrast, in the minimum wage regime, we have at most only one traverse to the left of the cycle which takes us to a smaller cycle and which no longer recurs. We conclude that combined wages represent an inferior policy proposal as compared to an economy-wide minimum wage regulation.

Capital's and Labor's Responsibility: Upper Bounds for Real Wage Increases

One may ask how the lower floor to real wage payments is in fact monitored in a society where wage negotiations are about money wages and not about real wages and are subject to collective bargaining (tariff autonomy). The answer to this question is, however, on the theoretical level not a difficult one, since it only demands that wages have to increase exactly with price inflation (as in the Italian scala mobile case or in the French adjustment rule for the minimum wage) when minimum real wages are reached (as long as employment is below the NAIRU). The problem may of course be to reach agreement between capital and labor on the management of wage inflation in this phase of the distributive cycle, here primarily concerning capital, since labor is in a weak position.

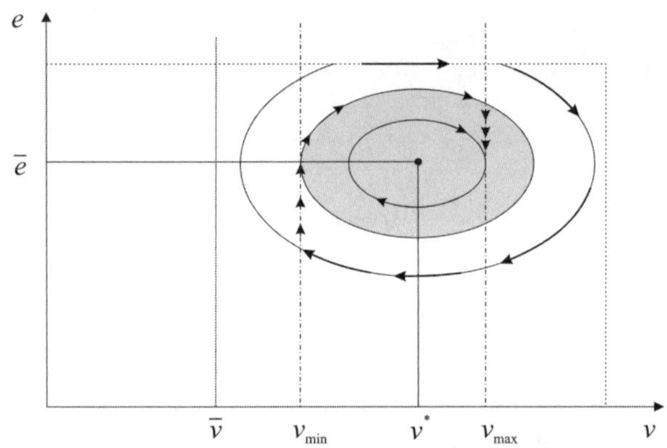

Fig. 2.9: The distributive cycle with a maximum wage restriction

A compensation that can be offered by labor is that a similar rule is applied when labor is in a strong position, that is when the maximum real wage shown in Figure 2.9 has been reached. Wage inflation is then higher than price inflation (since the real wage is increasing) and it now demands a compromise primarily from the side of workers' unions to accept that there will be only inflationary compensation until the NAIRU level $\bar{e}$ has been reached again (now from above). If such an agreement can be reached between capital and labor we get what is shown in Figure 2.9 and thus a further improvement in the cyclical behavior that is generated by the wage–price Phillips curve mechanisms and the pace of capital accumulation this implies.

The choice of the correct levels of minimum (and maximum) wages may, however, run into problems when set to close to the unobserved steady state level. Though this may dampen, on the one hand, the fluctuations in the rate of employment further if it really stays below $\omega^\star$ it will, on the other hand, lead to disastrous consequences if set above the steady state level, since profits are then not sufficient to maintain even the current level of the employment rate which will fall without limit if this choice of the minimum wage level is not revised. It may therefore be wise to use the minimum with sense of proportion and look for help from the maximum real wage level in order to tailor the fluctuations in growth and employment in the best achievable way.

Automatic Stabilizers: Blanchard and Katz Error Correction Terms

Blanchard and Katz's (1999) microfoundation of the wage Phillips curve (PC) extends the PC in the following way:

$$\hat{\omega} = \beta_{we}(e - \bar{e}) - \beta_{wv}(v - v^\star) + \hat{p}. \tag{2.19}$$

The parameter β_{wv} is strictly positive if labor productivity plays a role both in the formulation of reservation wages as well as the real wages targeted by unions in their wage negotiations.

Making use again of the Liapunov function of Section 2.3:

$$H(v,e) = \int_{e^\star}^{e} \beta_{we}(\tilde{e} - e^\star)/\tilde{e}\, d\tilde{e} - \int_{v^\star}^{v} (y(1-\tilde{v}) - n)/\tilde{v}\, d\tilde{v},$$

we get with respect to the above extended Phillips curve (which implies $\hat{v} = \beta_{we}(e - \bar{e}) - \beta_{wv}(v - v^\star)$) the result:

$$\begin{aligned}
\dot{H} &= H_v \dot{v} + H_e \dot{e} \\
&= -(\bar{y}(1-v) - n)\hat{v} + \beta_w(e - \bar{e})\hat{e} \\
&= -(\bar{y}(1-v) - n)(-\beta_{wv}(v - v^\star)) \\
&= (\bar{y}(v^\star - v)\beta_{wv}(v - v^\star) = -\bar{y}\beta_{wv}(v - v^\star)^2 \leq 0.
\end{aligned}$$

The unrestricted Goodwin growth cycle is therefore now globally convergent to the steady state of the economy by the arguments we use in Section 2.5 for the case $\eta < 1$. Since the cycles that so far resulted from either minimum or maximum real wages are tangent to these restrictions we get from the above that they are only needed once to restrict the unrestricted excessive cycle. Thereafter such bounds are no longer necessary, since the next cycle remains inside these bounds and converges to the steady state eventually. We thus get from the microfounded and estimated wage PC of the Blanchard and Katz (1999) type, at least for Europe as far as their study is concerned, that minimum and maximum wages will dampen the fluctuations of the unrestricted reserve army mechanism significantly and make it thereafter convergent to its long-run equilibrium position.

2.5 Minimum Wages in an Extended Goodwin Growth Cycle Model

We shall now introduce new aspects into the Goodwin's growth cycle model based on:

1. A representation of this model must be found which exhibits local instability and which takes account of the fact that the employment rate cannot exceed and the share of wages cannot reach the value 1, which here will guarantee global stability. This is a situation which is more in line with Marx's characterization of the profit squeeze mechanism than the common variants of Goodwin's growth cycle which are still unsatisfactory in this regard.

A well-known extension of the Goodwin model of cyclical growth toward a treatment of nominal magnitudes is given by the following two dynamic equations:

$$\hat{v} = h(e) - m - (1-\eta)\beta[(1+a)v - 1], \tag{2.20}$$
$$\hat{e} = s_p y - (n+m) - s_p y v = h(v). \tag{2.21}$$

These equations model the dynamic interaction of money–wage fixing, price-setting, profits and accumulation in a technological world with fixed proportions. In these equations we denote by:

v the share of wages (steady state $v^\star$),
e the employment rate (steady state $e^\star$),
m the growth rate of labor productivity ($z = Y/L$) (a constant),
n the growth rate $\hat{L^s}$ of (labor) population,
L^s (a constant),
$g^\star$ $n + m$,
y the output–capital ratio Y/K (a constant),

s_p the savings rate (with respect to profit income; $s_w = 0$),
$\hat{w}$ the growth rate of money wages w,
$\hat{p}$ the rate of inflation $\dot{p}/p$,
a mark-up factor on wage-unit-costs (a constant $(A = 1 + a)$.

The above dynamics is based on the following new structural equations and assumptions for the Goodwin growth cycle model:

$$\hat{w} = h(e) + \eta\hat{p} \qquad \text{(a money–wage Phillips curve),}$$
$$\hat{p} = \beta[(1 + a)v - 1] \qquad \text{(a mark-up theory of inflation).}$$

Here, η and β denote positive parameters. The function $h(e)$ is of the same form as in the preceding section. Yet, instead of a real wage Phillips curve we have now assumed a nominal form of it which explicitly shows how inflation enters real wage determination. Note that we are back at the situation of a real wage curve as employed in the preceding section in the often assumed case $\eta = 1$. In general, however, this new labor market curve demands the addition of a theory of inflation. This is done here in the particularly simple way of assuming that the time rate of change of prices p is given by the discrepancy between marked up unit wage costs and actual prices p (β the speed of adjustment):[20]

$$\dot{p} = \beta(AwL/Y - p).$$

We note finally that we added Harrod-neutral technical progress in comparison to our earlier Goodwin approaches. This assumption is standard for these types of models.

In sum, equations (2.20) and (2.21) state that the percentage change of the share of wages v depends positively on the rate of employment e and (for $\eta < 1$) negatively on the level of v (because of the assumed mark-up theory of inflation) and that the percentage change of the rate of employment e is governed by savings out of profits per unit of capital $s_p y(1 - v)$ diminished by the growth rates m, n of the labor force and labor productivity.

It is easily shown, by means of employing the following Liapunov function (in the case where $Av^\star = 1$ holds true):

$$H = \int_{e^\star}^{e} (f(x) - m)/x dx - \int_{v^\star}^{v} h(\xi)/\xi d\xi$$

which gives

$$\dot{H} = (1-\eta)\beta[Au-1]h(v) \gtreqless 0 \quad \text{for} \quad \eta \gtreqless 1, v \neq v^{\star},$$

so that the behavior of the above model can be characterized as depicted in Figure 2.10.

The depicted behavior is valid locally as well as globally and it is incomplete in the same way the unrestricted (linear) multiplier-accelerator model is not complete, since it does not remain restricted to economically meaningful values of v, e in the case $\eta > 1$ (of explosive cycles) and it is not yet a complete endogenous theory of the 'business cycle' in the case of $\eta < 1$ (implosive cycles).

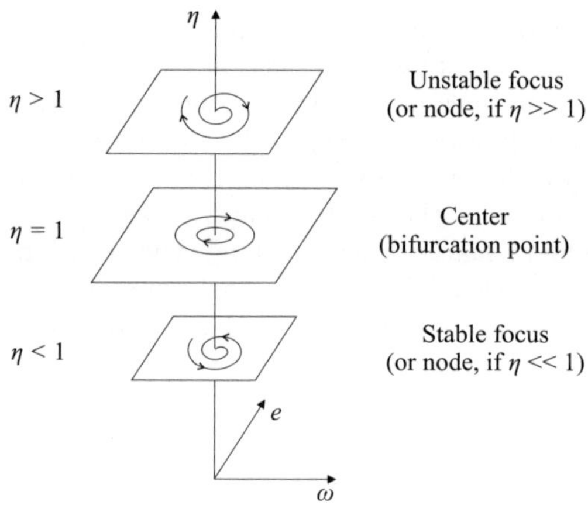

Fig. 2.10: A 'quasi-linear' Hopf bifurcation diagram

Let us consider the asymptotically stable case $\eta < 1$ first. In this case the Liapunov approach implies that all trajectories point inward with respect to the closed orbits of the original Goodwin model. The situation shown in Figure 2.8 here implies that the then generated trajectories must enter the grey area sooner or later after real wages have started to rise again. They will then converge to the steady state by an inwardly directed crossing of the closed orbits of the Goodwin case inside. Note here, however, that the law of motion

$$\hat{v} = \beta_w(e-\bar{e}) + (\eta-1)\beta_p[Av-1]$$

now implies an upward sloping $\dot{v} = 0$ isocline in place of a horizontal one (with an unchanged steady state) which means that real wages start rising earlier than in the case $\eta = 1$, moving the economy into the grey area in Figure 2.8 after some time.

In the unstable case $\eta > 1$ we instead have a declining $\dot{v} = 0$ isocline which means that real wages start rising later than in the case $\eta = 1$. In this case the trajectory generated thereafter hits the minimum wage barrier outside the Goodwin closed orbit corresponding to its starting point and is thus moving along the real wage barrier a longer way until real wages start rising again as before. This now generates a single closed orbit – with a recurrent minimum wage regime – and thus removes the explosiveness of the unrestricted case. The economy is thus made a viable one in the long-run through a minimum real wage restriction, see Figure 2.11.

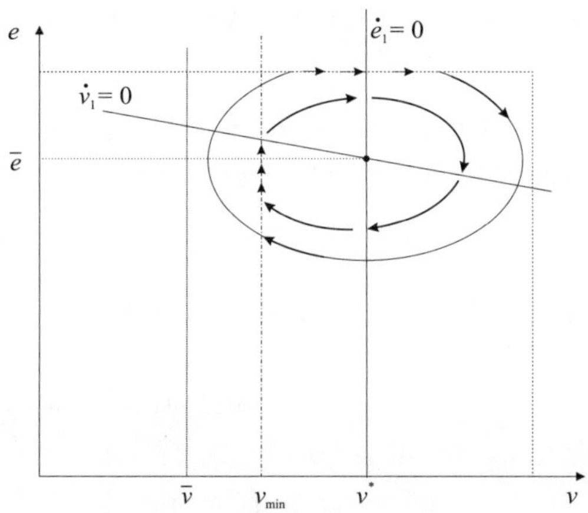

Fig. 2.11: The unstable distributive cycle with a minimum wage (η >1)

We conclude that minimum real wages contribute significantly to an improvement of the classical growth cycle in the cases where convergence to the steady state is not given originally. It may, however, well be that such an additional restriction to falling real wages – when based on an agreement between capital and labor – also modifies the behavior of agents in the case of the unrestricted wage–price dynamics. If convergence to the steady state is thereby obtained, this can only be welcomed as an additional contribution to the stability of the economy. If this is not happening, the arguments in the case $\eta > 1$ can, however, again be applied and imply as before that the severe fluctuations in employment and wage income of the unrestricted classical growth cycle are dampened to a degree that is acceptable from the societal point of view.

It is our opinion that a locally unstable steady state (here caused by $\eta > 1$) should be a key characteristic of a model of the Marxian theory of accumulation, yet that in addition to this feature reproductiveness (namely outward stability or economic viability) should also be true is not yet included into such a model (as is the case for the above dynamics (2.20), (2.21)!). In order to introduce such viability mechanisms which attempt to model the idea of the reproducibility of capitalism along the lines described in Marx (1954, p. 582):

> The rise of wages therefore is confined within limits that not only leave intact the foundations of the capitalistic system, but also secure its reproduction on a progressive scale.

we here start with the following simple extension of the above model (2.20), (2.21):

$$\hat{v} = h(e) - (1 - \eta(v)) \cdot \beta(v)[(1+a)v - 1] - m, \tag{2.22}$$

$$\hat{e} = s_p i(e) \cdot (1 - v)y - (m + n), \tag{2.23}$$

where

1. $\beta(v) \geq 0, \quad \beta'(v) \geq 0, \quad \beta(v) \to \infty$ for $v \to 1$, and $\beta(v) = 0$ if $v \leq \frac{1}{1+a}$,
2. $\eta(v)$ fulfills $\eta(v^\star) > 1, \eta'(v) \leq 0$ (and $\eta(v) < 1$ for $v > v^\star$ and near to 1),
3. $i(e) = \begin{cases} 1 \text{ for } & 0 \leq e \leq 1 - \varepsilon, \quad \varepsilon > 0 \quad \text{small} \\ 0 \text{ for } & e \qquad\qquad \geq 1 \end{cases}$

(all functions are supposed to be sufficiently smooth).

The mark-up pricing rule behind the term $\hat{p}(v)$ in (2.22), i.e.

$$\dot{p} = \beta(v)\left[\frac{(1+a)w}{z} - p\right],$$

is modified by assumption 1 to that extent that it is now assumed that the adjustment speed β of price changes (which are driven by the discrepancy between marked-up wage costs per unit of output and actual prices) increases (to infinity) as the share of wages approaches 1. Furthermore, the occurrence of deflation has been excluded from the present form of the model which helps to avoid the existence of problematic types of steady states. Assumption 2 states that wage earners demand more than just the rate of inflation $\hat{p}$ in their money–wage claim if the wage share is at its steady value $v^\star (m > 0!)$. This and the negative relationship between the aspiration factor η and the share of wages v can be motivated as follows:

Since the output–capital ratio y is constant, we have

$$g = \hat{Y} = \hat{K} = s_p i(e)(1-v)\frac{Y}{K} = s_p i(e)(1-v)y.$$

Therefore $g \gtreqless g^\star = m + n$ if $v \gtreqless v^\star$. It is thus implicitly assumed in assumption 2 that η relates positively to the actual rate of growth g with $\eta = 1$ already occurring at a point below normal growth $g^\star$. Assumption 3, finally, says that it is of no use to further accumulate capital if there is no labor force available for the new capital goods.

Model (2.22), (2.23) represents an elementary completion of (2.20), (2.21) by projecting the reaction patterns of the distributional conflict and the accumulation process into the price and wage sector and a simple capital formation equation. Inflation is the means by which the rate of profit is defended against money wage claims which are too high and a simple fall in the rate of growth of capital is here assumed as a reaction to the full employment barrier.[21]

Theorem 1 *Assume $s_p = 1$ for simplicity and also that $h(e^\star) = (1 - \eta(v^\star)) \cdot \beta(v^\star)(Av^\star - 1) + m$,[22] $v^\star = 1 - g^\star/y$ has a meaningful solution $(v^\star, e^\star) \in (0,1)^2$ within the range where $i(e)$ is still constant ($\equiv 1$). Assume further: $\eta^{'}(v^\star) = 0$ (or small). The model (2.22), (2.23) then has at least one (stable) limit cycle around its unique and unstable steady state solution $v^\star, e^\star$.*

This proposition represents a fairly obvious application of the Poincaré–Bendixson Theorem. Calculating the Jacobian of (2.22), (2.23) at the steady state gives[23]

$$J_1 = \begin{pmatrix} -(1-\eta(v^\star))\hat{p}^{'}(v^\star) \cdot v^\star & f^{'}(e^\star)v^\star \\ -ye^\star & 0 \end{pmatrix},$$

that is, we have $\det J > 0$ and trace $J > 0$. The steady state $(v^\star, e^\star)$ is thus an unstable node or focus.[24] And with regard to an analysis of global stability and the existence of limit cycles we will put up with the following phase portrait shown in Figure 2.12 (and skip the details of the proof):[25]

Remarks:

1. Note, that the $\dot{v} = 0$ isocline should not touch the horizontal axis (see assumption 2 in this regard).

2. We do not assume here $A = 1/v^\star$, that is a non-inflationary steady state: $\hat{p}(v^\star) = 0$.
3. $\hat{p} < 0$, i.e. deflation is, however, excluded in order to avoid that $\hat{v}$ may depend negatively on v for small v and e near full employment (this would imply a falling share of wages despite a situation of near full employment). Furthermore, additional interior and stable points of rest are avoided thereby.

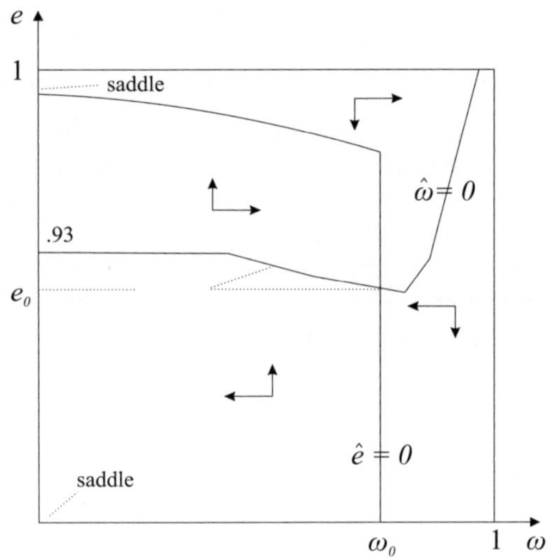

Fig. 2.12: A simple, but complete version of the Marxian growth cycle

The above model shows explicitly (some of) the forces which keep the dynamics of a Marxian growth cycle within economically meaningful bounds. Paired with the instability of the steady state this implies that each trajectory will be attracted by some closed curve in the relevant (v, e) domain. The model therefore provides a simple example for Marx's view on capitalistic accumulation as it is expressed in the above quotation from *Capital.* Note that this explanation of positive profits is quite different in nature from the type of 'explanation' that is offered by the so-called Fundamental Marxian Theorem on the equivalence of positive profits and positive surplus values (which in fact gives no explanation at all, but only establishes a relationship between two different basic magnitudes of Marx's *Capital*).

We conclude this simple analysis of a more appropriate representation of the 'Marxian growth cycle' as it is given by the model (2.20), (2.21) with a simulation study of the model (2.22), (2.23). To do so the following parameter values and functions are assumed: $m = 0.03$, $n = 0.02$, $y = 0.2$, $a = 0.5$ $(v^\star = 0.66)$, $h(e) = \rho e - \gamma$, $\rho = 1$, $\gamma = 0.9$, $i(e) = -50e + 50$ on $[0.98, 1]$ and $\equiv 0$ or 1 outside this interval, $e(v) = 1 - \eta(v)$ the continuous piecewise linear function with $e(o) = -0.5$, $e(0.72) = -0.05$, $e(0.78) = -0.05$, $e(1) = 0.5$, $\beta(v)$ the continuous function with $\beta' \equiv 0$ on $[0, v^\star]$, $\beta' \equiv 4$ on $(0.66, 0.75]$, $\beta' \equiv 400$ on $(0.75, 1]$. Figure 2.13 shows the outcome of this simulation.

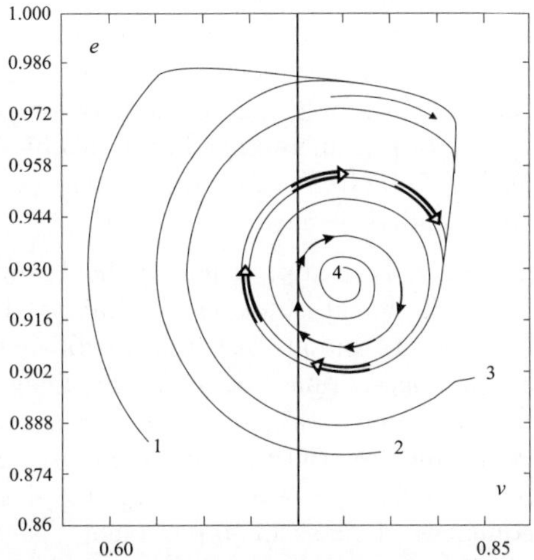

Fig. 2.13: A limit cycle in a Marxian analysis of cyclical accumulation and its minimum wage bound

2.6 Conclusions

In this chapter we departed from the conventional discussion of the impact of minimum wage legislation, which is only partial in nature, by considering the macroeconomic effects of such legislation on agreements between capital and labor. We think that sector-specific rules concerning minimum wages can only be discussed against the background of such macrofoundations where the medium- and long-run consequences of minimum wages are the focus of interest and not so much the short-run adjustment problems such a legislation may cause.

We conclude from what has been shown in this chapter that the introduction of a general level of minimum (or maximum) real wages into a supply-side macro model of fluctuating growth does not do much harm even in the shorter run to capital accumulation and employment as described through this model type, and does definitely and significantly improve the performance of the implied cyclical growth path in the course of time. We have not only got less severe fluctuations in income distribution than in the unrestricted case (where there is an unlimited working of the wage–price spiral and the reserve army mechanism), but can also avoid the social consequences of mass unemployment through basic income payments – and an employer of last resort, if meaningful activities of the unemployed are added to the reformulated social structure of accumulation. An educated society, in which the principle of equal opportunities holds in its schooling system, may also be a very important ingredient in the working of such a social structure, where partial workforce degradation is avoided by meaningful qualification processes of the unemployed and also life-long learning of the employed, see Flaschel, Greiner and Luchtenberg (2008) for further details on such an extended scenario.

The advantage of the Goodwin approach to cyclical growth employed as the reference case here is that it is not biased against capitalist interest, since it entails that workers' unions bear responsibility for overshooting wage shares in the prosperity phase of the cycle. They therefore might have avoided the subsequent stagnant phase to a certain degree by prudent upper real wage restrictions. By contrast, minimum wages come to the help of workers' unions in stagnant phases by avoiding the severe consequences of mass unemployment. We note that both minimum and maximum real wages are easier to implement in the prosperity phase of the cycle than in its stagnant or depressed phase.

Of course, there may be obstacles on the way towards such a social structure of accumulation, given by the factual sclerosis of existing social structures (degraded long-term unemployed persons, segmented labor markets, degrading job offers and more). Globalization may also represent a big challenge for our reformulated Goodwin growth cycle dynamics, concerning international competition for traded commodities and services, workforce migration, outsourcing and more. This, however, essentially demands that the very basic flexi(bility sec)curity system discussed in this chapter needs further refinements along the lines proposed in Flaschel, Greiner, Luchtenberg and Nell (2008).

Notes

[1] Third Edition: 1821 (Chapter IV); see P. Sraffa (1970) for details.

[2] Contrast this with Domar's analysis that a capitalist economy must grow in order to avoid economic crisis.

3 Here based on the assumption of a uniform rate of profits r and of wages ω due to Classical competition.

4 Since we have $L^s = L = K$ in competitive equilibrium, we can neglect the symbol L in the following.

5 Note with regard to this figure that the above implies:

$$R = f(K) - f'(K)K = \int_0^K f'(\zeta)d\zeta - f'(K)K,$$

which justifies the following graphical representation of total rent R.

6 We interpret the passage following 'Either ...' as characterizing a particular phase of such a cycle.

7 Compare here Marx's (1954, pp.600 ff.) description of the segments of the labor market.

8 Local stability analysis or stability in the first approximation is based on the following approximation of the original dynamics $\dot{z} = f(z)$:

$$\dot{z} \approx f(z^\star) + f'(z^\star) \cdot (z - z^\star), f(z^\star) = 0, J = f'(z^\star),$$

see Arrowsmith and Place (1982) for details.

9 Note here, that the variable transformation $\zeta = \ln K, \xi = \ln \omega$ transforms system (2.7), (2.8) into $\dot{\zeta} = \alpha(f'(e^\zeta) - e^\xi - \overline{r}), \quad \dot{\xi} = h(e^\zeta / L^s)$ which has the same type of Jacobian as the above growth rate system and which allows for an application of the Olech theorem in its original form (see the appendix for details).

10 See for example Amann (1983) for details.

11 Note here, that the above Jacobian has now been recalculated to include the terms that follow from the growth rate formulation on the left-hand side of the above dynamics.

12 We here assume for simplicity that there are 'poor laws' which guarantee the subsistence level to the unemployed (paid out of rent).

13 We shall not consider here Marx's attempt to derive his own version of a falling rate of profit by means of technical change which increases labor productivity at the cost of an increasing capital–output ratio.

14 $\dot{H}$ the derivative along the trajectories of this system, and L_e, L_ω the partial derivatives of the Liapunov function H.

15 That the equilibrium point $z^\star$ is a local minimum of the function H is easily shown by means of: $L'(z^\star) = 0$ and $L''(z^\star)$ positive definite.

16 Marx's characterization of such a growth cycle mechanism, however, differs in at least one very important respect from the analysis of this section, since Marx (1954, p.581) asserts that the rate of accumulation (investment) has to be considered as the independent variable in this industrial cycle which surely is not the case for the growth cycle we consider in this section.

[17] The Liapunov function is in this case given by $\int_{e^\star}^{e} h(\zeta)/\zeta d\zeta - \int_{v^\star}^{v} g(\xi)/\xi d\xi$.

[18] See Goodwin (1967, pp.57–58) for a brief verbal description of this growth cycle result.

[19] Since there are not yet financial assets present in the model. Note that we assume here that the parameter τ has been chosen such that these stocks are not exhausted in the course of the considered growth fluctuations.

[20] There is here no self-reference of the rate of inflation onto itself (or its expected value), since there is no exogenous driving force for the formation of the rate of inflation in this model. By a specific choice of the parameter A, it is assumed in addition to the above that the steady state rate of inflation $\hat{p}^\star$ is zero which provides a further reason for this lack of self-reference.

[21] This assumption can be justified through a simple reinterpretation of the standard one-good model by assuming that it includes luxury goods as well. In a sufficiently small neighborhood of full employment capitalists then simply prefer to use their inputs as (non-transferable) luxury goods instead of investing them (irreversibly) into capital formation.

[22] $A = 1 + a \geq 1/v^\star$.

[23] We here assume $\eta'(v^\star) = 0$ for simplicity and thus neglect the term $\eta'(v^\star)\hat{p}(v^\star)v^\star$ in J_{11}.

[24] These assumptions (which imply local instability) do not yet look very convincing. Further destabilizers can, however, easily be introduced, for example by means of production lags, wage drift lags, etc., yet they are difficult to treat from a purely qualitative point of view.

[25] The following picture corresponds approximately to the numerical values of the simulation example of this section.

3. Segmented Labor Markets and Low Income Work

3.1 Introduction

In recent times a controversial debate about the establishment of minimum wages in certain sectors or even throughout the economy has taken place at several levels (in parliament, in the media and between economists) of the German society. This controversy has been triggered by the significant rise of jobs with low salaries at or even below the subsistence level since the 1990s – documented in Rhein and Stamm (2006) and Bosch and Kalina (2007) – on the one hand, as well as by the fact that the income of top managers has been rising drastically faster than the average income of employees over the last decades. For example, according to Klesse and Voss (2007), the annual income of top managers of the largest 100 companies in Germany with total revenues exceeding 5 billion Euro has increased by the factor 8 over the last 30 years, while the general level of earned income in the same period (GDP) has risen by the factor 4.5.

In the minimum wage debate, its opponents have argued, along the neoclassical tradition, with the employment costs of such a regulation (see for example Sinn 2007). The main argument is well known: According with the underlying notion that employers always hire labor up to the point where real wages equal their marginal product, a lower bound on the real wage rate reduces employment and, thus, raises unemployment with all its negative effects for the economy (assuming that the marginal product at the current point of employment is below the minimum real wage rate).

There are, however, important arguments which speak for a much weaker causal relationship between real wage increases and higher unemployment than is predicted by the neoclassical framework. On the one hand, there is nowadays a broad consensus on the fact that institutions play a more important role than the for a real wage effect (for a long time the only aspect considered) in the determination of employment (the change of perspectives between the *OECD Jobs Study* (1994) and the *OECD Employment Outlook* (2006) in these respects is overwhelming). On the other hand, the rise in aggregate demand generated by the higher disposable income of low wage workers resulting from the establishment of a minimum wage is also likely to counteract the eventual decrease in employment, so that the final effect on output is not unambiguous a priori, as many neoclassical economists still state. However, last but not least, the question of whether and to what extent societies succeed in achieving the fulfillment of human rights for all their citizens (since social progress implies an evolution of societies that comprises more than just economic goals in a narrow sense) is an important issue which should also be addressed in the minimum wage debate and on general terms which should be a major concern for policy makers (an aspect often neglected by economists who look only at the economic sub-system of societies when enunciating policy recommendations).

In this chapter we will therefore show in a supply side framework that minimum (real) wages can be beneficial to the working of a modern capitalist economy (characterized by a high state of labor productivity and income per worker), at least in the longer run.[1] First of all, we would stress, in solving this task, that such a topic can only be treated in a dynamic framework that includes the forces of employment and income distribution, and thus not by means of static arguments or even static and partial ones. Secondly, as we will discuss, when the minimum wage barrier is chosen properly, its introduction can lead to economic and social outcomes that clearly dominate the situation of no minimum wages (delaying at most the rise in employment to a certain degree). Since solutions to the mass unemployment problems should involve an active participation of both capital and labor, upper bounds in real wage evolution also may be of help in such a context (see also the analysis in the last chapter). In addition, we emphasize, however (from the perspective of the model of this chapter), that proper minimum real wages and unemployment benefits should be accompanied by working regulations that allow flexible hiring and firing on the part of employers in the economy (as assumed by the model). Hence, employers should be able to react flexibly and quickly to changes in the economic situation. We stress, however, that this demands income security on the side of the workers' position and thus a flexicurity architecture in the economy to a certain degree similar to what is considered in Flaschel, Greiner, Luchtenberg and Nell (2008).

Extending the work by Flaschel and Greiner (2009), we introduce in this chapter low-skilled labor, with a money wage formation of a different type than in the high-skilled labor market. As we will show, since an additional minimum wage for this type of labor does not alter the macro-behavior of the economy to a significant extent, the introduction of such a minimum wage barrier in the low-skilled segment is likely to improve the overall performance of the economy, namely through the less severe fluctuations in economic activity as discussed in Flaschel and Greiner (2009). In addition, this measure is likely to increase the low-skilled workers' social acceptance of their situation, which in this case is not completely decoupled from the normal path of the economy, since in this new framework the employers cannot exploit the weak bargaining power situation of the former without limits any more. Temporarily, employment in this segment may suffer from such minimum real wages. Yet, in the longer run the economy is likely to function in a better way and, thus, also to bring about improvements in the situation of low-skilled workers.

On the other hand, the ideas of some trade unions in Germany concerning minimum wages and other regulations of the labor market are to be considered also as rather detrimental for the functioning of market economies. This concerns both a minimum real wage level that is above the steady state position of the economy[2] as well as the number of working hours per week, since this is just another side of the same coin.

The remainder of this chapter is organized as follows. In Section 3.2 we extend the classical Goodwin model of such an employment cycle – to be used in this chapter as point of reference – with a labor market characterized by queuing features between two groups of workers, skilled and unskilled, and show how they react to low reservation wages and mass unemployment in particular. Section 3.3 considers then a segmented dual labor market with the same two groups of workers and how general regulations concerning basic income needs, minimum wages, but also maximum wages modify (and improve) the employment dynamics of the Goodwin model. Section 3.4 concludes.

In this chapter we assume real wage-setting behavior (in a fixed proportions technology environment).[3]

3.2 The Classical Employment Cycle with a Low Wage Income Sector

In this section we provide an extended version of the Goodwin (1967) employment cycle model of the interaction of income distribution and (un-)employment, as measured by the wage share and the employment rate. This model will serve as a baseline framework for our subsequent discussion of the role of base income payments (unemployment benefits) for all unemployed members of the workforce and minimum wages for the employed part of the workforce.

An empirical example of what is meant by the reserve army mechanism is provided by Figure 3.1.

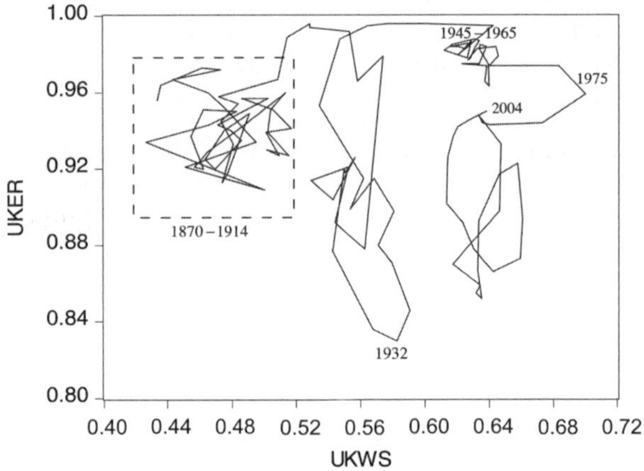

Fig. 3.1: UK distributive cycles 1870–2004: WS=wage share, ER=employment rate

Considerations along these lines are still of great relevance. As Figure 3.1 clearly shows, one insight that can be obtained for the UK (1855–1965) is that while Goodwin cycle in the UK seems to have been significantly shorter before 1914 (with larger fluctuations in employment during each business cycle), there has been a major change in it after 1945.[4] As illustrated in Figure 3.1 by the data taken from Groth and Madsen (2007), it is clear that employment fluctuations have experienced an increase in their amplitude during the last 70 years in the UK economy. In fact, we see in Figure 3.1 two periods of excessive over employment (in the language of the theory of the NAIRU) which were followed by periods of dramatic long underemployment, both started by periods of the more or less pronounced occurrence of stagflation.

Generating order and economic viability in market economies by large swings in the unemployment rate (mass unemployment with human degradation of part of the families that form the society) is one way to make capitalism work, but it must surely be critically reflected with respect to its social and political consequences. From these alternative perspectives, such a reproduction mechanism does not appear to be compatible in the long-run with an advanced and democratic society.

The functioning of a capitalist market economy must therefore be contrasted with alternative social structures of accumulation and labor market institutions which allow combining the situation of a highly competitive market economy (free hiring and firing) with a human rights bill that includes the right (and the obligation) to do (social) work (including the preservation of workforce skills), and to obtain an income from this work that at the least supports basic needs and basic happiness.[5] By contrast, a laissez-faire capitalistic society that ruins family structures to a considerable degree (through alienated work, degrading unemployment and education- and value-decomposing visual media) cannot be made compatible with a democratic society in the long-run, since it produces conflicts ranging from social segmentation to class and racial clashes and more.

This classical prototype model of fluctuating employment, now based on two labor markets adjustment processes (in Goodwin (1967), a single labor market was assumed) and as in Goodwin (1967) one accumulation dynamics, was originally written in purely real terms (this can be justified in a nominal framework through the assumption of myopic perfect foresight concerning the price inflation rate). In this chapter we want to discuss the working of the economy under the assumption of a normal Goodwinian labor market (workers of type 1) that is supplemented by (and interacts with) a low wage income labor market (workers of type 2) where we assume labor supply as being so abundant that there is no bottleneck created for the economy through this low income labor market. We can show in this framework that minimum real wages provide extra stability to such dynamics by decreasing the amount of overshooting in employment and distribution they are otherwise subject to. The labor market in this section is characterized by queuing features; when the skilled workers (type 1) do not find a job in the first labor market, they always find one in the second labor market and thus evict unskilled workers (type 2), which are then unemployed. In this simple model, if there is at first no redistribution scheme from the employed to the unemployed, then the unemployed have no income at all; we can assume that the unemployed have such a low utility value (concave utility function in terms of income) that any redistribution to them will increase the overall aggregate utility. Both working populations are stationary in time (and given by $\bar{L}_1, \bar{L}_2$) and we consider a fixed proportions technology with a given output–capital ratio $\bar{x} = Y/K$ and two given employment functions of the type $L_1^d = Y/\bar{y}_1, L_2^d = Y/\bar{y}_2$ for the two types of work corresponding to two labor markets that are performed in the industrial sector of the economy. The functioning of the labor market is illustrated in graphical form in Figure 3.2.

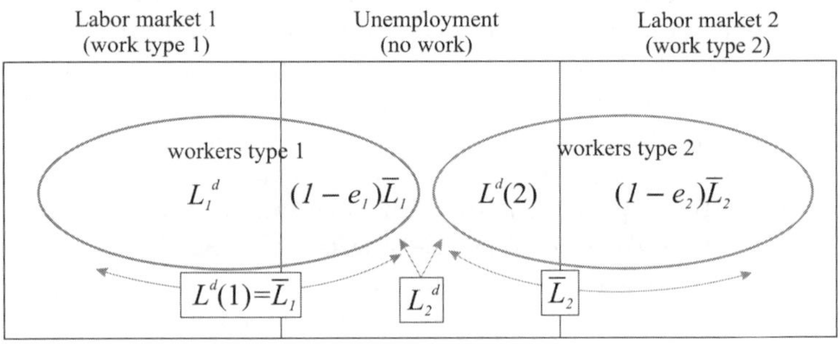

Fig. 3.2: Labor market system in graphical form

Let us start with the detailed formulation of the model. The growth rate of the money wage of workers of type 1 is given by:

$$\hat{w}_1 = \beta_{we}(e_1 - \bar{e}_1) + \beta_{wv}(\omega_2 - \bar{\omega}_2) + \pi^e, \quad \hat{w}_1 = \dot{w}_1/w_1. \tag{3.1}$$

For workers of type 2 we assume that their real wage is in principle fixed to the one of workers of type 1 by a factor a but that there will be additions to or substraction from it, depending on the state of the business cycle in the first labor market:

$$\omega_2 = a\omega_1 + b(e_1 - \bar{e}_1). \tag{3.2}$$

Workers of type 2 are therefore not actively involved in wage negotiations, on the one hand, and have to suffer from income losses in the case of a depressed first labor market (and vice versa), on the other hand. Workers of type 1 are negotiating nominal wages as in Goodwin (1967), but do this with more success when their reservation wage (the one of the second labor market) is increasing.

Assuming myopic perfect foresight with respect to price inflation ($\hat{p} = \pi^e$), the labor market dynamics can be reduced to the following two equations:[6]

$$\hat{v}_1 = \beta_{we}(e_1 - \bar{e}_1) + \beta_{wv}\bar{y}_2(v_2 - v_2^*), \quad v_1 = \frac{w_1 L_1^d}{pY} = \frac{\omega_1}{\bar{y}_1}, \tag{3.3}$$

$$v_2 = av_1\frac{\bar{y}_1}{\bar{y}_2} + (b/\bar{y}_2)(e_1 - \bar{e}_1), \quad v_2 = \frac{w_2 L_2^d}{pY} = \frac{\omega_2}{\bar{y}_2}, \tag{3.4}$$

where we now use the steady state value of v_2 (i.e. v_2^*) as point of reference for the reservation wage effect in the wage Phillips curve of workers of type 1.

Goodwin's accumulation equation for the rate of return on capital $\hat{K}$ reads in the considered framework on the basis of a linear technology with no technical change, (that is on the basis of the given input–output proportions $\bar{x} = Y/K = \text{const.}$, $\bar{y}_i = Y/L_i^d = \text{const.}$), and of its extremely classical savings and investment assumptions ($s_c = 1; s_w = 0$) as follows:

$$\hat{K} = \dot{K}/K = \frac{Y - \delta K - \omega_1 L_1^d - \omega_2 L_2^d}{K} = \bar{x}(1 - v_1 - v_2) - \delta, \tag{3.5}$$

with δ the depreciation rate of the capital stock.

Given the fixed input–output proportions $\bar{x}$ and $\bar{y}_1$, we get from the definitional equation $e_1 = L_1^d/\bar{L}_1$ the law of motion of this employment rate of workers of type 1:

$$\begin{aligned} \hat{e}_1 = \hat{K} &= \bar{x}(1 - v_1 - v_2) - \delta \\ &= \bar{x}\left(1 - v_1 - av_1\frac{\bar{y}_1}{\bar{y}_2} - (b/\bar{y}_2)(e_1 - \bar{e}_1)\right) - \delta. \end{aligned} \tag{3.6}$$

From the above expression we obtain an autonomous 2D system of differential equations in the state variables v_1, e_1:

$$\dot{v}_1 = [\beta_{we}(e_1 - \bar{e}_1) + \beta_{wv}\bar{y}_2(av_1\bar{y}_1/\bar{y}_2 + (b/\bar{y}_2)(e_1 - \bar{e}_1) - v_2^*)]v_1 \tag{3.7}$$

$$\dot{e}_1 = [\bar{x}(1 - (1 + a\bar{y}_1/\bar{y}_2)v_1 - (b/\bar{y}_2)(e_1 - \bar{e}_1)) - \delta]e_1 \tag{3.8}$$

as the basis for our discussion of classical unemployment cycles and their later modification through unemployment benefits and minimum wage payments.

The uniquely determined interior steady state solution of this system is

$$v_1^* = \frac{(\bar{x} - \delta)\bar{y}_2}{(\bar{y}_2 + a\bar{y}_1)\bar{x}}, \quad e_1^* = \bar{e}_1. \tag{3.9}$$

With respect to this steady state position there holds:

Proposition 1:

1. *The determinant of the Jacobian matrix of the dynamics at the steady state is positive for all positive parameter values of the dynamics (5), (6).*
2. *At the parameter values*

$$\beta_{wv}^H = \frac{b}{a}\frac{e_1^* \bar{x}/\bar{y}_2}{\bar{y}_1 v_1^*}, \quad b^H = \frac{\beta_{wv}\bar{y}_1 a v_1^*}{e_1^* \bar{x}/\bar{y}_2}$$

there occurs a (degenerate) Hopf bifurcation where explosive fluctuations are turned into damped ones for smaller β_{wv} and larger b. The interior steady state of the 2D dynamical system is then in particular locally asymptotically stable.

Proof: The Jacobian matrix of the considered dynamics reads at the steady state:

$$J = \begin{pmatrix} \beta_{wv}\bar{y}_1 a v_1^* & [\beta_{we} + \beta_{wv} b] v_1^* \\ -\bar{x}(1 + a\bar{y}_1/\bar{y}_2)e_1^* & -\bar{x}(b/\bar{y}_2)e_1^* \end{pmatrix}. \tag{3.10}$$

For the determinant of this Jacobian we therefore get:

$$\begin{aligned} \det J =& [-\beta_{wv} ab\bar{y}_1/\bar{y}_2 + \beta_{we}(1 + a\bar{y}_1/\bar{y}_2) + \beta_{wv}(1 + a\bar{y}_1/\bar{y}_2)b]\bar{x}v_1^* e_1^* \\ =& (\beta_{we} + \beta_{wv} b + a\beta_{we}\bar{y}_1/\bar{y}_2)\bar{x}v_1^* e_1^* > 0. \end{aligned} \tag{3.11}$$

This proves the first part of the proposition. Due to this fact the system can only lose stability when the trace of J passes through zero and becomes positive. The above two bifurcation values exactly characterize such a situation.

The proposition states that increasing sensitivity of workers of type 1 to their reservation wage in the second labor market (that is increasing β_{wv}) can lead the economy towards instability, while an increase in the strength by which the state in the first labor market changes the remuneration conditions in the second labor market (that is increasing b) outside the steady state stabilizes the economy.[7]

We have assumed with respect to workers of type 1 that they are always fully employed (though not necessarily in the first labor market). This implies for the employment $L^d(2)$ of low-income workers in the second labor market the situation ($\bar{L}_1, \bar{L}_2$ given magnitudes):

$$L^d(2) = L_2^d - (1 - e_1)\bar{L}_1, \tag{3.12}$$

$$\Rightarrow e_2 = L^d(2)/\bar{L}_2 = (L_2^d/K)(K/\bar{L}_2) - (1 - e_1)\bar{L}_1/\bar{L}_2. \tag{3.13}$$

This gives (with $l_1 = \bar{L}_1/K = \frac{\bar{x}/\bar{y}_1}{e_1}, l_2 = \frac{\bar{L}_2}{\bar{L}_1} l_1, l = l_1 + l_2$):

$$\bar{e}_2 = \bar{x}/\bar{y}_2(K/\bar{L}_2) - (1-\bar{e}_1)(\bar{L}_1/\bar{L}_2) = \bar{x}/\bar{y}_2/l_2 - (1-\bar{e}_1)(l_1/l_2) \quad (3.14)$$

if everything is expressed in per unit of capital and evaluated at the steady state. This expression shows the many parameters that are involved in the determination of the steady state rate of employment of the low income workers.

In order to draw a phase diagram of the dynamics considered in Proposition 1 we now calculate the isoclines of their two laws of motion. These isoclines are given by straight lines defined by:

$$\begin{aligned} \dot{v}_1 &= 0 \\ &= [\beta_{we}(e_1 - \bar{e}_1) + \beta_{wv}\bar{y}_2(av_1\bar{y}_1/\bar{y}_2 + b/\bar{y}_2(e_1 - \bar{e}_1) - v_2^*)]v_1, \quad (3.15) \\ \dot{e}_1 &= 0 \\ &= [\bar{x}(1 - (1 + a\bar{y}_1/\bar{y}_2)v_1 - (b/\bar{y}_2)(e_1 - \bar{e}_1)) - \delta]e_1. \quad (3.16) \end{aligned}$$

This implies as explicit representation for the two partial equilibrium curves:

$$e_1|_{\dot{v}=0} = \bar{e}_1 - \frac{\beta_{wv}(av_1\bar{y}_1 - v_2^*\bar{y}_2)}{\beta_{we} + \beta_{wv}b} = \bar{e}_1 - \frac{av_1\bar{y}_1 - v_2^*\bar{y}_2}{\beta_{we}/\beta_{wv} + b}, \quad (3.17)$$

$$e_1|_{\dot{e}=0} = \bar{e}_1 + \frac{\bar{x}(1 - (1 + a\bar{y}_1/\bar{y}_2)v_1) - \delta}{\bar{x}b/\bar{y}_2}. \quad (3.18)$$

We see that both lines are negatively sloped and that the second isocline is steeper than the first one. This implies as the phase plot of the dynamics the situation shown in Figure 3.3. Note that the steady state is in the north-west corner of the square shown in Figure 3.3. Its placement in the middle of it is only due to graphical reasons. Note that there are two more steady states of the dynamics on the axes of the phase space which, however, will play no role in the following.

Figure 3.3 shows the usual clockwise rotation of the Goodwin distributive cycle mechanism which may be damped or explosive depending on the conditions stated in Proposition 1. In the explosive case we need, however, at least one additional mechanism that keeps the dynamics bounded within an economically meaningful part of the phase space. Since the axes of the phase space are invariant subsets, convergence to the axes can only take place if there is a steady state position as limit of this process. This can be excluded for the vertical axes since the interior dynamics is moving away from this steady state.

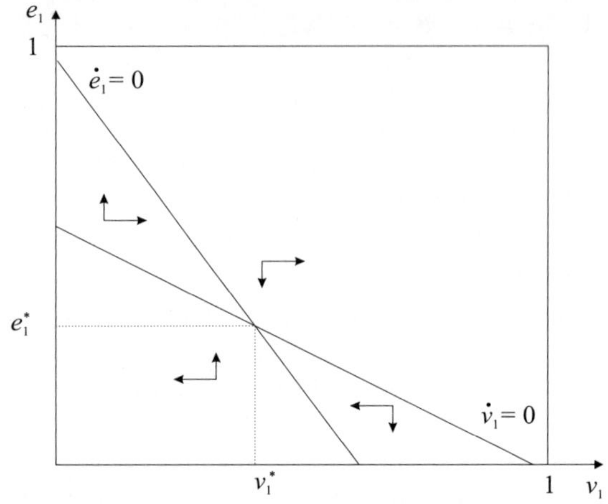

Fig. 3.3: The phase diagram of the Goodwin wage spread cycle

With respect to the steady state on the horizontal axes, we assume that the dynamics is bounded to the right as shown by the dotted line in Figure 3.4. The motivation for this bound is that we may have mathematical adjustment process there that can lead the wage share v_1 by accelerating wage (price) dynamics to 1. Even before this point is reached, the economy is no longer capable of reproducing itself so that in one way or another the behavior of economic agents will change (or be changed) before such a situation can arise.

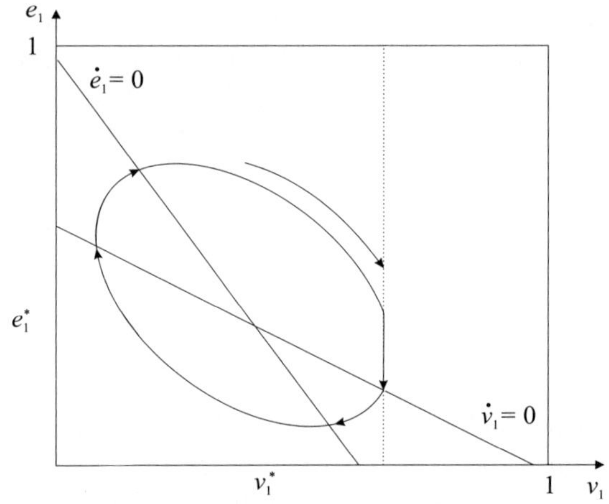

Fig. 3.4: A 'Nixon' type wage–price freeze and the generation of persistent fluctuations in employment and income distribution

For reasons of simplicity we have here assumed a wage–price freeze (as for example imposed on the US economy by President Nixon in 1971). The dotted line in Figure 3.4 shows a perfect wage–price freeze once its corresponding wage share level has been reached. As it is illustrated, the economy moves along it in a downward direction until the $\dot{v}_1 = 0$ isocline is reached from where it starts moving inside again. Since the axes of the positive quadrant cannot be approached in this area the economy must automatically have a lower turning point (in the rate of employment) and a turning point to the left (in the wage share). As the figure shows, it must also automatically have an upper turning point (in the rate of employment). If not, it would (similarly to the wage share) hit a ceiling (of absolute full employment) and move along it until it would again turn inside when the $\dot{e}_1$ isocline has been crossed.

Taken together, the model therefore implies in the explosive case the existence of a limit cycle as shown in Figure 3.4, which is rapidly approached from the outside in the case of an overheated economy. The model is therefore capable of explaining damped oscillations or persistent oscillation in the wage share and the employment rate of workers of type 1 (the ones that are employed in the first labor market) as well as the possibility of crisis scenarios which would call for drastic political reactions, as the system might be incapable of finding its way back to stability.

For the employment rate of the workers of type 2 we get on this basis as satellite system:[8]

$$e_2 = \frac{\bar{x}/\bar{y}_2 - e_1 l_1}{l_2}, \quad v(2) = \frac{\omega_2}{\bar{y}_2} - \omega_2(1-e_1)l_1\frac{1}{\bar{x}}. \qquad (3.19)$$

Of course we need further modifications of the model, should one of these expression pass through zero. Note here that the model exhibits increasing wage differentials in times of depressed activity ($e_1 < \bar{e}_1$) and that the wage share of workers of type 2 is in addition reduced by the workers of type 1 that are employed in the second labor market (namely the $(1 - e_1)$ term).

Let us now assume that there is a government wanting to mitigate the recurrent situations of mass unemployment (which means extreme poverty for workers of type 2 as they have then no income) and low wages in the second labor market by means of unemployment benefits as well as combined wages, for workers of type 2 respectively for workers in the labor market 2. We assume specifically that workers of type 1 working in the first labor market (who are never unemployed during the normal course of the established cyclical fluctuations in employment and income) have to pay a 'solidarity' contribution of size $\tau\omega_1 L_1^d$ out of their wage income $\omega_1 L_1^d$ into a fund R out of which unemployment benefits and combined wages for the other workers are paid. The redistribution scheme is therefore intra-redistributive among workers type 1 as well as inter-redistributive between the two worker types. This gives as law of accumulation for these funds R :

$$\dot{R} = \underbrace{\tau\omega_1 L_1^d}_{\text{contributions}} - \underbrace{\psi_1(r)\omega_u(L_2 - L^d(2))}_{\text{unemployment benefits}} - \underbrace{\psi_2(\omega_{min} - \omega_2)L_2^d}_{\text{wage subventions}}. \quad (3.20)$$

with $1 - \tau > a$

The parameter ψ_2, regulating minimum wage payments to workers in the second segment of the labor market, is equal to zero for $\omega_{min} < \omega_2$ and it is equal to one for $\omega_{min} \geq \omega_2$. Moreover, there may be times when the funds R get exhausted (become zero). In order to prevent this over the normal course of the cycle, we assume that unemployment benefits ($\psi_1(r)\omega_u$) are a linearly increasing function of $r = R/K$ (in the range $[0, r^*]$), with $\psi_1(0) = 0, \psi_1(r^*) = 1$ and r^* the steady state value of r (to be determined still). This assumes that unemployment benefits are reduced linearly to zero if the fund for supporting workers of type 2 gets exhausted. Of course, other schemes are equally easy to introduce, for example schemes that take the duration of unemployment into account. It here only serves the purpose that funds R can stay positive in principle if appropriate parameters are used to simulate the model. The justification for such a statement is that they have to be chosen such that combined wage payments can always be covered out of the new payments $\tau\omega_1 L_1^d$ during the period where they are actually paid.

For the evolution of funds $r = R/K$ per unit of capital this gives[9]

$$\begin{aligned} \dot{r} = \tau v_1 \bar{x} - \frac{r}{r^*}\omega_u(l - \bar{x}/\bar{y}_1 - \bar{x}/\bar{y}_2) - \psi_2(v_{min} - v_2)\bar{x} \\ -(\bar{x}(1 - v_1 - v_2) - \delta)r, \end{aligned} \quad (3.21)$$

with $v_{min} = \omega_{min}/\bar{y}_2 < v_2^*$ and ω_u given magnitudes. If the state variables v_1, e_1 are in their steady state position we get as a special case

$$\dot{r} = \tau v_1^*/\bar{x} - \frac{r}{r^*}\omega_u(l^* - \bar{x}/\bar{y}_1 - \bar{x}/\bar{y}_2). \quad (3.22)$$

We here assume finally that the value of r^* is given from the outside and that the value of ω_u is chosen such that $\dot{r} = 0$ holds at $r = r^*$.

This set of assumptions for the evolution of the variable r simply tailors the situation such that unemployment benefit payments and combined wages can actually be realized according to the rules just described. They serve the purpose to show how the Goodwinian cycle dynamics with two types of workers can be augmented such that basic needs of the workers of type 2 can be met in order to avoid their human degradation during the downswings of the cycle, with respect to employment by the benefits and with respect to wages in the second segment in the labor market by extra wage payments out of the funds R.

The important issue here is that these solidarity payments between workers employed in the first labor market and those temporarily or permanently in the second labor do not at all alter the accumulation dynamics shown in Figure 3.4, since they only represent a redistribution of wages between workers that does not alter their total consumption of produced goods. The inclusion of such transfer payments therefore mitigates the lot of the poor workers, but does not question at all the two-level distributive reserve army mechanism of the Goodwin type (with its typical overshooting effects in income distribution and employment at the aggregate) we have introduced in the previous section.

3.3 Free Hiring and Firing, Income Security and Socially Acceptable Reserve Army Fluctuations

3.3.1 Human Rights: Basic Income and Minimum Wages

Our purpose in this section is to show that Article 23 from the United Nations' declaration of human rights, quoted in detail in Section 2.4, does not only represent a normative political statement, but can also be justified from the economic point of view in the context of analysis of the process of capital accumulation of this chapter. We believe that capitalism is a very robust system of resource allocation and income distribution that can adjust to many social restrictions if these restrictions are justified from a normative point of view.[10]

In this section, we therefore augment the analysis of the working of the reserve army mechanism in a capitalist economy of the preceding section by two fundamental human rights: the right for basic (of course: real) income when becoming unemployed (that cannot and need not be adjusted to lower values as in the preceding section), and the right to earn fair wages, namely, that do not fall below a certain real minimum level. Of course, there are also obligations connected with the formulations of these rights which concern the obligation to work, the need of skill preservation when unemployed and the provision of adequate social services for the considered society (as in a workfare system). In this chapter, however, our focus relies on the macroeconomic sustainability of these minimum restrictions on the working of a capitalist economy and not on the detailed analysis on how such a system can work at the micro level. We will argue that the social costs of reproduction mechanisms as they are shown in Figures 3.3 and 3.4 are much higher than those produced within the above minimum restrictions by a capitalist economy and that it is the duty of capital as well as of labor to provide the necessary behavior such that these restrictions can be realized not only theoretically, but also – at least – in actual (advanced) capitalist democracies.

3.3.2 Capital's and Labor's Responsibility: Minimum Wages, Basic Income Needs and Upper Bounds for Real Wage Increases

We saw that in the queuing model neither the dynamics of the model nor its equilibrium values are altered if a redistribution scheme is introduced although the lot of the workers of type 2 greatly increase. In this section we consider another type of labor market which involves segmentation features and therefore is perhaps more realistic for European economies. In this market type workers of type 1 if they do not find a job on the labor market 1 now become unemployed (they do not evict workers of type 2 from their job positions in the labor market 2). Both labor markets functions in the same way and are represented graphically in Figure 3.5.

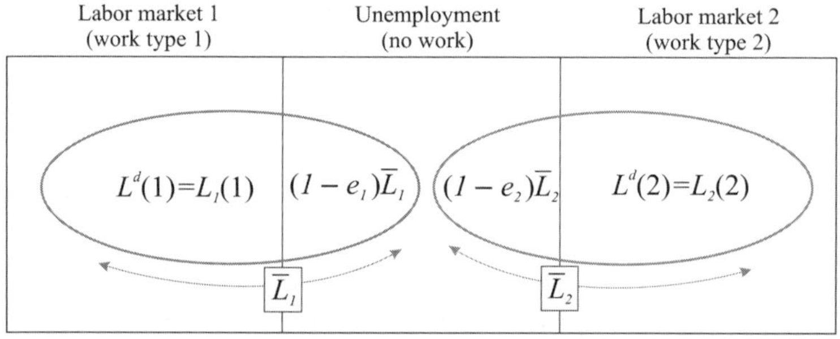

Fig. 3.5: Labor market system with a fraction of type 1 workers unemployed.

Wages are still bargained in labor market 1 only and along a slightly modified Phillips curve:

$$\hat{w}_1 = \beta_{we}(e_1 - \bar{e}_1) + \hat{p}. \tag{3.23}$$

This simplification is justified, since we will now assume that unemployment benefits for workers of the first type are higher than the wages paid to workers of the second type. The real wages of workers of type 2 are assumed now to be fully fixed to the one of workers of type 1 by a factor a and thus no longer overproportionally shrinking in periods of a depressed economy:

$$\omega_2 = a\omega_1, \qquad \omega_1 > \omega_1^{min}. \tag{3.24}$$

Workers of type 2 are still not actively involved in wage negotiations, while workers of type 1 are negotiating nominal wages as in Goodwin (1967). Workers of type 1 do not enter the second labor market now,[11] that is the employment rates in both sectors are now the ones of the two types of workers as pictured in Figure 3.5. Following the new wage equation of the worker of type 2, the wage share of workers of type 2 is now given by:

$$v_2 = \frac{w_2 L_2^d}{pY} = \frac{\omega_2}{\bar{y}_2} = av_1\frac{\bar{y}_1}{\bar{y}_2} \tag{3.25}$$

Goodwin's accumulation equation is unchanged and reads:

$$\begin{aligned} \hat{K} = \dot{K}/K &= \frac{Y - \delta K - \omega_1 L_1^d - \omega_2 L_2^d}{K} \\ &= \bar{x}(1 - (1 + a\bar{y}_1/\bar{y}_2)v_1) - \delta. \end{aligned} \tag{3.26}$$

Using again Y/K = const. and Y/L_1^d = const., we get from the definitional equation $e_1 = L_1^d/\bar{L}_1$ the law of motion of this employment rate of workers of type 1 ($\bar{L}_1$ = const.):

$$\hat{e}_1 = \hat{K} = \bar{x}(1 - v_1 - v_2) - \delta = \bar{x}(1 - v_1 - a\bar{y}_1/\bar{y}_2 v_1) - \delta. \tag{3.27}$$

From the above equation we get an autonomous 2D system of differential equations in the state variables v_1, e_1:

$$\dot{v}_1 = \beta_{we}(e_1 - \bar{e}_1)v_1 \tag{3.28}$$

$$\dot{e}_1 = [\bar{x}(1 - (1 + a\bar{y}_1/\bar{y}_2)v_1) - \delta]e_1. \tag{3.29}$$

This system is of the original Goodwin (1967) type and no longer subject to the intimidating effects we considered in the preceding section with respect to workers of types 1 and 2.[12]

For the evolution of unemployment funds $r = R/K$ per unit of capital we now assume:

$$\dot{r} = \tau_1 v_1/\bar{x} - \omega_{1u}(1-e_1)l_1 + \tau_2 v_2 \bar{x} - \omega_{2u}(1-e_2)l_2, \qquad (3.30)$$

where $l_i = \bar{x}/(\bar{y}_i e_i), i = 1, 2$ now. There are no further deductions here, since minimum wages

$$\omega_1 > \omega_1^{min}, \qquad \omega_2 > \omega_2^{min} = a\omega_1^{min}$$

have to be paid by firms now due to legislation. We assume that the contributions to the unemployment benefits are regulated such that they are equal to benefits payments for each group separately in the steady state[13] defined as:

$$v_1^* = \frac{\bar{x}-\delta}{1+a}, \; v_2^* = av_1\frac{\bar{y}_1}{\bar{y}_2}, \; e_1^* = \bar{e}_1, \; e_2^* = \frac{\bar{y}_1 L_1}{\bar{y}_2 L_2} e_1^*. \qquad (3.31)$$

We thus now have in sum a standard Goodwinian dynamics augmented by unemployment benefits for the two groups of workers which, depending on the size of the cycle that is in operation, demand a certain initial value of R in order to get the sustainability of benefits payments over the cycle. Here the redistribution scheme is only intra-redistributive for each type of worker separately.[14]

The question now, however, is how the dynamics of the original Goodwin model are modified in the large through the assumption of a minimum wage rate for the employed workers that is not organized via wage subventions, but that has to be paid by firms. The answer to that question is basically the same as in the last chapter. The introduction of minimum wages does not change the dynamics of the model economy as long as they are not binding. But, if the minimum wage becomes binding, the economy will move along this boundary until the NAIRU is reached. Once the NAIRU has been attained real wages will rise again. Thus, excessive fluctuations of the employment rate in the economy can be avoided. In addition, transfer payments can be introduced in order to further alleviate the social consequences which accompany declining employment rates.

Instead of pursuing such a strategy, this chapter would propose a further reflection of the strategies that will make the distributive cycle even less severe and maybe also convergent to the steady state of the economy. The addition of Blanchard and Katz's (1999) error correction may be a candidate here, with neoclassical smooth factor substitution being another stabilizing mechanism[15] (and, of course, any dialogue between workers' unions and capitalists' unions can also be of help). The advantage of the Goodwin approach to the employment cycle is that it is not biased against capitalist interest, since it entails that workers' unions bear responsibility for overshooting wage share and unemployment rates in the prosperity phase of the cycle.[16] Minimum wages come to the help of workers' unions in stagnant phases by avoiding more severe unemployment situations.

The reverse image to that situation may be obtained when a maximum real wage is introduced in this economy. As for the minimum wage nothing changes in the economy as long as the upper bound of the real wage is not binding. However, when the maximum real wage becomes binding wage inflation is higher than price inflation and the upper bound of the wage rate makes the economy return faster to the NAIRU level of employment.

3.3.3 A Microfounded Phillips Curve

As in Chapter 1, we now make use of Blanchard and Katz's (1999) microfoundation of the wage Phillips curve (PC) which adds a wage share error correction term to the wage PC of this section. This microfounded type of Phillips curve extends the wage PC in the following way:

$$\hat{w}_1 = \beta_{we}(e_1 - \bar{e}_1) - \beta_{wv}(v_1 - v_1^*) + \hat{p}. \tag{3.32}$$

We stress that the Blanchard and Katz (1999) approach makes use of a reservation wage (in a wage curve not Phillips curve setup) that is independent from the other labor market so that we now have v_1 in the implied wage Phillips curve in place of its extension by a v_2 expression in the preceding section. The dynamics to be investigated now read:

$$\dot{v}_1 = [\beta_{we}(e_1 - \bar{e}_1) - \beta_{wv}(v_1 - v_1^*)]v_1, \tag{3.33}$$

$$\dot{e}_1 = [\bar{x}(1 - (1 + a\bar{y}_1/\bar{y}_2)v_1) - \delta]e_1. \tag{3.34}$$

Making use of the Liapunov function:

$$H(v_1, e_1) = \int_{e_1^*}^{e_1} \beta_{we}(\tilde{e_1} - e_1^*)/\tilde{e_1}\, d\tilde{e}_1 - \int_{v_1^*}^{v_1} (\bar{x}(1 - (1 + a\bar{y}_1/\bar{y}_2)\tilde{v}_1) - \delta)/\tilde{v}_1\, d\tilde{v}_1$$

we get with respect to these dynamics the result:

$$\begin{aligned}
\dot{H} &= H_{v_1}\dot{v}_1 + H_{e_1}\dot{e}_1 \\
&= -(\bar{x}(1 - (1 + a\bar{y}_1/\bar{y}_2)\tilde{v}_1) - \delta)\hat{v}_1 + \beta_{we}(e_1 - \bar{e}_1)\hat{e}_1 \\
&= -(\bar{x}(1 - (1 + a\bar{y}_1/\bar{y}_2)\tilde{v}_1) - \delta)(-\beta_{wv}(v_1 - v_1^*)) \\
&= \bar{x}(1 + a)(v_1^* - v_1)\beta_{wv}(v_1 - v_1^*) = -\bar{x}\beta_{wv}(v_1 - v_1^*)^2 \leq 0.
\end{aligned}$$

The above potential function H is easily shown to be of the form illustrated in Figure 3.6.

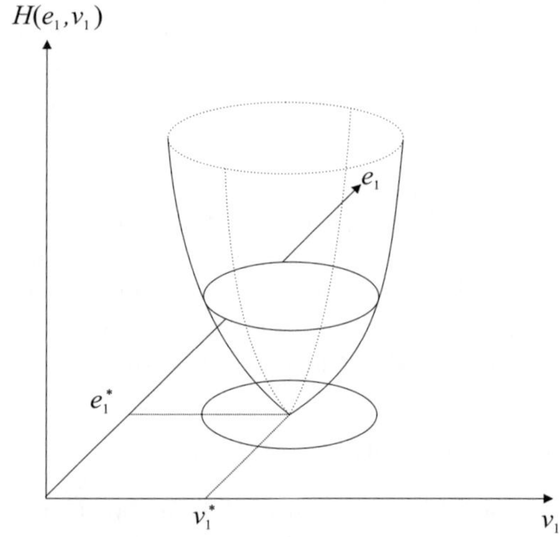

Fig. 3.6: A Liapunov function for the dynamics of this section

Setting $\beta_{wv} = 0$ implies – due to the above – that the function $H(v_1, e_1)$ is constant along the trajectories of the simple Goodwin model this implies. The orbits of the above dynamics are then (as is well known) all closed curves, obtained by projecting the height lines in Figure 3.6 into the phase space of v_1, e_1.

The unrestricted Goodwin employment cycle with $\beta_{wv} > 0$ is, however, losing height in the graph shown of the function H. Adding the Blanchard and Katz error correction term implies therefore that the dynamics are then globally convergent to the steady state of the economy, due to the facts that a) the function H is a global sink and b) the value of H is decreasing along the trajectories as was calculated above. To put it differently: the trajectories of the dynamics with the Blanchard and Katz error correction switched on are (nearly) always pointing inwards with respect to the closed orbits structure of the original Goodwin model. They must therefore converge to the steady state.

Since the cycles that so far resulted from either minimum or maximum real wages are tangent to these restrictions, we get from the above that they are only needed once to restrict the unrestricted excessive cycle to them. Thereafter such bounds are no longer necessary, since the next cycle remains inside of these bounds and converges to the steady state eventually. We thus get from the microfounded wage PC of the Blanchard and Katz (1999) type, at least for Europe as their study is concerned, that minimum and maximum wages will dampen the fluctuations of the unrestricted reserve army mechanism significantly and make it thereafter convergent to its long-run equilibrium position.

3.4 Conclusions

In this chapter we departed from the conventional discussion of the impact of minimum wage legislation, which is only partial in nature, by considering the macroeconomic effects of such legislation on agreements between capital and labor. We think that sector-specific rules concerning minimum wages can only be discussed against the background of such macrofoundations where the medium- and long-run consequences of minimum wages are the focus of interest and not so much the short-run adjustment problems such legislation may cause.

Especially, we have shown that for both labor market specifications (with queuing and with segmentation features) the introduction of a redistribution scheme (unemployment benefit and eventually wage subvention from a fund) change neither the equilibrium values of the system nor its dynamics. We modified for the segmentation model, as it is a more realistic model for Europe, the redistribution scheme by introducing a minimum wage, that is a wage level that will not vary with the state of the fund but that is exogenously fixed by law. In this case, the equilibrium values are not altered, provided the minimum wages (for workers type 1 and 2 respectively) are not set too high. The dynamics are reduced within bounds (defined by these minimum wages). So far, the minimum wage increases welfare in reducing the volatility of the cyclical ups and downs. The introduction of an error-correction term à la Blanchard and Katz (1999) in the Phillips curve even dampens the cyclical volatility toward the equilibrium values, still without affecting their levels.

We conclude, however, from what has been shown in this chapter that the introduction of a general level of minimum (or maximum) real wages for both skilled and unskilled labor into a supply-side macro model of fluctuating employment does not do much harm to capital accumulation and employment even in the shorter run and definitely and significantly improves the performance of the implied cyclical employment path in the course of time. The introduction of a minimum wage not only decreases to a larger extent the severity of fluctuations in the unemployment rates compared to the unrestricted case (where there is an unlimited functioning of the wage-price spiral and the reserve army mechanism), but can also avoid the social consequences of mass unemployment through basic income payments – and an employer of last resort, if meaningful activities of the unemployed are added to the reformulated social structure of accumulation. An advanced society, in which the principle of equal opportunities holds in its schooling system, and where the unskilled/skilled distinction is turned into a skilled/high skilled distinction, may be a very important ingredient in the working of such a social structure, where partial workforce degradation is avoided by meaningful qualification processes of the unemployed and also life-long learning of the employed (see Flaschel, Greiner and Luchtenberg (2008) for further details on such a scenario).

The traverse to such an educated flexicurity system, where the notion of unskilled labor no longer applies, is, however, much more difficult to analyze than the simple traverses shown in the preceding section that led us away from ruthless advantage-taking (by workers in the boom and by capital in the depression) towards a workfare type social structure of accumulation with considerably less severe fluctuations in employment rates and income distribution. Of course, there are practical obstacles on the way towards such a social structure of accumulation, given, for example, by the factual sclerosis of existing social structures (degraded long-term unemployed persons, segmented labor markets, degrading job offers and more). Globalization may also represent a big challenge for our reformulated Goodwin employment cycle dynamics, concerning international competition for traded commodities and services, workforce migration, outsourcing and more. This, however, essentially demands that the baseline workfare system discussed in this chapter needs further refinements, for example along the lines proposed in Flaschel (2009, Ch. 10).

Notes

[1] This chapter provides a – for the purposes of this book – revised version of Flaschel, Greiner, Logeay and Proaño (2011).

[2] See the following analysis.

[3] in place of a neoclassical production function, where employment would be determined by the slightly more general formula $w/p = F_L(K, L^d)$ with no change in the general conclusions of the chapter.

[4] This may be explained by significant changes in the adjustment processes of market economies for these two periods: primarily price adjustment before 1914 and primarily quantity adjustments after 1945.

5 'Basic' in the sense of 'socially acceptable, socially desirable' rather than just 'physical'.

6 Note here that v_1, v_2 represent the wage shares of the workers employed in sectors 1,2 and not the wage share of workers of type 1,2.

7 Note that assuming that output per unit of capital, x, depends to a certain degree on the relative living standard of the low-income workers as variant of an efficiency wage hypothesis:

$$x = x(v_2 - v_2^*) = x(b(e_1 - \bar{e}_1)), \quad x' > 0$$

would make the economy even more vulnerable in its stabilizing potential.

8 Due to our assumption that workers of type 1 are always fully employed if both labor markets are considered.

9 Due to $\dot{r} = \dot{R}/K - \hat{K}r$.

10 For more detailed discussions of such an approach, the reader is referred to Bowles, Gordon and Weisskopf's (1983) work *Beyond the Waste Land* and in particular to their chapter on 'an economic bill of rights'.

11 This requires the validity of $\omega_{1u} > a\omega_1$ for the admissible employment cycles of the model.

12 Figures 3.3 and 3.4 are further valid in the aggregate. The fluctuations in the employment rate of the workers of type 2 are, however, smaller.

13 This is guaranteed if $\tau_i = \omega_{iu}/\omega_i^* e_i^*$, $i = 1, 2$, holds true; those expressions can be shown to be smaller than 0.05 for reasonable parameter constellations.

14 This may be seen as an unrealistic specification but a modification where the funds payments would be pooled and redistributed to all unemployed according to their respective type (which match much more the European unemployment benefits systems) would not alter the results.

15 See Flaschel (2009, Ch. 4).

16 See Wörgötter (1986) for the details of such an observation.

4. Atypical Employment and Smooth Factor Substitution

In this chapter we argue that the model of a flexicurity economy comes close to the vision of competitive socialism as envisaged by Schumpeter when suitably adjusted to modern labor market institutions. We then present a growth model that contains minimum wages as one important element of a flexicurity economy where we allow for heterogenous labor and for real wage rigidities. It is demonstrated that the wage setting process, in its reference to the reservation wage of the first labor market, is crucial as regards stability of the economy and we prove that persistent or explosive oscillations occur for certain parameter constellations, in particular when the influence of the reservation wage on wage formation in the first labor market becomes too large. In addition, we shown that minimum wages can alleviate the negative consequences of economic downturns and help to stabilize the economy by always transforming explosive dynamics into persistent business fluctuations.

4.1 Introduction

Questioning the viability of Eastern state socialism existing at his time from the viewpoint of immaturity, Schumpeter (1942) developed a concept of socialism for Western countries in the state of maturity characterized as a type of competitive socialism. Schumpeter discusses the question of whether this type of socialism can work, what the corresponding socialist blueprints should look like and to what extent they are superior to the capitalist mark II blueprints (of the mega-corporations) that he conceived as having made obsolescent the entrepreneurial functioning of his view of capitalism mark I, the dynamic entrepreneur and the process of creative destruction which is conducted by this leading form of an economic agent.

Schumpeter answered the question of the workability of his model of socialism with a definite yes, but viewed from today's perspective we would at least question his solution of the coordination problem under socialism, which by and large is of a static Walrasian type. However, both capitalism and a competitive form of socialism, are of a very dynamic type, leading to radically transformed social structures of accumulation within the range of fifty to sixty years in a wave-like fashion as, for example, the period after World War II clearly shows. Therefore, its modeling must be done in a strictly dynamic context which is not visible in Schumpeter's (1942) discussion of late capitalism, socialism and democracy.

However, a form of competitive capitalism that comes close to what Schumpeter had in mind – when suitably adjusted towards modern labor market reforms – may be given by the system of flexicurity capitalism. The word flexicurity is obtained from combining flexibility with security and refers to an economy characterized by flexibility on goods markets as well as by social security. The flexicurity model has attracted much attention in public debates, but there is no clear consensus on its definition (see Zhou 2007). According to Wilthagen et al. (2004), flexibility on the labor market implies, among other things, both external flexibility, that is hiring and firing, as well as internal flexibility, such as flexible working hours and the possibility of working overtime and part-time work. As concerns security, essential characteristics of the flexicurity model are income security, that is income protection in the event of job loss, and the guarantee of a minimum wage rate in the low-wage sector and the ability to combine paid work with other social responsibilities and obligations.

Thus, the central message of Schumpeter's (1942) work *Capitalism, Socialism and Democracy* – that socialism is created out of Western capitalist economies, and not on the basis of the (now past) Eastern type of socialism – can be carried over to the current debate on the possibility of flexicurity capitalism.

In this chapter we intend to contribute to the line of research that tries to shed light on the question of how the basic ingredients of a flexicurity economy affect capitalistic economies.[1] In our contribution we focus on the labor market and we first analyze how the wage-setting process affects the dynamics of a market economy. In a second step we introduce minimum wages and study their implications on the evolution of wages and of the employment ratio. To do so we combine the approaches of Solow (1956) and of Goodwin (1967) which we extend by allowing for heterogenous labor and by taking into account real wage rigidities that give rise to unemployment.

The rest of the chapter is organized as follows. In the next section we introduce the structure of our economy. Section 4.3 analyzes the impact of the wage setting process on the dynamics of our model and Section 4.4 discusses policy implications as regards the wage setting process as well as implications of introducing minimum wages. Section 4.5 concludes.

4.2 The Model

In this section, we present the structure of our model economy. The starting point of our model is the contributions by Solow (1956) and by Goodwin (1967) where we integrate heterogenous labor and real wage inertia (see also Flaschel and Greiner, 2011).

4.2.1 Factor Substitution, Income, Real Wage Inertia, and a Low Wage Sector

Our synthesis of the growth models of Solow (1956) and Goodwin (1967) into a model of the minimum wage variety with a low-income labor market in addition to the normal one consists of four basic building blocks: the three factor production function of the industrial sector, the marginal productivity theory of real wages, and the dynamics of the real wages of the workers in the first labor market, describing the degree of labor market rigidity existing with respect to normal labor in the industrial sector of the economy. With respect to low wage work we assume that their real wage is a portion of the normal real wage and that it depends on the employment gap in the first labor market (in a positive way).

Thus, the growth dynamics of the model consists of the following four structural equations (plus the usual natural growth assumption for the labor of the first labor market):

$$Y = F(K, L_1, L_2), \tag{4.1}$$

$$\omega_1 = F_2(K, L_1, L_2), \quad \omega_2 = F_3(K, L_1, L_2), \tag{4.2}$$

$$\hat{w}_1 = \beta_{we}(e_1 - \bar{e}_1) + \hat{p} + \beta_{ww}(\omega_2 - \bar{\omega}_2), \quad e_1 = L_1/L_1^w, \tag{4.3}$$

$$\omega_2 = a\omega_1 + b(e_1 - \bar{e}_1), \tag{4.4}$$

$$\dot{L}_1^w = nL_1^w \quad (= nL_2^w), \quad n = const. \tag{4.5}$$

The first two equations provide a three-factor production function, built on standard assumptions, coupled with the conditions for profit maximization with respect to its two instantaneously variable inputs, the labor L_1 worked by workers L_1^w in the first labor market segment and the work done by part of the workforce L_2^w that is employed by firms from the second labor market. We assume that both groups of workers grow with the natural rate n and that unemployed workers in the first labor market totally crowd out workers of type 2. Therefore, there is full employment for workers of type 1, but not necessarily all in the first labor market, while workers of type 2 get the remaining jobs for work of type 2 or are unemployed. We do not yet consider an unemployment benefit system for the idle workers of type 2. The structure of the labor market is illustrated in Figure 3.2 in the last chapter.

The third equation is a conventional expectations augmented money-wage Phillips curve, based on the actual employment of workers of type 1 working in the first labor market, and based on myopic perfect foresight concerning price inflation. This latter assumption avoids the explicit consideration of a price Phillips curve, since we can then reduce the wage–price dynamics of this model type to a real wage dynamics $\hat{\omega}_1, \omega_1 = w_1/p$, and need not consider nominal effects in the framework chosen. Note, however, that we have augmented this law of motion for the real wage by a term that accounts for the deviation of real wages of workers of type 2, ω_2, from its steady state level, $\bar{\omega}_2$. This term expresses the influence of the reservation wage of workers of type 1, that is the wage they have to accept when they become unemployed in the first labor market.

Real wages of workers of type 2 are in the first place a fixed proportion of the real wage in the first labor market, but increase beyond this level if there is excess employment (according to the natural rate hypothesis) in the first labor market and they decrease below this level in the opposite situation.

Aggregate demand is always equal to aggregate supply in the chosen framework, since all savings are product-oriented and since all profits are invested (that is Say's law holds). Therefore, we have that actual output is supply driven, depending on the level of real wages ω_1, ω_2 and on the capital stock K as shown above.

4.2.2 Intensive Form

In the intensive form of the model we have to consider the statically endogenous variables $l_1, l_2, y, , e_1 = l_1/l_1^w, \omega_2$ in their interaction with the two dynamically endogenous variables ω_1, l_1^w. We stress that the indices $1, 2$ used here have to be distinguished from the same indices used for other relationships that will then denote partial derivatives.

$$y = F(1, l_1, l_2) = f(l_1, l_2), \tag{4.6}$$
$$\omega_1 = f_1(l_1, l_2), \quad \omega_2 = f_2(l_1, l_2), \tag{4.7}$$
$$\hat{\omega}_1 = \beta_{we}\left(\frac{l_1}{l_1^w} - \bar{e}_1\right) + \beta_{ww}(\omega_2 - \bar{\omega}_2), \tag{4.8}$$
$$\omega_2 = a\omega_1 + b\left(\frac{l_1}{l_1^w} - \bar{e}_1\right), \tag{4.9}$$
$$\hat{l}_1^w = n - \hat{K} = n - \rho(l_1, l_2), \tag{4.10}$$

with

$$\rho(l_1, l_2) = f(l_1, l_2) - f_1(l_1, l_2)l_1 - f_2(l_1, l_2)l_2,$$

the profit rate of firms.

Equations (4.7) can be solved for l_1, l_2 giving

$$l_1 = g(\omega_1, \omega_2), \tag{4.11}$$
$$l_2 = h(\omega_1, \omega_2), \tag{4.12}$$

with all partial derivatives of these functions being negative, since we have:[2]

$$f_{11}(l_1, l_2)f_{22}(l_1, l_2) - f_{12}(l_1, l_2)f_{21}(l_1, l_2) = f_{11}f_{22} - f_{12}^2 > 0,$$

and since we get in this case by the implicit function theorem from the total derivatives $d\omega_i = f_{i1}dl_1 + f_{i2}dl_2, i = 1, 2$:[3]

$$\begin{pmatrix} dl_1 \\ dl_2 \end{pmatrix} = \frac{1}{f_{11}f_{22} - f_{12}f_{21}} \begin{pmatrix} f_{22} & -f_{12} \\ -f_{21} & f_{11} \end{pmatrix} \begin{pmatrix} d\omega_1 \\ d\omega_1 \end{pmatrix} = \frac{1}{+} \begin{pmatrix} - & - \\ - & - \end{pmatrix} \begin{pmatrix} d\omega_1 \\ d\omega_1 \end{pmatrix}.$$

Mathematical rearrangement of the equations of the model in intensive form yields

$$\hat{\omega}_1 = \beta_{we}\left(\frac{l_1(\omega_1, \omega_2)}{l_1^w} - \bar{e}_1\right) + \beta_{ww}(\omega_2 - \bar{\omega}_2), \tag{4.13}$$
$$\hat{l}_1^w = n - \hat{K} = n - \rho(l_1(\omega_1, \omega_2), l_2(\omega_1, \omega_2)), \tag{4.14}$$

with

$$\omega_2 = a\omega_1 + b\left(\frac{l_1(\omega_1, \omega_2)}{l_1^w} - \bar{e}_1\right),$$

as the equation for the real wage of workers of type 2 now. This latter equation must again be solved by the implicit function theorem and then gives as expression for ω_2 :

$$\omega_2 = \omega_2(\omega_1, l_1^w), \quad \text{with} \quad \frac{\partial \omega_2}{\partial \omega_1} > 0, \frac{\partial \omega_2}{\partial l_1^w} < 0$$

for sufficiently low values of the parameter b. This follows from the following application of the implicit function theorem:

$$(1 - bl_{1\omega_2}/l_1^w)d\omega_2 = (a + bl_{1\omega_1}/l_1^w)d\omega_1 - bl_1/(l_1^w)^2 dl_1^w$$

obtained by totally differentiating the function

$$H(\omega_2, \omega_1, l_1^w) = a\omega_1 + b\left(\frac{l_1(\omega_1, \omega_2)}{l_1^w} - \bar{e}_1\right) - \omega_2 = 0, \quad i.e.,$$

we get

$$\frac{\partial \omega_2}{\partial \omega_1} = \frac{al_1^w + bl_{1\omega_1}}{l_1^w - bl_{1\omega_2}} > 0$$

if $b < al_1^w/(-l_{1\omega_1})$ holds true.

4.2.3 The Profit Rate Function

We have already considered the profit rate function ρ in the preceding section which (since all profits are reinvested and there is no debt financing) determines the growth rate of the capital stock and, thus, the law of motion of the labor intensity ratio $l_1^w = L_1^w/K$. The profit function is given by:

$$\rho(l_1, l_2) = f(l_1, l_2) - f_1(l_1, l_2)l_1 - f_2(l_1, l_2)l_2. \tag{4.15}$$

We now show that ρ depends positively on the two labor intensity ratios chosen by profit maximizing firms. For the derivative ρ_{l_1} we get, for example:

$$\begin{aligned} \rho_{l_1}(l_1, l_2) =& f_1(l_1, l_2) - f_1(l_1, l_2) - f_{11}(l_1, l_2)l_1 - f_{21}(l_1, l_2)l_2 \\ =& - f_{11}(l_1, l_2)l_1 - f_{21}(l_1, l_2)l_2. \end{aligned}$$

Making use of the adding up property of production functions which are homogeneous of degree 1 we can show that this expression is positive by making use of

$$Y = F_k K + F_{L_1} L_1 + F_{L_2} L_2, \quad i.e., \quad F_K + f_1 l_1 + f_2 l_2 = y.$$

This gives

$$F_{KL_1} + f_{11} l_1 + f_1 + f_{21} l_2 = f_1, \quad i.e., \quad F_{KL_1} + f_{11} l_1 + f_{21} l_2 = 0.$$

This implies that $f_{11}l_1 + f_{21}l_2$ must be negative, since F_{KL_1} is positive for conventional types of production functions. This shows that profits depend positively on the profit maximizing choice of the labor intensity for workers of type 1 and thus, of course, also for the one for workers of type 2.

Combining these results with the previous proof that these labor intensities both depend negatively on the real wages of workers of types 1 and 2 gives the result we were looking for, namely:[4]

$$\begin{aligned} \rho(\omega_1, \omega_2) =& \rho(l_1(\omega_1, \omega_2), l_2(\omega_1, \omega_2)) \\ & \text{with} \quad \rho_{\omega_1} < 0, \; \rho_{\omega_2} < 0. \end{aligned} \tag{4.16}$$

4.3 Dynamics

In this section we study the dynamic behavior of the model we introduced in the last section. First, we derive the laws of motion that describe our economy.

4.3.1 Laws of Motion

Inserting the static relationships into the two laws of motion gives rise to the following system of two autonomous differential equations (when multiplied by ω_1, l_1^w in order to replace the growth rate expression by time derivatives).

$$\hat{\omega}_1 = \beta_{we} \left(\frac{l_1(\omega_1, \omega_2(\omega_1, l_1^w))}{l_1^w} - \bar{e}_1 \right) + \beta_{ww}(\omega_2(\omega_1, l_1^w) - \bar{\omega}_2), \tag{4.17}$$

$$\hat{l}_1^w = n - \rho(\omega_1, \omega_2(\omega_1, l_1^w)). \tag{4.18}$$

The interior steady state the stability of which we investigate in the remainder of the chapter is constructed as follows:

$$0 = \beta_{we} \left(\frac{l_1(\omega_1, \omega_2(\omega_1, l_1^w))}{l_1^w} - \bar{e}_1 \right) + \beta_{ww}(\omega_2(\omega_1, l_1^w) - \bar{\omega}_2), \tag{4.19}$$

$$\text{with} \quad \beta_{ww} = 0$$

$$0 = n - \rho(\omega_1, \omega_2(\omega_1, l_1^w)). \tag{4.20}$$

This gives

$$\bar{e}_1 = l_1(\omega_1, \omega_2(\omega_1, l_1^w))/l_1^w, \tag{4.21}$$

$$n = \rho(\omega_1, \omega_2(\omega_1, l_1^w)). \tag{4.22}$$

The first equation defines a downward sloping function as long as $J_{11} < 0$ holds true, while the second relationship defines an upward sloping curve; see the signs of the Jacobian shown below. We assume that these curves intersect which provides us with a unique point $(\omega_1^o, l_1^{wo}) > 0$ where both equations are simultaneously fulfilled. On this basis the wage rate $\bar{\omega}_2$ is then given by $a\omega_1^o$. This triple then provides us with a steady state solution of the above two laws of motion which is locally unique, since the determinant of the Jacobian of the above system at the steady state is positive (as we shall show below).

For the matrix J_o of partial derivatives of this system of differential equations we get at the steady state the expressions:

$$J_o = (J_{ij}^o) = \begin{pmatrix} J_{11}^o & J_{12}^o \\ J_{21}^o & J_{22}^o \end{pmatrix} = \begin{pmatrix} \pm & - \\ + & - \end{pmatrix}$$

with

$$J_{11}^o = \frac{\partial \left(\beta_{we} \frac{l_1(\omega_1, \omega_2(\omega_1, l_1^w))}{l_1^w} + \beta_{ww}\omega_2(\omega_1, l_1^w)\right)}{\partial \omega_1} \omega_1^o$$

$$J_{12}^o = \frac{\partial \left(\beta_{we} \frac{l_1(\omega_1, \omega_2(\omega_1, l_1^w))}{l_1^w} + \beta_{ww}\omega_2(\omega_1, l_1^w)\right)}{\partial l_1^w} \omega_1^o$$

$$J_{21}^o = -\frac{\partial \rho(\omega_1, \omega_2(\omega_1, l_1^w))}{\partial \omega_1} l_1^{wo}$$

$$J_{22}^o = -\frac{\partial \rho(\omega_1, \omega_2(\omega_1, l_1^w))}{\partial l_1^w} l_1^{wo}$$

due to what has been shown in the preceding sections.

We consider the following substructure of the matrix J_o obtained by splitting its first row into two separate expressions:

$$\begin{pmatrix} \frac{\beta_{ww}\partial \omega_2(\omega_1, l_1^w)}{\partial \omega_1}\omega_1^o & \frac{\beta_{ww}\partial \omega_2(\omega_1, l_1^w)}{\partial l_1^w}\omega_1^o \\ -\rho_1 - \rho_2 \frac{\partial \omega_2(\omega_1, l_1^w)}{\partial \omega_1} l_1^{wo} & -\rho_2 \frac{\partial \omega_2(\omega_1, l_1^w)}{\partial l_1^w} l_1^{wo} \end{pmatrix}.$$

For the determinant of this matrix we get, after removing linear dependencies from its rows:

$$\begin{vmatrix} 0 & \frac{\beta_{ww}\partial\omega_2(\omega_1,l_1^w)}{\partial l_1^w}\omega_1^o \\ -\rho_1 & 0 \end{vmatrix} = \begin{vmatrix} 0 & - \\ + & 0 \end{vmatrix} > 0.$$

We have isolated the second terms in the first row of the determinant of J_o and shown that they imply a positive determinant. The full determinant of J_o is (due to its multilinearity) then obtained by calculating the value of

$$\begin{vmatrix} \frac{\beta_{we}\partial\frac{l_1(\omega_1,\omega_2(\omega_1,l_1^w))}{l_1^w}}{\partial\omega_1}\omega_1^o & \frac{\beta_{we}\partial\frac{l_1(\omega_1,\omega_2(\omega_1,l_1^w))}{l_1^w}}{\partial l_1^w}\omega_1^o \\ -\frac{\partial\rho(\omega_1,\omega_2(\omega_1,l_1^w))}{\partial\omega_1}l_1^{wo} & -\frac{\partial\rho(\omega_1,\omega_2(\omega_1,l_1^w))}{\partial l_1^w}l_1^{wo} \end{vmatrix} = \begin{vmatrix} - & - \\ + & - \end{vmatrix}.$$

We thus have shown by means of splitting the determinant of J_o into the sum of two expressions that this determinant is always strictly positive. Stability can therefore only get lost by way of limit of explosive cycles through so-called Hopf bifurcations as we will argue in the subsequent section.

4.3.2 Cyclical Loss of Stability for Strong Reservation Wage Effects

In this section we characterize the parameter domain where convergence to the steady state is given and show by means of the parameter β_{ww} when and how this local asymptotic stability gets lost. We find that weak effects of reservation wages on wage negotiations and also weak effects of the business cycle on the formation of the low wage income does guarantee the asymptotic stability of the steady state of the model. In the next section we discuss the economic implications of this result in detail. But before we state the outcome in the following proposition.

Theorem 1 *Assume (as before) that $e_1 = l_1/l_1^w$ is a negative function of both ω_1 and l_1^w and the ω_2 depends positively on ω_1 and negatively on l_1^w. Then the following holds true:*

1. *The determinant of the Jacobian matrix of the dynamics at the steady state is positive for all positive parameter values of the dynamics.*
2. *At the parameter value*

$$\beta_{ww}^H = \frac{\rho_2\frac{\partial\omega_2(\omega_1,l_1^w)}{\partial l_1^w}\frac{l_1^{wo}}{\omega_1^o} - \frac{\beta_{we}\partial(l_1(\omega_1,\omega_2(\omega_1,l_1^w))/l_1^w)}{\partial\omega_1}}{\partial\omega_2/\partial\omega_1} > 0$$

there occurs a Hopf bifurcation where damped fluctuations are turned into persistent or explosive cycles when the parameter β_{ww} is passing through this threshold value from below. The interior steady state of the 2D dynamical system is then in particular no longer locally asymptotically stable.

Proof: Straightforward on the basis of what has already been shown in this chapter.

Remark: We have for this bifurcation a value that is – formally seen – determined by $J^o_{11} + J^o_{22} = 0$, i.e., it is determined by a positive J^o_{11}, since J^o_{22} is negative. The slope of the $\dot{\omega}_1 = 0$ isocline (see Figure 4.1) by contrast is given by $-J^o_{12}/J^o_{11}$ and is therefore negative as long as $J^o_{11} < 0$ holds. Moreover the slope of the $\dot{l}^w_1$ isocline is given by $-J^o_{22}/J^o_{21}$ and is thus positive. Finally, assuming $\beta_{ww} \to \infty$ still keeps the determinant of J^o positive, namely the slope of the $\dot{\omega}_1 = 0$ isocline is always larger than the slope of the $\dot{l}^w_1$ isocline. This gives rise – in the case $J_{11} < 0$ – to the following phase plot of the considered dynamical system shown in Figure 4.1 where the parameters are such that convergence is assured.[5]

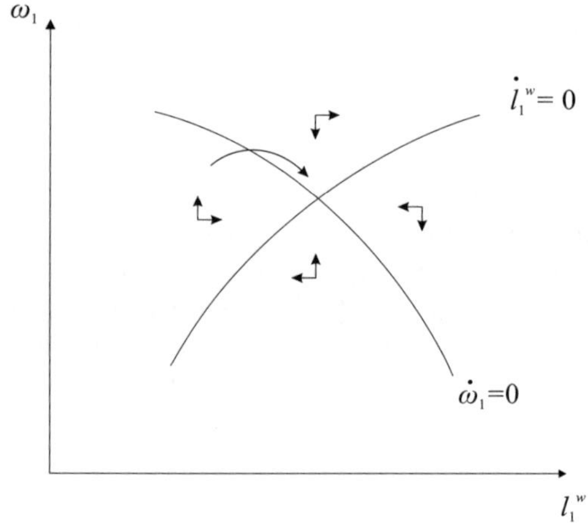

Fig. 4.1: The phase plot of the convergent dynamics in the case $J_{11} < 0$

4.4 Policy Issues and Minimum Wage Restrictions

To achieve convergence to the steady state the parameter b should – as it was assumed in this chapter – be chosen sufficiently small such that $\partial\omega_2/\partial\omega_1 > 0$ holds. This assumption states that the wage rate in the second labor market should not depend too strongly on the employment situation in the first labor market. It also implies that, otherwise, we would have the situation that the wage spread is not only increasing in the boom, but that real wages would even move into opposite directions, that is low income wages would be falling in the boom. Hence, a positive value for $\partial\omega_2/\partial\omega_1 > 0$ does make sense from an economic point of view.

In order to guarantee stability one should in addition attempt to move the parameter β_{we} to higher values and the parameter β_{ww} to lower ones. This means that the growth rate of the real wage should strongly depend on the employment situation in the first labor market whereas the wage rate in the second labor market should not affect the evolution of the wage rate in the first labor market.

It should also be noted that the limit case $b = 0$ so that $\omega_2 = a\omega_1$ and $\beta_{ww} = 0$ removes unnecessary complications from the considered dynamics. The situation $b = 0$ and $\beta_{ww} = 0$ indeed reduces the considered dynamics to the case

$$\hat{\omega}_1 = \beta_{we}\left(\frac{l_1(\omega_1, a\omega_1^o)}{l_1^w} - \bar{e}_1\right), \tag{4.23}$$

$$\hat{l}_1^w = n - \rho(\omega_1, a\omega_1^o), \quad i.e., \tag{4.24}$$

of the conventional Solow model with a real wage rigidity in the first labor market. This model is much simpler in its structure and dynamics, since it avoids the complicated feedback structure of the model when there is a flexible reservation wage spread of workers of type 1 (to which they respond negatively when it decreases) and when there is downward pressure on low wage incomes in the case of slack in the economy.

In our view this not only simplifies the working of the economy (where increasing normal wage flexibility increases its stability[6]), but also makes the working of it socially more acceptable, since it does not degrade low skilled work in the bust, but gives a real wage guarantee at the low end of the labor markets where wages may be close to still acceptable minimum wages.

It may be asked, however, why one does not do the same with normal wage payments, that is with wages that are above the minimum level? A possible answer here is that real wages in this segment of the labor market should be flexible from the microeconomic point of view, since sectoral changes may need flexible real wages for their proper working. The issue here only is that such a flexibility is not socially acceptable at the low end of the labor market where one has to protect the workforce from physical and mental degradation in order to secure proper citizenship behavior in a democratic society.

What is actually supporting stable economic growth is not so much the integration of a second labor market with its complicated interaction with the first one, but in fact a regulated second labor market and its positive influence on the working of the first labor market.

We add here that, with a fixed minimum low income real wage $\underline{\omega}_2$, the strict regime $\underline{\omega}_2 < \bar{\omega}_2$ is characterized by a steady state situation where the employment rate of worker of type 1 is higher than in the unrestricted case. In case of cyclical convergence the economy will only temporarily stay in the regime where the minimum wage is binding, since real wages ω_2 will sooner or later start to rise again whereby this regime is left and change into the unrestricted case. Fixed minimum real wages of low-income workers are therefore at best temporarily a problem for the economy. But they have the advantage of a better treatment of the low-income groups which is to be preferred in a democratic society from the societal point of view.

To be more precise we consider the dynamics of the general model when $\omega_2 = \underline{\omega}_2$ holds and where $b, \beta_{ww} \neq 0$, given by

$$\hat{\omega}_1 = \beta_{we}\left(\frac{l_1(\omega_1, \underline{\omega}_2)}{l_1^w} - \bar{e}_1\right) + \beta_{ww}(\underline{\omega}_2 - \bar{\omega}_2), \tag{4.25}$$

$$\hat{l}_1^w = n - \rho(\omega_1, \underline{\omega}_2). \tag{4.26}$$

Since $\underline{\omega}_2 < \bar{\omega}_2 = a\omega_{1o}$ holds, we get for the steady state position (denoted by a tilde) of this restricted system in comparison to the steady state of the unrestricted system via the second and then the first law of motion:[7]

$$\tilde{\omega}_{1o}(\underline{\omega}_2) > \omega_{1o} \quad \text{with} \quad \tilde{\omega}_{1o}'(\underline{\omega}_2) < 0, \tag{4.27}$$

$$\tilde{e}_{1o}(\underline{\omega}_2) > e_{1o} \quad \text{with} \quad \tilde{e}_{1o}'(\underline{\omega}_2) < 0, \tag{4.28}$$

$$e_{2o} = \frac{l_2(\tilde{\omega}_{1o}, \underline{\omega}_2)}{\alpha l_{1o}^w} + \frac{\tilde{e}_{1o} - 1}{\alpha}, \tag{4.29}$$

if we define $\alpha = L_1^w/L_2^w = l_1^w/l_2^w$. This gives the result that workers of type 1 working in the first labor market are better off in the long-run in this restricted case than in the unrestricted one, and increasingly so the lower the minimum wage in the second labor market, while the situation in the second labor market is not so easy to understand.

However, this is the long-run aspect if convergence to this new steady state is ensured. The latter seems, however, to be an easy to answer issue, since the Jacobian at the above steady state is characterized by:

$$\begin{pmatrix} - & - \\ + & 0 \end{pmatrix}.$$

Yet, in the background of the model, we have the working of the adjustment rule

$$\omega_2 = a\omega_1 + b(e_1 - \bar{e}_1).$$

Therefore, when the steady state value

$$\tilde{\omega}_{1o}(\underline{\omega}_2) > \omega_{1o}$$

is approached, this adjustment rule comes into being again and the economy is switching back to the unrestricted case. The assumed floor to the real wage in the second segment of the labor market therefore only serves the temporary purpose to avoid situations where workers of type two are thrown into misery and does not at all characterize the working of the economy in the longer run.

Minimum wages for low income workers are therefore in the worst case a temporary problem for the economy and are definitely superior to the alternative of their removal from the societal point of view where social cohesion and full citizen participation in a progressive democratic society is desirable.

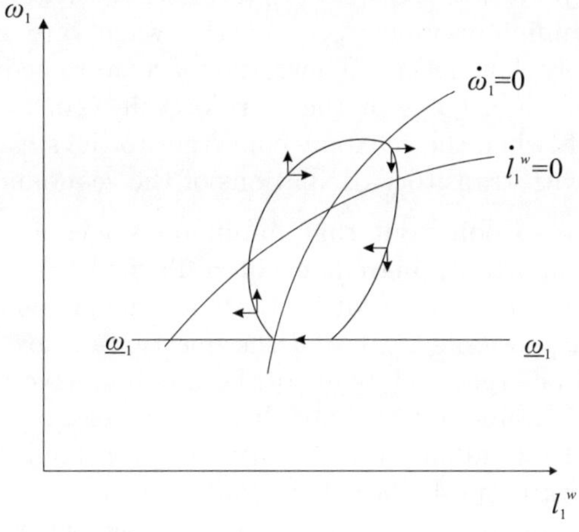

Fig. 4.2: The phase plot of the locally explosive, but downwards bounded dynamics ($J_{11} > -J_{22}$)

In case the parameters of the model are such that the economy is characterized by limit cycles, that is by persistent oscillations of the wage rate and of the employment share, a fixed minimum low income real wage rate prevents the wage from falling to its lower turning point. As in the case of convergence the lower bound is only temporarily binding before the economy leaves the restricted regime. After a certain time period the wage rate starts to rise again, leaves the restricted regime and enters the unrestricted regime. Figure 4.2 illustrates this case.

4.5 Conclusions

In this chapter we have analyzed an economy with heterogenous labor and real wage rigidities. We have demonstrated that the wage setting process is crucial as regards stability of the economy. Hence, we could show that a small influence of the reservation wage tends to stabilize the economy, that is the economy converges to the steady state when the wage rate of the second labor market has only a minor effect on the growth rate of the wage rate in the first labor market. In addition it turned out that a small effect of the employment situation in the first labor market on the wage rate in the second market exerts a stabilizing effect, too.

In addition, we also demonstrated that the economy may generate endogenous cycles for a certain parameter constellation. In such a situation, minimum wages prevent the wage rate from declining to unacceptably low levels. Thus, they are a remedy against the degradation of large parts of the workforce in economic downturns. The same holds when the economy converges to the steady state in the long-run but with transitory oscillations of the economic variables.

We should like to point out that minimum wages are just one, but nevertheless important, ingredient of a flexicurity economy. Other elements that we have not dealt with are an unemployment insurance, for example, a pension system and the question of how the education system should be organized. Some of these points have been addressed in Flaschel and Greiner (2011a) but there is still a lot of work to be done in order to understand how a flexicurity economy should be designed so that it can work properly. We think that a flexicurity economy comes close to that economy Schumpeter had in mind when speaking of a competitive form of socialism in his book *Capitalism, Socialism and Democracy* in 1942.

Appendix A: Fixed Proportions in Production

We shall show in this appendix that the assumption of a Leontief technology (the exclusion of smooth factor substitution) significantly simplifies the analysis of the dynamical system of this chapter, but that it also removes the additional stabilizing feature that results from the existence of a production function with smooth factor substitution.

In the case of fixed proportions we have that l_1 is a given magnitude $\bar{l}_1$ and thus get in this case the dynamical system:

$$\begin{aligned}\hat{\omega}_1 &= \beta_{we}(\bar{l}_1/l_1^w - \bar{e}_1) + \beta_{ww}(\omega_2(a\omega_1, l_1^w) - \bar{\omega}_2)\\ &= (\beta_{we} + b + \beta_{ww})(\bar{l}_1/l_1^w - \bar{e}_1) + \beta_{ww}(a\omega_1 - \bar{\omega}_2), \qquad (A.1)\\ \hat{l}_1^w &= n - \rho(\omega_1, \omega_2(a\omega_1, l_1^w)). \qquad (A.2)\end{aligned}$$

The interior steady state is here constructed as follows:

$$\begin{aligned}0 &= (\beta_{we} + b + \beta_{ww})(\bar{l}_1/l_1^w - \bar{e}_1) + \beta_{ww}(a\omega_1 - \bar{\omega}_2), \quad \beta_{ww} = 0, \qquad (A.3)\\ 0 &= n - \rho(\omega_1, \omega_2(a\omega_1, l_1^w)). \qquad (A.4)\end{aligned}$$

This gives

$$\begin{aligned}\bar{e}_1 &= \bar{l}_1/l_1^w \to l_1^{wo} = \bar{l}_1/\bar{e}_1, \qquad (A.5)\\ n &= \rho(\omega_1, \omega_2(a\omega_1, l_1^{wo})) \to \omega_1^o. \qquad (A.6)\end{aligned}$$

For the matrix J_o of partial derivatives of this system of differential equations we get at the steady state the expressions:

$$J_o = \begin{pmatrix} \frac{\partial \beta_{ww}\omega_2(a\omega_1, l_1^w)}{\partial \omega_1}\omega_1^o & \frac{\partial(\beta_{we}\bar{l}_1/l_1^w + \beta_{ww}\omega_2(a\omega_1, l_1^w))}{\partial l_1^w}\omega_1^o \\ -\frac{\partial \rho(\omega_1, \omega_2(a\omega_1, l_1^w))}{\partial \omega_1} l_1^{wo} & -\frac{\partial \rho(\omega_1, \omega_2(a\omega_1, l_1^w))}{\partial l_1^w} l_1^{wo} \end{pmatrix} = \begin{pmatrix} \pm & - \\ + & - \end{pmatrix}.$$

We consider the following substructure of the matrix J_o obtained by splitting its first row into two separate expressions:

$$\begin{pmatrix} \frac{\beta_{ww}\partial \omega_2(a\omega_1, l_1^w)}{\partial \omega_1}\omega_1^o & \frac{\beta_{ww}\partial \omega_2(a\omega_1, l_1^w)}{\partial l_1^w}\omega_1^o \\ \bar{l}_1 - \bar{l}_2\frac{\partial \omega_2(a\omega_1, l_1^w)}{\partial \omega_1} l_1^{wo} & -\bar{l}_1\frac{\partial \omega_2(a\omega_1, l_1^w)}{\partial l_1^w} l_1^{wo} \end{pmatrix}.$$

For the determinant of this matrix we get after removing linear dependencies from its rows:

$$\begin{vmatrix} 0 & \frac{\beta_{ww}\partial \omega_2(a\omega_1, l_1^w)}{\partial l_1^w}\omega_1^o \\ \bar{l}_1 & 0 \end{vmatrix} = \begin{vmatrix} 0 & - \\ + & 0 \end{vmatrix} > 0.$$

We have isolated the second terms in the first row of the determinant of J_o and shown that they imply a positive determinant. The full determinant of J_o is (due to its multilinearity) then obtained by calculating the value of

$$\begin{vmatrix} 0 & \beta_{we}\frac{\partial \bar{l}_1/l_1^w}{\partial l_1^w}\omega_1^o \\ \bar{l}_1 - \bar{l}_2\frac{\partial \omega_2(a\omega_1, l_1^w)}{\partial \omega_1}l_1^{wo} & -\bar{l}_1\frac{\partial \omega_2(a\omega_1, l_1^w)}{\partial l_1^w}l_1^{wo} \end{vmatrix} = \begin{vmatrix} - & - \\ + & - \end{vmatrix}.$$

We thus have shown by means of splitting the determinant of J_o into the sum of two expressions that this determinant is always strictly positive. Stability can therefore only get lost by way of limit of explosive cycles through so-called Hopf bifurcations.

Proposition A1:

1. *The determinant of the Jacobian matrix of the dynamics at the steady state is positive for all positive parameter values of the dynamics.*
2. *At the parameter value*

$$\beta_{ww}^H = \frac{\bar{l}_2\frac{\partial \omega_2(a\omega_1, l_1^w)}{\partial l_1^w}\frac{l_1^{wo}}{\omega_1^o}}{a} > 0$$

there occurs a Hopf bifurcation where damped fluctuations are turned into persistent or explosive cycles when the parameter β_{ww}^H is passing through this threshold value from below. The interior steady state of the 2D dynamical system is then in particular no longer locally asymptotically stable.

There is, however, one additional advantage of the presently considered case which makes it indeed very easy to analyze from the global perspective. This advantage stems from the fact that in the case of a fixed proportions technology we have the simple relationship $\hat{e}_1 = -\hat{l}_1^w$ which allows transforming the dynamics into the following quasi-linear form:

$$\hat{\omega}_1 = (\beta_{we} + b\beta_{ww})(e_1 - \bar{e}_1) + \beta_{ww}(a\omega_1 - \bar{\omega}_2), \tag{A.7}$$

$$\hat{e}_1 = \bar{y} - \omega_1\bar{l}_1 - (a\omega_1 - \bar{\omega}_2 + b(e_1 - \bar{e}_1))\bar{l}_2 - n. \tag{A.8}$$

This system has been analyzed in detail in Flaschel, Greiner, Logeay and Proaño (2011) also from the global perspective. Complications of the case of smooth factor substitution may therefore to a certain degree be better understood by making use of the limit case of a rigid Leontief technology.

Appendix B: The Low Wage Adjustment Process

In this section we consider the adjustment process of the low income real wage if it is not yet at its equilibrium value as we have assumed it to be the case in the body of the chapter. In this case there is (for the assumed sufficiently small values of the parameter b) a simple stable iteration routine – as shown in Figure B.1 – that will lead the economy to the assumed equilibrium value of the real wage ω_2.

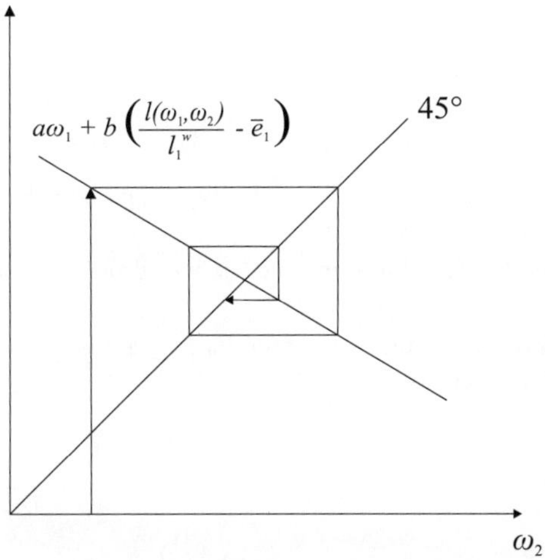

Fig. B.1: The low wage adjustment process

This iteration routine – or updating process for the lower real wage – is a cyclical one, but it is nevertheless converging and this the stronger the smaller the value of the parameter b

Notes

[1] This chapter is based on Flaschel, P. and A. Greiner (2011), 'Dual labor markets and the impact of minimum wages on atypical employment', *Metroconomica*, forthcoming.

[2] The critical point is to check whether the determinant $f_{11}f_{22} - (f_{12})^2$ is always positive. This holds true because the production function in extensive form $F(K, L, H)$ is linear-homogenous. Using the Euler theorem $F_{L_1}L_1 + F_{L_2}L_2 + F_K K = F$ and differentiating both sides with respect to L_1, L_2, and K we get a 3-dimensional system of equations in these three variables with determinant equal to zero. This yields $F_{L_1L_1}F_{L_2L_2} - F_{L_1L_2}F_{L_2L_1} > 0$. Since the expression in intensive form is just the latter term multiplied by $(1/K)^2$ the positive sign also holds for that term.

[3] In the case of a Cobb–Douglas production function $Y = K^{\alpha_o} L_1^{\alpha_1} L_2^{\alpha_2}$ one gets the expressions:

$$l_1 = \left(\frac{\alpha_1 \frac{\alpha_2}{\alpha_1} \frac{\omega_1}{\omega_2}}{\omega_1} \right)^{1/\alpha_o}, \quad l_2 = \frac{\alpha_2}{\alpha_1} \frac{\omega_1}{\omega_2} l_1$$

and on this basis

$$\begin{pmatrix} f_{22} & -f_{12} \\ -f_{21} & f_{11} \end{pmatrix} = l_1^{\alpha_1 - 1} l_2^{\alpha_2 - 1} \begin{pmatrix} (\alpha_2 - 1)\alpha_2 l_1/l_2 & -\alpha_1\alpha_2 \\ -\alpha_1\alpha_2 & (\alpha_1 - 1)\alpha_1 l_2/l_1 \end{pmatrix}$$

and

$$f_{11} f_{22} - f_{12} f_{21} = (l_1^{\alpha_1 - 1} l_2^{\alpha_2 - 1})^2 \alpha_1 \alpha_2.$$

[4] This result can also be derived by investigating the expression $F_K(l_1(\omega_1, \omega_2), l_2(\omega_1, \omega_2))$.

[5] The case of locally unstable dynamics converging to a limit cycle is shown in the next section.

[6] A sufficient increase in the parameter β_{we} even makes convergence to the steady state non-cyclical.

[7] $l_1(\tilde{\omega}_{1o}, \underline{\omega}_2)/e_{1o} = \tilde{l}_{1o}^w$.

PART III

Unemployment and Welfare Issues in Models of Endogenous Growth

5. Economic Growth with an Employer of Last Resort: A Simple Model of Flexicurity Capitalism

5.1 Introduction

Many European countries experience persistent unemployment in spite of permanently growing GDPs. An exception is the Nordic welfare states, which comprise Denmark, Finland, Norway and Sweden. These countries have been characterized by relatively small unemployment rates and a high standard of social security. In particular, Denmark has established social security programmes together with a high flexibility on factor markets, including the labor market, which has been termed the flexicurity model. Frictions on the labor market are made acceptable through a publicly organized labor market where all workers not employed by the private sector get remuneration and meaningful occupation from the government so that societies remain socially stable. Hence, these countries demonstrate that flexibility and security need not be contradictory but may well be compatible and can also go along with low unemployment rates.

The flexicurity model has attracted much attention in public debates as already pointed out in the last chapter. According to Wilthagen et al. (2004), flexibility on the labor market implies, among other things, both external flexibility, that is hiring and firing, as well as internal flexibility, such as flexible working hours and the possibility of working overtime and part-time work. As concerns security, essential characteristics of the flexicurity model are income security, that is income protection in the event of job loss, and the ability to combine paid work with other social responsibilities and obligations.

In this chapter we intend to present a standard model of economic growth where the idea of flexicurity is incorporated[1]. Thus, we assume that the productive sector of the economy, which is modeled by a representative firm, maximizes profits taking the wage rate and the interest rate as given. The firm demands two types of labor: skilled labor on the first labor market that is supplied by household one and simple or unskilled labor on the second labor market, supplied by household two, which receives a lower wage rate. The firm maximizes profits so that the marginal products of labor equal the wage rates, respectively, implying that there are no restrictions for the firm as concerns hiring and firing.

Wages adjust according to demand on the labor markets but the labor market is not sufficiently flexible to guarantee full employment. The government acts as an employer of unemployed labor, thus providing income security for households. In addition, the government pays transfers to the household supplying simple labor and it finances general government spending. In order to finance its spending, the government levies a distortionary income tax rate.

Households in the economy, finally, inelastically supply labor on the first and on the second labor market, respectively, and they both save a certain fraction of their income which is subject to income tax. Households may become unemployed but, if so, are hired by the government and produce services that raise the utility of the households. It should be pointed out that households have the right to be given occupation by the government but also the obligation to accept the work offered to them.

The rest of the chapter is organized as follows. In the next chapter, we present the basic structure of our growth model. Section 5.3 analyzes our model where we first study the model assuming that growth is exogenous. Section 5.4 presents and analyzes an endogenous growth model and Section 5.5 concludes and points out possible extensions of our model.

5.2 A Baseline Flexicurity Model of Economic Growth

Our economy consists of three sectors: a household sector which receives labor income and income from its saving, a productive sector and the government. First, we describe the productive sector and the wage adjustment process.

5.2.1 The Productive Sector and the Wage Adjustment Process

The productive sector is represented by one firm which behaves competitively and which maximizes static profits. Production of the firm at time t is given by a Cobb–Douglas production function as

$$Y(t) = AK(t)^{(1-\alpha)} L_1^d(t)^{\beta_1} L_2^d(t)^{\beta_2}, \tag{5.1}$$

where[2] Y gives output, K denotes physical capital, $(1-\alpha)$ is the capital share and A is a technology parameter. L_1^d denotes labor demand for skilled labor in the first labor market and L_2^d gives labor demand for simple labor in the second labor market. The coefficients $\beta_1 \in (0,1)$ and $\beta_2 \in (0,1)$ give the elasticity of production with respect to skilled and with respect to simple labor, respectively. In addition $(1-\alpha)+\beta_1+\beta_2 \leq 1$ holds. If the latter inequality is strict, the firm makes profits which we assume are invested in the formation of physical capital.

As concerns the wage rate for simple labor we posit that it is a certain fraction $\epsilon \in (0,1)$ of the wage rate for skilled labor, denoted by ω. Profit maximization, then, gives demand for the two types of labor as

$$L_1^d = c_1\, \beta_1\, \omega^{-1/(1-\beta_1-\beta_2)}\, K^{(1-\alpha)/(1-\beta_1-\beta_2)} \tag{5.2}$$

$$L_2^d = c_1\, \beta_2\, \omega^{-1/(1-\beta_1-\beta_2)}\, K^{(1-\alpha)/(1-\beta_1-\beta_2)}/\epsilon, \tag{5.3}$$

with $c_1 = A^{1/(1-\beta_1-\beta_2)} \beta_1^{\beta_1/(1-\beta_1-\beta_2)} \beta_2^{\beta_2/(1-\beta_1-\beta_2)} \epsilon^{-\beta_2/(1-\beta_1-\beta_2)}$.

Equations (5.2) and (5.3) yield $L_1^d/L_2^d = \epsilon\, \beta_1/\beta_2$, showing that the demand for labor in the first labor market relative to demand in the second labor market is determined by the elasticities of production with respect to labor in these two markets and by the wage rate in the second labor market relative to that in the first labor market, ϵ. The higher the elasticity of production with respect to skilled labor and the higher the wage rate in the second labor market relative to the first labor market, the higher is the demand for skilled labor relative to unskilled labor.

Denoting by r the return to capital, profit maximization yields

$$r = (1-\alpha)AK^{-\alpha}(L_1^d)^{\beta_1}(L_2^d)^{\beta_2}, \tag{5.4}$$

with L_1^d and L_2^d determined by (5.2) and (5.3).

We should like to point out that the use of a Cobb–Douglas production function implies that the elasticity of substitution between capital and labor and between the two types of labor is each equal to one. Although the elasticity of substitution between capital and labor crucially affects the speed of convergence (see Turnovsky 2007), the use of a Cobb–Douglas function seems to be justified because it characterizes the aggregate economy quite well for many countries. The same holds for the substitution between the two types of labor in our model, where the use of a Cobb–Douglas function can serve as a reasonable working hypothesis.[3]

The evolution of the wage rate is assumed to follow a simple type of Phillips curve relationship where the change in the wage rate negatively depends on the rate of unemployment.[4] Thus, we posit that labor demand on the two labor markets relative to labor supply affects the dynamics of the wage rate. The growth rate of the wage rate is described by

$$\frac{\dot{\omega}}{\omega} = \beta_{L1}\left(\frac{L_1^d - \bar{L}_1}{L_1}\right) + \beta_{L2}\left(\frac{L_2^d - \bar{L}_2}{L_2}\right), \tag{5.5}$$

with L_i, $i = 1, 2$, labor supply on the first and second labor market, respectively, and $\bar{L}_i$, $i = 1, 2$, the normal levels of employment in the two markets in the sense that there is no tendency for a change in the wage rate if labor demand is equal to those values. The parameters $\beta_{L1} > 0$ and $\beta_{L2} > 0$ determine the speed of adjustment. Since we allow for substitution between the two types of labor we suppose that demand on both labor markets influences the wage adjustment process.

We should also point out that there is one good in our economy that can be either consumed or invested. Consequently all variables are real including the return to capital and the wage rate so that equation (5.5) describes the evolution of the real wage rate. Next, we describe the household sector.

5.2.2 The Household Sector

The household sector is represented by two households that maximize their discounted streams of utility arising from per-capita consumption, C_i, $i = 1, 2$, over an infinite time horizon subject to their budget constraints, taking factor prices as given. The utility function of both households is assumed to be logarithmic, $U(C_i) = \ln C_i$, $i = 1, 2$, and the households supply labor inelastically. Both households may become unemployed but, if so, are occupied by the government at the market wage rate so that there is no income uncertainty. Thus, we intend to model in a very simple way the security aspect of our flexicurity model, described in the introduction.

The maximization problem of the household in the first labor market, then, can be written as

$$\max_{C_1} \int_0^{\infty} e^{-\rho t} \left(\ln C_1 + \ln C_p\right) dt, \tag{5.6}$$

subject to

$$(1-\tau)\left(\omega L_1 + r K_1\right) = \dot{K}_1 + \delta K_1 + C_1. \tag{5.7}$$

The parameters $\rho > 0$, $\tau \in (0,1)$ and $\delta \in (0,1)$ are the subjective discount rate, the income tax rate and the depreciation rate of capital, respectively, and $K_1 > 0$ and $C_1 > 0$ give the capital stock owned by the household in the first labor market and its level of consumption. The variable C_p gives public services that are supplied by the government and produced by that part of the labor force that is hired by the government. As concerns those services we assume that they have the character of a purely public good.

To solve this problem we formulate the current-value Hamiltonian which is written as

$$H_1 = \left(\ln C_1 + \ln C_p\right) + \gamma_1\left((1-\tau)\left(\omega L_1 + r K_1\right) - \delta K_1 - C_1\right) \tag{5.8}$$

The necessary optimality conditions are given by

$$C_1^{-1} = \gamma_1, \tag{5.9}$$

$$\dot{\gamma}_1 = (\rho+\delta)\gamma_1 - \gamma_1(1-\tau)\, r. \tag{5.10}$$

If the transversality condition $\lim_{t\to\infty} e^{-\rho t} K_1/C_1 = 0$ holds, which is fulfilled for a time path on which capital grows at the same rate as consumption, the necessary conditions are also sufficient.

The maximization problem of the household in the second labor market is given by

$$\max_{C_2} \int_0^{\infty} e^{-\rho t} \left(\ln C_2 + \ln C_p\right) dt, \tag{5.11}$$

subject to

$$(1-\tau)\left(\epsilon\, \omega L_2 + r K_2\right) + T_p = \dot{K}_2 + \delta K_2 + C_2. \tag{5.12}$$

The capital stock owned by household two is denoted by $K_2 > 0$ and $C_2 > 0$ is its consumption. The household in the second labor market also saves but we assume that it disposes of a smaller capital stock than the household in the first labor market, that is $K_2 < K_1$. Further, it receives transfer payments from the government, T_p, in addition to its market income.

Again, we formulate the current-value Hamiltonian which is

$$H_2 = (\ln C_2 + \ln C_p) + \gamma_2((1-\tau)(\epsilon\,\omega L_2 + rK_2) + T_p - \delta K_2 - C_2). \quad (5.13)$$

The necessary optimality conditions are obtained as

$$C_2^{-1} = \gamma_2, \quad (5.14)$$
$$\dot{\gamma}_2 = (\rho + \delta)\gamma_2 - \gamma_2(1-\tau)\,r. \quad (5.15)$$

These conditions are again sufficient if the transversality condition $\lim_{t\to\infty} e^{-\rho t} K_2/C_2 = 0$ is fulfilled.

The growth rates of consumption of the households are obtained from (5.9)–(5.10) and (5.14)–(5.15) as

$$\frac{\dot{C}_i}{C_i} = -\rho + (1-\tau)r,\ i = 1, 2. \quad (5.16)$$

Using $C_1 + C_2 = C$, the growth rate of aggregate consumption is given by

$$\frac{\dot{C}}{C} = \frac{\dot{C}_1}{C_1}\frac{C_1}{C} + \frac{\dot{C}_2}{C_2}\frac{C_2}{C} = (-\rho + (1-\tau)\,r)\left(\frac{C_1}{C} + \frac{C_2}{C}\right), \quad (5.17)$$

with $C_1/C + C_2/C = 1$.

5.2.3 The Government

The government in our economy receives tax revenues from income taxation it uses for public consumption, G, that neither yields utility nor raises the productivity of the economy but is only a waste of resources. Further, the government finances transfer payments and hires unemployed labor and it runs a balanced budget at any moment in time. Hence, the budget constraint of the government can be written as

$$\tau(rK + \omega L_1 + \epsilon\,\omega L_2) = G + T_p + \omega(L_1 - L_1^d) + \epsilon\,\omega(L_2 - L_2^d). \quad (5.18)$$

The left-hand side of (5.18) gives revenues of the government and the right-hand side gives its spending. The terms $\omega(L_1 - L_1^d)$ and $\epsilon\,\omega(L_2 - L_2^d)$ give public spending due to employing labor that cannot find employment in the regular labor markets. That labor is employed in the production of public services C_p and raises the utility of the households but does not affect the allocation of resources of the households.

We also should mention that we limit our analysis to the case where both labor markets are characterized by an excess supply of labor, that is, $L_i > L_i^d$, $i = 1, 2$. In principle, one could also imagine situations where demand exceeds supply of labor. However, for the last decades this situation has been of less relevance for most countries in the EU so that we exclude this possibility.

In the next section we analyze our baseline model assuming that growth is exogenous.

5.3 Analysis of the Model with Exogenous Growth

Given our production function (5.1) it can be realized that there are decreasing returns to physical capital implying that the marginal product of capital declines as capital rises. This implies that the baseline model does not generate ongoing growth unless exogenous parameters change. To study our model in this case, we first have to derive the differential equations describing the aggregate economy.

The economy-wide resource constraint is obtained by combining the budget constraints of the two households, (5.7) and (5.12), with that of the government, (5.18), and taking into account that profits, possibly made by the firm, are invested. Doing so, gives the evolution of the physical capital stock as

$$\begin{aligned}\dot{K} = Y(1-\tau(1-\alpha)) - C - \delta K - \omega((L_1^d + \epsilon\, L_2^d) \\ -(1-\tau)(L_1 + \epsilon\, L_2)) + T_p\end{aligned} \tag{5.19}$$

where we used $G = \tau(1-\alpha)Y + \omega((L_1^d + \epsilon\, L_2^d) - (1-\tau)(L_1 + \epsilon\, L_2)) - T_p$ from the budget constraint of the government.

The evolution of aggregate consumption is obtained from (5.17) as

$$\dot{C} = C\left(-(\rho+\delta) + (1-\tau)\, r\right), \tag{5.20}$$

with r determined by (5.4). The differential equation describing the change of the real wage rate is given by (5.5) as

$$\dot{\omega} = \omega\left(\beta_{L1}\left(\frac{L_1^d - \bar{L}_1}{L_1}\right) + \beta_{L2}\left(\frac{L_2^d - \bar{L}_2}{L_2}\right)\right), \tag{5.21}$$

with L_1^d and L_2^d from (5.2) and (5.3).

A rest point of the differential equations (5.19)–(5.21) yields a steady state for the exogenous growth model. Proposition 1 gives results as to the existence and stability of our exogenous growth model.

Proposition 1: *There exists a unique steady state for the system described by equations* (5.19)–(5.21)*. A sufficient but not necessary condition for the Jacobian matrix at the steady state to have exactly two negative real eigenvalues or two eigenvalues with negative real parts is* $\delta = 0$.

Proof: See appendix.

Proposition 1 demonstrates that the exogenous growth model is characterized by global determinacy.[5] From an economic point of view global determinacy implies that economies converge to the same steady state in the long-run, independent of initial conditions.

The transitional growth paths of the variables, however, can be different showing that the model is locally indeterminate. Thus, two economies endowed with the same initial physical capital stocks, and the same fiscal parameters, may be characterized by different transitional growth rates of capital and consumption, depending on the initial choice of the level of consumption, $C(0)$, and on the initial wage rate, $\omega(0)$. For example, an economy with an initially lower wage rate has a higher marginal product of capital and, consequently, higher transitory growth rates of consumption. From a technical point of view, local indeterminacy is given if the number of negative eigenvalues, or negative real parts of the eigenvalues, is larger than the number of variables that cannot be set at time $t = 0$ but must be taken as given, in our model the physical capital stock. That holds typically for state variables in optimal control problems.

We should also point out that the condition $\delta = 0$ is sufficient but not necessary for two negative real eigenvalues or two eigenvalues with negative real parts. This means that the Jacobian matrix is likely to have two negative real eigenvalues also for a strictly positive depreciation rate as the proof in the appendix suggests. Below we present a numerical example in order to illustrate our analytical model.

Another aspect in exogenous growth models is the question of whether private steady state consumption attains its maximum value implied by the golden rule capital stock (see for example Blanchard and Fischer 1989, ch. 2). Since the answer to this question is needed in order to determine the effect of variations in the income tax rate we state the result as a lemma. Lemma 1 shows that in our model consumption at the steady state is always below the maximum value, as in the standard neoclassical growth model of this type with full employment.

Lemma 1 *The steady state capital stock in the model with unemployment is smaller than the golden rule steady state capital stock.*

Proof: See appendix.

Since the government plays an important and active role in our economy, we will next analyze the effects of fiscal policy. The effects of varying public transfers to the household in the second labor market and the effects of a change in the income tax rate are given in proposition 2.

Proposition 2: *A rise in public transfer payments leaves the aggregate steady state capital stock unchanged and raises the steady state level of private consumption. An increase in the tax rate reduces both the steady state capital stock and the steady state level of private consumption.*

Proof: See appendix.

The first part of proposition 2 shows that higher transfers to the household in the second labor market raises private consumption at the steady state. The economic reason for this outcome is that a rise in public transfers implies less public spending because the government has to stick to its budget constraint. Less public spending goes along with higher private consumption, given a fixed capital stock. The physical capital stock at the steady state is not affected by variations in public transfer payments since neither public transfers nor public consumption affect production possibilities.

The second part of proposition 2 demonstrates that raising the distortionary income tax rate reduces both private consumption at the steady state and the steady state private capital stock. Private consumption declines because a higher tax rate raises public consumption and reduces physical capital. The physical capital stock at the steady state declines because the after tax return to capital is reduced as the income tax rate increases. Since the after tax return to capital equals the exogenously give rate of time preference plus the depreciation rate at the steady state, a higher tax rate implies that the return to capital before taxation must rise which can be only achieved by a reduction of the capital stock.

Proposition 2 suggests that the government can raise capital and consumption and, thus, welfare by reducing the income tax rate. But it must be stated that there exists a lower value for the income tax rate which is obtained from the government budget constraint when we set $G = T_p = 0$. The minimum rate of income taxation, τ_{min}, is obtained as

$$\tau_{min} = \frac{\omega(L_1 - L_1^d) + \epsilon\,\omega(L_2 - L_2^d)}{rK + \omega L_1 + \epsilon\omega L_2}. \tag{5.22}$$

Equation (5.22) states that the value below which the income tax rate cannot fall equals payments for unemployed labor relative to potential national income. Intuitively, this is plausible because in our growth model with unemployment the government must finance the payments for unemployed work.

Before we analyze our growth model with endogenous growth we present a numerical example in order to illustrate our exogenous growth model. In the example we set the parameters of the production function as follows, $A = 0.5$, $(1 - \alpha) = 0.3$, $\beta_1 = 0.35$, and $\beta_2 = 0.2$. These values imply that the capital share equals 30 percent and the total labor share is 55 percent, which are realistic values. The depreciation rate of capital is set to 7.5 percent, $\delta = 0.075$, and the rate of time preference is 5 percent, $\rho = 0.05$. Households in the second labor market are assumed to earn 75 percent of the wage rate of households in the first labor market, $\epsilon = 0.75$, and the income tax rate is $\tau = 0.25$ and transfers are set to $T_p = 0.05$. The coefficients determining the speed of adjustment are set to 2 percent each, $\beta_{L1} = \beta_{L2} = 0.02$. The remaining parameters of the wage adjustment function are $\bar{L}_1 = 1.7$, $\bar{L}_2 = 1.75$ and $L_1 = L_2 = 2$.

With these parameter values the steady state values[6] for capital, consumption and for the wage rate are given by $\{K^\star, C^\star, \omega^\star\} = \{1.35, 0.58, 0.13\}$. The eigenvalues of the Jacobian matrix are $\lambda_1 = -0.537$, $\lambda_2 = 0.215$ and $\lambda_3 = -0.187$. When we increase the depreciation rate δ, two eigenvalues become complex conjugate with negative real parts for about $\delta > 0.2$, implying that for very high depreciation rates the economy is characterized by transitory cycles until it reaches the steady state.

In the next section, we study our growth model with endogenous growth.

5.4 The Model with Endogenous Growth

In order to generate sustained growth endogenously the economy must be characterized by constant returns to capital as the stock of physical capital grows over time. One possibility to achieve that is to assume that capital is associated with positive externalities as in the seminal paper by Romer (1986). Since one of the main stylized facts in economic growth is the observation of ongoing per-capita growth without a tendency for declining growth rates, it seems indeed important to construct models that replicate that fact. This holds all the more because theoretical models are to replicate stylized facts.

Assuming that physical capital is associated with positive externalities, the production function of the representative firm can be written as

$$Y = AK^{(1-\alpha)}\bar{K}^{\alpha}(L_1^d)^{\beta_1}(L_2^d)^{\beta_2}, \tag{5.23}$$

where $\bar{K}$ denotes the economy-wide capital stock the firm takes as given in solving its optimization problem.

Profit maximization now gives demand for labor as

$$L_1^d = c_1\,\beta_1\,\omega^{-1/(1-\beta_1-\beta_2)}\,K^{1/(1-\beta_1-\beta_2)}, \tag{5.24}$$
$$L_2^d = c_1\,\beta_2\,\omega^{-1/(1-\beta_1-\beta_2)}\,K^{1/(1-\beta_1-\beta_2)}/\epsilon, \tag{5.25}$$

where we used that in equilibrium $\bar{K} = K$ must hold. Maximizing with respect to capital yields the return to capital as,

$$r = (1-\alpha)A(L_1^d)^{\beta_1}(L_2^d)^{\beta_2}, \tag{5.26}$$

with L_1^d and L_2^d determined by (5.24) and (5.25).

Equation (5.26) shows that the return to capital does not decline but is a constant if the wage rate grows at the same rate as physical capital. A constant return to capital implies that the incentive to invest does not diminish as capital grows and can generate sustained per-capita growth in the long-run. It can also be realized that the return to capital is the larger the smaller the wage rate because labor demand negatively depends on the wage rate whereas a higher labor input raises the return to capital.

The household behavior is equivalent to the one of the last section so that the evolution of aggregate consumption is again described by equation (5.20). The government is also modeled as in the last section as well as the wage adjustment process. Thus, our economy is now described by the following equations,

$$\begin{aligned}\dot{K} =& Y(1-\tau(1-\alpha)) - C - \delta K - \omega((L_1^d + \epsilon\, L_2^d) \\ &- (1-\tau)(L_1 + \epsilon\, L_2)) + T_p, \quad (5.27)\\ \dot{C} =& C\left(-(\rho+\delta) + (1-\tau)\, r\right), \quad (5.28)\\ \dot{\omega} =& \omega\left(\beta_{L1}\left(\frac{L_1^d - \bar{L}_1}{L_1}\right) + \beta_{L2}\left(\frac{L_2^d - \bar{L}_2}{L_2}\right)\right), \quad (5.29)\end{aligned}$$

where we used $G = \tau(1-\alpha)Y + \omega((L_1^d + \epsilon\, L_2^d) - (1-\tau)(L_1 + \epsilon\, L_2)) - T_p$ from the budget constraint of the government and with L_1^d and L_2^d given by (5.24) and (5.25). The return to capital is obtained from (5.26) and production is described by (5.23), with $\bar{K} = K$.

In case of endogenous growth the left-hand side of equations (5.27)–(5.29) is strictly positive. Hence, in order to be able to analyze our economy we define the new variables $x = C/K$ and $y = \omega/K$. This leads to a new two-dimensional differential equation system. Using equations (5.24) and (5.25) this system can be written as,

$$\begin{aligned}\dot{x} =& x\Big(c - \rho - t_p - y(1-\tau)(L_1 + \epsilon\, L_2) + \\ & y^{(-\beta_1-\beta_2)/(1-\beta_1-\beta_2)} c_1(\beta_1 + \beta_2 - \alpha)\Big) \quad (5.30)\\ \dot{y} =& y\Big(c + \delta - y(1-\tau)(L_1 + \epsilon\, L_2) + \\ & y^{-1/(1-\beta_1-\beta_2)}\left((\beta_1\beta_{L1}/L_1) + (\beta_2\beta_{L2}/(\epsilon\, L_2))\right)\Big) + \\ & y\Big(y^{(-\beta_1-\beta_2)/(1-\beta_1-\beta_2)} c_1(\beta_1 + \beta_2 - (1-\tau(1-\alpha))) - t_p\Big), \quad (5.31)\end{aligned}$$

with $t_p = T_P/K$ public transfers to the household in the second labor market relative to the capital stock. A rest point of (5.30)–(5.31) where $\dot{x} = \dot{y} = 0$ holds[7] gives a balanced growth path (BGP) where all variables grow the same constant growth rate. Proposition 3 gives results as concerns existence and stability of a BGP for our model economy with endogenous growth.

Proposition 3: *Assume that the time preference of the household sector and the depreciation rate are sufficiently small. Then, for* $\rho + \delta < (\beta_{L1}\bar{L}_1/L_1) + (\beta_{L2}\bar{L}_2/L_2)$ *there exists a unique balanced growth path with positive growth which is a saddle point. For* $\rho + \delta > (\beta_{L1}\bar{L}_1/L_1) + (\beta_{L2}\bar{L}_2/L_2)$ *there exists no balanced growth path or there exist two balanced growth paths. The balanced growth path yielding the higher growth rate is a saddle point, the balanced growth giving the lower* *growth rate has two positive eigenvalues or two eigenvalues with positive real parts.*

Proof: See appendix.

Before we discuss this proposition we point out that the requirement that the rate of time preference and the depreciation rate must not be too large for a BGP with a strictly positive growth rate to exist can be seen from (5.28). This is not a strict assumption. It just states that the after-tax return to capital must be sufficiently large so that growth does not come to a standstill.

Proposition 3 demonstrates that there exists a unique BGP or possibly two BGPs. From an economic point of view a unique BGP emerges if the speed of adjustment of the wage rate, determined by the parameters β_{L1} and β_{L2}, are relatively large. With a unique BGP the economy is globally determinate and locally indeterminate, meaning that the long-run growth rate is the same for different countries but with identical initial capital stocks, the growth rates on the transition path, however, can differ depending on the value of initial consumption and on the initial wage rate the economies choose at the starting point $t = 0$.

For relatively small adjustment speeds we can observe possibly two BGPs. Then, our model is characterized by global indeterminacy implying that the initial choices of consumption and of the wage rate cannot only determine the transitional growth rates but also the long-run balanced growth rate. In this case, the BGP yielding the higher growth rate is again locally indeterminate while the BGP giving the lower growth rate is locally determinate. The latter means that there exists a unique value for initial consumption and a unique value for the initial wage rate such that the economy grows at the lower balanced growth rate. In that case, there are no transitional dynamics because the economy instantaneously jumps on the BGP. We should also like to mention that in case of two BGPs, one BGP may yield a positive growth rate while the other BGP can be associated with a negative growth rate.

In order to illustrate the possibility of two BGPs mentioned in proposition 3 we now resort to a numerical example. The structural parameters of the production function are the same as in the last section, that is we set $A = 0.5$, $(1 - \alpha) = 0.3$, $\beta_1 = 0.35$, and $\beta_2 = 0.2$. The depreciation rate of capital is $\delta = 0.075$ and the rate of time preference is $\rho = 0.05$. Households in the second labor market are again assumed to earn 75 percent of the wage rate of households in the first labor market, $\epsilon = 0.75$, and the income tax rate is

$\tau = 0.25$. Public transfers relative to capital are set to $t_p = 0.03$ and the coefficients determining the speed of adjustment are now $\beta_{L1} = 0.075$ and $\beta_{L2} = 0.045$. The remaining parameters of the wage adjustment function are $\bar{L}_1 = 1.14$, $\bar{L}_2 = 1.75$ and $L_1 = 3$ and $L_2 = 4$. With these parameters we get two BGPs. The first yields a balanced growth rate of 5.5 percent and is saddle point stable with the eigenvalues given by $\lambda_4 = 0.124$ and $\lambda_5 = -0.044$. The balanced growth rate on the second BGP is 3.7 percent and the eigenvalues are $\lambda_{6,7} = 0.049 \pm 0.054\sqrt{-1}$, demonstrating that this BGP is unstable.

In the following we analyze the effect of varying some parameters as concerns the balanced growth rate. The discussion following proposition 3 has demonstrated that the size of the speed of adjustment of the wage rate may be crucial as to whether there exists a unique BGP or possibly two BGPs, given other parameters. Therefore, we next study the effects of the speed of adjustment as concerns the balanced growth. Proposition 4 gives the result of that analysis.

Proposition 4: *If there is a unique BGP, a higher adjustment speed* β_{Li}, $i = 1, 2$, *implies a higher balanced growth rate if and only if* $L_i^d < \bar{L}_i$, $i = 1, 2$, *holds.*

If there are two BGPs, a higher adjustment speed β_{Li}, $i = 1, 2$, *implies a higher balanced growth rate at the BGP associated with the larger growth rate and goes along with a lower growth rate at the BGP with the smaller growth rate if and only if* $L_i^d < \bar{L}_i$, $i = 1, 2$.

Proof: See appendix.

This proposition shows that in case of a unique BGP, a higher adjustment speed leads to a higher (lower) long-run growth rate if labor demand is smaller (larger) than the normal level of labor input, defined as that value where there is no pressure for a change in the wage rate. The economic mechanism is obvious. If labor demand is below (above) the normal level, an increase in the speed of adjustment implies that the differential between labor demand and the normal level of labor becomes a larger weight in the wage equation. Since the differential is negative (positive), this reduces (raises) the growth rate of the wage rate. As a consequence, the wage rate relative to capital declines (increases) which raises (reduces) the demand for labor and, thus, the return to capital. Therefore, the long-run balanced growth rate increases. It should also be mentioned that on a BGP with a positive growth rate, labor demand can exceed the normal level of labor only on one of the two markets but not on both markets simultaneously. Otherwise, the growth rate of the wage rate would be negative.

If there are two BGPs, the mechanism as to the BGP with the higher growth rate is the same as the one in case of a unique BGP. As concerns the effect for the BGP with the lower growth rate, it is just reverse. In order to illustrate the mechanism behind it we assume that labor, say on the first labor market, is below its normal level and we consider the effect of an increase in the adjustment speed on that labor market. Then, a higher adjustment speed reduces the growth rate of the wage rate. Consequently, the wage rate relative to capital declines and raises the demand for labor. The higher demand for labor, in a second step, raises the growth rate of the wage rate. The higher labor demand also raises the growth rate of capital. However, this increase is smaller than that of the wage rate so that the wage rate relative to capital rises. The rise in the wage rate relative to capital exceeds the initial decrease, so that the economy ends up with a larger wage rate relative to capital, leading to a decline in the return to investment and, therefore, in the balanced growth rate.[8]

As in the last section, we want to analyze how fiscal policy affects the economy in the long-run. Proposition 5 summarizes the growth effects of varying public transfers to the household in the second labor market and of variations in the income tax rate.

Proposition 5: *Variations in public transfers do not affect the balanced growth rate. An increase in the income tax rate leads to a lower balanced growth rate in case of a unique BGP.*

If there are two BGPs, a rise in the income tax rate reduces the balanced growth rate at the BGP with the higher growth rate but may increase or reduce the growth rate at the BGP with the lower growth rate.

Proof: See appendix.

The interpretation of that proposition is as follows. Since transfer payments do not affect the allocation of resources on the balanced growth path they have no effect on the investment share and on the long-run growth rate. Hence, a higher transfer share only raises the income of the household in the second labor market but, since it is lump-sum, it does not lead to a reallocation of resources leaving the growth rate unchanged. It should also be recalled that a rise in public transfers implies a reduction in government consumption.

In case of a unique BGP, the income tax rate negatively affects the balanced growth rate because a higher tax rate reduces the return to capital. Therefore, economic agents shift resources from investment to consumption when the income tax rate is increased, leading to a lower investment share and lower growth. The same mechanism holds for the BGP associated with the higher growth rate, in case of two BGPs.

If there are two BGPs, the growth rate at the BGP with the smaller growth rate may decline or rise as the income tax rate is increased. The economic mechanism behind this result is as follows. First, from equation (5.28) we see that there is always a negative direct effect of the income tax rate on the balanced growth rate. On the other hand, a higher income tax rate reduces the growth rate of the capital stock while it does not affect the growth rate of the wage rate directly. That effect raises the wage rate relative to capital and reduces the demand for labor. This decline in the demand for labor, then, reduces the growth rate of the wage rate so that the economy ends up with a lower wage rate relative to capital.[9] This lower wage rate relative to capital exceeds the initial increase in the wage to capital ratio and raises the marginal product of capital. This indirect positive growth effect can dominate the negative direct growth effect of a higher income tax rate, implying that a higher tax rate can raise the balanced growth rate.

In our numerical example, presented above, the balanced growth rate monotonically declines with a higher income tax rate at the BGP with the larger growth rate while it monotonically rises at the BGP associated with the lower growth rate. This process can be observed for income tax rates up to $\tau \approx 0.2505$. For income tax rates larger than that value, there does not exist a BGP any longer with the other parameter values as given above.

5.5 Conclusion

In this chapter we have presented and analyzed a standard model of economic growth with unemployment. There are no restrictions on labor markets as concerns hiring and firing but unemployment is made socially acceptable through the government employing idle labor, thus providing the household sector with income security. Thereby, we intended to model in a simple growth framework the flexicurity capitalism of Scandinavian countries.

We could demonstrate that there exists a unique steady state for the exogenous growth model which is stable. As concerns the model with endogenous growth we have shown that it is characterized by a unique balanced growth path which is saddle point stable or possibly by two balanced growth paths where one is again saddle point stable while the other is unstable. In addition we have shown that the government may essentially affect the long-run outcome in both the exogenous growth model as well as in the model with endogenous growth.

To conclude, we should like to point out that our model is, as far as we know, a first framework that integrates the idea of flexicurity in a formal model of economic growth. Hence, our approach is a very basic one that could be reasonably extended in several directions. One possibility could be to allow for human capital allocation by one type of household which would endogenize the difference in the types of labor. Another reasonable and realistic extension would be to assume that the government only guarantees a certain percentage of the market income for unemployed. These topics, however, are left for future research.

Appendix

Proof of Proposition 1

To prove this proposition we note that $\dot{\omega} = 0$ gives

$$\omega^{-1/(1-\beta_1-\beta_2)} = (c_2/c_1)K^{-(1-\alpha)/(1-\beta_1-\beta_2)},$$

with

$$c_2 = \frac{(\bar{L}_1\beta_{L1}/L_1) + (\bar{L}_2\beta_{L2}/L_2)}{(\beta_1\beta_{L1}/L_1) + (\beta_2\beta_{L2}/(\epsilon\, L_2))}.$$

Using this gives labor demand at the steady state as $L_1^d = c_2\beta_1$ and $L_2^d = c_2\beta_2/\epsilon$. Inserting these values in $\dot{C}$ yields

$$\dot{C} = C\left(-(\rho+\delta) + (1-\tau)(1-\alpha)K^{-\alpha}(c_2\beta_1)^{\beta_1}(c_2\beta_2/\epsilon)^{\beta_2}\right).$$

It is immediately seen that there exists a unique K that solves $\dot{C} = 0$ (we neglect the economically meaningless possibility $C = 0$). Consumption at the steady state, then, is obtained from $\dot{K} = 0$.

To analyze stability we compute the Jacobian matrix which is given by

$$J_1 = \begin{bmatrix} \partial\dot{K}/\partial K & -1 & \partial\dot{K}/\partial\omega \\ \partial\dot{C}/\partial K & 0 & \partial\dot{C}/\partial\omega \\ \partial\dot{\omega}/\partial K & 0 & \partial\dot{\omega}/\partial\omega \end{bmatrix}.$$

The determinant of that matrix is computed as

$$\det J_1 = -(\partial\dot{C}/\partial\omega)(\partial\dot{\omega}/\partial K) + (\partial\dot{C}/\partial K)(\partial\dot{\omega}/\partial\omega).$$

It is easy to see that $\partial\dot{C}/\partial\omega < 0$, $\partial\dot{\omega}/\partial K > 0$, $\partial\dot{C}/\partial K \leq 0$ and $\partial\dot{\omega}/\partial\omega < 0$ hold so that $\det J_1 > 0$.

Defining the constant W as

$$W = \begin{vmatrix} \partial\dot{K}/\partial K & \partial\dot{K}/\partial\omega \\ \partial\dot{\omega}/\partial K & \partial\dot{\omega}/\partial\omega \end{vmatrix} + \begin{vmatrix} 0 & \partial\dot{C}/\partial\omega \\ 0 & \partial\dot{\omega}/\partial\omega \end{vmatrix} + \begin{vmatrix} \partial\dot{K}/\partial K & -1 \\ \partial\dot{C}/\partial K & 0 \end{vmatrix}$$

a characterization of the eigenvalues can be given. For $\det J_1 > 0$ and $W < 0$, there are two negative real eigenvalues or two eigenvalues with negative real parts (see Wirl 1997).

The second term of W is equal to zero and the third term is given by $\partial\dot{C}/\partial K \leq 0$. To obtain the first term of W we compute the derivatives as

$$\begin{aligned}
\frac{\partial\dot{K}}{\partial K} &= \left(\frac{1-\alpha}{1-\beta_1-\beta_2}\right) K^{-1+(1-\alpha)/(1-\beta_1-\beta_2)} \omega^{(-\beta_1-\beta_2)/(1-\beta_1-\beta_2)} c_1 \cdot \\
&\quad (1-\tau(1-\alpha)-\beta_1-\beta_2)-\delta,
\end{aligned}$$

$$\begin{aligned}
\frac{\partial\dot{K}}{\partial\omega} &= \left(\frac{-\beta_1-\beta_2}{1-\beta_1-\beta_2}\right) \omega^{-1/(1-\beta_1-\beta_2)} K^{(1-\alpha)/(1-\beta_1-\beta_2)} c_1 \cdot \\
&\quad (1-\tau(1-\alpha)-\beta_1-\beta_2)+(1-\tau)(L_1+\epsilon L_2),
\end{aligned}$$

$$\begin{aligned}
\frac{\partial\dot{\omega}}{\partial K} &= \left(\frac{1-\alpha}{1-\beta_1-\beta_2}\right) K^{-1+(1-\alpha)/(1-\beta_1-\beta_2)} \omega^{(-\beta_1-\beta_2)/(1-\beta_1-\beta_2)} c_1 \cdot \\
&\quad ((\beta_1\beta_{L1}/L_1)+(\beta_2\beta_{L2}/(\epsilon L_2))),
\end{aligned}$$

$$\begin{aligned}
\frac{\partial\dot{\omega}}{\partial\omega} &= \left(\frac{-1}{1-\beta_1-\beta_2}\right) K^{(1-\alpha)/(1-\beta_1-\beta_2)} \omega^{-1-1/(1-\beta_1-\beta_2)} c_1 \cdot \\
&\quad ((\beta_1\beta_{L1}/L_1)+(\beta_2\beta_{L2}/(\epsilon L_2))).
\end{aligned}$$

After some calculations we get with these derivatives

$$0 \gtreqless \frac{\partial\dot{K}}{\partial K}\frac{\partial\dot{\omega}}{\partial\omega} - \frac{\partial\dot{K}}{\partial\omega}\frac{\partial\dot{\omega}}{\partial K} \leftrightarrow$$

$$\begin{aligned}
0 &\gtreqless (-1)K^{(1-\alpha)/(1-\beta_1-\beta_2)}\omega^{-1/(1-\beta_1-\beta_2)} \cdot \\
&\quad (1-\alpha)(1-\tau(1-\alpha)-\beta_1-\beta_2)+\delta K + \\
&\quad (-1)(1-\alpha)(1-\tau)\omega(L_1+\epsilon L_2).
\end{aligned}$$

For $\delta = 0$ we always have $W < 0$. But even for $\delta > 0$ it is very likely that W is negative. In all our numerical examples the Jacobian either had two negative eigenvalues or two eigenvalues with negative real parts. In particular, we could not find parameter constellations such that $W > 0$ so that a Hopf bifurcation cannot occur. □

Proof of Lemma 1

Public spending at the steady state can be written as

$$\begin{aligned} G^\star &= \tau(1-\alpha)Y + \tau\omega L_1^d + \tau\epsilon\omega L_2^d - \omega(1-\tau)\cdot \\ &\quad ((L_1 - L_1^d) + \epsilon(L_2 - L_2^d)) - T_p \\ &= \tau(Y-\pi) - Y c_1^{-\beta_1-\beta_2} c_2^{\beta_1+\beta_2-1}(1-\tau)\cdot \\ &\quad ((L_1 - L_1^d) + \epsilon(L_2 - L_2^d)) - T_p \end{aligned}$$

where we used that in steady state $Y = c_1 K^{(1-\alpha)}$ and $\omega = (c_1/c_2)^{1-\beta_1-\beta_2} K^{(1-\alpha)}$ (from the proof of proposition 1). This gives steady state consumption as (from $\dot{K} = 0$),

$$\begin{aligned} C^\star &= Y(1-\tau) - \delta K^\star + \tau\pi + Y\, c_1^{-\beta_1-\beta_2} c_2^{\beta_1+\beta_2-1}(1-\tau)\cdot \\ &\quad ((L_1 - L_1^d) + \epsilon(L_2 - L_2^d)) + T_p \end{aligned}$$

with $L_1^d = c_2\beta_1$ and $L_1^d = c_2\beta_2/\epsilon$ at the steady state (from the proof of proposition 1). The golden rule capital stock is given for $\partial C/\partial K = 0$ at $\dot{K} = 0$ which is equivalent to

$$\begin{aligned} &\frac{\delta}{\left(1 + c_1^{-\beta_1-\beta_2} c_2^{\beta_1+\beta_2-1}(1-\tau)\left((L_1 - L_1^d) + \epsilon(L_2 - L_2^d)\right)\right)} \\ &= (1-\tau)\frac{\partial Y}{\partial K} \end{aligned} \tag{A.1}$$

with $L_1 > L_1^d$ and $L_2 > L_2^d$.

At the steady state we have $\dot{C} = 0$ which implies

$$\delta + \rho = (1-\tau)\frac{\partial Y}{\partial K}. \tag{A.2}$$

For the steady state capital stock to be smaller than the golden rule capital stock, the left-hand side in (A.1) must be smaller than the left-hand side in (A.2). Subtracting the left-hand side of (A.2) from the left-hand side in (A.1) gives

$$\frac{-(\delta+\rho)c_1^{-\beta_1-\beta_2}c_2^{\beta_1+\beta_2-1}(1-\tau)\left((L_1-L_1^d)+\epsilon(L_2-L_2^d)\right)-\rho}{\left(1+c_1^{-\beta_1-\beta_2}c_2^{\beta_1+\beta_2-1}(1-\tau)\left((L_1-L_1^d)+\epsilon(L_2-L_2^d)\right)\right)}<0.$$

This shows that the left-hand side in (A.1) is smaller than the left-hand side in (A.2) implying that the steady state capital stock is smaller than the golden rule capital stock in our model with unemployment. □

Proof of Proposition 2

To prove proposition 2 we note from the proof of proposition 1 that the steady state value $K^\star$ is that value of K which satisfies

$$\dot{C}/C = 0 = -(\rho+\delta) + (1-\tau)(1-\alpha)K^{-\alpha}(c_2\beta_1)^{\beta_1}(c_2\beta_2/\epsilon)^{\beta_2}.$$

This shows that variations in transfer payments do not affect the steady state capital stock and that higher values of τ reduce the steady state capital stock.

Public spending in steady state is given by

$$\begin{aligned} G^\star &= Y\Big(\tau(1-\alpha) + (\beta_1+\beta_2)(c_2/c_1)^{\beta_1+\beta_2} - \\ &\quad c_1^{-\beta_1-\beta_2}c_2^{1-\beta_1-\beta_2}(1-\tau)(L_1+\epsilon\, L_2)\Big) - T_p. \end{aligned}$$

Using that steady state production can be written as $Y = c_1K^{(1-\alpha)}$, steady state consumption is obtained as

$$\begin{aligned} C^\star &= T_p - \delta K^\star + c_1(K^\star)^{(1-\alpha)} \\ &\quad \Big(1-\tau(1-\alpha) - (\beta_1+\beta_2)(c_2/c_1)^{\beta_1+\beta_2} + \\ &\quad c_1^{-\beta_1-\beta_2}c_2^{1-\beta_1-\beta_2}(1-\tau)(L_1+\epsilon\, L_2)\Big). \end{aligned}$$

Since variations in T_p do not affect the steady state capital stock, it is immediately seen from this expression that a rise in T_p raises steady state consumption.

The effect of an increase in τ is calculated as

$$\begin{aligned} \frac{\partial C^\star}{\partial \tau} &= -c_1(K^\star)^{(1-\alpha)}\left(1-\alpha + c_1^{-\beta_1-\beta_2}c_2^{1-\beta_1-\beta_2}(L_1+\epsilon\, L_2)\right) \\ &\quad + \frac{\partial C^\star}{\partial K^\star}\frac{\partial K^\star}{\partial \tau}. \end{aligned}$$

Since the steady state capital stock is below its golden rule value, $\partial C^\star/\partial K^\star > 0$ holds, showing that a rise in τ reduces $C^\star$. □

Proof of Proposition 3

Setting $\dot{x}/x = 0$ gives

$$x = \rho + \alpha c_1 y^{(-\beta_1-\beta_2)/(1-\beta_1-\beta_2)} + t_p + y(1-\tau)(L_1 + \epsilon L_2) - y^{(-\beta_1-\beta_2)/(1-\beta_1-\beta_2)} c_1(\beta_1+\beta_2).$$

Inserting that term in $\dot{y}$ leads to

$$q \equiv \rho + \delta - \left((\beta_{L1}\bar{L}_1/L_1) + (\beta_{L2}\bar{L}_2/L_2)\right) - y^{(-\beta_1-\beta_2)/(1-\beta_1-\beta_2)} c_1(1-\alpha)(1-\tau) + y^{-1/(1-\beta_1-\beta_2)} c_1\left((\beta_1\beta_{L1}/L_1) + (\beta_2\beta_{L2}/(\epsilon L_2))\right).$$

A solution $y^\star$ such that $q(\cdot) = 0$ gives a BGP. It is easily seen that the following holds,

$$\lim_{y\to 0} q(\cdot) = +\infty, \quad \lim_{y\to\infty} q(\cdot) = \rho + \delta - \left((\beta_{L1}\bar{L}_1/L_1) + (\beta_{L2}\bar{L}_2/L_2)\right).$$

The first and the second derivative of $q(\cdot)$ with respect to y are

$$\frac{\partial q}{\partial y} = \frac{-1}{1-\beta_1-\beta_2} y^{-1-1/(1-\beta_1-\beta_2)} c_1\left((\beta_1\beta_{L1}/L_1) + (\beta_2\beta_{L2}/(\epsilon L_2))\right) + \frac{\beta_1+\beta_2}{1-\beta_1-\beta_2} y^{-1+(-\beta_1-\beta_2)/(1-\beta_1-\beta_2)} c_1(1-\alpha)(1-\tau).$$

$$\frac{\partial q^2}{(\partial y)^2} = \frac{2-\beta_1-\beta_2}{(1-\beta_1-\beta_2)^2} y^{-2-1/(1-\beta_1-\beta_2)} c_1\left((\beta_1\beta_{L1}/L_1) + (\beta_2\beta_{L2}/(\epsilon L_2))\right) + \frac{-\beta_1-\beta_2}{(1-\beta_1-\beta_2)^2} y^{-1-1/(1-\beta_1-\beta_2)} c_1(1-\alpha)(1-\tau).$$

Therefore, in case of $\rho + \delta - \left((\beta_{L1}\bar{L}_1/L_1) + (\beta_{L2}\bar{L}_2/L_2)\right) < 0$ the function $q(\cdot)$ starts from $+\infty$ for $y = 0$ declines with rising y, intersects the horizontal axis then rises and has a unique turning point at y_T where $\partial q^2/(\partial y)^2 = 0$ and converges to $\rho + \delta - \left((\beta_{L1}\bar{L}_1/L_1) + (\beta_{L2}\bar{L}_2/L_2)\right) < 0$ for $y \to \infty$. Note that $q(\cdot)$ can intersect the horizontal axis only once. This holds because otherwise more than one turning points would have to exist which is not possible.

In case of $\rho + \delta - \left((\beta_{L1}\bar{L}_1/L_1) + (\beta_{L2}\bar{L}_2/L_2)\right) > 0$ the function $q(\cdot)$ starts from $+\infty$ for $y = 0$ declines with rising y, intersects the horizontal axis from above then rises, intersects the horizontal axis from below and converges to $\rho + \delta - ((\beta_{L1}\bar{L}_1/L_1) + (\beta_{L2}\bar{L}_2/L_2)) > 0$ for $y \to \infty$. Note that $q(\cdot)$ can intersect the horizontal axis only two times because otherwise more than one turning point would have to exist which is not possible. But it must be pointed out that it is also possible that the function $q(\cdot)$ has no intersection point with the horizontal axis. In that case no BGP exists.

To prove stability we compute the Jacobian J_2 at the BGP as,

$$J_2 = \begin{bmatrix} x \; x\,(\partial(\dot{C}/C)/\partial y - \partial(\dot{K}/K)/\partial y) \\ y \; y\,(\partial(\dot{\omega}/\omega)/\partial y - \partial(\dot{K}/K)/\partial y) \end{bmatrix}.$$

The determinant can easily be calculated as

$$\det J_2 = x\,y\,\left(\partial(\dot{\omega}/\omega)/\partial y - \partial(\dot{C}/C)/\partial y\right),$$

and it is immediately seen that the sign of $\det J_2$ is equivalent to the sign of $\partial q(\cdot)/\partial y$. If there is a unique BGP, $\partial q(\cdot)/\partial y < 0$ holds so that the BGP is saddle point stable because $\det J_2 < 0$ is necessary and sufficient for saddle point stability.

If there are two BGPs, $\partial q(\cdot)/\partial y < 0$ holds at the first intersection point that yields the lower value of $y^\star$ and, consequently, the higher growth rate, so that this BGP is saddle point stable, too. At the second intersection point $q(\cdot)$ intersects the horizontal axis from below so that $\partial q(\cdot)/\partial y > 0$, showing that this BGP cannot be a saddle point. To show that this BGP is unstable we compute the trace of the Jacobian, $\mathrm{tr}\, J_2$. The trace is given by

$$\mathrm{tr} J_2 = \frac{\partial \dot{y}}{\partial y} + x = \frac{\partial q}{\partial y} + \rho + t_p + \alpha c_1 y^{(-\beta_1-\beta_2)/(1-\beta_1-\beta_2)} - \frac{\beta_1+\beta_2}{1-\beta_1-\beta_2} y^{(-\beta_1-\beta_2)/(1-\beta_1-\beta_2)} c_1 (1-\alpha),$$

with x from $\dot{x}/x = 0$. Since $\partial q(\cdot)/\partial y > 0$, a sufficient condition for $\mathrm{tr}\, J_2 > 0$ to hold is, $\alpha - (1-\alpha)(\beta_1+\beta_2)/(1-\beta_1-\beta_2) \geq 0$. Because of constant or decreasing returns to scale we have $(1-\alpha) + \beta_1 + \beta_2 \leq 1$ so that the latter inequality is always fulfilled. □

Proof of Proposition 4 and of Proposition 5

To prove proposition 4 we compute $\partial y/\partial \beta_{Li}$, $i = 1, 2$, by implicit differentiation from $q(\cdot) = 0$, with $q(\cdot)$ defined in the proof of proposition 3. This gives

$$\frac{\partial y}{\partial \beta_{Li}} = -\frac{(L_i^d - \bar{L}_i)/L_i}{\partial q/\partial y}, \quad i = 1, 2,$$

where we used that L_i^d, $i = 1, 2$, is given by (5.24) and (5.25), respectively. If the BGP is unique, we have $\partial q/\partial y < 0$, if there are two BGPs, $\partial q/\partial y < (>)\, 0$ holds at the BGP giving the higher (smaller) growth rate. Noting that the balanced growth rate, given by (5.28), is a negative function of y proposition 4 is proven.

To prove proposition 5 we note that $\partial q/\partial t_p = 0$, showing the first part. For the second part we compute $\partial y/\partial \tau$ as

$$\frac{\partial y}{\partial \tau} = -\frac{c_1(1-\alpha)y^{(-\beta_1-\beta_2)/(1-\beta_1-\beta_2)}}{\partial q/\partial y}.$$

Again, with a unique BGP we have $\partial q/\partial y < 0$, if there are two BGPs, $\partial q/\partial y < (>)\, 0$ holds at the BGP giving the higher (smaller) growth rate. Since the balanced growth rate (5.28) negatively depends on τ directly and negatively on y, the proposition is proven. □

Notes

1 This chapter is based on Greiner, A. and P. Flaschel (2009), 'Economic growth with an employer of last resort. A simple model of flexicurity capitalism', *Research in Economics*, **63**(2), 102–113.

2 From now on we omit the time argument t if no ambiguity arises.

3 The role of the elasticity of substitution between two types of labor for the wage differential is studied in Greiner et al. (2004) for example.

4 An extensive discussion of the role of the Phillips curve in dynamic macroeconomics can be found for example in Flaschel et al. (1997).

5 As to the definition of global and local determinacy and indeterminacy, see, for example, Benhabib and Farmer (1994).

6 The * denotes steady state values.

7 Since y is raised to a negative power in (5.30) the solution $y^\star = 0$ is not possible and we also exclude the economically meaningless solution $x^\star = 0$.

8 This feedback mechanism is also present in the case of a unique BGP and at the BGP with the higher growth rate. But there, the feedback effect does not compensate the initial change in the wage rate.

9 The smaller labor demand also reduces the growth rate of capital but less than the growth rate of the wage rate.

6. Economic Policy in a Growth Model with Human Capital, Heterogenous Agents and Unemployment

6.1 Introduction

With the publication of the paper by Lucas (1988) the role of human capital has become increasingly popular in building models of economic growth. The paper by Lucas, which is based on the contribution by Uzawa (1965), asserts that the accumulation of human capital is the major source of ongoing growth. Empirical research analyzing the role of human capital indeed seems to find supportive evidence for this view. For example, the survey by Krueger and Lindahl (2001) shows that there is strong evidence that education is positively correlated with income growth at the microeconomic level and the positive correlation seems to be quite robust. However, this does not necessarily hold for the macroeconomic level where the findings are more fragile. For example, human capital is not a robust variable in explaining economic growth according to the study by Sala-i-Martin (1997). But the lack of explanatory power of human capital may be due to measurement errors as pointed out by Krueger and Lindahl (2001) who demonstrate that cross-country regressions show a positive and statistically significant correlation with economic growth if measurement errors are taken into account. It should also be pointed out that Levine and Renelt (1992) have demonstrated that human capital, measured by the secondary enrollment rate, is a robust variable in growth regressions, in contrary to the result found in Sala-i-Martin (1997). Because of that, building endogenous growth models with human capital as the engine of sustained growth is certainly justified.

As concerns the formation of human capital, one can find two approaches in the economics literature. On the one hand, there are approaches where human capital formation is only financed by the private sector and, on the other hand, there exist studies where only the public sector spends resources for the formation of human capital. In addition, there also exist contributions where human capital formation is the result of both public and private expenditures. For example, Glomm and Ravikumar (1992) and Blankenau and Simpson (2004) assume that human capital accumulation results from both private and public services. Glomm and Ravikumar present an OLG model with heterogenous agents where human capital accumulation is the result of formal schooling. They demonstrate that public education leads to a faster decline of income inequality whereas private education may lead to higher per-capita incomes. Blankenau and Simpson present an endogenous growth model with both private and public inputs in the process of human capital accumulation. They demonstrate that the response of growth to public education depends on the tax structure, on the level of government spending and on parameters of the production function.

On the other side, Ni and Wang (1994) and Beauchemin (2001) present models where human capital is the result of public spending alone. Ni and Wang assume homogenous agents, as the contribution by Glomm and Ravikumar (1992), and present an OLG model where human capital is the result of public education which is financed by an income tax. Using calibration exercises they derive that the optimal income tax rate is in the range of 6–10 percent. Beauchemin presents a political-economic OLG model of growth and human capital accumulation where human capital accumulation is the result of public education. The paper demonstrates that a sufficiently rapid population growth may generate economic stagnation. In Greiner (2008) a growth model with public education and public debt is presented and analyzed. There, the question of how public debt and deficits affect human capital formation and economic growth is analyzed.

An early contribution that studies optimal fiscal policy in an endogenous growth model with human capital and productive public spending is the paper by Corsetti and Roubini (1996). These authors present a general framework where public spending may either enter the production of final goods or the production function of human capital formation. The goal of their paper is to derive optimal tax rates that can replicate the first best optimum. They show that in optimum tax rates are positive so that the externality related rents are taxed away and no public debt is necessary to attain the first-best solution. If there are restrictions as concerns the available tax instruments, the optimal policy may be obtained only if the government borrows or lends in order to smooth distortions over time.

All that these contributions have in common is that they assume full employment on the labor market. However, many European countries experience persistent unemployment in spite of permanently growing GDPs, due to downward labor rigidities. Although wages adjust according to demand on the labor markets, the labor markets are not sufficiently flexible to guarantee full employment. Therefore, allowing for unemployment in an economic growth model seems to be justified. In addition to that most European countries are characterized by relatively high standards of transfer payments and social security that make frictions on the labor market acceptable so that societies remain socially stable.

Therefore, the goal of this chapter is to analyze how fiscal policies, in particular unemployment benefits and social transfers, and labor market rigidities affect growth and welfare in economies that are characterized by features typical of European economies.[1] In addition, we also study stability properties of the model. Thus, we intend to present a general endogenous growth model that captures important features of European economies and to gain insight into how fiscal policy works in such economies.

To achieve this goal, we will present an endogenous growth model with human and physical capital where investment in human capital is the result of public spending for education (see also Greiner and Flaschel, 2009a). In addition, we consider an economy with two different types of households. One household supplies skilled labor, due to human capital formation, whereas the other household supplies low-skilled labor but benefits from human capital accumulation through spill-over effects. Households inelastically supply labor on the first and on the second labor market, respectively, and they both save a certain fraction of their income which is subject to income tax. Both types of households may become unemployed but, if so, they receive unemployment benefits, thus providing income security for households.

The government pays unemployment benefits and pays transfers to the household supplying simple labor, besides financing human capital accumulation. In order to finance its spending, the government levies a distortionary income tax rate. The firm demands two types of labor: skilled labor on the first labor market that is supplied by household one and simple or low-skilled labor on the second labor market, supplied by household two, which receives a lower wage rate. The firm maximizes profits so that the marginal products of labor equal the wage rates, respectively.

The rest of the chapter is organized as follows. In the next section, we present the basic structure of our growth model. Section 6.3 studies growth and welfare effects of fiscal policy along the balanced growth path. Section 6.4, Section 6.5 and Section 6.6 analyze stability properties and Section 6.7 concludes.

6.2 The Structure of the Growth Model

Our economy consists of three sectors: a household sector which receives labor income and income from its saving, a productive sector and the government. First, we describe the productive sector and the wage adjustment process.

6.2.1 The Productive Sector and the Wage Adjustment Process

The productive sector is represented by one firm which behaves competitively and which maximizes profits. Production of the firm at time t is given by a Cobb–Douglas production function as

$$Y(t) = AK(t)^{1-\alpha-\beta} \left(h_c(t)L_1^d(t)\right)^{\alpha} \left(\xi h_c(t)L_2^d(t)\right)^{\beta}, \qquad (6.1)$$

where[2] Y gives output, K denotes physical capital and h_c gives per-capita human capital. L_1^d denotes labor demand for skilled labor in the first labor market and L_2^d gives labor demand for simple labor in the second labor market. The parameter $\xi \in (0,1)$ determines the spill-over effect of human capital implying that, due to externalities, low-skilled labor benefits to a certain degree from human capital of skilled labor. The coefficients $\alpha \in (0,1)$ and $\beta \in (0,1)$ give the elasticity of production with respect to skilled and with respect to simple labor, respectively, so that $(1-\alpha-\beta)$ is the capital share and A is a technology parameter.

As concerns the wage rate for simple labor we posit that it is a certain fraction $\epsilon \in (0,1)$ of the wage rate for skilled labor, denoted by ω. The assumption that the wage rate for low-skilled labor is a constant fraction of that for high-skilled certainly is a very simplified way of representing the relative wage generation process. But, we think that for the purpose of this chapter this can be justified as a first approach.

Static profit maximization, then, gives demand for the two types of labor as

$$L_1^d = \quad c_1\,\alpha\,\omega^{-1/(1-\alpha-\beta)}\,(h_c/K)^{(\alpha+\beta)/(1-\alpha-\beta)} \tag{6.2}$$
$$L_2^d = \quad c_1\,\beta\,\omega^{-1/(1-\alpha-\beta)}\,(h_c/K)^{(\alpha+\beta)/(1-\alpha-\beta)}/\epsilon, \tag{6.3}$$

with $c_1 = A^{1/(1-\alpha-\beta)}\alpha^{\alpha/(1-\alpha-\beta)}\beta^{\beta/(1-\alpha-\beta)}(\xi/\epsilon)^{\beta/(1-\alpha-\beta)}$.

Equations (6.2) and (6.3) yield $L_1^d/L_2^d = \epsilon\,\alpha/\beta$, showing that the demand for labor in the first labor market relative to demand in the second labor market is determined by the elasticities of production with respect to labor in these two markets and by the wage rate in the second labor market relative to that in the first labor market, ϵ. The higher the elasticity of production with respect to skilled labor and the higher the wage rate in the second labor market relative to the first labor market, the higher is the demand for skilled labor relative to low-skilled labor.

Denoting by r the return to capital, profit maximization yields

$$\begin{aligned} r =& (1-\alpha-\beta)A(h_c/K)^{(\alpha+\beta)/(1-\alpha-\beta)}(\omega/K)^{(-\alpha-\beta)/(1-\alpha-\beta)}\,\cdot \\ & (c_1\alpha)^{\alpha}(c_1\beta/\epsilon)^{\beta}, \end{aligned} \tag{6.4}$$

with L_1^d and L_2^d substituted by the expressions given in (6.2) and (6.3).

We should like to point out that the use of a Cobb–Douglas production function implies that the elasticity of substitution between capital and labor and between the two types of labor is each equal to one. This implies that the two types of labor can be substituted by each other to a certain degree.

As concerns the evolution of the wage rate, we assume that it depends negatively on the unemployment rate on the two labor markets and positively on the growth rate of physical capital. The reason for this assumption is that the change in the wage rate will be the smaller the higher the unemployment rate in an economy, as described by a Phillips curve relationship.[3] In addition, in a growing economy wage demands of unions will be the higher the larger the growth rate of the economy. Further, the capital stock positively affects labor productivity so that a higher growth rate of capital implies a higher growth rate of labor productivity. It should also be noted that our assumption as to the wage formation implies that, along a balanced growth path, the wage rate grows at the same rate as capital and GDP.

With this assumption, the growth rate of the wage to capital ratio, $x \equiv \omega/K$, can be described by

$$\frac{\dot{x}}{x} = \beta_{L1}\left(\frac{L_1^d - L_1^n}{(1-u)L_1}\right) + \beta_{L2}\left(\frac{L_2^d - L_2^n}{L_2}\right), \tag{6.5}$$

with $(1-u)L_1$ and L_2 labor supply on the first and on the second labor market, respectively, and L_i^n, $i = 1, 2$, the natural levels of employment in the two markets. This means that the wage rate grows at the same rate as the capital stock if skilled and simple labor demand is equal to its natural level, respectively. It must also be mentioned that uL_1, $u \in (0, 1)$, of the skilled labor is hired by the government as teachers in the educational sector, that is described in detail in the next subsection, so that $(1-u)L_1$ of skilled labor is available in the final goods sector. The parameters $\beta_{L1} > 0$ and $\beta_{L2} > 0$ determine the speed of adjustment and reflect labor market rigidities. The less flexible labor markets are, the smaller will be the parameters, implying that changes in labor demand affect the growth of the wage rate only to a minor degree. Further, since we allow for substitution between the two types of labor we suppose that demand on both labor markets influences the wage adjustment process.

We should also point out that there is one good in our economy that can be either consumed or invested. Consequently all variables are real including the return to capital and the wage rate. Next, we describe the government sector and human capital accumulation.

6.2.2 Human Capital Formation and the Government

Human capital in our economy is produced in the schooling sector where an exogenously given number of students is educated. As mentioned above, the government hires the fraction u of the skilled labor force as teachers. Additionally, the government uses public resources for education in the schooling sector, like expenditures for books and other teaching material, which is an input in the process of human capital formation, too. Thus, the input in the schooling sector is composed of teachers and of schooling expenditures and we assume decreasing returns to scale to each input but constant returns to both inputs. The evolution of per capita human capital, then, is a function of teachers per student and of expenditures per student.

It should be noted that human capital, which is embodied in students, becomes available to the whole active skilled labor force in the economy, once students become employees. The reason for this assumption is to be seen in spill-over effects of knowledge, which leads to a diffusion of knowledge among the labor force. At first sight, this seems to be a strong assumption. But if one takes into account that in reality newly hired employees interact with existing staff and both learn from each other, this assumption becomes comprehensible.

As concerns the production function for human capital formation we assume a Cobb–Douglas specification. The differential equation describing the change in human per capita capital can be written as

$$\dot{h}_c = \kappa(uh_cL)^{\psi}(I_E)^{1-\psi}/S - \delta_h h_c, \tag{6.6}$$

where I_E is public resources used in the schooling sector, $\kappa > 0$ a technology parameter and $0 < \psi < 1$ is the elasticity of human capital formation with respect to teachers. The parameter δ_h gives depreciation taking into account that a certain fraction of human capital gets lost, for example due to unemployment. Finally, the variable S gives the number of students in the economy.

The government in our economy receives tax revenues from capital and labor income taxation it then uses for the remuneration of the teachers, for public spending in the schooling sector, for transfer payments to low-skilled labor, T_P, and for unemployment benefits, U_p. The budget of the government is balanced at each point in time. Thus, the period budget constraint of the government is given by

$$T = I_E + \omega uL + T_p + U_b, \tag{6.7}$$

with T denoting tax revenue. As concerns transfer payments, T_p, we assume that this variable makes a certain part of the tax revenue, i.e. $T_p = \phi T$, with $0 < \phi < 1$.

6.2.3 The Household Sector

The household sector is composed of two types of households. The first household supplies skilled labor, which is employed either in the production of the final good or in the educational sector, while the second household supplies low-skilled labor. We assume that both households behave as immortal families corresponding to finite-lived individuals who are connected via intergenerational transfers that are based on altruism. Thus, although individuals have finite lives each family is considered as a dynasty where the decision maker behaves as if he had an infinite time horizon (see Barro and Sala-i-Martin 1995, Chapter 2.1).

The overall number of skilled people is composed of a stock of students, S, and of a stock of employees, L, who constitute the active labor force and produce goods or are hired as teachers. At each point of time a certain number of students, which is determined exogenously, enter the stock of students and a certain number of students become employees. We assume that the number of students becoming employees just equals the number of new students so that the overall stock of students is constant. Further, the number of students becoming employees equals the number of employees leaving the active labor force, so that the active labor force and, thus, the total stock of skilled labor is constant, too, just like the number of low-skilled labor.

The household sector maximizes the discounted streams of utility arising from per-capita consumption, C_i, $i = 1, 2$, over an infinite time horizon subject to their budget constraints, taking factor prices as given. The utility function of both households is assumed to be logarithmic, $U(C_i) = \ln C_i$, $i = 1, 2$, and the households supply labor inelastically. Both households may become unemployed but, if so, receive unemployment benefits from the government that make a certain percentage of the market wage rate.

The maximization problem of the household in the first labor market, then, can be written as

$$\max_{C_1} \int_0^\infty e^{-\rho t} \ln C_1 dt, \tag{6.8}$$

subject to

$$\begin{aligned}&(1-\tau)\left(\omega L_1^d + u\omega L_1 + rK_1 + \lambda\omega(L_1 - L_1^d - uL_1)\right)\\ &= \dot{K}_1 + \delta K_1 + C_1.\end{aligned} \tag{6.9}$$

The parameters $\rho > 0$, $\tau \in (0, 1)$ and $\delta \in (0, 1)$ are the subjective discount rate, the income tax rate and the depreciation rate of capital, respectively, and $K_1 > 0$ and $C_1 > 0$ give the capital stock owned by the household in the first labor market and its level of consumption. $\lambda \in (0, 1)$ gives that part of the market wage that is paid by the government as unemployment benefit and we assume that the total income, including unemployment benefits, is subject to the income tax.

To solve this problem we formulate the current-value Hamiltonian which is written as

$$\begin{aligned}H_1 =& \ln C_1 + \gamma_1((1-\tau)\big(\omega L_1^d + u\omega L_1 + rK_1 +\\ &\lambda\omega(L_1 - L_1^d - uL_1)\big) - \delta K_1 - C_1),\end{aligned} \tag{6.10}$$

with γ_1 the shadow-price of capital for household 1. Necessary optimality conditions are given by

$$C_1^{-1} = \gamma_1, \tag{6.11}$$
$$\dot{\gamma}_1 = (\rho + \delta)\gamma_1 - \gamma_1(1-\tau)\, r. \tag{6.12}$$

If the transversality condition $\lim_{t\to\infty} e^{-\rho t} K_1/C_1 = 0$ holds, which is fulfilled for a time path on which capital grows at the same rate as consumption, the necessary conditions are also sufficient.

The maximization problem of the household in the second labor market is given by

$$\max_{C_2} \int_0^{\infty} e^{-\rho t} \ln C_2 dt, \tag{6.13}$$

subject to

$$(1-\tau)\left(\epsilon\,\omega L_2 + rK_2 + \lambda\,\epsilon\,\omega(L_2 - L_2^d)\right) + T_p = \dot{K}_2 + \delta K_2 + C_2. \tag{6.14}$$

The capital stock owned by household two is denoted by $K_2 > 0$ and $C_2 > 0$ is its consumption. The household in the second labor market also saves but we assume that it disposes of a smaller capital stock than the household in the first labor market, that is, $K_2 < K_1$. Further, it receives transfer payments from the government, T_p, in addition to its market income.

Again, we formulate the current-value Hamiltonian which is

$$\begin{aligned} H_2 = &\ln C_2 + \gamma_2((1-\tau)\big(\epsilon\,\omega L_2^d + rK_2 + \\ &\lambda\,\epsilon\,\omega(L_2 - L_2^d)\big) + T_p - \delta K_2 - C_2), \end{aligned} \tag{6.15}$$

with γ_2 the shadow-price of capital for household 2. Necessary optimality conditions are obtained as

$$C_2^{-1} = \gamma_2, \tag{6.16}$$
$$\dot{\gamma}_2 = (\rho + \delta)\gamma_2 - \gamma_2(1-\tau)\, r. \tag{6.17}$$

These conditions are again sufficient if the transversality condition $\lim_{t\to\infty} e^{-\rho t} K_2/C_2 = 0$ is fulfilled.

The growth rates of consumption of the households are obtained from (6.11)–(6.12) and (6.16)–(6.17) as

$$\frac{\dot{C}_i}{C_i} = -\rho + (1-\tau)r,\ i = 1, 2. \tag{6.18}$$

Using $C_1 + C_2 = C$, the growth rate of aggregate consumption is given by

$$\frac{\dot{C}}{C} = \frac{\dot{C}_1}{C_1}\frac{C_1}{C} + \frac{\dot{C}_2}{C_2}\frac{C_2}{C} = (-\rho + (1-\tau)\,r)\left(\frac{C_1}{C} + \frac{C_2}{C}\right), \tag{6.19}$$

with $C_1/C + C_2/C = 1$.

6.3 The Balanced Growth Path

An equilibrium allocation is defined as an allocation such that the firm maximizes profits implying that factor prices equal their marginal products (equations (6.2), (6.3) and (6.4)), the households solve (6.8) subject to (6.9) and (6.13) subject to (6.14), respectively, the wage rate relative to capital evolves according to (6.5) and the budget constraint of the government (6.7) is fulfilled and the limiting transversality conditions hold.

The economy-wide resource constraint in this economy is obtained by combining the budget constraint of private households, equations (6.9) and (6.14), with the budget constraint of the government (6.7) as

$$\frac{\dot{K}}{K} = \frac{Y}{K} - \frac{C}{K} - \frac{I_E}{K} - \delta, \tag{6.20}$$

where I_E is given by

$$I_E = T(1-\phi) - \omega u L_1 - \lambda\omega(L_1(1-u) - L_1^d + \epsilon(L_2 - L_2^d)). \tag{6.21}$$

Aggregate consumption evolves according to equation (6.19) with r given by (6.4) so that the growth rate of aggregate consumption can be written as

$$\frac{\dot{C}}{C} = (1-\tau)\,(1-\alpha-\beta)\left(\frac{Y}{K}\right) - (\rho+\delta), \tag{6.22}$$

with Y/K given by

$$\frac{Y}{K} = A\,h^{(\alpha+\beta)/(1-\alpha-\beta)} x^{(-\alpha-\beta)/(1-\alpha-\beta)} (c_1\alpha)^{\alpha}(c_1\beta/\epsilon)^{\beta}, \tag{6.23}$$

where we defined $h \equiv h_c/K$.

Human capital, finally, grows according to

$$\frac{\dot{h}_c}{h_c} = (\kappa/S)(u\,L_1)^{\psi}\left(\frac{I_E}{h_c}\right)^{1-\psi} - \delta_h. \tag{6.24}$$

Thus, the economy is completely described by equations (6.5), (6.20), (6.22) and (6.24) plus the limiting transversality conditions of the households and initial conditions with respect to the capital stocks.

A balanced growth path (BGP) is defined as a path on which all endogenous variables grow at the same constant rate, that is, $\dot{K}/K = \dot{C}/C = \dot{h}_c/h_c = \dot{\omega}/\omega = g > 0$ holds, with $g = constant$. To analyze our economy around a BGP we define the new variable $c \equiv C/K$ and we use $h = h_c/K$. Differentiating these variables with respect to time and using $x = \omega/K$ from (6.5), a three dimensional system of differential equations results, given by $\dot{c}/c = \dot{C}/C - \dot{K}/K$, $\dot{h}/h = \dot{h}_c/h_c - \dot{K}/K$ and $\dot{x}/x$ which can be written as follows,

$$\begin{aligned}\dot{c} =& c\Bigg((1-\tau)(1-\alpha-\beta)\left(\frac{Y}{K}\right) - \rho - u\omega L_1 - \lambda\omega(L_1(1-u)- \\ & L_1^d + (L_2 - L_2^d)\epsilon)\Bigg) + c\left(c + (1-\phi)\left(\frac{T}{K}\right) - \left(\frac{Y}{K}\right)\right), \end{aligned} \tag{6.25}$$

$$\begin{aligned}\dot{h} =& h\left((\kappa/S)(u\,L_1)^{\psi}\left(\frac{I_E}{h_c}\right)^{1-\psi} - \delta_h - u\omega L_1 - \lambda\omega(L_1(1-u)- \right. \\ & \left. L_1^d + (L_2 - L_2^d)\epsilon)\right) + h\left(\delta + c + (1-\phi)\left(\frac{T}{K}\right) - \left(\frac{Y}{K}\right)\right), \end{aligned} \tag{6.26}$$

$$\begin{aligned}\dot{x} =& x\left(h^{(\alpha+\beta)/(1-\alpha-\beta)}x^{(-\alpha-\beta)/(1-\alpha-\beta)}\, c_1\, (\alpha\beta_{L1}/(L(1-u))+ \right. \\ & \left.\beta\beta_{L2}/(\epsilon L_2))\right) + x\left(\rho + \delta - (1-\tau)(1-\alpha-\beta)\left(\frac{Y}{K}\right) - \right. \\ & \left. \beta_{L1}L_1^n/(L(1-u)) - \beta_{L2}L_2^n/(\epsilon L_2)\right), \end{aligned} \tag{6.27}$$

with L_1^d, L_2^d, I_E and Y/K given by (6.2), (6.3), (6.21) and (6.23), respectively. The expression for T/K is $T/K = \tau(1-\alpha-\beta)(Y/K) + \tau h^{(\alpha+\beta)/(1-\alpha-\beta)}x^{(-\alpha-\beta)/(1-\alpha-\beta)}(1-\lambda)c_1(\alpha+\beta) + \tau x(uL_1 + \lambda L_1(1-u) + \lambda\epsilon L_2)$. It should be noted that the tax revenue T grows at the same rate as capital K on the BGP, because the return to capital r is constant and the wages grow at the same rate as capital. Thus, T/K is constant along the BGP.

A solution of $\dot{c} = \dot{h} = \dot{x} = 0$ with respect to h, c, x gives a BGP for our model and the corresponding ratios $h^\star, c^\star, x^\star$ on the BGP.[4] Proposition 1 gives results as concerns existence of a BGP.

Proposition 1: *Assume that* $I_E/h_c > (\kappa(uL)^{\psi}/\delta_h)^{1/(\psi-1)}$ *holds in equilibrium. Then, there exists a unique balanced growth path for the model economy.*

Proof: See appendix.

This proposition shows that the balanced growth path for this economy is unique provided that public investment in the educational sector is large enough. The fact that educational investment has to be positive and sufficiently large for sustained growth is not too surprising because human capital formation is the source of ongoing growth in this model. It should also be pointed out that along the BGP total employment equals its natural level which is due to the formulation of the Phillips curve in equation (6.5). But, since we use a Cobb–Douglas production function that allows substitution between the two types of labor, labor demand for one type of labor can be below its natural level while the other type of labor exceeds its natural level of employment.

6.4 Comparative Statics of the Balanced Growth Path

In this section we want to study how the balanced growth rate reacts to changes in parameters. In particular, we are interested in the question of how labor market rigidities, modeled in our approach by the parameters $\beta_{L,i}$, $i = 1, 2$, affect the balanced growth rate as well as how transfer payments and unemployment benefits influence growth. Thus, we first analyze variations in the adjustment speed. Proposition 2 gives the result.

Proposition 2: *A rise in the adjustment speed for skilled labor raises (leaves unchanged, reduces) the balanced growth rate if and only if* $L_1^n/L_2^n > (=, <)\, \alpha\,\epsilon/\beta$. *A rise in the adjustment speed for low-skilled labor raises (leaves unchanged, reduces) the balanced growth rate if and only if* $L_2^n/L_1^n < (=, >)\, \beta/(\alpha\,\epsilon)$.

Proof: See appendix.

To interpret that proposition we first note that variations in the speed of adjustment do not affect the ratio of human capital to physical capital on the BGP. Thus, it is the relation of labor demand relative to its natural level that determines whether a rise in the adjustment speed raises the balanced growth rate. For example, if labor demand for skilled labor is smaller than its natural level, a higher speed of adjustment for skilled labor will raise the growth rate. The reason for that outcome is that a more flexible labor market reduces unemployment, thus raising the balanced growth rate. This interpretation becomes obvious when it is recalled that $\alpha\epsilon/\beta = L_1^d/L_2^d$.

Of course, the same holds for low-skilled labor. If low-skilled labor is employed below its natural level, a higher speed of adjustment for low-skilled labor will increase the balanced growth rate because it implies a smaller rate of unemployment. Thus, a more flexible labor market for that type of labor that is in excess supply, that is where demand is below its natural level, leads to a higher balanced growth rate.

In the next two propositions, we analyze how fiscal policy affects the balanced growth rate.[5] The next proposition deals with growth effects of raising transfer payments.

Proposition 3: *A shift of resources to transfer payments reduces the balanced growth rate.*

Proof: See appendix.

Proposition 3 shows that more transfer payments imply a decline in the balanced growth rate. The economic mechanism behind that result is obvious. Due to the budget constraint of the government a rise in transfers leads to a decline in public spending for education. As a consequence, the balanced growth rate declines because investment in human capital is reduced.

When analyzing growth effects of increasing unemployment benefits, the outcome changes. Proposition 4 gives the result.

Proposition 4: *A rise in unemployment benefits λ reduces (leaves unchanged) the balanced growth rate if and only if $c_1(\alpha+\beta) < (=) L_1(1-u) + \epsilon L_2$.*

Proof: See appendix.

In order to interpret that proposition we note that the condition in the proposition can be rewritten as $(L_1^d - L_1(1-u)) + \epsilon(L_2^d - L_2) < (=)\, 0$. This shows that higher unemployment benefits reduce the balanced growth rate if labor demand is smaller than labor supply. The economic mechanism behind that result is the same as in Proposition 3. More unemployment benefits reduce public investment in education and, as a consequence, the ratio of human to physical capital on the BGP and, thus, economic growth. Only in case of full employment variations in unemployment benefits do not affect the balanced growth rate which is obvious since, in that case, unemployment payments of the government are equal to zero anyhow.

In the next section we analyze how fiscal policy affects welfare on the BGP.

6.5 Welfare Effects of Fiscal Policy

We analyze welfare effects of fiscal policy by comparing welfare on the balanced growth path for different fiscal policy parameters. Further, we have to introduce a social welfare function. In this chapter, we use a Bernoulli–Nash function that gives social welfare W and that is written as

$$W = W_1^{\mu_1} \cdot W_2^{\mu_2}, \tag{6.28}$$

with W_1 and W_2 welfare of household 1 and household 2, respectively, and $\mu_i \geq 0$, $i = 1, 2$, weights given to the welfare of the households, where we set $\mu_1 = \mu_2 = 1$ so that welfare of the two households receive the same weight.

Along the BGP, individual welfare is given by

$$W_i = \int_0^\infty e^{-\rho t} \ln C_i(t) = \frac{g}{\rho^2} + \frac{\ln C_i(0)}{\rho}, \; i = 1, 2, \tag{6.29}$$

with g denoting the balanced growth rate. It should be noted that along the BGP, consumption and the capital stocks of the two households grow at the same rate as the economy. Hence, we have $\dot{K}_i/K_i = \dot{C}_i/C_i = g = (1-\tau)r - (\rho + \delta)$. This gives initial consumption of the two households as $C_1 = \rho K_1 + (1-\tau)\omega(uL_1 + L_1^d + \lambda(L_1(1-u) - L_1^d))$ and $C_2 = \rho K_2 + (1-\tau)\epsilon\omega(L_2^d + \lambda(L_2 - L_2^d)) + T_p$. Of course, we have $C_1 + C_2 = C$ and $K_1 + K_2 = K$. Along the BGP, the distribution of capital between the two households is constant because all capital stocks grow at the same rate. Therefore, on the BGP the initial value of consumption of the two households depends on the initial distribution of the capital stocks, on the initial value of the aggregate capital stock and on the wage rate relative to capital on the BGP.

In order to study how fiscal policy affects welfare in this economy we resort to a numerical example. As regards the parameter values we use the following values as benchmark, $A = 1$, $\alpha = 0.4$ and $\beta = 0.2$. Those values for α and β imply an elasticity of output with respect to skilled labor and with respect to low-skilled labor of 40 and 20 percent, respectively, and the elasticity with respect to physical capital is 40 percent. The parameter determining spill-overs of human capital in the production is set to $\xi = 0.15$. Labor supply is set to 0.1 for both types of labor, i.e. $L_1 = L_2 = 0.1$, and low-skilled labor gets 50 percent of the wage rate of skilled labor, $\epsilon = 0.5$. The natural rate of unemployment is assumed to be 2.5 percent for skilled labor and 7.5 for low-skilled so that we set $\bar{L}_1 = 0.0975$ and $\bar{L}_2 = 0.0925$. It should be noted that this implies that low-skilled labor is more likely to become unemployed than skilled labor.

The adjustment speed for both types of labor is set to 1 percent, $\beta_{L1} = \beta_{L2} = 0.01$. Further, we assume that the number of students relative to total labor supply is 10 percent, implying $S = 0.02$ and 7 percent of skilled labor supply is employed in the education sector, $u = 0.07$. The elasticity of human capital formation with respect to educational investment is 50 percent, i.e. $\psi = 0.5$, and we set $\kappa = 0.14$. The depreciation rates of physical and human capital are 5 percent, $\delta = \delta_h = 0.05$, and the rate of time preference is $\rho = 0.05$. Finally, the fiscal parameters are set to $\tau = 0.15$, $\phi = 0.1$ and $\lambda = 0.7$, giving an income tax rate of 15 percent and implying that 10 percent of the tax revenue is paid as transfers and unemployed receive 70 percent of the wage rate.

With these parameter values we first compute welfare for different values of transfers paid to the relatively poor household. Table 6.1 shows the outcome for different values of the parameter ϕ, where we set $K_1/K = 0.75$ implying that the first household owns 75 percent of the capital stock in this economy[6] and we set $K(0) = 100$.

Table 6.1: Welfare, initial consumption and the growth rate for different values of ϕ.

	$\phi = 0.05$	$\phi = 0.1$	$\phi = 0.15$	$\phi = 0.2$
W	3364.29	3287.2	3202.69	3110.46
W_1	71.3246	70.2074	69.039	67.8124
W_2	47.1688	46.8212	46.3895	45.8686
$C_1(0)$	20.1651	19.894	19.6114	19.3158
$C_2(0)$	6.0265	6.1787	6.3195	6.4478
g	2.8%	2.6%	2.4%	2.1%

Table 6.1 shows that a rise in transfer payments reduces both the balanced growth rate and welfare in this economy. The increase in

transfer raises initial consumption of the relatively poorer household; however, this increase is not sufficiently large to compensate the decline in the growth rate. As a consequence, the welfare of the poorer household declines although transfers are increased. The level of initial consumption of the relatively rich household declines as transfers to the poor rises and, of course, its welfare, too.

In Table 6.2 we report the results of varying the unemployment benefits.

Table 6.2: Welfare, initial consumption and the growth rate for different values of λ.

	$\lambda = 0.6$	$\lambda = 0.7$	$\lambda = 0.8$	$\lambda = 0.9$
W	3284.96	3287.2	3289.45	3291.65
W_1	70.2433	70.2074	70.172	70.1363
W_2	46.7656	46.8212	46.877	46.9322
$C_1(0)$	19.917	19.894	19.8711	19.8481
$C_2(0)$	6.1576	6.1787	6.1998	6.2209
g	2.6%	2.6%	2.6%	2.6%

Table 6.2 shows that welfare in the economy rises as unemployment benefits become higher. It can also be seen that the relatively rich household is worse off with higher unemployment benefits. Thus, both its initial consumption and its welfare decline as λ rises. The poor household, however, has both higher initial consumption and higher welfare, the larger unemployment benefits are. Further, the increase in welfare of the poorer household outweighs the decline in welfare of the richer household so that total welfare rises.

The economic mechanism behind that outcome is that the quantitative decline of the balanced growth rate is only small. Hence, the balanced growth rate is reduced but the decline is less than 0.1 percent. This is due to the fact that both households get unemployment benefits and pay taxes on their total income. Therefore, the decline in the tax revenue and, thus, the reduction of public investment in education, is smaller compared to the case when transfer payments are increased that are not subject to the income tax. Consequently, the negative effect of a smaller balanced growth rate is negligible and this measure raises welfare in the economy.

Up to now, we have studied growth and welfare effects along the BGP. In the next section, we analyze stability the properties of our model.

6.6 Stability of the Balanced Growth Path

In order to find how fiscal parameters affect stability we resort to the numerical example from the last section and compute the eigenvalues of the Jacobian matrix. As in the last section we study the effects of varying transfer payments and unemployment benefits. Table 6.3 shows the signs of the eigenvalues of the Jacobian matrix for different values of transfer payments, ϕ.

Table 6.3: Eigenvalues of the Jacobian for different values of ϕ ($a, b > 0$, $i = \sqrt{-1}$).

	$\phi = 0.05$	$\phi = 0.1$	$\phi = 0.2$	$\phi = 0.35$
eigenvalues	$+; -a \pm bi$	$+; -a \pm bi$	$+; -a \pm bi$	$+; +a \pm bi$

Table 6.3 demonstrates that more transfer payments, that is a higher value for ϕ, tends to make the economy unstable. Hence, this table suggests that higher spending for education and less for unproductive purposes do not only raise economic growth but also tend to stabilize the economy. Thus, for values of ϕ larger than about 35 percent all eigenvalues are positive or have positive real parts. It should also be mentioned that the economy is characterized by transitory oscillations until it reaches the BGP in the long run since the eigenvalues are complex conjugate.

However, the question of for which parameter values the economy becomes unstable also depends on the flexibility of the wage adjustment process, that is on the value of β_{L1} and β_{L2}. This is illustrated in Table 6.4, where we set $\beta_{L1} = \beta_{L2} = 0.1$ which is ten times as high as in the benchmark case.

Table 6.4: Eigenvalues of the Jacobian for different ϕ, $\beta_{L1} = \beta_{L2} = 0.1$ ($a, b > 0, i = \sqrt{-1}$).

	$\phi = 0.05$	$\phi = 0.25$	$\phi = 0.55$	$\phi = 0.75$
eigenvalues	$-; -; +$	$-; -; +$	$+; -a \pm bi$	$+; +a \pm bi$

With higher values for the coefficients β_{L1} and β_{L2} the economy is stable even for relatively large transfer payments. Thus, only for values of ϕ larger than about 75 percent the economy is now unstable. But it must also be pointed out that the balanced growth rate becomes negative if ϕ becomes larger than 55 percent. In that case, educational investment is not sufficiently high to compensate the decline in human capital, due to oblivion, and the economy is characterized by a declining GDP on the BGP.

An additional result is that the economy is not characterized by transitory oscillations if transfer payments are sufficiently small, ϕ smaller than about 25 percent. Hence, fiscal policy may also be decisive as to whether the economy shows transitory cycles on the transition path or whether the adjustment is monotonic. In the next two tables we analyze effects of varying the amount of unemployment benefits.

Qualitatively, the results are the same as in the case of varying transfer payments. Hence, for small values of λ, determining the amount of unemployment benefits, the economy is stable with two negative real roots. If the parameter λ is increased, the eigenvalues become complex with two negative real roots. That means that the economy is stable but it shows transitory oscillations until it reaches the BGP in the long-run. If unemployment benefits are further increased the economy again becomes unstable.[7] Table 6.5 illustrates this case.

Table 6.5: Eigenvalues of the Jacobian for different values of λ $(a, b > 0, i = \sqrt{-1})$.

	$\lambda = 0.4$	$\lambda = 0.5$	$\lambda = 0.9$	$\lambda = 0.95$
eigenvalues	$+; -a \pm bi$	$+; -a \pm bi$	$+; -a \pm bi$	$+; +a \pm bi$

Finally, Table 6.6 shows that the economy is always stable for $\beta_{L1} = \beta_{L2} = 0.1$.

Table 6.6: Eigenvalues of the Jacobian for different λ, $\beta_{L1} = \beta_{L2} = 0.1$ $(a, b > 0, i = \sqrt{-1})$.

	$\lambda = 0.5$	$\lambda = 0.75$	$\lambda = 0.8$	$\lambda = 1$
eigenvalues	$-; +; -$	$-; -; +$	$+; -a \pm bi$	$+; -a \pm bi$

Again, for small values of λ all eigenvalues are real with two being negative, for larger values of λ two eigenvalues become complex conjugate with negative real parts. Hence, the economy may produce transitory oscillations, but it always converges to the BGP in the long-run.

6.7 Conclusion

In this chapter we have presented an endogenous growth model with human capital and unemployment. Human capital is the result of public spending for education and the government sector also finances transfers to the poorer household and unemployment benefits.

The analysis of our model has demonstrated that more flexible labor markets – flexible in the sense that changes in labor demand imply a stronger reaction in the wage rate – go along with a higher balanced growth rate if labor demand is smaller than the natural level of employment. Further, higher transfer payments reduce the balanced growth. The same holds for higher unemployment benefits unless labor demand equals labor supply. The reason for the latter two results is that, due to the budget constraint of the government, higher transfers and unemployment spending reduce productive investment in the educational sector.

As concerns welfare, numerical examples have shown that higher transfer payments reduce welfare in the economy due to the large decline in the growth rate so that welfare of both rich as well as poor households declines. However, this does not necessarily hold for unemployment benefits. The reason for that outcome is that variations in unemployment benefits affect economic growth to a lesser extent than variations in transfer payments. In that case, a rise in unemployment benefits reduces the welfare of the rich household but raises that of the poor so that overall welfare can rise.

Hence, the general conclusion that can be drawn from our analysis is that social spending programs that benefit poorer households can raise welfare provided that the growth rate does not decline too strongly, even if these policy measures reduce the welfare of relatively rich households.

Finally, a study of the stability properties has demonstrated that fiscal policy affects stability properties of the model economy as well. We found that higher unproductive public spending for transfers and for unemployment benefits can make the economy unstable. But, the more flexible labor markets are, in the sense that the wage rate adjusts quickly to variations in labor demand, the more social spending is feasible without endangering stability.

Appendix

Proof of Proposition 1

To prove this proposition we note that $\dot{c}/c = 0$ gives $c + \delta - uL_1\omega - \lambda\omega(L_1(1-u) - L_1^d + \epsilon(L_2 - L_2^d)) + (1-\phi)T/K - Y/K = (\rho+\delta) - (1-\tau)(1-\alpha-\beta)(Y/K)$.

Using this, we can rewrite $\dot{h}/h$ as

$$\dot{h}/h = (\kappa/S)(u\,L_1)^{\psi}\left(\frac{I_E}{h_c}\right)^{1-\psi} - \delta_h + \rho + \delta - (1-\tau)(1-\alpha-\beta)\left(\frac{Y}{K}\right)$$

with

$$\frac{Y}{K} = A\,h^{(\alpha+\beta)/(1-\alpha-\beta)}x^{(-\alpha-\beta)/(1-\alpha-\beta)}(c_1\alpha)^{\alpha}(c_1\beta/\epsilon)^{\beta}.$$

From (6.21) we get for I_E/h_c :

$$\begin{aligned} I_E/h_c =& h^{-1+(\alpha+\beta)/(1-\alpha-\beta)}x^{(-\alpha-\beta)/(1-\alpha-\beta)}\big((1-\phi)\tau \\ &\cdot(1-\alpha-\beta)(Y/K) + (\lambda + (1-\phi)\tau(1-\lambda))c_1(\alpha+\beta)\big) \\ &+ h^{-1}x\big((1-\phi)\tau(uL_1 + \lambda L_1(1-u) + \lambda\epsilon L_2) - uL_1 \\ &- \lambda(L_1(1-u) + \epsilon L_2)\big). \end{aligned}$$

Further, from $\dot{x}/x = 0$ we get

$$x = h^{\alpha+\beta}\left(\frac{c_1(\alpha\beta_{L1}/(L(1-u)) + \beta\beta_{L2}/(\epsilon L_2))}{\beta_{L1}L_1^n/(L(1-u)) + \beta_{L2}L_2^n/L_2}\right)^{1-\alpha-\beta}.$$

Replacing x in Y/K and in I_E/h_c leads to

$$\frac{\dot{h}}{h} \equiv q(h,\cdot) = (\kappa/S)(u\,L_1)^{\psi}h^{-(1-\alpha-\beta)(1-\psi)}\,C_1^{1-\psi} + (\rho+\delta-\delta_h) - h^{\alpha+\beta}\,C_2,$$

with $C_i > 0$ $i = 1, 2$, constants, given by

$$\begin{aligned} C_1 =& \tau(1-\phi)(1-\alpha-\beta)A(c_1\alpha)^{\alpha}(c_1\beta/\epsilon)^{\beta} + (1-\lambda)c_1(\alpha+\beta) + uL \\ &+ \lambda L_1(1-u) + \lambda\epsilon L_2 + \lambda c_1(\alpha+\beta) - uL - \lambda(L_1(1-u) + \epsilon L_2) \end{aligned}$$

and

$$C_2 = (1-\tau)(1-\alpha-\beta)A(c_1\alpha)^{\alpha}(c_1\beta/\epsilon)^{\beta}.$$

Thus $\dot{h}/h \to +\infty$, for $h \to 0$, $\dot{h}/h \to -\infty$, for $h \to \infty$ and $\partial(\dot{h}/h)/\partial h < 0$ such that there exists a unique $h^{\star}$ with $q(h^{\star}, \cdot) = 0$. □

Proof of Proposition 2

To prove that proposition, we note that the balanced growth rate is given by equation (6.22). Using (6.23) and $x = x(h, \cdot)$ obtained from solving $\dot{x}/x = 0$ in the proof of Proposition 1, we get

$$\frac{\dot{C}}{C} = -(\rho+\delta) + (1-\tau)(1-\alpha-\beta)A(c_1\alpha)^{\alpha}(c_1\beta/\epsilon)^{\beta}h^{\alpha+\beta} \cdot \left(\frac{\beta_{L1}L_1^n/(L(1-u)) + \beta_{L2}L_2^n/L_2}{c_1(\alpha\beta_{L1}/(L(1-u)) + \beta\beta_{L2}/(\epsilon L_2))}\right)^{\alpha+\beta} \tag{A.30}$$

From the proof of Proposition 1 it is easily seen that h on the BGP is invariant with respect to variations in $\beta_{L,i}$, $i = 1, 2$. Using that and differentiating (A.1) with respect to $\beta_{L,i}$, $i = 1, 2$, it is easily seen that we get the result in Proposition 2. □

Proof of Proposition 3

From (A.1) one realizes that transfer payments do not directly affect the balanced growth rate but only through variations in h. The effect of varying ϕ on the value of h along the BGP is obtained by implicitly differentiating $q(h, \cdot)$ from Proposition 1. It is easily seen that $\partial q(h, \cdot)/\partial \phi < 0$ and $-\partial q(h, \cdot)/\partial h > 0$ so that a rise in ϕ implies a decrease in h on the BGP and, therefore, a lower balanced growth path. □

Proof of Proposition 4

Unemployment benefits λ do not directly affect the balanced growth rate (A.1). Implicitly differentiating $q(h, \cdot)$ from Proposition 1 gives $-\partial q(h, \cdot)/\partial h > 0$ and $\partial q(h, \cdot)/\partial \lambda < (=) 0$ for $c_1(\alpha+\beta) < (=) L_1(1-u) + \epsilon L_2$. □

Notes

[1] This chapter is based on Greiner, A. and P. Flaschel (2009a), 'Economic policy in a growth model with human capital, heterogenous agents and unemployment', *Computational Economics*, **33**, 175–192.

[2] From now on we omit the time argument t if no ambiguity arises.

[3] An extensive discussion of the role of the Phillips curve in dynamic macroeconomics can be found for example in Flaschel et al. (1997). As regards the Phillips curve see also Blanchard and Katz (1999).

[4] The * denotes BGP values and we exclude the economically meaningless BGP $h^\star = c^\star = x^\star = 0$.

[5] We do not study effects of varying the income tax rate. Since the government uses its tax revenues to finance productive investment in education, there will exist a growth maximizing income tax rate as in growth models with public infrastructure (see for example Greiner and Hanusch, 1998). The same holds for human capital employed in the educational sector.

[6] The ratio K_1/K is not decisive. For example, setting $K_1/K = 0.9$ gives the same qualitative results.

[7] In Tables 6.3, 6.4 and 6.5, the dynamic system (6.25)–(6.27) undergoes a Hopf bifurcation leading to unstable limit cycles for $\phi = 0.3119$, $\phi = 0.7409$ and for $\lambda = 0.9093$, respectively.

7. Public Debt, Public Expenditures and Endogenous Growth with Real Wage Rigidities

7.1 Introduction

The book by Arrow and Kurz (1970) was the first that introduced productive public capital in modern models of economic growth. However, these authors did not analyze models that are characterized by endogenously determined growth rates in the long-run. The latter was achieved by Futagami et al. (1993) who studied the structure of an endogenous growth model with a productive public capital stock.

After the publication of the paper by Futagami et al. (1993) a great many contributions were published that studied the effects of fiscal policy within that class of model. But most papers assume that the budget of the government is balanced at each point in time. Exemptions are provided by the approaches by Greiner and Semmler (2000) as well as by Ghosh and Mourmouras (2004). In these papers the government may run deficits but it has to stick to some well-defined budgetary regimes.[1] It is shown that more strict budgetary regimes reduce the debt ratio and imply higher growth and welfare. An interesting contribution is also provided by the paper by Futagami et al. (2006) who study an endogenous growth model with productive public spending and government debt but assume that government debt must converge to an exogenously given debt ratio asymptotically, as determined in the Maastricht treaty, for example. They show that there exist two balanced growth paths in their model to which the economy can converge asymptotically, with one being saddle point stable and the other being saddle point stable or asymptotically stable.

While the assumption of institutional constraints that limit the scope of the government to run deficits is plausible and certainly realistic, they may nevertheless be considered as ad hoc. This does not hold for the inter-temporal budget constraint of the government that is in a way a natural constraint to which any government must stick. Examples where the inter-temporal budget constraint of the government is explicitly taken into account are the contributions by Greiner (2007, 2008, 2008a). In the first paper it is assumed that the primary surplus of the government is a positive linear function of the debt to gross national income ratio which guarantees that the inter-temporal budget constraint of the government is fulfilled. The paper, then, defines a balanced growth path as a path on which all endogenous variables, including public debt, grow at the same constant growth rate and presents an extensive analysis of the model. In the second paper a different topic is analyzed. There, a scenario with a zero debt ratio in the long-run is compared to a scenario where debt grows in the long-run and the question of which of these two scenarios performs better in terms of growth and welfare is analyzed.

In this chapter we take up the approach by Greiner (2008, 2008a).[2] However, in contrast to that latter contribution we suppose that labor markets may be characterized by real wage rigidities and unemployment. We then consider two cases. First, we analyze the case with flexible real wages as a benchmark implying that the unemployment rate is equal to the natural rate of unemployment. The goal, then, is to analyze the model assuming a balanced government budget and to compare the growth performance to a scenario with persistent deficits. In addition, growth effects of deficit-financed public investment are studied as well. In a next step, real wages are assumed to be rigid and the growth rate of the wage rate is described by a Phillips curve. The chapter again compares a balanced budget scenario to a scenario with permanent deficits and analyzes the effects of deficit-financed investment.

The motivation to allow for wage rigidities and unemployment in an endogenous growth model is the observation that many European countries experience persistent unemployment in spite of permanently growing GDPs (see also Greiner and Flaschel, 2010). Therefore, constructing a growth model featuring that characteristic and analyzing effects of fiscal policy within such a model seems to be justified.

The rest of the chapter is organized as follows. In the next section, we present the basic structure of our model. Section 7.3 analyzes our model where we assume flexible wages and in Section 7.4 we study the model assuming wage rigidities. Section 7.5 discusses the economic mechanisms behind the results in detail and compares the outcome to that in the model where unemployment is absent. Section 7.6 concludes.

7.2 The Structure of the Growth Model

Our economy consists of three sectors: a household sector which receives labor income and income from its saving, a productive sector and the government. First, we describe the household sector.

7.2.1 The Household Sector

The household sector is represented by one household which maximizes the discounted stream of utility arising from per-capita consumption, $C(t)$, over an infinite time horizon subject to its budget constraint, taking factor prices as given. The utility function is assumed to be logarithmic, $U(C) = \ln C$, and the household inelastically supplies L units of labor of which L^d is demanded by the productive sector. The rest $L - L^d$ is unemployed and the household receives unemployment benefits of $\lambda\omega$ per unemployed labor, where ω is the wage rate and $\lambda \in (0, 1)$.[3] We assume that unemployment payments in our economy are strictly positive and sufficiently high so that unemployed can lead dignified lives. In addition, unemployed must pursue simple activities, organized by the government, that are skill preserving. Hence, unemployment does not lead to a loss of human capital and unemployed labor can again be employed in the production process in the economy. Total labor supply L is constant over time. The maximization problem of the household can be written as,

$$\max_C \int_0^\infty e^{-\rho t} \ln C \, dt, \tag{7.1}$$

subject to

$$(1-\tau)\left(\omega L^d + rK + r_B B\right) + \lambda\omega(L - L^d) = \dot{W} + C + \delta K. \tag{7.2}$$

The coefficient ρ is the household's rate of time preference, r is the return to capital and r_B is the interest rate on government bonds. $W \equiv B + K$ gives wealth which is equal to public debt, B, and private capital, K, which depreciates at the rate δ. Finally, $\tau \in (0, 1)$ is the constant income tax rate[4] and we assume that unemployment benefits are not subject to the income tax. The dot over a variable gives the derivative with respect to time.

A no-arbitrage condition requires that the return to capital equals the return to government bonds yielding $r_B = r - \delta/(1-\tau)$. Thus, the budget constraint of the household can be written as

$$\dot{W} = (1-\tau)\left(\omega L^d + rW\right) + \lambda\omega(L - L^d) - \delta W - C. \tag{7.3}$$

To solve this problem we formulate the current-value Hamiltonian which is written as

$$\mathcal{H} = \ln C + \gamma \left((1-\tau) \left(\omega L^d + rW \right) + \lambda \omega (L - L^d) - C - \delta W \right). \quad (7.4)$$

Necessary optimality conditions are given by

$$C^{-1} = \gamma, \quad (7.5)$$

$$\dot{\gamma} = \rho\gamma - \gamma(1-\tau)\, r. \quad (7.6)$$

If the transversality condition $\lim_{t\to\infty} e^{-\rho t} W/C = 0$ holds, which is fulfilled for a time path on which assets grow at the same rate as consumption, the necessary conditions are also sufficient.

7.2.2 The Productive Sector and the Wage Adjustment Process

The productive sector is represented by one firm which behaves competitively and which maximizes static profits. The production function of the firm is

$$Y = K^{1-\alpha} \left(GL^d \right)^{\alpha}. \quad (7.7)$$

Y is output, G denotes public capital and $\alpha \in (0,1)$ gives the elasticity of output with respect to public capital and $(1-\alpha)$ is the private capital share. With this formulation public capital is labor augmenting implying that it raises the productivity of labor input. Profit maximization gives the interest rate as

$$r = (1-\alpha)(Y/K). \quad (7.8)$$

In case of flexible wages, implying a vertical Phillips curve, labor demand equals its natural level, L^n, and the wage rate, as well as its growth rate, are determined by the marginal productivity rule. Thus, we get

$$\omega = \alpha (L^n)^{\alpha-1} K^{1-\alpha} G^{\alpha}. \quad (7.9)$$

The unemployment rate, then, is equal to its natural rate and is given by $1 - L^n/L$. At this point we should like to point out that we assume throughout the chapter that labor supply exceeds labor demand, that is, $L \geq L^d$ holds. Thus, there is no rationing of the productive sector in the economy.

In case of rigid real wages, labor demand is again obtained from the firm maximizing profits. This leads to

$$L^d = \alpha^{1/(\alpha-1)}(\omega/K)^{1/(\alpha-1)}(G/K)^{\alpha/(1-\alpha)}. \tag{7.10}$$

In this case, the evolution of the wage rate is assumed to follow a simple Phillips curve relationship where the change in the wage rate negatively depends on the rate of unemployment.[5] Thus, we posit that labor demand on the labor market relative to labor supply affects the dynamics of the wage rate. The growth rate of the wage rate is described by

$$\frac{\dot{\omega}}{\omega} = \beta_L \left(\frac{L^d - \bar{L}}{L} \right), \tag{7.11}$$

with $\bar{L}$ the normal level of employment in the labor market in the sense that there is no tendency for a change in the wage rate if labor demand is equal to that value. The parameter $\beta_L > 0$ determines the speed of adjustment.

We should also point out that there is one good in our economy that can be either consumed or invested. Consequently all variables are real including the return to capital and the wage rate so that equation (7.11) describes the evolution of the real wage rate. Next, we describe the public sector.

7.2.3 The Government

The government in our economy receives tax revenues from income taxation and has revenues from issuing government bonds. Public spending is composed of public investment, I_p, spending for unemployment benefits, $\lambda\omega(L - L^d)$, and of public consumption, C_p, that is neither productive nor welfare enhancing. Further, the government sets the primary surplus such that it is a positive linear function of public debt which guarantees that public debt is sustainable. In order to see this, we note that the accounting identity describing the accumulation of public debt in continuous time is given by:[6]

$$\dot{B} = r_B B(1 - \tau) - S, \tag{7.12}$$

where S is government surplus exclusive of net interest payments.

The inter-temporal budget constraint of the government is fulfilled if

$$\begin{aligned} B(0) &= \int_0^\infty e^{-\int_0^\mu (1-\tau) r_B(\nu) d\nu} S(\mu) d\mu \\ &\leftrightarrow \lim_{t\to\infty} e^{-\int_0^t (1-\tau) r_B(\mu) d\mu} B(t) = 0 \end{aligned} \tag{7.13}$$

holds. Equation (7.13) is the present-value borrowing constraint which states that public debt at time zero must equal the future present-value surpluses.

Now, assume that the ratio of the primary surplus to GDP ratio is a positive linear function of the debt to GDP ratio and of a constant. The primary surplus ratio, then, can be written as

$$\frac{S}{Y} = \phi + \beta \, \frac{B}{Y} = \frac{\tau Y - I_p - C_p - \lambda\omega(L - L^d)}{Y}, \tag{7.14}$$

where $\phi \in \mathbb{R}$, $\beta \in \mathbb{R}_{++}$ are constants. The parameter β determines how strong the primary surplus reacts to changes in public debt and ϕ determines whether the level of the primary surplus rises or falls with an increase in GDP.

Using (7.14) the differential equation describing the evolution of public debt can be written as

$$\dot{B} = (r_B(1-\tau) - \beta)\, B - \phi Y. \tag{7.15}$$

Solving this differential equation and multiplying both sides by $e^{-\int_0^t (1-\tau) r_B(\mu) d\mu}$ to get the present-value of public debt leads to

$$\begin{aligned} & e^{-\int_0^t (1-\tau) r_B(\mu) d\mu} B(t) \\ & = e^{-\beta t} B(0) - \phi Y(0) \, \frac{\int_0^t e^{\beta\mu} \, e^{-\int_0^\mu ((1-\tau) r_B(\nu) - g_Y(\nu)) d\nu} d\mu}{e^{\beta t}}, \end{aligned} \tag{7.16}$$

with $B(0) > 0$ public debt at time $t = 0$ and g_Y the growth rate of GDP.

Equation (7.16) shows that $\beta > 0$ is necessary for $\lim_{t\to\infty} e^{-\int_0^t (1-\tau) r_B(\mu) d\mu} B(t) = 0$. Further, if the numerator in the second expression in (7.16) remains finite the second term converges to zero. If the numerator in the second expression in (7.16) becomes infinite, l'Hôpital gives the limit as $e^{-\int_0^t ((1-\tau) r_B(\nu) - g_Y(\nu)) d\nu} / \beta$. This shows that $\beta > 0$ and $\lim_{t\to\infty} \int_0^t ((1-\tau) r_B(\nu) - g_Y(\nu)) d\nu = \infty$ are sufficient for sustainability of public debt. It should be noted that for t sufficiently large, $(1-\tau) r_B - g_Y > 0$ always holds in our model if the growth rate of GDP converges to the balanced growth rate because we assume a logarithmic utility function.

These considerations demonstrate that a positive linear dependence of the primary surplus to GDP ratio on the debt ratio, that is $\beta > 0$, is a necessary condition for the inter-temporal budget constraint of the government to be met. Therefore, we posit that the government sets the primary surplus according to (7.14) so that the evolution of public debt is given by (7.15).

Using that the evolution of public debt is given by $\dot{B} = r_B B(1-\tau) + I_p + C_p + \lambda\omega(L - L^d) - \tau Y = r_B B(1-\tau) - \beta B - \phi Y$ public investment can be written as

$$I_p = \psi(\tau - \phi)Y - \psi\beta B - \psi\lambda\omega(L - L^d)\,, \qquad (7.17)$$

where we assumed that public consumption relative to public investment is constant, $C_p/I_p = \kappa = constant$, $\psi = 1/(1+\kappa)$.

Denoting by δ_G the depreciation rate of public capital, the differential equation describing the evolution of public capital, then, is written as

$$\dot{G} = \psi(\tau - \phi)Y - \psi\beta B - \psi\lambda\omega(L - L^d) - \delta_G G\,. \qquad (7.18)$$

7.2.4 The Balanced Growth Path

The description of our economy is completed by deriving the growth rate of consumption and by deriving the economy-wide resource constraint. The growth rate of consumption is obtained from (7.5) and (7.6) as

$$\frac{\dot{C}}{C} = -(\rho + \delta) + (1-\tau)(1-\alpha)(Y/K). \qquad (7.19)$$

with Y/K given by $Y/K = (L^n)^\alpha (G/K)^\alpha$ in case of a vertical Phillips curve and by $Y/K = \alpha^{\alpha/(\alpha-1)}(\omega/K)^{-\alpha/(1-\alpha)}(G/K)^{\alpha/(1-\alpha)}$ if the Phillips curve has a negative slope, where the latter is obtained by using the optimality condition (7.10).

The economy-wide resource constraint is derived by combining the budget constraint of the household with that of the government as

$$\frac{\dot{K}}{K} = \frac{Y}{K} - \frac{C}{K} + \beta\,\frac{B}{K} + (\phi - \tau)\,\frac{Y}{K} + \lambda(L - L^d)\,\frac{\omega}{K} - \delta\,, \qquad (7.20)$$

with $L \geq L^d$.

Hence, the economy is completely described by equations (7.15), (7.18), (7.19) and (7.20), with r given by (7.8). The wage rate is either determined by (7.9) or by (7.11) with L^d given by (7.10), depending on whether the Phillips curve is vertical or negatively sloped.

A balanced growth path (BGP) is given when the conditions shown in definition 1 are fulfilled.

Definition 1 *A balanced growth path (BGP) is a path such that consumption, private capital, public capital and the wage rate grow at the same strictly positive constant growth rate, i.e.* $\dot{C}/C = \dot{K}/K = \dot{G}/G = \dot{\omega}/\omega = g$, $g > 0$, $g =$ *constant, and either*
(i) $\dot{B} = 0$ *or*
(ii) $\dot{B}/B = g$.

This definition shows that, as usual, consumption, private capital, public capital and, thus, output, as well as the wage rate, grow at a constant and strictly positive rate over time. Public debt may also grow at the same rate as output or it may be constant. The latter holds when the government pursues a balanced budget. In the next two sections we analyze our model, first for the case of an exogenously given Phillips curve and, second, assuming that the Phillips curve is negatively sloped.

7.3 Analysis of the Model with Real Wage Flexibility

In this section we study the structure of our model assuming that labor demand equals its natural level, $L^d = L^n$, such that the unemployment rate equals its natural rate, $1 - L^n/L$. The wage rate is determined by the marginal productivity rule (7.9).

In this case, the economy is completely described by equations (7.15), (7.18), (7.19) and (7.20), with r and ω given by (7.8) and (7.9), with $L^d = L^n$. To analyze our economy around a BGP we define the new variables $c \equiv C/K$, $b \equiv B/K$ and $x \equiv G/K$. Differentiating these variables with respect to time leads to a three-dimensional system of differential equations given by

$$\begin{aligned}\dot{c} = {} & c\big((1-\alpha)x^\alpha (L^n)^\alpha (1-\tau) - \rho + c - x^\alpha (L^n)^\alpha \\ & - (\phi - \tau)x^\alpha (L^n)^\alpha - \beta b\big) - c\left(\lambda \alpha x^\alpha (L^n)^{\alpha-1}(L - L^n)\right), \quad (7.21)\end{aligned}$$

$$\begin{aligned}\dot{b} = {} & b\big((1-\alpha)x^\alpha (L^n)^\alpha (1-\tau) - \beta - \phi x^\alpha (L^n)^\alpha / b + c - x^\alpha (L^n)^\alpha \\ & - (\phi - \tau)x^\alpha (L^n)^\alpha\big) - b\left(\beta b + \lambda \alpha x^\alpha (L^n)^{\alpha-1}(L - L^n)\right), \quad (7.22)\end{aligned}$$

$$\begin{aligned}\dot{x} = {} & x\big(\psi(\tau - \phi)(L^n)^\alpha x^{\alpha-1} - \psi\beta b/x - \psi\lambda\alpha x^{\alpha-1}(L^n)^{\alpha-1}(L - L^n) \\ & - \delta_G - x^\alpha (L^n)^\alpha\big) + x\left(c + \delta - \beta b - (\phi - \tau)x^\alpha (L^n)^\alpha \right. \\ & \left. - \lambda\alpha x^\alpha (L^n)^{\alpha-1}(L - L^n)\right). \quad (7.23)\end{aligned}$$

A solution of $\dot{c} = \dot{b} = \dot{x} = 0$ with respect to c, b, x gives a BGP for our model and the corresponding ratios $x^\star, b^\star, c^\star$ on the BGP.[7]

In the following we consider two situations. First, we analyze the economy with a balanced budget, then for the case of permanent deficits.

Balanced Government Budget

The balanced budget scenario, scenario (i), is obtained by setting the reaction coefficient β equal to the net return on capital, $(1-\tau)r-\delta$, making β an endogenous variable. Further, ϕ is set equal zero for all times, i.e. $\phi = 0$, for $t \in [0, \infty)$. For this scenario, Proposition 1 gives results as concerns uniqueness and stability of a balanced growth path.

Proposition 1: *Assume that there exists a balanced growth path for scenario (i). Then, the balanced growth path is unique and saddle point stable.*

Proof: See appendix.

This proposition demonstrates that the balanced budget scenario is characterized by a unique BGP which is saddle point stable, in case of ongoing growth. The fact that the existence of a BGP cannot be shown for the analytical model is due to unemployment benefits paid by the government and due to depreciation of public capital. Thus, if unemployment benefits exceed a certain threshold sustained growth may not be feasible because public resources devoted to growth-enhancing public investment are not sufficiently large.

It should also be pointed out that saddle point stability implies, in case of a vertical Phillips curve, that there exists a unique value $c(0)$ such that the economy converges to the balanced growth path. If one takes both $x(0)$ and $b(0)$ as given, since both x and b are state variables, this means that the economy is determinate, implying that two economies with identical initial capital stocks and the same initial level of public debt have the same transitional growth rates.

Permanent Public Deficits

As concerns scenario (ii), the deficit scenario, where public debt grows at the same rate as consumption and capital in the long-run, the analytical model turns out to be quite complicated and no unambiguous results can be derived. But it is possible to derive a result as concerns the public debt to private capital ratio for the analytical model. This is done in Proposition 2.

Proposition 2: *Assume that there exists a balanced growth path in scenario (ii). Then, the ratio of public debt to private capital is given by*

$$b^{\star} = \frac{\phi\,(x^{\star})^{\alpha}(L^{n})^{\alpha}}{\rho - \beta}\,.$$

Proof: See appendix.

From Proposition 2 one can realize that in case of a relatively low reaction coefficient β, so that $\beta < \rho$, the coefficient ϕ must be positive for sustained growth with a positive government debt to be feasible.[8] This implies that the primary surplus must rise as GDP increases if the reaction of the government to higher public debt is relatively small. If the reverse holds, namely for $\beta > \rho$, the coefficient ϕ must be negative. In this case, the reaction of the government to higher debt is relatively large implying that the government pays too much attention to stabilizing debt and does not attach sufficient weight to fostering economic growth through public investment. Therefore, the primary surplus must decline with a higher GDP, implying that public investment rises, so that sustained growth is feasible.

An interesting result can be obtained when the deficit scenario is compared to the balanced budget scenario. It turns out that the balanced budget scenario always is associated with a higher growth rate. Proposition 3 gives the result.

Proposition 3: *The balanced growth rate in scenario (ii), the deficit scenario, is lower than the balanced growth rate in the balanced budget scenario, scenario (i).*

Proof: See appendix.

From an economic point of view, the result in Proposition 3 is due to the fact that in the deficit scenario the government must devote resources to the debt service that cannot be used for productive public investment. The latter does not hold for the balanced budget scenario so that this scenario goes along with a higher balanced growth rate.

In order to get additional insight in our model we perform simulations. We should like to point out that our model is a highly stylized one so that we do not intend to make calibration exercises or replicate real economies. The simulations are intended to derive results that cannot be obtained for the analytical model. In particular, we are interested in growth effects of deficit-financed public investment and in the question of how the reaction coefficient, β, affects stability of the model.

In the simulations, the subjective discount rate is set to 3.5 percent and the depreciation rates of private and of public capital are 3.5 and 7.5 percent, respectively, that is, $\rho = 0.035$, $\delta = 0.035$, $\delta_G = 0.075$. Labor supply is normalized to one, $L = 1$, and the natural rate of employment is 0.98 giving a natural rate of unemployment of 2 percent. The parameter ψ is set to $\psi = 0.65$, implying that the ratio of public consumption to public investment is about 55 percent. The income tax rate is set to 10 percent and the unemployment benefit per labor is 80 percent, that is $\tau = 0.1$, $\lambda = 0.8$. The elasticity of output with respect to public capital is set to 30 percent. It must be pointed out that this implies that the elasticity of output with respect to labor is also 30 percent while the elasticity of output with respect to capital is 70 percent. This can be justified by supposing that labor is raw labor and that capital is interpreted in a broad sense so that capital comprises both private physical and human capital.[9]

In Table 7.1 we report the balanced growth rate, g, and the signs of the eigenvalues of the Jacobian for different values of ϕ, with β set $\beta = 0.01$.

Table 7.1: Balanced growth rate, g, and eigenvalues for different ϕ with $\beta = 0.01$.

	$\phi = 0.065$	$\phi = 0.055$	$\phi = 0.045$
g	5%	11.8%	15.2%
eigenvalues	$+; -; +$	$-; +; +$	$-; +; +$

In order to interpret Table 7.1 we note that a deficit-financed increase in public investment is modelled by a decline in ϕ which can be seen from equation (7.17). Hence, Table 7.1 shows that a deficit-financed increase in public investment leads to a higher balanced growth rate with the parameters underlying the simulation. However, it can also be seen that only one eigenvalue is negative implying that the economy is unstable in this case. Consequently, the government must levy an additional non-distortionary tax in order to control public debt so that the economy can converge to the BGP.

If ϕ is further increased in Table 7.1, the balanced growth rate declines and for $\phi \geq 0.068$ no BGP exists any longer. If ϕ is decreased, the balanced growth rate rises and for $\phi \to 0$ the balanced growth rate approaches its maximum value of about 24 percent which is equal to the growth rate obtained in the balanced budget scenario.

Next, we choose a higher value for β and set $\beta = 0.05$ so that $\rho < \beta$ holds. Table 7.2 gives results for this example.

Table 7.2: Balanced growth rate, g, and eigenvalues for different ϕ with $\beta = 0.05$.

	$\phi = -0.01$	$\phi = -0.02$	$\phi = -0.03$
g	21.5%	18.3%	13.8%
eigenvalues	$+; -; -$	$+; -a \pm bi, a, b > 0$	$+; -a \pm bi, a, b > 0$

Table 7.2 shows that with a larger reaction coefficient β the economy is stable. For $\beta = 0.05$ there are either two negative real eigenvalues or two complex conjugate eigenvalues with negative real parts. But in this case, a deficit-financed increase in public investment reduces the balanced growth rate. The reason is that the initial deficit-financed increase in public investment is compensated by the strong reaction of the government to the higher public debt so that the economy ends up with a smaller growth rate. Hence, there is a trade-off between stability and positive growth effects of deficit-financed public investment.

If ϕ is increased the growth rate rises and again approaches its maximum value for $\phi \to 0$. If ϕ is decreased, the balanced growth rate declines and it turns out that for $\phi \leq -0.036$ the balanced growth becomes unstable, that is the Jacobian matrix has only positive eigenvalues or eigenvalues with positive real parts. For $\phi \leq -0.041$, finally, no BGP exists any longer.

In order to see that a lower reaction coefficient β destabilizes the economy, we set $\phi = -0.03$ and continuously decrease β starting from $\beta = 0.05$. Doing so shows that for $\beta = \beta_{crit} = 0.047649$ two eigenvalues are purely imaginary and for values of β smaller than β_{crit} one eigenvalue is positive and two are complex conjugate with positive real parts, implying that the BGP looses stability. In addition, a Hopf bifurcation can be observed at $\beta = \beta_{crit}$ leading to limit cycles. At the bifurcation point the first Lyapunov coefficient l_1 is negative, $l_1 \approx -1.089$, indicating that the emerging limit cycles are stable.[10]

Figure 7.1 shows a limit cycle in the $(x - b - c)$ phase space. The orientation of the cycle is as indicated by the arrow.

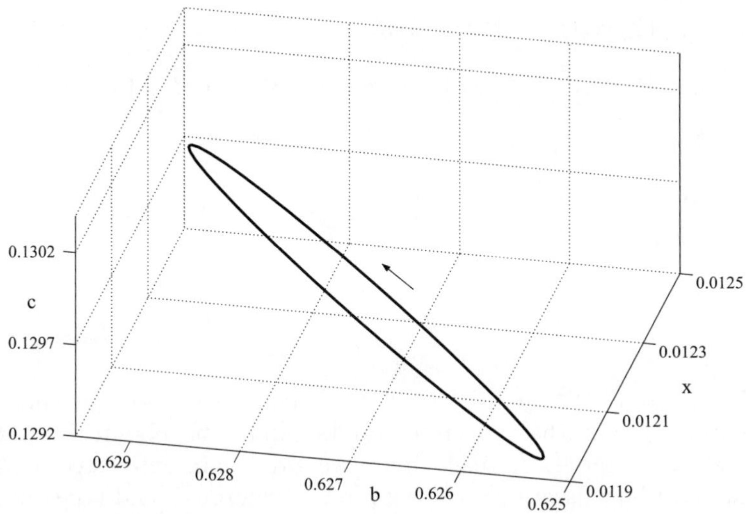

Fig. 7.1: Limit cycle in the $(x - b - c)$ phase space.

7.4 The Model with Real Wage Rigidities

In the case of real wage rigidities, labor demand is given by (7.10) and the wage adjustment is described by the Phillips curve (7.11). This implies that the growth rate of the wage rate is a negative function of the unemployment rate. In this case, the economy is completely described by the equations (7.11), (7.15), (7.18), (7.19) and (7.20), with r given by (7.8) and L^d given by (7.10).

In order to analyze the economy around a BGP we proceed as in the last section and define the variables $c \equiv C/K$, $b \equiv B/K$, $x \equiv G/K$ and, in addition, $y = \omega/K$. Differentiating these variables with respect to time gives a four-dimensional system of differential equations which is written as,

$$\begin{aligned}\dot{c} =& c\Big((1-\alpha)(1-\tau)(Y/K) - \rho - \beta b - \lambda y \Big(L - \alpha^{1/(1-\alpha)} \cdot \\ & y^{-1/(1-\alpha)} x^{\alpha/(1-\alpha)}\Big)\Big) + c\,(c - (Y/K)(1-\phi+\tau))\,, \qquad (7.24)\end{aligned}$$

$$\begin{aligned}\dot{b} =& b\Big((1-\alpha)(1-\tau)(Y/K) - \beta - \phi(Y/K)/b - \lambda y(L - \alpha^{1/(1-\alpha)} \cdot \\ & y^{-1/(1-\alpha)} x^{\alpha/(1-\alpha)})\Big) + b\,(c - \beta b - (Y/K)(1-\phi+\tau))\,, \qquad (7.25)\end{aligned}$$

$$\dot{x} = x\Big(\psi(Y/K)(\tau - \phi)/x - \psi\beta b/x - \delta_G - \psi\lambda y(L - \alpha^{1/(1-\alpha)} \cdot$$
$$y^{-1/(1-\alpha)}x^{\alpha/(1-\alpha)})/x\Big) + x\Big(c + \delta - \beta b - (Y/K)(1 - \phi + \tau) -$$
$$\lambda y(L - \alpha^{1/(1-\alpha)}y^{-1/(1-\alpha)}x^{\alpha/(1-\alpha)})\Big), \tag{7.26}$$
$$\dot{y} = y\Big(\beta_L\alpha^{1/(1-\alpha)}y^{-1/(1-\alpha)}x^{\alpha/(1-\alpha)}/L - \beta_L\bar{L}/L - (Y/K)\cdot$$
$$(1 - \phi + \tau) + \delta - \beta b\Big) +$$
$$y\left(c - \lambda y(L - \alpha^{1/(1-\alpha)}y^{-1/(1-\alpha)}x^{\alpha/(1-\alpha)})\right), \tag{7.27}$$

with $Y/K = \alpha^{\alpha/(1-\alpha)}y^{-\alpha/(1-\alpha)}x^{\alpha/(1-\alpha)}$. This system is rather complex and it turns out that concrete results cannot be obtained without numerical exercises. In particular, we are again interested in the question of how fiscal policy affects economic growth and the stability of the economy. First, we analyze the balanced budget scenario.

Balanced Government Budget

As in the last section, the balanced budget scenario, scenario (i), is obtained by setting the reaction coefficient β equal to the net return on capital, $(1-\tau)r-\delta$, and by setting $\phi = 0$. For this scenario, Proposition 4 gives information about stability properties of the dynamic system.

Proposition 4: *Assume that there exists a balanced growth path for scenario (i). Then, there is at least one negative real eigenvalue.*

Proof: See appendix.

If there is exactly one negative real eigenvalue the economy is unstable. In this case, the government again has to levy a non-distortionary tax and use the revenue to control public debt such that the economy can converge to the BGP in the long-run. If there are two negative eigenvalues or two eigenvalues with negative real parts, there exist unique initial values of consumption and of the wage rate the economy can choose, such that it converges to the BGP. In case of more than two negative real eigenvalues, the economy is indeterminate in the sense that the initial consumption and the initial wage rate are not uniquely determined. Next, we study the deficit scenario and try to find how fiscal policy may affect the economy.

Permanent Public Deficits

To analyze the economy with this scenario we again use numerical examples and take the same parameter values as in the last section and we set the parameter β_L, determining the adjustment speed of wages, to $\beta_L = 0.07$. In Table 7.3 we study the effects of raising deficit-financed public investment with a relatively small reaction coefficient β.

Table 7.3: Balanced growth rate, g, unemployment rate, u, and eigenvalues for different values of ϕ with $\beta = 0.01$.

	$\phi = 0.065$	$\phi = 0.055$	$\phi = 0.045$
g	1.5%	1.2%	0.8%
u	3.1%	8.3%	13%
eigenvalues	$+; -; +; +$	$+; -; +; +$	$+; -; +; +$

Table 7.3 shows that for a relatively small value of the reaction coefficient β, the model is unstable. In addition, it can be seen that a deficit-financed increase in public investment, modeled by a decrease in ϕ, reduces the balanced growth rate and raises the unemployment rate. If we set the reaction coefficient β to a higher value, implying that the government raises the primary surplus to a larger degree as public debt increases, the situation changes. Then, the economy becomes stable and a deficit-financed increase in public investment leads to a higher balanced growth rate and a smaller unemployment rate.

If the parameter ϕ is further decreased in Table 7.3, the growth rate becomes negative for $\phi \leq 0.0094$. If ϕ is still further reduced, the balanced growth rate continues to decline and it converges to the value of the balanced budget scenario which is -0.3 percent for $\phi \to 0$. Thus, a balanced budget would go along with a negative balanced growth rate and an unemployment rate of 28.9 percent. The Jacobian has exactly one negative eigenvalue implying that the BGP is unstable. If ϕ is increased the economy reaches the full employment state for $\phi = 0.0524$ with a growth rate of 2.1 percent. Next, Table 7.4 shows the results with β set to $\beta = 0.05$. Table 7.4 shows that the economy is saddle point stable with a larger value of β. The outcome that a higher reaction coefficient stabilizes the economy is equivalent to the result of the last section with flexible wages and a vertical Phillips curve. But, in contrast to the last section, the trade-off between positive growth effects of deficit-financed public investment and stability does not seem to exist any longer when real wages are rigid.

Table 7.4: Balanced growth rate, g, unemployment rate, u, and eigenvalues for different values of ϕ with $\beta = 0.05$.

	$\phi = -0.01$	$\phi = -0.02$	$\phi = -0.03$
g	0.07%	0.5%	1%
u	24%	17.9%	10.7%
eigenvalues	+; −; +; −	+; −; +; −	+; −; +; −

As Table 7.4 demonstrates, a deficit-financed rise in public investment, modeled by a decline in ϕ, raises the balanced growth rate and the economy is stable.

If we increase the parameter ϕ in Table 7.4 it turns out that for $\phi \geq -0.008$ the balanced growth rate becomes negative. If ϕ is reduced the growth rate rises and for $\phi = -0.0422$ it attains 1.7 percent that goes along with an unemployment rate equal to zero.

The difference to the outcome of the last section is clearly due to the difference in wage flexibility that determines the shape of Phillips curves. In the next section, we discuss in detail the economic mechanisms behind the different results.

7.5 Discussion and Comparison to the Model Without Unemployment

In the last two sections we have derived results for our model and we have seen that the outcome partly depends on the flexibility of the real wage rate, that is on whether the Phillips curve is vertical or whether it has a negative slope. In this section we want to identify economic mechanisms that generate the different results.

One result we derived was a trade-off between positive growth effects of higher deficit-financed public investment and stability of the model when the Phillips curve is vertical. The reason for that outcome is that a high reaction coefficient β implies that the increase in the primary surplus is large as public debt rises, which stabilizes the economy. But, with a large β, the initial increase in deficit-financed public investment is more than compensated by the rise in public debt implying that public investment declines again, so that the economy is characterized by a smaller growth rate in the long-run. Thus, the higher public debt requires more resources for the debt service which reduces public investment in the end.

If wages are rigid and the Phillips curve has a negative slope, the trade-off does not exist. In this case, a deficit-financed increase in public investment raises the ratio of public to private capital and labor demand. As a consequence, unemployment declines, reducing unemployment payments of the government which raises public investment. Thus, lower unemployment spending prevents a decline in public investment as public debt rises, even if the reaction coefficient β is large. Further, a large reaction coefficient β has a positive effect on the growth rate of private capital, which can be seen from the economy-wide resource constraint (7.20). Therefore, a deficit-financed increase in public investment raises the balanced growth rate for a large β.

With a small β, the positive effect of less unemployment payments on public investment, as a result of higher deficit-financed public investment, would be amplified. But, in this case, the crowding-out effect of an increase in public investment dominates in the economy-wide resource constraint so that private investment declines. This is again seen from the economy-wide resource constraint (7.20), where we recall that the initial deficit-financed increase in public investment is modeled by a lower ϕ. Therefore, a deficit-financed increase in public investment reduces the balanced growth, where $\dot{K}/K = \dot{G}/G$ holds, for a small reaction coefficient β in case the Phillips curve has a negative slope.

Hence, the different effects of higher deficit-financed public investment in our model are due to the fact that employment is equal to its natural level with flexible wages whereas employment varies if real wages are not flexible when deficit-financed public investment is increased. It should also be mentioned that a higher balanced growth rate goes along with a higher wage to private capital ratio if wages are flexible. In case of rigid real wages, the reverse holds. In this case, a higher balanced growth rate goes along with a smaller ratio of the wage rate to private capital implying a higher employment share and, thus, less unemployment.

Finally, comparing our model with the model where unemployment is not considered, analyzed in Greiner (2007, 2008), it can be realized that, from a qualitative point of view, the model with flexible wages produces the same results as the model without unemployment. This holds although the differential equations in the two models are of course different, due to unemployment in this model leading to unemployment payments from the government to the household sector. Nevertheless, if wages are flexible and the Phillips curve is vertical, employment is fixed at its natural rate and the wage rate equals the marginal product. Only if wages are rigid and the Phillips curve has a negative slope does fiscal policy affect the unemployment rate and unemployment payments. Then, the model gives rise to different outcomes, as mentioned above.

7.6 Conclusion

Should the government run deficits and finance productive public spending in order to promote growth and employment in an economy? The answer to this question crucially depends on whether real wages are flexible and the Phillips curve is vertical or whether wages are rigid and the Phillips has a negative slope.

With flexible real wages, there is a trade-off between stability and positive growth effects of deficit-financed increases in public investment. If a deficit-financed increase in public investment raises the balanced growth rate, the government has to levy a lump-sum tax in order to control public debt. Otherwise, convergence to the balanced growth path cannot be assured. If real wages are rigid and the Phillips curve has a negative slope, this trade-off does not exist. The reason for this is that fiscal policy affects the level of employment in this case and, therefore, the feedback effect of higher public debt is different from the situation where employment is fixed at its natural level.

A result that holds independent of the flexibility of real wages is that a stronger reaction of the government to higher public debt stabilizes the economy. Hence, if the reaction of the government to higher debt is large, the economy is stable and converges to the balanced growth path asymptotically, independent of whether real wages are flexible or rigid.

Appendix

Proof of Proposition 1

To prove this proposition, we set $\phi = 0$, $\beta = (1-\tau)(1-\alpha)x^{\alpha}(L^n)^{\alpha} - \delta$ and $b = 0$. Setting $\dot{x}/x = \dot{c}/c$ gives $q(x, \cdot) = (1-\alpha)x^{\alpha}(L^n)^{\alpha}(1-\tau)-(\rho+\delta) + \delta_G - \tau x^{\alpha-1}(L^n)^{\alpha} + \lambda\alpha x^{\alpha-1}(L^n)^{\alpha-1}(L-L^n)$. In case of sustained growth we have $g = \tau x^{\alpha-1}(L^n)^{\alpha} - \delta_G - \lambda\alpha x^{\alpha-1}(L^n)^{\alpha-1}(L-L^n) > 0$ which is only possible for $\tau > \lambda\alpha(L-L^n)/L^n$. With this, it is easily seen that $\lim_{x\to 0} q(x,\cdot) = -\infty$ and $\lim_{x\to\infty} q(x,\cdot) = +\infty$. Further, we have $\partial q(\cdot)/\partial x > 0$. Thus, uniqueness of a BGP is shown.

To show saddle point stability, we compute the Jacobian matrix evaluated at the rest point of (7.21)–(7.23). The Jacobian is given by

$$\mathrm{J} = \begin{bmatrix} c\ \partial\dot{c}/\partial b & \partial\dot{c}/\partial x \\ 0\ \partial\dot{b}/\partial b & 0 \\ x\ \partial\dot{x}/\partial b & \partial\dot{x}/\partial x \end{bmatrix},$$

with $c = c^\star$ and $x = x^\star$. One eigenvalue of this matrix is given by $\lambda_1 = \partial\dot{b}/\partial b = -\dot{K}/K = -g < 0$. Thus, we know that one eigenvalue, λ_1, is negative. Further, $c(\partial\dot{x}/\partial x) - x(\partial\dot{c}/\partial x)$ can be computed as $c(\partial\dot{x}/\partial x) - x(\partial\dot{c}/\partial x) = -\alpha(1-\alpha)x^{\alpha-1}(L^n)^\alpha(1-\tau) + (\alpha-1)x^{-1}\left(\tau x^{\alpha-1}(L^n)^\alpha - \lambda\alpha x^{\alpha-1}(L^n)^{\alpha-1}(L-L^n)\right)$. $g > 0$ implies $\tau x^{\alpha-1}(L^n)^\alpha - \lambda\alpha x^{\alpha-1}(L^n)^{\alpha-1}\ (L-L^n) > \delta_G > 0$. Thus, the determinant of J is negative. Since the product of the eigenvalues equals the determinant, $\lambda_1 \cdot \lambda_2 \cdot \lambda_3 = \det J > 0$, and because of $\lambda_1 < 0$, we know that two eigenvalues are negative and one is positive. □

Proof of Proposition 2

To prove Proposition 2, $\dot{b}/b = 0$ is solved with respect to c giving $c = c(x, b, \cdot)$. Inserting $c = c(x, b, \cdot)$ in $\dot{c}/c$ and solving $\dot{c}/c = 0$ with respect to b gives $b^\star$ as in Proposition 2. □

Proof of Proposition 3

To prove this proposition we note that we set $\phi = 0$, $\beta = (1-\tau)(1-\alpha)x^\alpha(L^n)^\alpha - \delta$ and $b = 0$ to get scenario (i). Further, the balanced growth rate is given by $\dot{C}/C = -(\rho+\delta) + (1-\tau)(1-\alpha)x^\alpha(L^n)^\alpha$. Along a BGP we have $\dot{C}/C = \dot{G}/G$ which implies

$$(1-\tau)(1-\alpha)x^\alpha(L^n)^\alpha - (\rho+\delta) = \psi\,\tau x^{\alpha-1}(L^n)^\alpha - \psi\,\lambda\alpha x^{\alpha-1}(L^n)^{\alpha-1}(L-L^n) - \delta_G. \tag{A.1}$$

A value $x_i^\star$ such that the left-hand side (l.h.s.) in (A.1) equals the right-hand side (r.h.s.) gives a BGP for scenario (i).

Using that b on the BGP is given by $b = \phi \cdot (x^\star)^\alpha(L^n)^\alpha/(\rho-\beta)$, the condition $\dot{C}/C = \dot{G}/G$ can be written for scenario (ii) as

$$(1-\tau)(1-\alpha)x^{\alpha}(L^n)^{\alpha} - (\rho+\delta) =$$
$$\psi\tau x^{\alpha-1}(L^n)^{\alpha} - \psi\lambda\alpha x^{\alpha-1}(L^n)^{\alpha-1}(L-L^n) - \delta_G - \rho\psi b/x. \quad \text{(A.2)}$$

A value $x^{\star}_{ii}$ such that the l.h.s. in (A.2) equals the r.h.s. gives a BGP for scenario (ii).

The function on the l.h.s. of equation (A.1) and of equation (A.2) are identical. The graph of the function on the r.h.s. of (A.1), however, is above the graph of the function on the r.h.s. of (A.2) for all $b > 0$. Therefore, the l.h.s. and the r.h.s. in (A.1) intersect at a larger value of x than the l.h.s. and the r.h.s. in (A.2), giving a higher balanced growth rate for scenario (i). □

Proof of Proposition 4

To prove this proposition, we compute the Jacobian matrix evaluated at the rest point of system (7.25) – (7.27). The Jacobian has the following form,

$$\mathrm{J} = \begin{bmatrix} c\ \partial\dot{c}/\partial b & \partial\dot{c}/\partial c & \partial\dot{c}/\partial y \\ 0\ \partial\dot{b}/\partial b & 0 & 0 \\ x\ \partial\dot{x}/\partial b & \partial\dot{x}/\partial c & \partial\dot{x}/\partial y \\ y\ \partial\dot{y}/\partial b & \partial\dot{y}/\partial c & \partial\dot{y}/\partial y \end{bmatrix},$$

with $c = c^{\star}$, $x = x^{\star}$ and $y = y^{\star}$. One eigenvalue of this matrix is given by $\lambda_1 = \partial\dot{b}/\partial b = -\dot{K}/K = -g < 0$. □

Notes

1 A survey of budgetary regimes studied in the economics literature is given by van Ewijk (1991)

2 This chapter is based on Greiner, A. and P. Flaschel (2010), 'Public debt and public investment in an endogenous growth model with real wage rigidities', *Scottish Journal of Political Economy*, **57**, 68–89.

3 From now on we omit the time argument t if no ambiguity arises.

4 We assume a constant tax rate since a time dependent rate would lead to welfare losses, see Barro (1979).

5 An extensive discussion of the role of the Phillips curve in dynamic macroeconomics can be found, for example, in Flaschel et al. (1997).

6 This is already shown in Bohn (1995) for discrete time and in Greiner (2007) for continuous time. We repeat it here for reasons of readability.

7 The $\star$ denotes BGP values and we exclude the economically meaningless BGP $x^{\star} = c^{\star} = 0$.

[8] We limit our consideration to $b \geq 0$ because there would be no need for the government to stick to the rule defined in (7.14) for $b < 0$, namely if it was a creditor.

[9] We made the simulations also with $\alpha = 0.6$. Qualitatively, the results are identical to those presented here.

[10] For those computations as well as for the depiction of the limit cycle we used the software CL_MATCONT, see Dhooge et al. (2003).

PART IV

The Road to Full-Employment Capitalism

8. Flexicurity: A Baseline Supply Side Model

8.1 Social Reproduction and the Reserve Army Mechanism

This chapter starts from the observation that Goodwin's (1967) classical growth cycle does not represent a process of social reproduction that can be considered as adequate for a social and democratic society in the long-run. The chapter therefore derives from this background a basic macrodynamic framework where this form of cyclical growth and social reproduction is overcome by an employer of 'first' resort, added to an economic reproduction process that is highly competitive and flexible and thus not of the type of the past Eastern socialism. Instead, there is high capital and labor mobility (concerning 'hiring' and 'firing' in particular) where fluctuations of employment in the first labor market of the economy (in the private sector) are made socially acceptable through a second labor market where all remaining workers (and even pensioners) find meaningful occupation. The resulting economic system with its detailed transfer payment schemes is in its essence comparable to the flexicurity model developed for the Nordic welfare states and Denmark in particular. We show that this economy exhibits a balanced growth path that is globally attracting. Moreover, credit financed investment can be easily added without disturbing the prevailing situation of full capacity growth. We thus do not get demand-, but only supply-driven business fluctuations in such an environment with both factors of production always fully employed. This combines flexible factor adjustment in the private sector of the economy with high employment security for the labor force and thus shows that the flexicurity variety of capitalist reproduction can work in a balanced or at least fairly stable manner.

We start from the (in 1995) still weak empirical evidence for the existence of a long-phase cycle in the state variables e and v, the employment rate and the wage share, that we have presented in Flaschel and Groh (1995) for a number of industrialized market economies. We do this on the basis of fifteen years of further observations and now also partly based on quite modern econometric techniques. Our brief findings will be that the Goodwin growth cycle model of Flaschel and Groh (1995) provides indeed a useful approach to the explanation of the distributive cycle as it was observed in the US, the UK and in other countries after World War II. In Kauermann et al. (2007) we have obtained by specifically tailored econometric techniques the graphical representation of the long-phase wage share v/employment rate e cycle (as centers of the business fluctuations around them) for the US economy over the period 1955–2004.

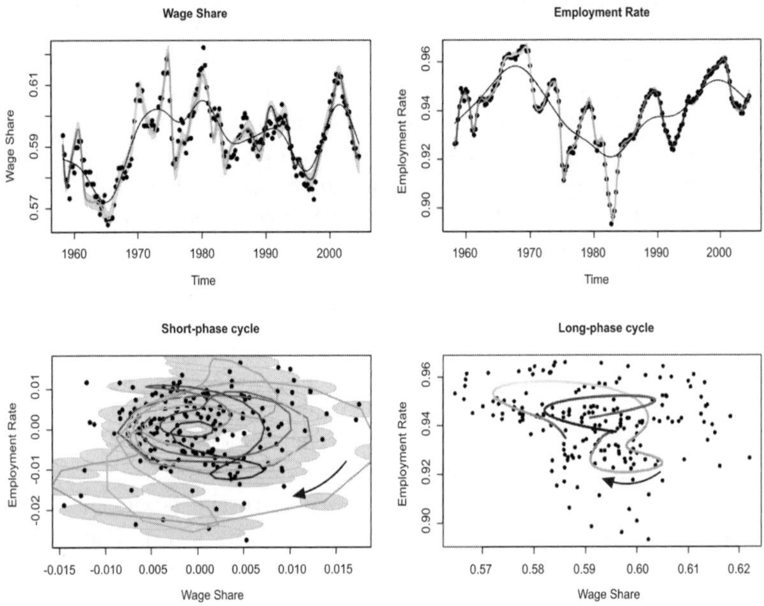

Fig. 8.1: Goodwinian wage share/employment rate dynamics (bottom plots) with estimated long-phase cycle to the right. Top graphs show the data plotted against time

Figure 8.1 shows (bottom right) a single estimated long-phase core cycle (within the scatter plot of v, e observations) for a period length of approximately 50 years and (bottom left) the 6–7 cycles of business cycle frequency (approximately 8 years each) that fluctuate around this long-phase cycle. We ignore the shorter cycles in the following and concentrate on the observation that there is evidence for a long-phase overshooting (non-monotonic) interaction between the share of wages v in national income and the employment rate e, the core of which is shown in Figure 8.1, bottom right. This clockwise oriented long-phase cycle appears to be more complex in situations of a high employment rate and is relatively simply structured in the opposite situations. The reader is referred to Kauermann et al. (2007) for details on the applied econometric technique and the results that can be obtained from it.

In order to briefly present a simple model of such a long-phase accumulation cycle in the variables v and e we make use of the seminal growth cycle model of Goodwin (1967). From this perspective, the envisaged cycle-generating feedback structure can be based on the following two laws of motion:

$$\hat{v} = \dot{v}/v = \beta_{ve}(e - \bar{e}) - \beta_{vv}(v - \bar{v}), \tag{8.1}$$

$$\hat{e} = \dot{e}/e = -\beta_{ev}(v - \bar{v}), \tag{8.2}$$

where v denotes real unit wage costs (or the share of wages in GDP) and e the employment rate and the parameters $\beta_{ve} > 0$, $\beta_{ev} > 0$, $\beta_{vv} \geq 0$ determine the speed of adjustment. The coefficients $\bar{e}$ and $\bar{v}$ denote the normal levels of employment and the wage share, respectively, meaning that employment and the wage share are constant at those values. We justify eq. (8.1) by means of the wage dynamics investigated in Blanchard and Katz (1999), with perfect anticipation of price inflation, however (implying a real wage Phillips curve), where in addition to demand pressure we have unit wage costs acting as an error correction mechanism on their own evolution. In the second law of motion we focus on a goods market behavior that is profit-led, that is increases in unit wage costs act negatively on aggregate demand and thus negatively on the growth rate of the rate of employment e.

If $\beta_{vv} = 0$ holds, as Blanchard and Katz assert it for the US economy, we have the cross-dual dynamics of the Goodwin (1967) growth cycle model and thus a center type dynamics that is stable, but not asymptotically stable. In the case $\beta_{vv} > 0$ we can apply Olech's Theorem, see Flaschel (1984), and obtain from it global asymptotic stability of the dynamics in the positive orthant of the phase plane with respect to the uniquely determined interior steady state position $\bar{e}, \bar{v}$. For weak Blanchard and Katz (1999) error correction terms we thus get a somewhat damped long-phased cyclical motion in the wage share/employment rate phase space as shown in Figure 8.2. We have a clockwise rotation in the considered phase space with approximately one cycle in 50 years.[1]

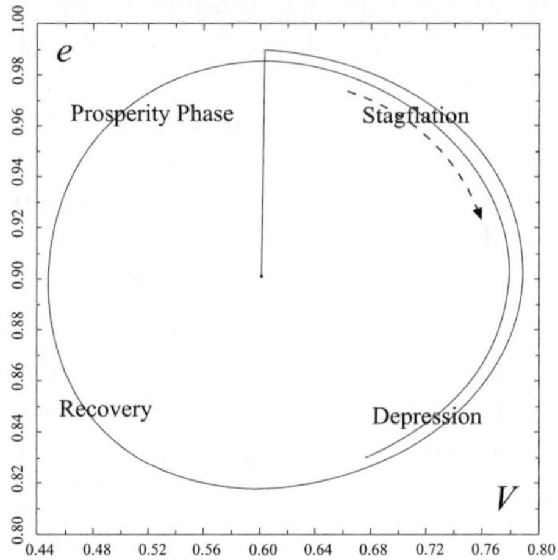

Fig. 8.2: Goodwin-type long-phased wage share/employment dynamics

We can see that the theoretical 2D dynamics mirrors the empirical phase plot to a certain degree. The Goodwin growth cycle mechanism where employment growth depends negatively on income distribution (is profit-led) and where wage share growth depends positively on the state of the labor market thus not only explains the clockwise orientation observed in the data, but also the long-phased nature of the cycle when adjustment speeds are crudely chosen from an empirical perspective. The unique observation of a single long cycle in income distribution and employment that we have available for the US economy after World War II is thus in fairly close correspondence to the Classical growth cycle model and its suggestion of a long-phase accumulation cycle.[2]

Generating order and economic viability in market economies by large swings in the unemployment rate (mass unemployment with human degradation of part of the families that form the society), as shown above, is one way to make capitalism work, but it must surely be critically reflected with respect to its social consequences. Moreover, it must be contrasted with alternative economic systems that allow combining the situation of a highly competitive market economy with a human rights bill that includes the right (and the obligation) to work, and to get income from this work that at the least supports basic needs and basic happiness. The Danish flexicurity system provides a typical example for such an alternative. By contrast, a laissez-faire capitalistic society that ruins family structures to a considerable degree (through alienated work, mass unemployment and unlimited media programs) cannot stay a democratic society in the long-run, since it produces conflicts that can range from social segmentation to class clashes, racial clashes and more.

In the next section, we augment the Goodwin model by a second labor market where the state acts as the employer of 'first' resort[3] and thus guarantees full employment by specific actions. We show that this extension not only removes the reserve army mechanism from the labor market, despite the possibility of a wage–price spiral mechanism in the first labor market, but also makes the economy convergent to its long-run balanced growth path and this the faster the more flexible the labor market is adjusting. Apart from the (important) microeconomic problem of how the second labor market that is added here to the Goodwin growth cycle model can work in an efficient and socially acceptable manner, we thus get the result that the macroeconomic performance is not only improved by this reformulation of the Goodwin model, but indeed turned into a state that can be considered as socially superior to the actual working of capitalist market economies like the USA and the UK.

8.2 Flexicurity: A Baseline Structure

We have considered from the theoretical and the empirical perspective a long-phase growth cycle that in the theoretical model of Flaschel and Groh (1995) was based – as a modification of the simple Goodwin growth cycle approach discussed in the preceding section – on a repelling steady state and behavioral nonlinearities far off the steady state that tame the explosive dynamics and make it viable and that is confirmed in its qualitative features through econometric measurements for the US economy after World War II. This reserve army mechanism, the distributive cycle as well as the accompanying inflation/unemployment cycle, is obviously a fairly archaic way to provide boundedness and order in a advanced capitalist market economy and its democratic institutions. We are therefore now designing as an alternative to the preceding one a growth model that rests in place of overaccumulation (in the prosperity phase) and mass unemployment (in the stagnant phase) on a second labor market which, through its institutional setup, guarantees full employment in its interaction with the first labor market, the employment in the industrial sector of the economy that is modelled as highly flexible and competitive.

We therefore first reconsider the sector of firms in such an economy:

Table 8.1: Firms: production and income account

Uses	Resources
δK	δK
$\omega_1 L_1^d,\ L_1^d = Y^p/z$	$C_1 + C_2 + C_r$
$\omega_2 L_{2f}^w$	G
$\Pi \quad (= Y^f)$	$I \quad (= Y^f)$
$\delta_1 R + \dot{R}$	S_1
Y^p	Y^p

This account is a very simple one. Firms use their capital stock (at full capacity utilization as we shall show later on) to employ the amount of labor (in hours): L_1^d in its operation, at the real wage ω_1, the law of motion of which is to be determined in the next section from a model of the wage–price level interaction in the manufacturing sector. They in addition employ labor force $L_{2f}^w = \alpha_f L_1^d, \alpha_f = const.$ from the second labor market at the wage ω_2, which is a constant fraction α_ω of the market wage in the first labor market. This labor force L_{2f}^w is working the normal hours of a standard workday, while the workforce L_1^w from the first labor market may be working overtime or undertime depending on the size of the capital stock in comparison to its own size. The rate $u_w = L_1^d/L_1^w$ is therefore the utilization rate of the workforce in the first labor market, the industrial workers of the economy (all other employment comes from the working of households occupied in the second labor market). Note, finally, that we allow for capital stock depreciation at the rate δ.

Firms produce full capacity output[4]

$$Y^p = C_1 + C_2 + C_r + I + \delta K + G + S_1$$

that is sold to the two types of consumers (and the retired households), the investing firms and the government. The demand side of the model is formulated here in a way such that indeed this full capacity output can be sold in this way, see the next section on this matter. Deducting from this output Y^p of firms their real wage payments to workers from the first and the second labor market (and depreciation)[5] we get the profits of firms which are here assumed to be invested fully into capital stock growth $\dot{K} = I = \Pi$. We thus have classical (direct) investment habits in this basic approach to a model with an employer of first resort.

There is therefore not yet debt or equity financing of investment in this model type.

We assume a fixed proportions technology with $y^p = Y^p/K$ the potential output–capital ratio and with $z = Y^p/L_1^d$ the given value of labor productivity (which determines the employment L_1^d of the workforce L_1^w of firms).

We next consider the households sector of our social growth model which is composed of worker households working in the first labor market and the remaining ones that are all working in the second labor market.

Table 8.2: Households 1 and 2 (primary and secondary labor market): income account

Households 1:

Uses	Resources
$C_1 = c_{h1}(1-\tau_h)\omega_1 L_1^d$	
$\omega_2 L_{2h}^w = c_{h2}(1-\tau_h)\omega_1 L_1^d$	
$T = \tau_h \omega_1 L_1^d$	
$\omega_2(L - (L_1^w + L_{2f}^w + L_{2h}^w + L_{2g}^w))$	
$\omega_2 L^r, L^r = \alpha_r L$	
S_1	$\omega_1 L_1^d$
$Y_1^w = \omega_1 L_1^d$	$Y_1^w = \omega_1 L_1^d$

Households 2:

Uses	Resources
C_2	$\omega_2 L_2^w, L_2^w = L - L_1^w$
Y_2^w	Y_2^w

Households of type 1 consume manufacturing goods of amount C_1 and services from the second labor market L_{2h}^w. They pay an (all) income tax T and they pay in addition – via further tax transfers – all workers' income in the labor market that is not coming from firms, from them and government (which is equivalent to an unemployment insurance). Moreover, they pay the pensions of the retired households ($\omega_2 L^r$) and accumulate their remaining income S_1 in the form of a company pension into a fund R that is administrated by firms (with inflow S_1, see the sector of households and outflow $\delta_1 R$).

The transfer $\omega_2(L - (L_1^w + L_{2f}^w + L_{2h}^w + L_{2g}^w)$ can be considered as solidarity payments, since workers from the first labor market that lose their job will automatically be employed in the second labor market where full employment is guaranteed by the government (as employer of first resort). We consider this employment as skill preserving, since it can be viewed as ordinary office or handicraft work (subject only to learning by doing when such workers return to the first labor market, that is, employment in the production process of firms).

The second sector of households is here modeled in the simplest way that is available: households employed in the second labor market, that is, $L_2^w = L_{2f}^w + L_{2h}^w + L_{2g}^w$ pay no taxes and totally consume their income. We have thus Classical saving habits in this household sector, while households of type 1 may have positive or negative savings S_1 as residual from their income and expenditures. We here assume that they can accumulate these savings (or dissave in case of a negative S_1) from the stock of commodities they have accumulated as inventories in the past.

In order to have a consistent distribution of the funds R that are accumulated by households of type 1 on the basis of their savings S_1, according to the stock–flow relationship $\dot{R} = S_1$ we have to modify this relationship as follows:

$$\dot{R} = S_1 - \delta_1 R,$$

where δ_1 is the rate by which these funds are depreciated through company pension payments to the 'officially retired' workers L^r assumed to be a constant fraction of the 'active' workforce $L^r = \alpha_r L$. These worker households are added here as not really inactive, but offer work according to their still existing capabilities that can be considered as an addition to the supply of work organized by the government $L - (L_1^w + L_{2f}^w + L_{2h}^w)$, that is the working potential of the officially retired persons remains an active and valuable contribution of the work hours that are supplied by the members of the society. It is obvious that the proper allocation of the work hours under the control of the government needs thorough reflection from the microeconomic and the social point of view, which, however, cannot be a topic in a chapter on the macroeconomics of such an economy.

As the income account of the retired households (see Table 8.3) shows, they receive pension payments as if they worked in the second labor market and they get in addition individual transfer income (company pensions) from the accumulated funds R in proportion to the time they have been active in the first labor market, and as an aggregate household group of the total amount $\delta_1 R$ by which the pension funds R are reduced in each period.

Table 8.3: Retired households: income account

Uses	Resources
C_r	$\omega_2 L^r + \delta_1 R, L^r = \alpha_r L$
Y^r	Y^r

There is finally the government sector which is also formulated in a very basic way:

Table 8.4: The government: income account

Uses	Resources
$G = \alpha_g T$	$T = \tau_h \omega_1 L_1^d$
$\omega_2 L_{g2}^w = (1 - \alpha_g)T$	
$\omega_2(L - (L_1^w + L_{2f}^w + L_{2h}^w + L_{2g}^w))$	$\omega_2 L_r^w$
$\omega_2 L^r$	$\omega_2 \alpha_r L$
Y^g	Y^g

The government receives income taxes, the solidarity payments (employment benefits) for the second labor market paid from workers in the first labor market and old-age pension payments. It uses the taxes to finance government goods demand G and the surplus of taxes over these government expenditures to actively employ the core workers in the government sector. In addition it employs the workers receiving employment benefits from the households in the first labor market and it in fact also employs the 'retired' persons to the extent they can still contribute to the various employment activities. We thus have that the total labor force in the second labor market is employed by firms, by households of type 1 and the remainder through the government as is obvious from the solidarity payments of households working in the first labor market. We thus have that the income payments to workers in the second labor market ($\omega_2 L_2^w$) that are not originating from their services to firms, to households of type 1 or through an excess of income taxes over government commodity expenditures (base government employment) are paid out of transfers from the household sector that works in industrial production to the government, and that on the basis of these payments the remaining work in the second labor market is organized by government (in the way it does this in the administration of the state in all modern market economies).

In sum we get that workers are employed either in the first labor market and if not there then by doing auxiliary work within firms, services for households of type 1 or services in the government sector concerning public administration, infrastructure services, educational services or other public services (in addition there is potential labor supply $\alpha_r L$ from the retired households, which due to the long life expectancy in modern societies can remain effective suppliers of specific work over a considerable span of time). In this way the whole workforce is always fully employed in this model of social growth (and the retired persons according to their capabilities) and thus does not suffer from human degradation in particular. Of course, there are a variety of issues concerning state organized work that point to problems in the organization of such work, but all such problems exist also in actual industrialized market economies in one way or another.

We thus have a classical growth model of the economy where full employment is not assumed, but actively constructed. To motivate the behavioral equations of the social growth model of this chapter we derive them as simplification from an advanced Goodwin–Kalecki growth cycle model where indeed the persistent long-phase cycle in employment and the wage share we derived and observed in Section 8.1 is augmented by Keynesian goods market dynamics and a Kaleckian reserve army mechanism that concerns the whole social structure of accumulation and in particular an explanation of the rise and the (partial) fall of the welfare state after World War II. We will introduce the behavioral equations of our social growth model by contrasting them – as we go along – with what has been assumed in Flaschel, Franke and Semmler (2008) within the Goodwin–Kaleckian growth cycle model of a distributive reserve army mechanism coupled with Kalecki's (1943) political aspects of full employment.

8.3 Goodwin–Kalecki Dynamics: Progress towards Consensus-driven Economies?

In this section we go on from the Goodwinian modeling of the Marxian reserve army mechanism to its extension as a Kaleckian model of the evolution of the welfare state after World War II as it was modeled in Flaschel, Franke and Semmler (2008). We progressed in this framework from the case of dissent economies (where in fact a Goodwinian and a Kaleckian type of reserve army mechanism were interacting) to the case of consensus-driven economies where we could show the existence of a high and attracting balanced growth path for such an economy. The following Table 8.5 shows the range of possibilities that was considered in Flaschel, Franke and Semmler (2008).

Table 8.5: Four types of market economies

	High steady state	Low steady state
Stable steady state	Nordic consensus-driven economy	Kaleckian market economy type I
Unstable steady state	Kaleckian market economy type II	Southern dissent economy

As conditions for the existence of a consensus-driven economy, we assumed Flaschel, Franke and Semmler (2008), see the behavioral equations below, that demand pressure in the labor market (both inside and outside of the firm) does not influence the rate of wage inflation very much, that is the wage level is a fairly stable magnitude. Furthermore, the Kaleckian reserve army mechanism was absent from the model ($i_e = 0$). Moreover, the benchmark values for demand pressures and the employment policy of firms are consistent with each other and all sufficiently high to not imply labor market segmentation and significant disqualification of unemployed workers. This can be coupled with flexible hiring and firing policies then, that is the parameter β_{eu} may be chosen as large as it is desirable.

This modified Kaleckian approach to consensus-driven economies is contrasted in the following with the dynamics and the balanced growth path of the model of flexicurity capitalism we have introduced in the preceding section. We there compare models of the distributive growth cycle (with more or less conflict between capital and labor) with the flexicurity variant of competitive capitalism. However, the important and difficult topic of the generation of socio-economic progress paths that lead from distributive conflict cycles to consensus-driven economies and from there towards the proper functioning of an employer of first resort economy, as the perspective of the flexicurity approach to social growth, must be left for future research here.

We derive the behavioral relationships of our model of flexicurity capitalism by contrasting them with the Kaleckian growth cycle model of Flaschel, Franke and Semmler (2008). We represent the laws of motion of the latter economy first in a framework of Goodwin–Kalecki type, before we show how these equations simplify in our model of social growth with an employer of first resort.

We consider first the wage–price dynamics in the first labor market, which is the only labor market in the Goodwin–Kalecki approach. For the description of these dynamics we start from a general formulation of a wage–price spiral as shown below, see Flaschel, Franke and Semmler (2007) for a detailed treatment of its structure.[6]

$$\hat{w} = \beta_{we}(e - \bar{e}) + \beta_{wu}(u_w - \tilde{u}_w) - \beta_{w\omega} \ln(\frac{\omega}{\omega^o}) + \kappa_w \hat{p} + (1 - \kappa_w)\pi^c,$$

$$\hat{p} = \beta_{py}(y - \bar{y}) + \beta_{p\omega} \ln(\frac{\omega}{\omega^o}) + \kappa_p \hat{w} + (1 - \kappa_p)\pi^c.$$

In these equations, $\hat{w}$, $\hat{p}$ denote the growth rates of nominal wages w and the price level p (their inflation rates) and π^c a medium-term inflation-climate expression which, however, is of no relevance in the following due to our neglect of real interest rate effects on the demand side of the model. We denote by e the rate of employment on the external labor market and by u_w the ratio of utilization of the workforce within firms. This latter ratio of employment is compared by the workforce in their negotiations with firms with their desired normal ratio of utilization $\tilde{u}_w$. We thus have two employment gaps, an external one, $e - \bar{e}$, and an internal one, $u_w - \tilde{u}_w$, which determine wage inflation rate $\hat{w}$ from the side of demand pressure within or outside of the production process. In the wage PC we in addition employ a real wage error correction term $\ln(\omega/\omega_0)$ as in Blanchard and Katz (1999), see Flaschel and Krolzig (2006) for details, and as a cost pressure term a weighted average of short-term (perfectly anticipated) price inflation $\hat{p}$ and the medium-term inflation climate π^c in which the economy is operating.

As the wage PC is constructed it is subject to an interaction between the external labor market and the utilization of the workforce within firms. Higher demand pressure on the external labor market translates itself here into higher workforce wage demand pressure within firms (and demand for a reduced length of the normal working day, etc.), an interaction between two utilization rates of the labor force that has to be and will be taken note of in the formulation of the employment policy of firms. Demand pressure on the labor market thus exhibits two interacting components that employed workers may make their behavior dependent upon.

We use the output–capital ratio $y = Y/K$ to measure the output gap in the price inflation PC and again the deviation of the real wage $\omega = w/p$ from the steady state real wage ω^o as an error correction expression in the price PC. Cost pressure in this price PC is formulated as a weighted average of short-term (perfectly anticipated) wage inflation and again our concept of an inflationary climate π^c. In this price Phillips curve we have three elements of cost pressure interacting with each other, a medium-term one (the inflationary climate) and two short-term ones, basically the level of real unit wage labor costs (a Blanchard and Katz (1999) error correction term) and the current rate of wage inflation, which taken by itself would represent a constant markup pricing rule. This basic rule is however modified by these other cost-pressure terms and in particular also made dependent on the state of the business cycle by way of the demand pressure term $y - \bar{y}$ in the market for goods.

In our social growth model the above wage–price inflation dynamics simplifies to the following form:

$$\hat{w} = \beta_{wu}(u_w - \tilde{u}_w) - \beta_{w\omega}\ln(\frac{\omega}{\omega^o}) + \kappa_w\hat{p} + (1 - \kappa_w)\pi^c \quad (8.3)$$

$$\hat{p} = \beta_{p\omega}\ln(\frac{\omega}{\omega^o}) + \kappa_p\hat{w} + (1 - \kappa_p)\pi^c \quad (8.4)$$

since we will have – by construction – full employment in this model type (and a NAIRU rate that is zero) and in addition a goods demand that is always equal to the potential output that is produced by firms.

On the demand side of the model the Kaleckian framework used for reasons of simplicity the conventional Keynesian dynamic multiplier process (in place of a full-fledged Metzlerian inventory adjustment mechanism) and extremely classical saving habits, together with a Kaleckian type of investment function, that is

$$\hat{Y} = \dot{Y}/Y = \beta_y(Y^d/Y - 1) + \bar{a}, \quad Y^d = \omega L^d + I(\cdot) + \delta K + G,$$

where Y^d, Y denote aggregate demand and supply and $\bar{a}$ a trend term in the behavior of capitalist firms. Assuming a fixed proportions technology with a given output–employment ratio $x = Y/L^d$, and potential output–capital ratio $y^p = Y^p/K$, allows us to determine from the output–capital ratio y the employment u_w of the workforce within firms that corresponds to this activity measure y:

$$u_w = y/(xle), \quad u_w = L^d/L^w, l = L/K, e = L^w/L$$

(with L^d hours worked, L^w the number of workers employed within firms and with L denoting labor supply). This relationship represents by and large a technical relationship (to be calculated by 'engineers') and relates hours worked to goods market activity as measured by y in the way shown above.

In the social growth model we always have the relationship $y^d = y = y^p$ per unit of capital and thus no dynamic on the goods market, and get on this basis then:

$$u_w = L_1^d/L_1^w = \frac{y^p}{zle_1} = \frac{y^p}{zl_1^w}, \qquad (8.5)$$
$$\text{with } l = L/K, l_1^w = L_1^w/K, e_1 = L_1^w/L.$$

This technological relationship must be carefully distinguished from the employment (recruitment) policy of firms that reads on the intensive form level:

$$\hat{e} = \beta_{eu}(u_w - \tilde{u}_f) - \beta_{e\omega}(\omega - \omega^o) + \bar{a} - \hat{L}, \text{ i.e.,}$$
$$\dot{e} = \beta_{eu}(y^p/(xl) - \tilde{u}_f e) - \beta_{e\omega}(\omega - \omega^o)e + (\bar{a} - \hat{L})e.$$

The basis of this formulation of an employment policy of firms in terms of the employment rate is – by assumption – the following level form representation of this relationship:

$$\dot{L}^w = \beta_{eu}(L^d - \tilde{u}_f L^w) - \beta_{e\omega}(\omega - \omega^o)L^w + \bar{a}L^w, \text{ i.e.,}$$
$$\hat{L}^w = \beta_{eu}(L^d/L^w - \tilde{u}_f) - \beta_{e\omega}(\omega - \omega^o) + \bar{a},$$

where $\bar{a}$ again integrates the trend term assumed by firms now into their employment policy and where $\tilde{u}_f$ represents the utilization ratio of the workforce of firms that is desired by them. In order to obtain the equation $\hat{e}$ as the resulting law of motion for the rate of employment one simply has to take note of the definitional relationship $\hat{e} = \hat{L}^w - \hat{L}$, where L denotes the labor supply in each moment in time. We have also included into the above recruitment policy a term that says that intended recruitment will be lowered in case of increasing real wage costs of firms.

In the social growth model the employment policy of firms (on the first labor market) is by and large the same as above. We stress, however, that the external and the internal labor market and the pressure they are exercising on money wage formation form a capillary system in the Goodwin–Kalecki approach and are handled by firms against this background. Such a situation is no longer present in the social growth model, since there is by construction full employment in this model type and since the second labor market here serves as a buffer for the fluctuations that occur in the employment of workers within firms.

Note that the label flexicurity assumes in this regard that firms are completely free in their choice of the hiring and firing parameter β_{eu}.

Now, we have

$$\hat{e}_1 = \beta_{eu}(u_w - \tilde{u}_w) + \rho^o - \hat{L}, \text{ i.e.,} \tag{8.6}$$

$$\dot{e}_1 = \beta_{eu}(y^p/(xl) - \tilde{u}_w e_1) + (\rho^o - \hat{L})e_1, \text{or simpler,} \tag{8.7}$$

$$\hat{l}_1^w = \beta_{eu}(y^p/(zl_1^w) - \tilde{u}_w) + (\rho^o - \rho) \tag{8.8}$$

since investment is equal to profits in this basic version of the social growth model. Note that we now use a common measure $\tilde{u}_w$ in the money wage PC and the recruitment policy of firms and that we assume now ρ^o to be the trend rate of growth of the economy which is used by firms in their trend labor recruitment policy (in place of the $\bar{a}$ used in the Goodwin–Kalecki model).

In the Keynesian Goodwin–Kalecki framework we assumed extremely classical saving habits ($s_w = 0, s_c = 1$) and for the investment behavior of firms:

$$I/K = i_\rho(\rho - \rho_o) - i_e(e - \bar{e}_f) + \bar{a},$$

with $\rho = y(1 - \omega/x)$ the current rate of profit. In this equation, the magnitude $\bar{a}$ denotes again the given trend investment rate (representing investor's 'animal spirits') from which firms depart in a natural way if there is excess profitability (and vice versa). Moreover, firms have a view of what the employment rate should be on the external labor market (Kalecki's (1943, ch.12) analysis of why 'bosses' dislike full employment) and thus reduce their (domestic) investment plans (driven by excess profitability) in situations of a tense labor market. They thus take pressure from the labor market in the future evolution of the economy by their implicit collective understanding that high pressure in the capillary system of internal and external labor markets we have considered above will lead to conditions in the capital–labor relationship, unwanted by firms, since persistently high employment rates may give rise to significant changes of workforce participation with respect to firms' decision making, in the hiring and firing decision of firms, in reductions in the worky day etc., not at all liked by 'industrial leaders' in the case of a Kaleckian dissent economy.

In the social growth model, the alternative and extension of this chapter to/of a Kaleckian consensus-driven economy, we have already assumed that workers of type 2 consume their whole income (they pay no taxes). With respect to the other type of workers we assume as their consumption function

$$C_1 = c_{h1}(1 - \tau_h)\omega_1 L_1^d, \tag{8.9}$$

c_h propensity to consume, τ_h tax rate

$$\omega_2 L_{2h}^w = c_{h2}(1 - \tau_h)\omega_1 L_1^d \tag{8.10}$$

consumption of household services.

Households' type 1 savings is on the basis of our accounting relationships given by

$$\begin{aligned} S_1 =& \omega_1 L_1^d - C_1 - \omega_2 L_{2h}^w - \\ & \omega_2 (L - (L_1^w + L_{2f}^w + L_{2h}^w + L_{2g}^w) - \omega_2 L^r) \end{aligned} \tag{8.11}$$

due to the assumed solidarity contribution they provide to the second labor market. Investment behavior is very simple in the basic form of the social growth model: all profits of firms are invested and there is no debt or equity financing yet. The growth rate of the capital stock is thus simply given by $\hat{K} = \rho = \Pi/K(\rho^o$ the steady state rate of profit). On the basis of what we have already assumed we thus get:

$$\begin{aligned} \hat{K} = \rho = y^p[1 - \omega_1(1 + \alpha_\omega \alpha_f)/z] - \delta, \\ \omega_2 = \alpha_\omega \omega_1, L_{2f}^w = \alpha_f L_1^d. \end{aligned} \tag{8.12}$$

See below with respect to the parameter α_f which characterizes the employment policy of firms with respect to the second labor market.

For government consumption we finally assume the simple relationship $G = \gamma I$, that is, government consumption per unit of capital grows at the same rate as the capital stock (which allows integrating fiscal policy with investment behavior in the intensive form of the model).

Since the government, workers from the second labor market and pensioners do not save; since all tax transfers are turned into consumption and the savings of households of type 1 into commodity inventories of firms from which company pensions are to be deducted; and since finally all profits are invested, it can easily be shown from what was presented in accounting form in the preceding section that we must have at all times:

$$Y^p = C_1 + C_2 + C_r + I + \delta K + G + S_1, \tag{8.13}$$

$$C_1 = c_{h1}(1 - \tau_h)\omega_1 L_1^d \tag{8.14}$$

if firms produce at full capacity $Y^p = y^p K, L_1^d = Y^p/z$ (which they can and will do in this case). There is thus no demand problem on the market for goods and thus no need to discuss a dynamic multiplier process as in the Goodwin–Kalecki model with which this model was compared here. Note that, moreover, we have by construction of the social growth model at all points in time:

$$L = L_1^w + L_{2f}^w + L_{2h}^w + L_{2g}^w + L_r^w = L_1^w + L_2^w \tag{8.15}$$
$$L_r = \alpha_r L.$$

We thus assume that households of type 1 must pay as solidarity contribution (employment benefits) those workers of type 2, whose wages are not paid by firms, through households type 2 service to households of type 1 and through the core employment in the government sector. The government employs in addition as administrative workers and infrastructure workers (public work and education) the remaining workforce in the second labor market (plus the L^r services from pensioners). This completes the discussion of the behavioral equations of the social growth model, the intensive form of which will now be derived in the following section. Compared to the Goodwin–Kalecki model of Flaschel, Franke and Semmler (2008) this model type will be shown to function very easily without the need of a discussion of conflict-driven upper and lower turning points in economic activity and income distribution which are necessary to keep the locally centrifugal dynamics of the Goodwin–Kalecki approach bounded and thus viable. There are only mildly conflicting income claims in the social growth model and also only mild conflicts about the role and the extent of the welfare state in such a framework (to be discussed below).

In the Goodwin–Kalecki growth cycle model we have (in the dissent situation) conflict-riddled turning points in economic and social activities than can end prosperity phases in a radical fashion and then lead the society into long-lasting depressions; processes that are harmful and wasteful with respect to human and physical capital and that may not work towards a recovery under all circumstances. The need for an alternative to such a situation is therefore a compelling one from the perspective of a social and democratic society and the potential it may contain for the evolution of mankind. We have already introduced in the previous and this section the economic contours of such an alternative. This alternative model of social reproduction will be analyzed in its macrodynamic features in the next two sections.

8.4 Balance Reproduction: Existence and Stability

The Dynamics and their Balanced Growth Path

Inserting the equations of the social growth model appropriately into each other gives rise to the following 3D dynamics in the state variables $\omega_1 = w/p, l_1^w = L_1^w/K$ and $l = L/K$ where the last variable does not, however, feed back into the first two laws of motion due to the construction of the labor markets of the model.[7]

$$\begin{aligned}\hat{\omega}_1 =&\kappa\left[(1-\kappa_p)\left(\beta_{wu}\left(\frac{y^p}{zl_1^w}-\tilde{u}_w\right)-\right.\right.\\ &\left.\left.\beta_{w\omega}\ln\left(\frac{\omega_1}{\omega_1^o}\right)\right)-(1-\kappa_w)\beta_{p\omega}\ln\left(\frac{\omega_1}{\omega_1^o}\right)\right],\end{aligned} \tag{8.16}$$

$$\begin{aligned}\hat{l}_1^w =&\beta_{eu}\left(\frac{y^p}{zl_1^w}-\tilde{u}_w\right)+n-\rho,\\ &\text{with } \rho = y^p[1-\omega_1(1+\alpha_\omega\alpha_f)/z]-\delta,\end{aligned} \tag{8.17}$$

$$\begin{aligned}\hat{l} =&n-(y^p[1-(1+\alpha_\omega\alpha_f)\omega_1/z]-\delta).\\ =&y^p[(1+\alpha_\omega\alpha_f)(\omega_1-\omega_1^o)/z]\end{aligned} \tag{8.18}$$

However, in order to get a stationary value of l in the long-run we must assume a special value for ω_1^o in the first two equations (as the steady state reference real wage in the first labor market), which is determined by:

$$\hat{l}=0, \quad \text{i.e.,} \quad y^p[1-(1+\alpha_\omega\alpha_f)\omega_1/z]=\delta+n. \tag{8.19}$$

The reference wage used in the first two laws of motion must therefore be chosen such that the capital stock grows with the natural rate n in the steady state, which is one of the conditions needed for steady growth in the Harrod (1939) growth model. Since our model is based on Say's law the other conditions of the Harrod model do not apply here.

Based on this assumption we get for the interior steady state or balanced growth path of the social growth economy the equations ($\tilde{u}_w = 1$ in the following for reasons of simplicity):

$$l_1^{wo} = \frac{y^p}{\tilde{u}_w z} = \frac{l_1^{do}}{\tilde{u}_w} = y^p/z, \tag{8.20}$$

$$\omega_1^o = \frac{1 - \frac{n+\delta}{y^p}}{1 + \alpha_f \alpha_\omega} z < z, \tag{8.21}$$

$$l^o = \text{arbitrary}. \tag{8.22}$$

Since we have a zero determinant for the 3D Jacobian of the above dynamics (since the third law of motion only depends on the first state variable) we have zero root hysteresis in the 3D system which in the given form allows us to treat and solve the first two equations independently of the third one, which when appended can converge to any value of l, depending on shocks to labor supply, capital formation and the like. Note, however, that this only applies if there is social consensus with respect to the steady state real wage ω_1^o as the benchmark for real wage negotiations in the first labor market. Choosing in addition (and for example) as parameter values[8] $\alpha_w = 0.5, n = 0.05, \delta = 0.1, y^p = 0.5$ gives for the ratio $v_1 = \omega_1/z$, the wage share in the first labor market, the approximate value $v_1 = 0.64$, and for the profit share Π^o/Y^p the value 0.1, which in sum implies for the shares of wages and government expenditures the value 90 percent. Note finally that the living standards in this society, as measured by real wages, depend of course on the value of the labor productivity of workers in the first labor market.

Monotonic Convergence towards Balanced Growth

For the Jacobian of the 3D dynamics evaluated at the steady state we get from the laws of motion:

$$J^o = \begin{pmatrix} -\kappa[(1-\kappa_p)\beta_{w\omega} + (1-\kappa_w)\beta_{p\omega}] & -\kappa(1-\kappa_p)\beta_{wu}\frac{y^p}{z}\frac{\omega_1^o}{(l_1^{wo})^2} & 0 \\ \frac{y^p(1+\alpha_\omega\alpha_f)}{z} l_1^{wo} & -\beta_{eu}\frac{y^p}{z l_1^{wo}} & 0 \\ \frac{y^p(1+\alpha_\omega\alpha_f)}{z} l & 0 & 0 \end{pmatrix}.$$

Since we only have to investigate the first two laws of motion, it suffices to consider the following matrix with respect to its eigenvalues:

$$J^o = \begin{pmatrix} J^o_{11} & J^o_{12} \\ J^o_{21} & J^o_{22} \end{pmatrix}$$

$$= \begin{pmatrix} -\kappa[(1-\kappa_p)\beta_{w\omega} + (1-\kappa_w)\beta_{p\omega}] & -\kappa(1-\kappa_p)\beta_{wu}\frac{y^p}{z}(l_1^{wo})^{-2}\omega_1^o \\ \frac{y^p(1+\alpha_\omega\alpha_f)}{z}l_1^{wo} & -\beta_{eu}\frac{y^p}{zl_1^{wo}} \end{pmatrix}$$

$$= \begin{pmatrix} - & - \\ + & - \end{pmatrix}.$$

From the sign structure in this matrix it is obvious that we always have locally asymptotically stable dynamics (that is, trace $J^o < 0, \det J^o > 0$). Furthermore, the condition trace $J^o = 4 \det J^o$, that is,

$$(J^o_{11} + J^o_{22})^2 = 4(J^o_{11}J^o_{22} + J^o_{21}J^o_{12})$$

separates monotonic convergence (for parameters β_{eu} sufficiently large) from cyclical convergence (parameters β_{eu} sufficiently small). Reformulated, this condition reads:

$$|J^o_{22}| = |J^o_{11}| + 2\sqrt{|J^o_{21}J^o_{12}|}, \quad \text{i.e.,} \quad \beta^H_{eu} = \frac{zl_1^{wo}}{y^p}[|J^o_{11}| + 2\sqrt{|J^o_{21}J^o_{12}|}].$$

We thus get for the bifurcation value β^H_{eu} that separates monotonic from cyclical convergence:

$$\begin{aligned} \beta^H_{eu} =& \kappa[(1-\kappa_p)\beta_{w\omega} + (1-\kappa_w)\beta_{p\omega}] + \\ & 2\sqrt{(1+\alpha_\omega\alpha_f)\kappa(1-\kappa_p)\beta_{wu}\omega_1^o l_1^{wo}}. \end{aligned} \tag{8.23}$$

This critical parameter for the hiring and firing speed parameter in our social growth economy is therefore in particular larger the larger the reaction of money wage inflation with respect to workforce utilization, that is the larger the parameter β_{wu} becomes. We thus get that economic fluctuations can be avoided in this type of economy if wages in the first labor market respond relatively sluggishly to demand pressure in this market (as measured by the utilization rate of the insiders) and if hiring and firing is a sufficiently flexible process as envisaged by the concept of flexicurity capitalism.

Global Viability

For the investigation of global asymptotic stability we will now analyze the core dynamical system by means of so-called Liapunov functions.

For this purpose we represent the 2D dynamics of the preceding section as follows.

$$\hat{\omega}_1 = G^1(\omega_1) + G^2(l_1^w), \quad G^{1'} < 0, G^{2'} < 0, \tag{8.24}$$

$$\hat{l}_1^w = H^1(\omega_1) + H^2(l_1^w), \quad H^{1'} > 0, H^{2'} < 0. \tag{8.25}$$

The Liapunov function to be used in the stability proof then reads as follows:

$$V(\omega_1, l_1^w) = \int_{\omega_1^o}^{\omega_1} H^1(\tilde{\omega}_1)/\tilde{\omega}_1 d\tilde{\omega}_1 + \int_{l_1^{wo}}^{l_1^w} -G^2(\tilde{l}_1^w)/\tilde{l}_1^w d\tilde{l}_1^w.$$

This function describes by its graph a 3D sink with the steady state of the economy as its lowest point, since the above integrates two functions that are negative to the left of the steady state values and positive to their right. For the first derivative of the Liapunov function along the trajectories of the considered dynamical system we moreover get:

$$\begin{aligned}
\dot{V} =& dV(\omega_1(t), l_1^w(t))/dt = \left(H^1(\omega_1)/\omega_1\right)\dot{\omega}_1 - \left(G^2(l_1^w)/l_1^w\right)\dot{l}_1^w \\
=& H^1(\omega_1)\hat{\omega}_1 - G^2(l_1^w)\hat{l}_1^w \\
=& H^1(\omega_1)(G^1(\omega_1) + G^2(l_1^w)) - G^2(l_1^w)(H^1(\omega_1) + H^2(l_1^w)) \\
=& H^1(\omega_1)G^1(\omega_1) - G^2(l_1^w)H^2(l_1^w) \\
=& - H^1(\omega_1)(-G^1(\omega_1)) - (-G^2(l_1^w))(-H^2(l_1^w)) \\
\leq& 0 \qquad [= 0 \quad \text{if and only if} \quad \omega_1 = \omega_1^o, l_1^w = l_1^{wo}],
\end{aligned}$$

since the multiplied functions have the same sign to the right and to the left of their steady state values and thus lead to positive products with a minus sign in front of them (up to the situation where the economy is already sitting in the steady state). We thus have proved that there holds:

Theorem 1 *The interior steady state of the dynamics*

$$\begin{aligned}
\hat{\omega}_1 =& \kappa\left[(1-\kappa_p)\left(\beta_{wu}\left(\frac{y^p}{zl_1^w} - \tilde{u}_w\right) - \beta_{w\omega}\ln\left(\frac{\omega_1}{\omega_1^o}\right)\right) - \right. \\
& \left.(1-\kappa_w)\beta_{p\omega}\ln\left(\frac{\omega_1}{\omega_1^o}\right)\right],
\end{aligned} \tag{8.26}$$

$$\hat{l}_1^w = \beta_{eu}\left(\frac{y^p}{zl_1^w} - \tilde{u}_w\right) + \rho^o + (y^p[(\omega_1 - \omega_1^o)(1 + \alpha_\omega\alpha_f)/z] - \delta), \tag{8.27}$$

is a global sink of the function V, defined on the positive orthant of the phase space, and is attracting in this domain, since the function V is strictly decreasing along the trajectories of the dynamics in the positive orthant of the phase space.

From the global perspective there may, however, be supply bottlenecks in the second labor market. Here we assume that the economy is working always in a corridor around the steady state where the government as the employer of first resort has still a sufficient amount of workforce working in the range of activities that is organized by it. Due to the stability results obtained in the present and the preceding section this is not a very restrictive assumption under the normal working of the economy.

8.5 Company Pension Funds

There is a further law of motion in the background of the model that needs to be considered in order to provide an additional statement on the viability of the considered model of flexicurity capitalism. This law of motion describes the evolution of the pension fund per unit of the capital stock $\eta = \frac{R}{K}$ and is obtained from the defining equation $\dot{R} = S_1 - \delta_1 R$ as follows:

$$\hat{\eta} = \hat{R} - \hat{K} = \frac{\dot{R}}{K}\frac{K}{R} - \rho = \frac{S_1 - \delta_1 R}{K}/\eta - \rho, \quad \text{i.e.:}$$
$$\dot{\eta} = \frac{S_1}{K} - (\delta_1 + \rho)\eta = s_1 - (\delta_1 + \rho)\eta$$

with savings of households of type I and profits of firms per unit of capital being given by:

$$\begin{aligned} s_1 =& (1 - (c_{h1} + c_{h2})(1 - \tau_h) - \tau_h)\omega_1 y^p/z - \alpha_\omega \omega_1 (l_x^w + l^r), \\ l_x^w =& l - (l_1^w + l_{2f}^w + l_{2h}^w + l_{2g}^w), \\ l^r =& \alpha_r l, \end{aligned}$$

that is, due to the financing of the employment terms $l_{2h}^w + l_{2g}^w$:

$$\begin{aligned} s_1 =& (1 - c_{h1}(1 - \tau_h) - \alpha_g \tau_h)\omega_1 y^p/z - ((1 + \alpha_r)l - (l_1^w + l_{2f}^w))\alpha_\omega \omega_1, \\ l_{2f}^w =& \alpha_f y^p/z, \\ \rho =& y^p[1 - (1 + \alpha_\omega \alpha_f)\omega_1/z] - \delta. \end{aligned}$$

For reasons of analytical simplicity we now assume that the government pursues an immigration policy that ensures for the total growth rate of the labor force the condition $n = \hat{K}$, that is, the total labor supply grows by this migration policy with the same rate as the capital stock. This keeps the ratio $l = L/K$ constant, a simplifying assumption that must be accompanied by the assumption that the actual $\bar{l}$ must be chosen in a certain neighborhood of a base value $\bar{l}_o$ that is to be determined later on. Since we are now no longer able to determine the steady state value of the real wage ω_1 from the law of motion for l, we have to supply it from the outside now: $\omega_1^o = \bar{\omega}_1 =$ given. This also provides us with the steady state value of the rate of profit $\rho^o = \bar{\rho} = y^p[1 - (1 + \alpha_\omega \alpha_f)\bar{\omega}_1/z] - \delta$ which also determines the steady value of natural growth $n_o = \bar{\rho}$. Moreover we also assume for simplicity $\delta_1 = \delta$ for the depreciation rates of the capital stock and the stock of pension funds.

This gives for the law of motion of the pension fund to capital ratio the differential equation:

$$\begin{aligned}\dot{\eta} =& (1 - c_{h1}(1 - \tau_h) - \alpha_g \tau_h)\omega_1 \frac{y^p}{z} - \left((1 + \alpha_r)\bar{l} - \left(l_1^w + \alpha_f \frac{y^p}{z}\right)\right) \alpha_\omega \omega_1 \\ & - \left(y^p - (1 + \alpha_\omega \alpha_f)\omega_1 \frac{y^p}{z}\right) \eta.\end{aligned}$$

We thus get that the trajectory of the pension fund ratio η is driven by the autonomous evolution of the state variables ω_1, l_1^w that characterize the dynamics of the private sector of the economy and that has been shown to be convergent to the steady state values $\bar{\omega}_1, l_1^{wo} = y^p/z$ as usual. Assuming that these variables have reached their steady state positions then gives

$$\begin{aligned}\dot{\eta} =& (1 - c_{h1}(1 - \tau_h) - \alpha_g \tau_h)\bar{\omega}_1 \frac{y^p}{z} - \\ & \left((1 + \alpha_r)\bar{l} - \left(l_1^{wo} + \alpha_f \frac{y^p}{z}\right)\right) \alpha_\omega \bar{\omega}_1 - (\delta + \bar{\rho})\eta,\end{aligned}$$

which gives a single linear differential equation for the ratio η. This dynamic is globally asymptotically stable around its steady state position ($l_1^{wo} = y^p/z$):

$$\eta_o = \frac{(1 - c_{h1}(1 - \tau_h) - \alpha_g \tau_h)\bar{\omega}_1 \frac{y^p}{z} - \left((1 + \alpha_r)\bar{l} - (1 + \alpha_f)\frac{y^p}{z}\right) \alpha_\omega \bar{\omega}_1}{\delta + \bar{\rho}}.$$

In this simple case we thus have monotonic adjustment of the pension-fund capital ratio to its steady state position, while in general we have a non-autonomous adjustment of this ratio that is driven by the real wage and employment dynamics of the first labor market. The steady state level of η is positive iff there holds for the full employment labor intensity ratio:

$$\bar{l} < \frac{(1 - c_{h1}(1 - \tau_h) - \alpha_g \tau_h)\bar{\omega}_1 y^p/z + ((1 + \alpha_f)y^p/z)\alpha_\omega \bar{\omega}_1}{(\delta + \bar{\rho})(1 + \alpha_r)\alpha_\omega \bar{\omega}_1}.$$

We now assume, moreover, that the additional company pension payments to pensioners should add the percentage $100 \cdot \alpha_c$ to their base pension $\omega_2 \alpha_r \bar{l}$ per unit of capital. We thus have as further restriction on the steady state position of the economy, if there is an α_c target given:

$$\delta \eta_o = \alpha_c \omega_2^o \alpha_r \bar{l}, \quad \omega_2^o = \alpha_\omega \bar{\omega}_1$$

Inserting the value for η_o then gives

$$\alpha_c = \frac{\delta}{(\delta + \bar{\rho})\omega_2^o \alpha_r \bar{l}} \cdot \Big((1 - c_{h1}(1 - \tau_h) - \alpha_g \tau_h)\bar{\omega}_1 y^p/z - ((1 + \alpha_r)\bar{l} - (1 + \alpha_f)y^p/z)\alpha_\omega \bar{\omega}_1\Big).$$

We thus get that a target value for α_c demands a certain labor intensity ratio $\bar{l}$ and vice versa. For a given total labor intensity ratio there is a given percentage by which company pensions compare to base pension payments. This percentage is the larger the smaller the ratio $l_1^{wo}/\bar{l}$ due to the following reformulation of the α_c formula:

$$\alpha_c = \frac{\delta}{(\delta + \bar{\rho})\alpha_r \alpha_\omega \bar{\omega}_1} \cdot \Big([(1 - c_{h1}(1 - \tau_h) - \alpha_g \tau_h)\bar{\omega}_1 + (1 + \alpha_f)\alpha_\omega \bar{\omega}_1] l_1^{wo}/\bar{l} - (1 + \alpha_r)\alpha_\omega \bar{\omega}_1\Big). \tag{8.28}$$

If this value of the total employment labor intensity ratio prevails in the considered economy (where it is of course as usual assumed that $c_{h1}(1 - \tau_h) + \alpha_g \tau_h < 1$ holds) we have that core pension payments to pensioners are augmented by company pension payments by a percentage that is given by the parameter α_c and that these extra pension payments are distributed to pensioners in proportion to their contribution to the time that they have worked in the private sector of the economy. There is thus a negative trade-off between the ratios $\bar{l}, \alpha_c$, as expressed by the relationship (8.28). This also shows that the total working population must have a certain ratio to the capital stock in order to allow for a given percentage of extra company pension payments. Due to $\delta\eta_o = \alpha_c\omega_2^o\alpha_r\bar{l}$ and $s_1^o = (\delta + \bar{\rho})\eta_o$ we also have the equivalence between positive savings per unit of capital of households of type I and positive values for α_c, η_o. Moreover, these values are in fact positive if there holds:[9]

$$\bar{l} < \frac{(1 - c_{h1}(1 - \tau_h) - \alpha_g\tau_h)\bar{\omega}_1 y^p/z + (1 + \alpha_f)y^p/z)\alpha_\omega\bar{\omega}_1}{(\delta + \bar{\rho})(1 + \alpha_r)\alpha_\omega\bar{\omega}_1}.$$

This inequality set limits to the total labor-supply capital–stock ratio $\bar{l}$ which allows for positive savings of households of type I in the steady state and thus for extra pension payments to them later on. Households of type I are by and large financing the second labor market through taxes and employment benefits (besides their contribution to the base income of the retired people). Since firms have a positive rate of profit in the steady state, since the government budget is always balanced and since only households of type I save in this economy, we have thus now established the condition under which such an economy accumulates not only capital, but also pension funds – under appropriate restrictions on labor supply – to a sufficient degree. We get from the above expressions that the extra pension payment ratio α_c will increase if y^p, α_f is increasing and it will decrease (among others) if the levels of $z, \bar{\omega}_1, \bar{l}, c_{h1}$ are increasing.

8.6 Pension Funds and Credit

In this section we will investigate the implications of the situation where pension funds are used for real capital formation instead of remaining idle except for being used for company pension payments (of amount δR at each point in time). The productive use of part of the pension fund R is here assumed to be rewarded at the constant interest rate r applied to the debt level D accumulated by the firms in the private sector of the economy.

Accounting Relationships

Pension funds act as quasi commercial banks who give credit to firms out of their funds and thus allow firms to invest in good times much beyond their retained earnings, that is profits net of interest payments on loans.

Table 8.6: Firms: production and income account

Uses	Resources
δK	δK
$\omega_1 L_1^d = \omega_1 Y^p/z$	$C_1 + C_2 + C_r$
$\omega_2 L_{2f}^w = \alpha_\omega \omega_1 \alpha_f Y^p/z$	G
rD	
Π	$I = (i_\rho(\rho - \rho_o) - i_d(d - d_o) + \bar{a})K$
$\delta_1 R + \dot{R}$	S_1
Y^p	Y^p

The behavior and financing of gross investment is shown in Table 8.7.

Table 8.7: Firms: investment and credit

Uses	Resources
δK	δK
$I = (i_\rho(\rho - \rho_o) - i_d(d - d_o) + \bar{a})K$	Π
	$\dot{D} = I - \Pi$
I^g	I^g

We assume as the investment behavior of firms the functional relationship:

$$I/K = i_\rho(\rho - \rho_o) - i_d(d - d_o) + \bar{a}.$$

This investment schedule states that investment plans depend positively on the deviation of the profit rate from its steady state level and negatively on the deviation of the debt to capital ratio from its steady state value. The exogenous trend term in investment is $\bar{a}$ and it is again assumed that it represents the influence of investing firms' 'animal spirits' on their investment activities.

Table 8.8: Firms' net worth

Assets	Liabilities
K	D
	Real Net Worth
K	K

In the management of pension funds we assume that a portion sR of them is held as minimum reserves and that a larger portion of them has been given as credit D to firms. The remaining amount is idle reserves D^s, not yet allocated to any interest-bearing activity.

Table 8.9: Pension funds and credit (stocks)

Assets	Liabilities
R	sR
	D
	X excess reserves
R	R

Pension funds receive the savings of households of type 1 (the other households do not save) and they receive the interest payments of firms. They allocate this into required reserve increases, payments to pensioners, new credit demand of firms and the rest as an addition or substraction to their idle reserves.

Table 8.10: Pension funds and credit (flows)

Resources	Uses
S_1	$s\dot{R}$
rD	$\delta R + rD$
	$\dot{D} = I - \Pi$
	$\dot{X}$
$S_1 + rD$	$S_1 + rD$

The above representation of the flows of funds in the pension funds system implies for the time derivative of accumulated funds R the relationship

$$\dot{R} = S_1 - \delta R - (I - \Pi) = S_1 + \Pi - \delta R - I,$$

that is, it is given by the excess of savings of households of type 1 over current company pension funds payments to retired households and the new credit that is given to firms to finance the excess of investment over retained profits.

Households in the first labor market consume with a constant marginal propensity out of the income after primary taxes and they employ households' services in constant proportions to the consumption habits. They pay the wages of the workers in the second labor market

Table 8.11: Households 1 (primary and secondary labor market): income account

Uses	Resources
$C_1 = c_{h1}(1-\tau_h)Y_1^w$	
$\omega_2 L_{2h}^w = c_{h2}(1-\tau_h)Y_1^w$	
$T = \tau_h Y_1^w$	
$\omega_2(L - (L_1^w + L_{2f}^w + L_{2h}^w + L_{2g}^w))$	
$\omega_2 L^r$	
S_1	$\omega_1 L_1^d$
Y_1^w	Y_1^w

that are not employed by firms, by them and the government as a quasi unemployment benefit insurance (a generational solidarity contribution) and they pay the common base rent of all pensioners (as intergenerational contribution). The remainder represents their contribution to the pension scheme of the economy, from which they will receive $\delta R + rD$ when retired. We consider this as a possible scheme of funding the excess employment and the pensioners, not necessarily the only one, however.

Table 8.12: Households 2 (primary and secondary labor market): income account

Uses	Resources
C_2	$\omega_2 L_2^w$
Y_2^w	Y_2^w

Table 8.13: Retired households: income account

Uses	Resources
C_r	$\omega_2 L^r + \delta R + rD$
Y^r	Y^r

Government gets primary taxes and spends them on goods as well as services in the government sector (which are here determined residually). It administrates the common base rent payments as well as the payments of those not yet employed in the sectors of the economy. Its workforce consists of all workers that are not employed by firms of households of type 1 and also of all pensioners that are still capable

Table 8.14: The government: income account – fiscal authority (employer of first resort)

Uses	Resources
$G = \alpha_g \tau_h Y_1^w$	$T = \tau_h Y_1^w$
$\omega_2 L_{2g}^w = (1-\alpha_g)\tau_h Y_1^w$	
$\omega_2 L_x^w$	$\omega_2(L - (L_1^w + L_{2f}^w + L_{2h}^w + L_{2g}^w))$
$\omega_2 L^r$	$\omega_2 L^r$
Y^g	Y^g

of working. The model therefore assumes not only that there is a work guarantee for all, but also a work obligation for all members in the workforce, with the addition of those that are retired but still able and willing to work.

Investment and Credit Dynamics

For simplicity we assume again that the government pursues an immigration policy that ensures for the growth rate of the labor force the condition $n = \hat{K}$, that is, the total labor supply grows by this migration policy with the same rate as the capital stock. This again keeps the ratio $l = L/K = \bar{l} =$ constant. Since we are again no longer able to determine the steady state value of the real wage ω_1 from the law of motion for l, we have to supply it again from the outside: $\omega_1^o = \bar{\omega}_1 =$ given. This, however, no longer also provides us with the steady state value of the rate of profit, since profits are now to be determined net of interest payments: $\rho = y^p[1-(1+\alpha_\omega\alpha_f)\bar{\omega}_1/z] - \delta - rd$, where $d = D/K$ denotes the indebtedness of firms per unit of capital. We assume again as a trend term in Okun's law the growth rate of the capital stock (that is this part of the new hiring is just determined by the installation of new machines or whole plants, under the assumption of fixed proportions in production. The normal level of the rate of employment of the workforce employed by firms is again set equal to '1' for simplicity.

On the basis of these assumptions we get from what was formulated in the preceding subsection (where investment was assumed to be given now by $I/K = i_\rho(\rho-\rho_o) - i_d(d-d_o) + \bar{a}$):

$$\hat{l}_1^w = \beta_{eu}\left(\frac{y^p}{zl_1^w} - 1\right)$$

$$\hat{\omega}_1 = \kappa\left[(1-\kappa_p)\left(\beta_{wu}\left(\frac{y^p}{zl_1^w}-1\right) - \beta_{w\omega}\ln\left(\frac{\omega_1}{\bar{\omega}_1}\right)\right)\right.$$
$$\left. -(1-\kappa_w)\beta_{p\omega}\ln\left(\frac{\omega_1}{\bar{\omega}_1}\right)\right]$$

$$\dot{d} = [i_\rho(\rho-\rho_o) - i_d(d-d_o) + \bar{a}](1-d) - \rho$$

$$\begin{aligned}\hat{\eta} =& s_1 + \rho - (\delta\eta + (1+\eta)[i_\rho(\rho-\rho_o) - i_d(d-d_o) + \bar{a}])\\ =&(1 - c_{h1}(1-\tau_h) - \alpha_g\tau_h)\omega_1 y^p/z - ((1+\alpha_r)\bar{l} -\\ &(l_1^w + \alpha_f y^p/z))\alpha_\omega\omega_1 + [y^p[1-(1+\alpha_\omega\alpha_f)\bar{\omega}_1/z] - \delta - rd] -\\ &(\delta\eta + (1+\eta)[i_\rho(\rho-\rho_o) - i_d(d-d_o) + \bar{a}]).\end{aligned}$$

The introduction of debt financing of firms thus makes the model considerably more advanced in its economic structure, but not so much from the mathematical point of view, due to the recursive structure that characterizes the dynamical system at this level of generality. We note that there is not yet an interest rate policy rule involved in these dynamics, but the assumption of an interest rate peg: $r = const.$

We make use in the following of the following abbreviations:

$$s_1^o = (1 - c_{h1}(1-\tau_h) - \alpha_g\tau_h)\bar{\omega}_1 y^p/z - ((1+\alpha_r)\bar{l} - y^p/z(1+\alpha_f))\alpha_\omega\bar{\omega}_1$$

and

$$\rho_{max} = y^p[1-(1+\alpha_\omega\alpha_f)\bar{\omega}_1/z] - \delta.$$

On the basis of such expressions we then have:

Theorem 2 *The interior steady state of the considered dynamics is given by:*[10]

$$l_1^{wo} = \frac{y^p}{z},\ \omega_1^o = \bar{\omega}_1,\ \eta_o = \frac{s_1^o + \rho_o - \bar{a}}{\delta + \bar{a}},$$

where d_o, ρ_o have to be determined by solving the two equations

$$\rho_o = \rho_{max} - rd_o, \quad \rho_o = \bar{a}(1-d_o)$$

which gives for the steady state values of d, ρ, η the expressions:

$$d_o = \frac{\bar{a} - \rho_{max}}{\bar{a} - r}, \quad \rho_o = \bar{a}\frac{\rho_{max} - r}{\bar{a} - r},$$

$$\eta_o = \frac{s_1^o + \bar{a}\frac{\rho_{max} - r}{\bar{a} - r}}{\delta + \bar{a}} = \frac{s_1^o(\bar{a} - r) - \bar{a}(\bar{a} - \rho_{max})}{(\delta + \bar{a})(\bar{a} - r)}.$$

We assume that both the numerator and the denominator of the fraction that defines d_o are positive, that is the trend term in investment is sufficiently strong (larger than the rate of profit before interest rate payments ρ_{max} and larger than the rate of interest r). Moreover, it is also assumed that $\rho_{max} > r$ holds so that all fractions shown above are in fact positive. In the case where $\bar{a} = \rho_{max} = y^p[1 - (1 + \alpha_\omega \alpha_f)\bar{\omega}_1/z] - \delta$ holds we have $d_o = 0$ and $\rho_o = \bar{a}$ in which case the value of η_o is the same as in the sections on investment without debt financing. Nevertheless the dynamics around the steady state remain debt financed and are therefore different from the one of the preceding section. We thus can have a 'balanced budget' of firms in the steady state while investment remains driven by $I/K = i_\rho(\rho - \rho_o) - i_d(d - d_o) + \bar{a}$ outside the steady state position.

For the fraction of company pension funds divided by base pension payments we now get as a relationship in the steady state

$$\alpha_c = \frac{\delta\eta_o + rd_o}{\alpha_\omega \alpha_r \bar{\omega}_1 \bar{l}},$$

an expression that in general does not give rise to unambiguous results concerning comparative dynamics. In the special case $d_o = 0$, however, we can state that this fraction depends positively on s_o^1 (also in general) and negatively on $\bar{a}, \delta, \bar{l}$.

The Jacobian at the interior steady state of the 4D dynamics considered here reads

$$J^o = \begin{pmatrix} -\beta_{eu}/l_1^{wo} & 0 \\ ? & -\kappa[(1-\kappa_p)\beta_{w\omega} + (1-\kappa_w)\beta_{p\omega}] \\ ? & ? \\ ? & ? \end{pmatrix.}$$

$$\begin{matrix} 0 & 0 \\ 0 & 0 \\ -(i_\rho + i_d)(1 - d_o)) - (\bar{a} - r) & 0 \\ ? & -\bar{a}(1+\delta) \end{matrix}\Bigg).$$

This lower triangular form of the Jacobian immediately implies that the elements on the diagonal of the matrix J^o are just equal to the four eigenvalues of this matrix which are therefore all real and negative. This gives:

Theorem 3 *The interior steady state of the considered dynamics is locally asymptotically stable and is characterized by a strict hierarchy in the state variables of the dynamics.*

Due to the specific form of the laws of motion considered we conjecture that the steady state is also a global attractor in the economically relevant part of the 4D phase space. We then would get again monotonically convergent trajectories from any starting point of this part of the phase space and thus fairly simple adjustment processes also in the case where investment is jointly financed by profits (retained earnings) and credit.

The stability of the steady state is increased (that is the eigenvalues of its Jacobian matrix become more negative) if the speed parameter characterizing hiring and firing is increased, if the Blanchard and Katz type error correction becomes more pronounced and if the parameters $i_\rho, i_d, \bar{a}$ in the investment function are increased.

8.7 Conclusion

We have considered in this chapter an alternative to the Marxian reserve army mechanism we have considered in detail in Part II and which was there mitigated through income policy measures concerning unemployment benefits and minimum (and maximum) wages. This alternative not only allows putting these wage income measures on a coherent and more extensive basis, but it also completely removed unemployment from the economy considered, by way of the construction of an employer of last resort (ELR). The obtained flexicurity model of a capitalist economy overcomes the one-sided conception of a welfare state and it also represents a wider perspective as compared to the construction of workfare systems, where welfare is combined with activating labor market policies. These latter policies are also at work in specific ways under a flexicurity regime, but are then designed from the perspective of an employer of first, not last, resort.[11]

In this chapter we have also seen that the formulated adjustment processes and their stability properties are very supportive for the working of our model of flexicurity type which is generally monotonically convergent with full capacity utilization of both capital and labor to a steady state position with a sustainable distribution of income between firms, our three types of households and the government. We conclude that flexicurity capitalism can be a workable alternative to current forms of capitalism and, in particular, can avoid severe social deformations and human degradations caused by the Marxian reserve army mechanism and the mass unemployment it implies for certain stages in a long-phase distributive and welfare state cycle, in the US and the UK more of a neoclassical cold turkey type and in Germany and in France more gradualistic in nature.[12]

Notes

1 The parameters underlying this simulation are: $\beta_{ve} = 0.06; \bar{e} = 0.9; \beta_{vv} = 0.01; \beta_{ev} = 0.1; \bar{v} = 0.6$; and are approximately obtained from simple OLS estimates of these dynamics (with no good statistical properties, however, but definitely more appropriately chosen compared to the case without any empirical reference).

2 Note with respect to Figure 8.2 that it is assumed there that an increasing wage share is accompanied by inflationary pressure as it is suggested by the conflicting income claims approach. Note furthermore that – as is shown in Flaschel, Tavani, Taylor and Teuber (2011) – this cycle can be more complicated in nature if empirically observed nonlinearities in the money wage Phillips curve are taken into account which in fact move the cycle of the theoretical model already fairly close to what is shown in Figure 8.1, bottom right.

3 And thus not yet of last resort, since this latter approach has been rightly criticized as being too passive and inventory-like in nature.

4 Augmented by company pension payments $\delta_1 R$. Note here also that savings are real savings in this framework.

5 The term S_1 is equal to $\delta_1 R + \dot{R}$.

6 The considered wage–price spiral will imply a law of motion for real wages which in simplified form also appears in the flexicurity model. As these models are formulated their dynamics are independent of the nominal levels of wages and prices, that is everything can be expressed in real terms. For the introduction of the monetary sector see Flaschel, Franke and Semmler (2008).

7 The steady state value, see below, is here assumed to underlie Blanchard and Katz (1999) type error correction in the first labor market.

8 The value of n must be chosen that high since technical change is still ignored in this baseline social growth model.

[9] Note that the numerator is easily shown to be not only positive, but even larger than 1 under standard Keynesian assumptions on expenditure and taxation rates.

[10] The steady state value of s_1^o is the same as in the preceding section.

[11] The reader is referred to Flaschel, Greiner and Luchtenberg (2010) for more details on this distinction.

[12] We refer the reader back to what is shown in Figure 8.1 where the postwar period up into the 1960s seemed to suggest that the working of the reserve army mechanism had been overcome, a suggestion that was disproved in the subsequent years in a striking way.

9. Factor Substitution, Okun's Law and Gradual Wage Adjustments

9.1 Introduction

Many European countries have been suffering from high and persistent unemployment over the last decades, significantly different from what happened in the USA. Notable further exceptions are, on the one hand, the Nordic welfare states, Denmark, Finland, Norway and Sweden and, on the other hand, Great Britain. While Great Britain pursued an Anglo-Saxon approach in its economic policy that is characterized by flexible hiring and firing conditions and by low social spending, the Nordic welfare states follow a different policy. Those economies also allow flexible hiring and firing, but have a high standard of social security, in contrast to Anglo-Saxon countries. These countries therefore show that flexibility and security need not be contradictory, but may well be compatible and can also go along with low unemployment rates. Often, this framework is called the flexicurity model which is obtained by merging the terms flexibility and security.

It is in particular in public debates that the flexicurity model has attracted great attention, although there is no clear consensus on its definition (see Zhou, 2007). In any case, an important aspect as regards flexibility on the labor market is that there is both external flexibility, namely hiring and firing, as well as internal flexibility, such as flexible working hours and the possibility of working overtime and part-time work, according to Wilthagen et al. (2004). Essential characteristics with respect to security are income security, that is income protection in the event of job loss, on the one hand, and the ability to combine paid work with other social responsibilities and obligations, on the other hand. Our goal in this chapter is to integrate the basic ideas of the flexicurity model into the basic neoclassical growth model as presented by Solow (1956) and to analyze the resulting model in its dynamic properties.

Solow's (1956) model of economic growth provided the baseline case for nearly all subsequent modelings of the phenomenon of economic growth in Western capitalist economies, where in place of fixed proportions in production a neoclassical production function and thus smooth factor substitution was assumed as the input–output relationship underlying the laws of motion of the economy. Solow assumed full employment and considered homogeneous labor as one of the factors of production. Goodwin's (1967) growth cycle model had quite a different starting point (Marx's reserve army mechanism) compared to Solow's contribution. It assumed – as in Marx (1954, ch. 23) – a real wage Phillips curve and considered its interaction with extremely classical savings behavior in a technological framework with fixed proportions in production. In place of monotonic convergence to the steady state it gave rise to persistent cycles around its steady state position of a structurally unstable center dynamics type that can be easily modified towards the occurrence of stable limit cycles (as in Rose's (1967) employment cycle model).[1]

It is not difficult to integrate the Solow growth model with the Goodwin growth cycle, since this basically only introduces real wage rigidities into the Solovian framework (or smooth factor substitution in the Goodwin model). The result is that we now get damped oscillations (close to Goodwinian cycles if the elasticity of substitution between capital and labor is low) and even monotonic convergence to the steady state in the opposite case (with respect to the state variables labor intensity and the real wage). One problem with this integrated model however is – if it creates periods of mass unemployment – that there is then the possibility that unemployed workers lose their skills, that labor markets become segmented, and so in particular older workers are subject to long-term or never ending unemployment and that workers' families become degraded in their social and emotional status that is difficult to reverse. There may be counteracting unemployment benefits, low wages for the degraded part of the workforce and more that then have to be considered in their consequences for the evolution of capitalist economies.

In this chapter we will not go into such an analysis of the consequences of mass unemployment, but will instead augment the above Solow–Goodwin synthesis by an employer of first (not last) resort, where all workers (and even pensioners) find reasonable employment if they are temporarily dismissed from the private sector of the economy, the sector of capitalist firms.[2] The model we shall build on this basis is providing a theoretical basis for the Danish approach to flexicurity, but one that is not subject to the pejorative reformulation of flexicurity as flexploitation as it is sometimes found in valuations of the concept of flexicurity in the political debate (see also Asada et al. 2011). Instead, we use the Solow model with the Goodwin real wage rigidity to construct full employment in this framework by means of (decentralized) government actions, with wage bargains in the industrial sector and with two implied laws of motion (for employment and the real wage) that under flexible hiring and firing in this sector will guarantee even monotonic convergence to the steady state in such a setup.

We view this model as an ideal towards which progress paths have to be found that are to be confirmed by elections in a democratic society and which therefore are subject to ratchet effects when some parties propose to abolish such an evolution (if it is successful). It is ideal in that it combines flexible hiring and firing (and job discontinuities in the first, the industrial labor market) with employment security through a second labor market that preserves the skills of the workforce and prevents their human degradation. We think that all modern market economies currently experiment with such progress paths, sometimes on a very low scale as the current discussion about minimum wage in Germany demonstrates. Yet, even such a discussion can be reflected from the perspective of the concept of flexicurity and be interpreted as a step forward towards flexicurity if a general minimum level of (real) wages can be established in Germany. We have shown in Chapter 2 in the context of Goodwin's growth cycle mechanism that minimum and also maximum wages (of workers) will dampen the employment fluctuations of the economy and will thus contribute to its stability after a transitory period of low employment (yet not so low as in the unrestricted case).

Flexicurity – properly understood – may thus be the modern equivalent to Solow's growth model and may – in the same ideal way – provide a perspective for the future of capitalism which is compatible with the social structure of democratic societies. To demonstrate the working of flexicurity capitalism we will provide in Section 9.2 the accounting framework for such an economy, will then consider the behavior of the agents in such a framework in very basic terms in Section 9.3 and show on this basis the global asymptotic stability of – and even monotonic convergence to – its steady state position with respect to its central state variables, the real wage in the first labor market and the utilization rate of workforce of firms (Sections 9.4 and 9.5). In Section 9.6 we consider the law of motion and the steady state positions of the (extra) company pension payments this model type allows for and thus consider conditions for the viability of the economy (which should allow for pension payments above the level of base pension payments). Yet, if credits conducted in nominal terms are added to the model we get that investment behavior can depart from savings behavior such that the coordination of these two magnitudes leads to Keynesian effective demand problems and thus to demand-driven business cycles. This is the stage where flexicurity capitalism must prove its superiority, since there are now existing business cycle fluctuations of a much larger extent than those that can originate from supply-side driven full capacity growth. Such problems must, however, be left for future research here.

9.2 Flexicurity

Flexicurity intends to combine two labor market components which – as many economists would argue – cannot be reconciled with each other: workplace flexibility in a very competitive environment with income and employment (but not job) security for workers. The basic aspects and problems of such a combination are:

- How much flexibility in:

  1.1 hiring and firing and job discontinuities?

  1.2 wage and price setting?

  1.3 technical change?

  1.4 globalization and financialization?

- How much security in:

  2.1 base income?

  2.2 employment?

  2.3 location of employment?

  2.4 atypical employment?

Moreover, in order to get social acceptance for such a combination of needs of capital and the needs of labor the following problems must also find a positive solution:

Basic aspects of social cohesion in a modern democratic market economy:

- consent-based cooperation between capital and labor?

- proper citizenship education and democratic evolution?
- the existence of equal opportunities to a larger degree?
- reflected and controlled institutional evolution?

In this chapter we will provide a model which reconciles the aspects 1.1/1.2 with the problems 2.1/2.2, where the other aspects of the enumerated points remain, however, excluded. Moreover we shall simply assume here that the societal issues in the last block are developed to such an extent that the proposed model is not only transparent to the citizens of the considered capitalist society, but have indeed led to basic agreement on how the economy is to be organized and the society to be developed further.

Against this background, we design the accounting framework (formulate the budget equations) of a growth model that marries the ideas of Solow (1956) and Goodwin (1967), but that rests on a second labor market in place of overaccumulation (in capitalistic prosperity phases) and mass unemployment (in stagnant phases). The second labor market guarantees full employment, through its institutional setup, in its interaction with the first labor market which represents the highly flexible and competitive industrial sector of the economy. The accounting framework is identical to that presented in Section 8.2 so that we do not repeat it here but just refer to the previous chapter. Instead, we continue with the analysis of this model where we allow for smooth factor substitution, in contrast to our analysis in the previous chapter.

9.3 Smooth Factor Substitution, Okun's Law and Real Wage Rigidities

Our synthesis of the growth models of Solow (1956) and Goodwin (1967) into a model of the flexicurity variety consists of three basic building blocks, the three factor production function of the industrial sector, Okun's law that relates the utilization of the workforce L_1^w to the hiring and firing decision of firms and the dynamic of the real wages of the workers in the first labor market, describing the degree of labor market rigidity existing in the industrial sector of the economy.

The module that describes the growth dynamics of the model therefore consists of the following three structural equations:

$$Y = F(K, L_1^d, L_{2f}^w),\ \omega_1 = F_2(K, L_1^d, L_{2f}^w),\ \omega_2 = F_3(K, L_1^d, L_{2f}^w), \quad (9.1)$$

$$\dot{L}_1^w = \beta_e(L_1^d - L_1^w) + nL_1^w, \quad (9.2)$$

$$\hat{w}_1 = \beta_w(u_w - 1) + \hat{p}, \quad u^w = L_1^d / L_1^w. \quad (9.3)$$

The first (set of) equation(s) provide a three factor neoclassical production function, built on standard assumptions, coupled with the conditions for profit maximization with respect to its two variable inputs, the labor hours worked by workers L_1^w in the first labor market segment and the normal working hours supplied by the workforce L_{2f}^w that is employed by firms from the second labor market. We stress that workers L_1^w of type 1 are providing over- or under-time work according to the needs of profit-maximizing firms (who will recruit additional workers or dismiss employed ones in view of the discrepancy $L_1^d - L_1^w$ described by Okun's law later on).[3]

The second equation describes, as already indicated, Okun's law in the given environment where only L_1^w is over- or under-employed (since capital is always fully employed and since we have an employer of first resort with respect to the second labor market). The time rate of change $\dot{L}_1^w$ is following the excess measure $L_1^d - L_1^w$ with an adjustment speed described by β_e, taking in account in addition that the natural growth rate n, a constant, of the total workforce L must be used as a trend term in this law of motion to provide a steady state solution later on (if further adjustment equations are to be avoided in this baseline model for reasons of simplicity).

The third equation is a standard money-wage Phillips curve, solely based on the actual inside employment of workers working on the first labor market, and on myopic perfect foresight concerning price inflation.[4] This latter assumption avoids the explicit consideration of a price Phillips curve, since we can then reduce the wage–price dynamics of this model type to a real wage dynamics $\hat{\omega}_1, \omega_1 = w_1/p$ and need not consider nominal effects in the chosen framework. For the real wage of workers in the second labor market we simply assume that it is a constant fraction of the real wage ω_1, which means that income distribution is driven by the insiders in the first labor market solely. Outsiders (the second labor market) play no role in the wage bargaining process.

Since aggregate demand is always equal to aggregate supply in the chosen framework, since all savings is product-oriented and since all profits are invested (that is Say's law holds), we have that actual output can be and is supply driven, depending on the level of real wages ω_1, ω_2 and on the capital stock K.

Supplement: On the Validity of Say's Law in Solovian Flexicurity Growth

In our social growth model, we have assumed that workers of type 2 consume their whole income (they pay no taxes). With respect to the other type of workers we have assumed as their consumption function

$$C_1 = c_{h1}(1-\tau_h)\omega_1 L_1^d, \quad c_h \text{ propensity to consume}, \tau_h \text{ tax rate}$$
$$\omega_2 L_{2h}^w = c_{h2}(1-\tau_h)\omega_1 L_1^d \qquad \text{consumption of household services}$$

Households' type 1 savings are, on the basis of our accounting relationships, given by

$$S_1 = \omega_1 L_1^d - C_1 - \omega_2 L_{2h}^w - \omega_2(L - (L_1^w + L_{2f}^w + L_{2h}^w + L_{2g}^w) - \omega_2 L^r)$$

due to the assumed solidarity contribution they provide to the second labor market. Since the government, workers from the second labor market and pensioners do not save; since all tax transfers are turned into consumption and the savings of households of type 1 into commodity inventories of firms from which company pensions are to be deducted; and since finally all profits are invested, it can easily be shown from what was presented in accounting form in the preceding section that we must have at all times:

$$Y = C_1 + C_2 + C_r + I + \delta K + G + S_1, \quad C_1 = c_{h1}(1-\tau_h)\omega_1 L_1^d$$

if firms produce at full capacity Y (which they can and will do in this case). There is thus no demand problem on the market for goods and thus no need to discuss a dynamic multiplier process as in Keynesian type models. Note, moreover, that we have by construction for our social growth model at all points in time:

$$L = L_1^w + L_{2f}^w + L_{2h}^w + L_{2g}^w + L_r^w = L_1^w + L_2^w \quad L_r = \alpha_r L.$$

We have assumed that households of type 1 must pay as solidarity contribution (employment benefits) to those workers of type 2, whose wages are not paid by firms, through households of type 2 services to households of type 1 and through the core employment in the government sector. The government employs in addition as administrative workers and infrastructure workers (public work and education) the remaining workforce in the second labor market (plus the L^r services from pensioners). This completes the discussion of the behavioral equations of the social growth model

9.4 Global Stability of Balanced Reproduction

Normalizing level magnitudes as usual by dividing through the capital stock K and using lower case letters for the ratios thereby obtained we get from the above the reduced form equations:

$$y = F(1, l_1^d, l_{2f}^w),\ \omega_1 = F_2(1, l_1^d, l_{2f}^w),\ \omega_2 = F_3(1, l_1^d, l_{2f}^w), \quad (9.4)$$

$$\hat{l}_1^w = \beta_e(l_1^d/l_1^w - 1) + n - \hat{K}, \quad \hat{K} = \rho = \Pi/K, \quad (9.5)$$

$$\hat{\omega}_1 = \beta_w(l_1^d/l_1^w - 1). \quad (9.6)$$

Since ω_2 is a constant fraction of ω_1 we get from the profit maximization condition of firms the proposition (due to $\rho = y - \delta - \omega_1 l_1^d - \omega_2 l_{2f}^w$):

Proposition 1: *Assume that there hold for the production function F*

$$\begin{aligned} F_2 >& 0, \quad F_3 > 0, \quad F_{22} < 0, \quad F_{33} < 0, \quad F_{23} \geqq 0, \\ \Delta =& F_{22}F_{33} - (F_{23})^2 > 0. \end{aligned} \quad (9.7)$$

The profit maximizing behavior of firms then implies the relationships:[5]

$$l_1^d = l_1^d(\omega_1), \quad (l_1^d)'(\omega_1) < 0, \quad (9.8)$$

$$l_{2f}^w = l_{2f}^w(\omega_1), \quad (l_{2f}^w)'(\omega_1) < 0, \quad (9.9)$$

$$y = y(\omega_1), \quad y'(\omega_1) < 0, \quad (9.10)$$

$$\rho = \rho(\omega_1), \quad \rho'(\omega_1) < 0. \quad (9.11)$$

Proof: See appendix.

On this basis, the dynamics implied by the model can be reduced to two nonlinear laws of motion for the state variables $\omega_1, l_1^w > 0$ of the type:

$$\hat{\omega}_1 = \beta_w(l_1^d(\omega_1)/l_1^w - 1), \quad (9.12)$$

$$\hat{l}_1^w = \beta_e(l_1^d(\omega_1)/l_1^w - 1) + n - \rho(\omega_1). \quad (9.13)$$

Proposition 2: *Assume that there holds* $\lim_{\omega_1 \to 0} \rho(\omega_1) = +\infty$ *and* $\lim_{\omega_1 \to +\infty} \rho(\omega_1) = 0$. *Then: the above dynamical system has a unique interior steady state that is given by:*

$$\omega_1^o = \rho^{-1}(n), \quad l_1^{wo} = l_1^d(\omega_1^o). \quad (9.14)$$

Proof: See appendix.

Proposition 3: *1. The above dynamical system can be reformulated as a planar system defined on the whole plane by using the logs* $\varpi_1, \ell_1^w > 0$ *of the state variables* $\omega_1, l_1^w > 0$ *which implies the equivalent system of differential equations*

$$\dot{\varpi}_1 = \beta_w(\exp(\ell_1^d)(\exp(\varpi_1))/\exp(\ell_1^w) - 1), \tag{9.15}$$

$$\dot{\ell}_1^w = \beta_e(\exp(\ell_1^d)(\exp(\varpi_1))/\exp(\ell_1^w) - 1) + n - \rho(\exp(\varpi_1)). \tag{9.16}$$

2. The unique interior steady state of these laws of motion is globally asymptotically stable.

Proof: An application of Olech's theorem (see the appendix).

Our model of social economic growth or flexicurity growth dynamics thus is always convergent to its unique balanced growth path. Just as the original Solow (1956) model it is based on supply side conditions solely, while the demand side is only of importance for the savings decision of households of type 1 and thus for the evolution of company pension funds, to be considered in the next section.

Supplement: Solovian Labor Intensity $l = L/K$ Dynamics (an Appended Law of Motion in Flexicurity Growth)

By definition we have the following further law of motion in our model of flexicurity growth:

$$\hat{l} = n - \rho(\omega_1).$$

For the Jacobian of the resulting 3D dynamics evaluated at the steady state we get from the laws of motion for ω_1, l_1^w, l:[6]

$$J^o = \begin{pmatrix} - & - & 0 \\ \pm & - & 0 \\ + & 0 & 0 \end{pmatrix}.$$

Proposition 4: *The above 3D dynamics are globally asymptotically stable, but exhibits zero root hysteresis with respect to the state variable* l.

Proof: See the appendix.

9.5 Increased Flexibility in Hiring and Firing is Stability-supporting

We now derive a local condition for the occurrence of monotonic convergence to the steady state of our model of flexicurity growth. According to the last proposition, we basically only have to investigate the first two laws of motion. It suffices therefore to consider the following matrix with respect to its eigenvalues:

$$J^o = \begin{pmatrix} J^o_{11} & J^o_{12} \\ J^o_{21} & J^o_{22} \end{pmatrix} = \begin{pmatrix} - & - \\ \pm & - \end{pmatrix}$$

where the $\pm$ sign reduces to $+$ in the calculation of the determinant of this matrix. It is obvious that we always have locally asymptotically stable dynamics (that is, trace $J^o < 0, \det J^o > 0$). Furthermore, the condition trace $J^o = 4 \det J^o$, that is,

$$(J^o_{11} + J^o_{22})^2 = 4(J^o_{11}J^o_{22} + J^o_{21}J^o_{12})$$

separates monotonic convergence (for parameters β_e sufficiently large) from cyclical convergence (parameters β_e sufficiently small). Reformulated, this condition reads:

$$|J^o_{22}| = |J^o_{11}| + 2\sqrt{|J^o_{21}J^o_{12}|}, \quad i.e., \quad \beta^H_e = const?[|J^o_{11}| + 2\sqrt{|J^o_{21}J^o_{12}|}].$$

This gives:

Proposition 5: *Assume that the parameter β_w fulfills the inequality:*

$$\beta_w \omega^o_1 \{(l^d_1)'(\omega^o_1)\}^2 < -4 l^d_1(\omega^o_1) \underset{(-)}{\rho'(\omega^o_1)} \, l^{wo}_1.$$

Then: there is a uniquely determined bifurcation value $\beta^H_e > 0$ that separates monotonic from cyclical convergence. Cyclical convergence to the balanced growth path occurs for all $\beta_e \in (0, \beta^H_e)$, and monotonic convergence to the balanced growth path occurs for all $\beta_e \in (\beta^H_e, +\infty)$.

Proof: See appendix.

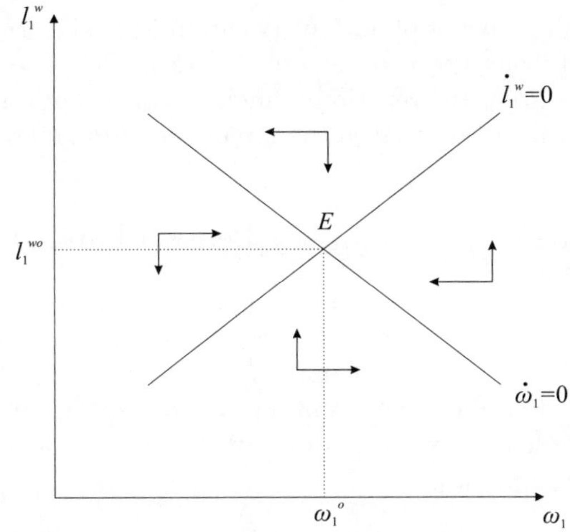

Fig. 9.1: The case of a small parameter β_e

The case of monotonic convergence is shown in Figure 9.2, while the case of cyclical convergence to the steady state is given in Figure 9.1.

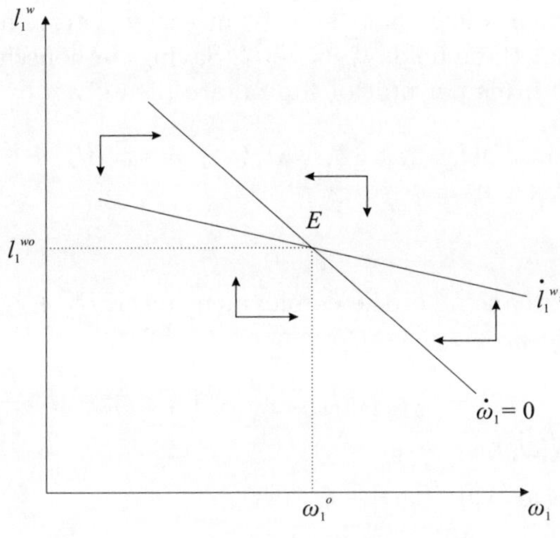

Fig. 9.2: The case of a large parameter β_e

We thus get that economic fluctuations can be avoided in this type of economy if wages in the first labor market respond relatively sluggishly to demand pressure in this market (as measured by the utilization rate of the insiders) and if hiring and firing is a sufficiently flexible process as envisaged by the concept of flexicurity capitalism. The critical value for the hiring and firing speed parameter in our model of social growth is the larger, the larger the reaction of money wage inflation with respect to workforce utilization, that is the larger the parameter β_w becomes.

9.6 The Dynamics of Company Pension Funds

There is a further law of motion in the background of the model that needs to be considered in order to provide an additional statement on the viability of the considered model of flexicurity capitalism.[7] This law of motion describes the evolution of the pension fund per unit of the capital stock $\eta = \frac{R}{K}$ and is obtained from the defining equation $\dot{R} = S_1 - \delta_1 R$ as follows:

$$\hat{\eta} = \hat{R} - \hat{K} = \frac{\dot{R}}{K}\frac{K}{R} - \rho = \frac{S_1 - \delta_1 R}{K}/\eta - \rho, \quad \text{i.e.:}$$
$$\dot{\eta} = \frac{S_1}{K} - (\delta_1 + \rho)\eta = s_1 - (\delta_1 + \rho)\eta$$

We assume now for reasons of simplicity a Cobb–Douglas production function. We then know that there is an easily determined constant $\alpha_f > 0$ such that there holds $l_{2f}^w = \alpha_f l_1^d$. Savings of households of type 1 and profits of firms per unit of capital are then given by:

$$\begin{aligned} s_1 =& (1 - (c_{h1} + c_{h2})(1 - \tau_h) - \tau_h)\omega_1 l_1^d(\omega_1) - \alpha_\omega \omega_1 (l_x^w + l^r) \\ l_x^w =& \, l - (l_1^w + l_{2f}^w + l_{2h}^w + l_{2g}^w) \\ l^r =& \, \alpha_r l, \end{aligned}$$

i.e., due to the financing of the employment terms $l_{2h}^w + l_{2g}^w$:

$$\begin{aligned} s_1 =& (1 - c_{h1}(1 - \tau_h) - \alpha_g \tau_h)\omega_1 l_1^d(\omega_1) - ((1 + \alpha_r)l - (l_1^w + l_{2f}^w))\alpha_\omega \omega_1, \\ l_{2f}^w =& \, \alpha_f l_1^d(\omega_1), \\ \rho =& \, y - (1 + \alpha_\omega \alpha_f)\omega_1 l_1^d(\omega_1)] - \delta. \end{aligned}$$

For reasons of analytical simplicity we now assume that the economy sits in its steady state with respect to the variables ω_1, l_1^w and that we also have a given ratio $l = L/K = const$, a simplifying assumption that must be accompanied later on by the assumption that the actual value of $l = \bar{l}$ must be chosen in a certain neighborhood of a base value l^o, see below. The above of course also provides us with a steady state value of the rate of profit $\bar{\rho}(\bar{\omega}_1) = \rho^o(\omega^o)$. Moreover we also assume for simplicity $\delta_1 = \delta$ for the depreciation rates of the capital stock and the stock of pension funds.

This gives for the law of motion of the pension fund per unit of capital the differential equation:

$$\begin{aligned}\dot{\eta} = &(1 - c_{h1}(1 - \tau_h) - \alpha_g \tau_h)\bar{\omega}_1 l_1^d(\bar{\omega}_1) - \\ &((1 + \alpha_r)\bar{l} - (\bar{l}_1^w + \alpha_f l_1^d(\bar{\omega}_1)))\alpha_\omega \bar{\omega}_1 - (\delta + \bar{\rho})\eta,\end{aligned}$$

which gives a single linear differential equation for the ratio η. This dynamical equation is globally asymptotically stable around its steady state position:

$$\begin{aligned}\eta_o = &\frac{1}{\delta + \bar{\rho}}\Big((1 - c_{h1}(1 - \tau_h) - \alpha_g \tau_h)\bar{\omega}_1 l_1^d(\bar{\omega}_1) \\ &- ((1 + \alpha_r)\bar{l} - (1 + \alpha_f)l_1^d(\bar{\omega}_1))\alpha_\omega \bar{\omega}_1\Big).\end{aligned}$$

In this case we thus have monotonic adjustment of the pension fund–capital ratio to its steady state position, while in general we have a non-autonomous adjustment of this ratio that is driven by the real wage and employment dynamics of the first labor market. The steady state level of η is positive iff there holds for the full employment labor intensity ratio:

$$\bar{l} < \frac{(1 - c_{h1}(1 - \tau_h) - \alpha_g \tau_h)\bar{\omega}_1 l_1^d(\bar{\omega}_1) + ((1 + \alpha_f)l_1^d(\bar{\omega}_1))\alpha_\omega \bar{\omega}_1}{(\delta + \bar{\rho})(1 + \alpha_r)\alpha_\omega \bar{\omega}_1}.$$

We now assume moreover that the additional company pension payments to pensioners should add the percentage $100\alpha_c$ to their base pension $\omega_2 \alpha_r \bar{l}$ per unit of capital. We thus have as further restriction on the steady state position of the economy, if there is an α_c target given:

$$\delta \eta_o = \alpha_c \omega_2 \alpha_r \bar{l}, \quad \omega_2 = \alpha_\omega \bar{\omega}_1.$$

Inserting the value for η_o then gives

$$\begin{aligned}\alpha_c = &\frac{\delta}{(\delta + \bar{\rho})\omega_2 \alpha_r \bar{l}}\Big((1 - c_{h1}(1 - \tau_h) - \alpha_g \tau_h)\bar{\omega}_1 l_1^d(\bar{\omega}_1) \\ &-((1 + \alpha_r)\bar{l} - (1 + \alpha_f)l_1^d(\bar{\omega}_1))\alpha_\omega \bar{\omega}_1\Big).\end{aligned}$$

We thus get that a target value for α_c demands a certain labor intensity ratio $\bar{l}$ and vice versa. For a given total labor intensity ratio there is a given percentage by which company pensions compare to base pension payments. This percentage is the larger the smaller the ratio $\bar{l}_1^w/\bar{l}$ due to the following reformulation of the α_c formula:

$$\begin{aligned}\alpha_c =&\frac{\delta}{(\delta+\bar{\rho})\alpha_r\alpha_\omega\bar{\omega}_1}\Big(\big[(1-c_{h1}(1-\tau_h)-\alpha_g\tau_h)\bar{\omega}_1 \\ &+(1+\alpha_f)\alpha_\omega\bar{\omega}_1\big]\frac{\bar{l}_1^w}{\bar{l}}-(1+\alpha_r)\alpha_\omega\bar{\omega}_1\Big).\end{aligned} \tag{9.17}$$

If this value of the total employment labor intensity ratio prevails in the considered economy (where it is of course as usually assumed that $c_{h1}(1-\tau_h)+\alpha_g\tau_h < 1$ holds) we have that core pension payments to pensioners are augmented by company pension payments by a percentage that is given by the parameter α_c and that these extra pension payments are distributed to pensioners in proportion to the time that they have worked in the private sector of the economy. There is thus a negative trade-off between the ratios $\bar{l}, \alpha_c$, as expressed by the relationship (9.17). It also shows that the total working population must have a certain ratio to the capital stock in order to allow for a given percentage of extra company pension payments. Due to $\delta\eta_o = \alpha_c\omega_2\alpha_r\bar{l}$ and $s_1^o = (\delta+\bar{\rho})\eta_o$ we also have the equivalence between positive savings per unit of capital of households of type 1 and positive values for α_c, η_o. Moreover, these values are indeed positive if there holds:[8]

$$\bar{l} < \frac{(1-c_{h1}(1-\tau_h)-\alpha_g\tau_h)\bar{\omega}_1 l_1^d(\bar{\omega}_1)+(1+\alpha_f)l_1^d(\bar{\omega}_1))\alpha_\omega\bar{\omega}_1}{(\delta+\bar{\rho})(1+\alpha_r)\alpha_\omega\bar{\omega}_1}.$$

This inequality set limits to the total labor–supply–capital stock ratio $\bar{l}$ which allows for positive savings of households of type 1 in the steady state and thus for extra pension payments to them later on. Households of type 1 are by and large financing the second labor market through taxes and employment benefits (besides their contribution to the base income of the retired people). Since firms have a positive rate of profit in the steady state, since the government budget is always balanced and since only households of type 1 save in this economy, we have thus now established the condition under which such an economy accumulates not only capital, but also pension funds – under appropriate restrictions on labor supply – to a sufficient degree.

9.7 Effective Demand Problems

We have shown in this chapter that a model of flexicurity capitalism can be formulated, exhibiting a second labor market (and an employer of first resort) where all workers not employed by firms in the industrial sector find meaningful employment. This economy is characterized by viable and attracting balanced reproduction schemes. In technical terms, the model therefore exhibits a unique interior steady state position which is globally asymptotically stable. We could show this by concentrating on the private sector of the economy, the dynamics of which are characterized by insider real wage adjustment dynamics of the type considered in Blanchard and Katz (1999)[9] and a type of Okun's Law that linked the level of utilization of the insiders of firms to their hiring and firing decision. Since both of these laws of motion only refer to the first labor market and thus only to part of the whole workforce, the fundamental equation of the Solow (1956) growth model here only has appeared as an appendix to this core dynamics, describing the evolution of the total labor supply per unit of capital in addition.

A further fundamental law concerning the viability of the economy was, however, the law of motion of company pension fund per unit of capital which was shown to lead us to a viable steady state level of it when the labor–supply–capital ratio was bounded by above in an appropriate way. The existence of such pension funds allows in principle to add credit (out of these funds) to the considered flexicurity model which, when credits are delivered in physical form, would not question the supply side orientation of the model (see Flaschel, Greiner, Luchtenberg and Nell (2008) for details).

This, however, changes when paper credit is added to the model implying that investment demand can now depart from the supply of savings in which case there is implied an IS equilibrium on the market for goods that generally differs from the profit-maximizing supply of goods through the firms. In place of savings-driven supply side fluctuations in economic activity we then have investment-driven demand side business fluctuations of probably much more volatile type. This situation is modeled and analyzed in Flaschel, Greiner, Luchtenberg and Nell (2008). It represents one litmus test for the proper working of flexicurity capitalism (not yet considering this situation from the viewpoint of globalization, however), since supply side growth may be too stable a situation in order to really test the strength of economies that are designed to work on the basis of the flexicurity approach. In such a situation it has to be tested in detail, also numerically (since the implied 5D dynamics are of a fully interdependent type), how the hiring and firing parameter β_e influences the performance of the economy. Moreover, prudent fiscal and monetary policy may then be needed in addition to preserve the stability features we have shown to exist for our supply side version of flexicurity growth of this chapter. The investigation of such topics must be left for future research here, however.

Appendix

Proof of Proposition 1

Since ω_2 is a constant fraction of ω_1, we set $\omega_2 = \alpha\omega_1$, where α is a positive constant. We can express then the rate of profit ρ as follows:

$$\rho = y - \delta - \omega_1 l_1^d - \omega_2 l_{2f}^w = F(1, l_1^d, l_{2f}^w) - \omega_1 l_1^d - \alpha\omega_1 l_{2f}^w. \qquad \text{(A.1)}$$

The first order conditions for the maximization of ρ with respect to l_1^d and l_{2f}^w are given by the following set of equations:

$$\partial\rho/\partial l_1^d = F_2(1, l_1^d, l_{2f}^w) - \omega_1 = 0, \qquad \text{(A.2)}$$

$$\partial\rho/\partial l_{2f}^w = F_3(1, l_1^d, l_{2f}^w) - \alpha\omega_1 = 0, \qquad \text{(A.3)}$$

where $F_2 = \partial F/\partial l_1^d$ and $F_3 = \partial F/\partial l_{2f}^w$. The second order conditions for the maximization of ρ can be written as follows:

$$F_{22} < 0, \quad F_{33} < 0, \quad \Delta = \begin{vmatrix} F_{22} & F_{23} \\ F_{23} & F_{33} \end{vmatrix} = F_{22}F_{33} - (F_{23})^2 > 0, \quad \text{(A.4)}$$

where $F_{22} = \partial^2 F/\partial l_1^{d2}$, $F_{33} = \partial^2 F/\partial l_{2f}^{w2}$, and $F_{23} = \partial^2 F/\partial l_{2f}^w \partial l_1^d = \partial^2 F/\partial l_1^d \partial l_{2f}^w$.

Assumption A1

$$F_2 > 0, \quad F_3 > 0, \quad F_{22} < 0, \quad F_{33} < 0, \quad F_{23} \gtreqless 0,$$
$$\Delta = F_{22}F_{33} - (F_{23})^2 > 0.$$

Remark A1

Suppose that the production function is of the Cobb–Douglas type such that

$$Y = AK^{1-\beta_1-\beta_2}(L_1^d)^{\beta_1}(L_{2f}^w)^{\beta_2} \quad (0 < \beta_1 < 1, 0 < \beta_2 < 1).$$

We then have

$$y = A(l_1^d)^{\beta_1}(l_{2f}^w)^{\beta_2}, \quad y = Y/K.$$

In this case, all of the inequalities in Assumption 1 are satisfied (and $F_{23} > 0$).

Given Assumption A1 we now prove Proposition 1.

Solving equations (A.2) and (A.3), we have $l_1^d = l_1^d(\omega_1)$ and $l_{2f}^w = l_{2f}^w(\omega_1)$. Totally differentiating equations (A.2) and (A.3), we get

$$\begin{pmatrix} F_{22} & F_{23} \\ F_{23} & F_{33} \end{pmatrix} \begin{pmatrix} dl_1^d/d\omega_1 \\ dl_{2f}^w/d\omega_1 \end{pmatrix} = \begin{pmatrix} 1 \\ \alpha \end{pmatrix}. \tag{A.5}$$

Solving this equation, we obtain the following inequalities.

$$(l_1^d)'(\omega_1) = dl_1^d/d\omega_1 = \begin{vmatrix} 1 & F_{23} \\ \alpha & F_{33} \end{vmatrix} /\Delta = (\underset{(-)}{F_{33}} - \alpha \underset{(-or0)}{F_{23}})/\underset{(+)}{\Delta} < 0, \tag{A.6}$$

$$(l_{2f}^w)'(\omega_1) = dl_{2f}^w/d\omega_1 = \begin{vmatrix} F_{22} & 1 \\ F_{23} & \alpha \end{vmatrix} /\Delta = (\alpha \underset{(-)}{F_{22}} - F_{23}^2)/\underset{(+)}{\Delta} < 0. \tag{A.7}$$

Therefore, we have $y = F(1, l_1^d(\omega_1), l_{2f}^w(\omega_1)) = y(\omega_1)$ and

$$y'(\omega_1) = dy/d\omega_1 = \underset{(+)}{F_2}\,\underset{(-)}{(dl_1^d/d\omega_1)} + \underset{(+)}{F_3}\,\underset{(-)}{(dl_{2f}^w/d\omega_1)} < 0. \tag{A.8}$$

It follows from Equation (A.1) that ρ is a linear decreasing function of ω_1 for any given values of $l_1^d > 0$ and $l_{2f}^w > 0$. Therefore, the graph of the function $\rho = \rho(\omega_1)$ becomes the outer envelope of downward sloping straight lines. This means that we have $\rho'(\omega_1) = d\rho/d\omega_1 < 0$.

Next, let us consider the phase diagram for the system (9.12), (9.12) in the text (see Figure 9.1). The locus of $\dot{\omega}_1 = 0$ is given by the following equation:

$$l_1^d(\omega_1) = l_1^w \tag{A.9}$$

Totally differentiating this equation and rearranging terms, we get

$$\left.\frac{dl_1^w}{d\omega_1}\right|_{\dot{\omega}_1=0} = (l_1^d)'(\omega_1) < 0. \tag{A.10}$$

The locus of $\dot{l}_1^W = 0$ is given by

$$\{l_1^d(\omega_1)/l_1^w - 1\} + \{n - \rho(\omega_1)\}/\beta_e = 0. \tag{A.11}$$

Totally differentiating this equation and rearranging terms, we obtain the following relationship.

$$\frac{dl_1^w}{d\omega_1}|_{\dot{l}_1^w=0} = \left((l_1^d)'(\omega_1) - \frac{\rho'(\omega_1)l_1^w}{\beta_e}\right)\left(\frac{l_1^w}{l_1^d(\omega_1)}\right). \tag{A.12}$$

Since $(l_1^d)'(\omega_1) < 0$ and $\rho'(\omega_1) < 0$, we have the following results from equations (A.11) and (A.12):

(1) $\left.\frac{dl_1^w}{d\omega_1}\right|_{\dot{l}_1^w=0}$ is a continuous decreasing function of the parameter value $\beta_e > 0$.

(2) $\lim_{\beta_e \to 0} \left.\frac{dl_1^w}{d\omega_1}\right|_{\dot{l}_1^w=0} = +\infty.$

(3) $\lim_{\beta_e \to +\infty} \left.\frac{dl_1^w}{d\omega_1}\right|_{\dot{l}_1^w=0} = (l_1^d)'(\omega_1) < 0.$

In other words, the slope of the locus of $\dot{l}_1^w = 0$ is positive for all sufficiently small values of β_e, and it is negative for all sufficiently large values of β_e, and the locus of $\dot{l}_1^w = 0$ coincides with that of $\dot{\omega}_1 = 0$ if β_e is infinitely large. On the other hand, we can easily see that $\partial\hat{\omega}_1/\partial\omega_1 < 0$ and $\partial\hat{l}_1^w/\partial l_1^w < 0$. Therefore, we obtain two types of the phase diagrams (see Figures 9.1 and 9.2 in the text) depending on the magnitude of the parameter value β_e.

Proof of Proposition 2

Assumption B1

$$\lim_{\omega_1 \to 0} \rho(\omega_1) = +\infty \text{ and } \lim_{\omega_1 \to +\infty} \rho(\omega_1) = 0.$$

Remark B1

The assumption B1 is in fact satisfied if the production function is of Cobb–Douglas type.

Given assumption B1 we can now prove the proposition. We first note that the equilibrium solution of this dynamical system is characterized by the following set of equations with the two unknowns ω_1 and l_1^w :

$$l_1^d(\omega_1) = l_1^w, \tag{B.1}$$

$$\rho(\omega_1) = n. \tag{B.2}$$

Equation (B.2) has the unique solution $\omega_1^o = \rho^{-1}(n) > 0$ because of Assumption B2 and the fact that the function $\rho(\omega_1)$ is a decreasing function. Substituting $\omega_1 = \omega_1^o$ into equation (B.1), we moreover get $l_1^{wo} = l_1^d(\omega_1^o) > 0$.

Proof of Proposition 3

Let us define

$$\tilde{\omega}_1 = \ln \omega_1, \quad \tilde{l}_1^d = \ln l_1^d, \quad \tilde{l}_1^w = \ln l_1^w. \tag{C.1}$$

We can then transform the dynamical system that is given by equations (9.12) and (9.13) in the text as follows:

$$\dot{\tilde{\omega}}_1 = \beta_w\{\exp(\tilde{l}_1^d)(\exp(\tilde{\omega}_1))/\exp(\tilde{l}_1^w) - 1\} = G_1(\tilde{\omega}_1, \tilde{l}_1^w), \tag{C.2}$$

$$\begin{aligned}\dot{\tilde{l}}_1^w =& \beta_e\{\exp(\tilde{l}_1^d)(\exp(\tilde{\omega}_1))/\exp(\tilde{l}_1^w) - 1\} + n - \rho(\exp(\tilde{\omega}_1)) \\ =& G_2(\tilde{\omega}_1, \tilde{l}_1^w).\end{aligned} \tag{C.3}$$

This system is well-defined for all $(\tilde{\omega}, \tilde{l}_1^w) \in R^2$. The Jacobian matrix of this system is given by

$$J_1 = \begin{pmatrix} G_{11} & G_{12} \\ G_{21} & G_{22} \end{pmatrix}, \tag{C.4}$$

where

$$G_{11} = \frac{\partial G_1}{\partial \tilde{\omega}_1} = \beta_w \{ \frac{\partial(\exp(l_1^d))}{\partial(\exp(\tilde{\omega}_1))} \frac{\exp(\tilde{\omega}_1)}{\exp(\tilde{l}_1^w)} \} < 0,$$

$$G_{12} = \frac{\partial G_1}{\partial \tilde{l}_1^w} = -\beta_w \{ \frac{\exp(\tilde{l}_1^d)}{\exp(\tilde{l}_1^w)} \} < 0,$$

$$G_{21} = \frac{\partial G_2}{\partial \tilde{\omega}_1} = [\beta_e \{ \frac{\partial(\exp(\tilde{l}_1^d))}{\partial(\exp(\tilde{\omega}_1))} \frac{1}{\exp(\tilde{l}_1^w)} \} - \frac{d\rho}{d(\exp(\tilde{\omega}_1))}] \exp(\tilde{\omega}_1),$$

and $G_{22} = -\beta_e \{ \frac{\exp(\tilde{l}_1^d)}{\exp(\tilde{l}_1^w)} \} < 0$ for all $(\tilde{\omega}_1, \tilde{l}_1^w) \in R^2$.

Therefore, we have the following set of inequalities for all $(\tilde{\omega}_1, \tilde{l}_1^w) \in R^2$:

$$\text{trace } J_1 = \underset{(-)}{G_{11}} + \underset{(-)}{G_{22}} < 0, \tag{C.5}$$

$$\begin{aligned} \det J_1 &= G_{11}G_{22} - G_{12}G_{21} \\ &= \underset{(-)}{G_{12}}(\exp(\tilde{\omega}_1)) \underset{(-)}{\frac{d\rho}{d(\exp(\tilde{\omega}_1))}} > 0, \end{aligned} \tag{C.6}$$

$$G_{11}G_{22} \neq 0. \tag{C.7}$$

This set of inequalities implies that all of Olech's sufficient conditions for global asymptotic stability of the two-dimensional system of differential equations are satisfied (see Gandolfo 1996, 354–355). This proves all assertions of Proposition 3.[10]

Proof of Proposition 4

Let us consider the global stability of the system of dynamical equations (9.12) and (9.13) in the text when appended by the following law of motion for l.

$$\hat{l} = n - \rho(\omega_1). \tag{D.1}$$

This system is a decomposable system, and we already know that the unique equilibrium point (ω_1^o, l_1^{wo}) of the independent subsystem that consists of equations (9.12) and (9.13) is globally stable (see

Proposition 3). In other words, we have $\lim_{t\to+\infty} \omega_1(t) = \omega_1^o$ so that we have $\lim_{t\to+\infty} \rho(\omega_1(t)) = \rho(\omega_1^o) = n$ (see Proposition 2). Therefore, we obtain:

$$\lim_{t\to+\infty} \hat{l}(t) = n - \lim_{t\to+\infty} \rho(\omega_1(t)) = n - n = 0. \tag{D.2}$$

This means that the whole system is globally stable in the sense that l also converges to some value although $\lim_{t\to+\infty} l(t)$ depends on the initial condition $l(0)$. We can prove the dependency of $\lim_{t\to+\infty} l(t)$ on $l(0)$ as follows. Let us define $\tilde{l} = \ln l$. Then, we can rewrite Equation (D.1) as

$$\dot{\tilde{l}} = n - \rho(\omega_1). \tag{D.3}$$

Integrating this equation with respect to time, we obtain

$$\tilde{l}(t) = \tilde{l}(0) + \int_0^t \{n - \rho(\omega_1(\tau)\}d\tau \tag{D.4}$$

so that we have

$$\lim_{t\to+\infty} \tilde{l}(t) = \tilde{l}(0) + \int_0^\infty \{n - \rho(\omega_1(\tau)\}d\tau. \tag{D.5}$$

This proves the assertion.

Proof of Proposition 5

We can rewrite the system of dynamical equations (9.12) and (9.13) in the text as follows:

$$\dot{\omega}_1 = \omega_1 \beta_w \{l_1^d(\omega_1)/l_1^w - 1\} = \tilde{G}_1(\omega_1, l_1^w) \tag{E.1}$$

$$\dot{l}_1^w = l_1^w[\beta_e\{l_1^d(\omega_1)/l_1^w - 1\} + n - \rho(\omega_1)] = \tilde{G}_2(\omega_1, l_1^w) \tag{E.2}$$

The Jacobian matrix of this system at the equilibrium point (ω_1^o, l_1^{wo}) can be written as follows:

$$J^o = \begin{pmatrix} J_{11}^o & J_{12}^o \\ J_{21}^o & J_{22}^o \end{pmatrix} \tag{E.3}$$

where

$$J_{11}^o = \omega_1^o \beta_w (l_1^d)'(\omega_1^o)/l_1^{wo} < 0,\ J_{12}^o = -\omega_1^o \beta_w l_1^d(\omega_1^o)/(l_1^{wo})^2 < 0,$$
$$J_{21}^o = l_1^{wo}[\beta_e\{(l_1^d)'(\omega_1^o)\}/l_1^{wo} - \rho'(\omega_1^o)],\ \text{and}\ J_{22}^o = -\beta_e l_1^d(\omega_1^o)/l_1^{wo} < 0.$$

Then, the characteristic equation of this system becomes

$$\Gamma^o(\lambda) = |\lambda I - J^o| = \lambda^2 + a_1\lambda + a_2 = 0, \tag{E.4}$$

where

$$\begin{aligned} a_1 &= -\,trace J^o = -J_{11}^o - J_{22}^o \\ &= [-\omega_1^o \beta_w (l_1^d)'(\omega_1^o)\} + \beta_e l_1^d(\omega_1^o)]/l_1^{wo} > 0, \end{aligned} \tag{E.5}$$

$$\begin{aligned} a_2 &= \det J^o = J_{11}^o J_{22}^o - J_{12}^o J_{21}^o \\ &= -\,\omega_1^o \beta_w l_1^d(\omega_1^o)\rho'(\omega_1^o)/l_1^{wo} > 0. \end{aligned} \tag{E.6}$$

The discriminant (D) of this system can be written as

$$D = a_1^2 - 4a_2 = D(\beta_e). \tag{E.7}$$

It is now obvious that cyclical fluctuations around the equilibrium point occur if and only if $D < 0$ holds true.

Assumption E1

The parameter β_w is so small that we have the following inequality (E.8):

$$\beta_w \omega_1^o \{(l_1^d)'(\omega_1^o)\}^2 < -4 l_1^d(\omega_1^o)\,\underset{(-)}{\rho'(\omega_1^o)}\, l_1^{wo}. \tag{E.8}$$

With Assumption E1, we now prove Proposition 5. We get for the uniquely determined bifurcation value that separates monotonic from cyclical convergence the inequality $\beta_e^H > 0$. Cyclical convergence to the balanced growth path occurs for all $\beta_e \in (0, \beta_e^H)$, and monotonic convergence to the balanced growth path occurs for all $\beta_e \in (\beta_e^H, +\infty)$.

We can easily see that $D(\beta_e)$ is a monotonically increasing continuous function of β_e with the following properties.

$$\lim_{\beta_e \to +\infty} D(\beta_e) = +\infty, \tag{E.9}$$

$$D(0) = (\omega_1^o \beta_w / l_1^{wo})[\beta_w \omega_1^o (l_1^d)'(\omega_1^o)^2 / l_1^{wo} + 4 l_1^d(\omega_1^o)\rho'(\omega_1^o)]. \qquad \text{(E.10)}$$

Assumption E1 implies that $D(0) < 0$. In this case, there exists unique positive value β_e^H such that we have $D(\beta_e^H) = 0$, $D(\beta_e) < 0$ for all $\beta_e \in (0, \beta_e^H)$, and $D(\beta_e) > 0$ for all $\beta_e \in (\beta_e^H, +\infty)$. This proves the assertion because we already proved the global convergence of the solution to the balanced growth path (see Proposition 3).

Notes

1 See also Solow (1990) for an interesting discussion of the Goodwin (1967) growth cycle model.

2 This chapter is based on Asada, Flaschel, Greiner and Proaño (2011).

3 We assume that the normal supply of labor by individual workers is measured by '1' for notational simplicity.

4 See Blanchard and Katz (1999) and Flaschel and Krolzig (2006) for its microfoundation and note that we do not use Blanchard and Katz's (1999) error correction terms here which, however, when added would not modify our stability results obtained in this chapter.

5 In the case of a Cobb–Douglas production function $K^\alpha (L_1^d)_1^\beta (L_2^w)_2^\beta$ we in particular have:

$$l_{2f}^w = \frac{\beta_2}{\beta_1 \alpha_\omega} l_1^d, \quad l_1^d = \left[\frac{\beta_2 \alpha_\omega}{\beta_1} \frac{\beta_2}{\beta_1}{}_2^\beta \omega_1 \right]^{\frac{1}{\beta_1 + \beta_2 - 1}}.$$

6 Note again that the $\pm$ term does not give rise to an ambiguous sign for the determinant of J^o (which is always positive).

7 This section is identical to that of section 8.5 except that we now have smooth factor substitution.

8 Note that the numerator is easily shown to be not only positive, but even larger than 1 under standard Keynesian assumptions on expenditure and taxation rates.

9 If myopic perfect foresight is added to their discussion of a wage Phillips curve and its theoretical underpinnings.

10 See also Flaschel (1984) for the application of Olech's theorem in the context of models of economic growth.

10. Skill Formation, Heterogeneous Labor and Investment-driven Business Fluctuations

10.1 From Marx's 'Law of Capitalist Accumulation' to Schumpeter's 'Competitive Socialism' and Beyond

This chapter starts from the hypothesis that Goodwin's (1967) Classical growth cycle, modeling the Marxian reserve army mechanism, does not represent a process of social reproduction that can be considered as adequate and sustainable in a social and democratic society in the long-run. The chapter derives on this background a basic macrodynamic framework where this form of cyclical growth and economic reproduction of capitalism is overcome by an employer of first resort, added to an economic reproduction process that is highly competitive and flexible and thus not of the type of the past Eastern socialism. Instead, there is high capital and labor mobility (concerning 'hiring' and 'firing' in particular), and thus flexibility, where fluctuations of employment in this first labor market of the economy (the private sector) are made socially acceptable through the security aspect of the flexicurity concept, that is by a second labor market where all remaining workers (and even pensioners) find meaningful occupation. The resulting model of flexicurity capitalism with its detailed transfer payment schemes is in its essence comparable to the flexicurity models developed for the Nordic welfare states and Denmark in particular.

We show that this economy exhibits a balanced growth path that is globally attracting. We also show that credit financed investment, and thus more flexible investment behavior, can be easily added without disturbing the prevailing situation of stable full capacity growth. However, we do not yet get demand- but only supply-driven business fluctuations in such an environment with both factors of production always fully employed. This combines flexible factor adjustments in the private sector with high employment security for the labor force and shows that the flexicurity variety of a capitalist economy, protected by the government, can work in a fairly balanced manner.

A similar framework for the modeling of flexicurity capitalism is also investigated in Flaschel, Greiner, Luchtenberg and Nell (2008). We here go beyond this modeling by the consideration of two types of workers in the first (and the public) labor market: skilled and high-skilled ones (as baseline representation of a full set of skill differentials). This makes the model comparable to the discussion of unskilled vs. skilled labor under contemporaneous capitalism and is intended to show that there is no systematic need for unskilled labor in a model of flexicurity growth. We do not deny, however, that there may also exist an employer of last resort (in addition to the employer of first resort) in such a framework, since there may always exist some people that are unwilling or incapable of providing work within the schemes set up in this model. Yet, the primary task of the schooling system is to provide equal opportunities for all school students in primary and secondary education and to minimize thereby the number of people who for one reason or another do not contribute to labor markets of the flexicurity model though illness or refusal may occur after school. The chapter here only considers the situation of where everybody passes successfully through the schooling system (as investigated in its components and environment in a later section of the chapter) and thus leaves the consideration of an employer of last resort to future research. However, it adds a tertiary education sector to the model where access is limited and that is responsible for the education of high-skilled workers of the model.

Solow's (1956) famous growth model is to a certain degree also of the flexicurity type, since competitive firms are always operating there on their profit-maximizing activity level and since the labor market is assumed to always guarantee full employment. We thus have employment flexibility again coupled with wage income 'security', through the assumed behavior of firms and through the assumption of perfectly flexible money wages (which may give rise to wage income fluctuations). The monetarist critique of Keynesianism and recent work by Blanchard and Katz (1999) and others suggest, however, a wage Phillips curve which, when coupled with the assumption of myopic perfect foresight regarding the price inflation rate, for example, implies a real wage Phillips curve where the growth rate of real wages depends positively on the employment rate and negatively on the level of the real wage rate. Adding such empirically supported real wage rigidity to the Solow model then gives rise to two laws of motion, now for labor intensity and the real wage, a dynamical system which approaches the situation of the overshooting Goodwin growth cycle mechanism if factor substitution in production is sufficiently inelastic and if the Blanchard and Katz (1999) real wage error correction term in the Phillips curve is sufficiently weak. Solow's growth model thus becomes thereby a variant of the Classical distributive growth cycle and its overshooting reserve army mechanism, the adequacy of which for a democratic society is questioned in this chapter.

An empirical example of what is meant by this latter statement is provided by Figure 3.1 in Chapter 3. The important insight that can be obtained from that figure for the UK 1855–1965 is that the Goodwin cycle must have been significantly shorter before 1914 (with larger fluctuations in employment during each business cycle), and that there has been a major change in it after 1945. This may be explained by significant changes in the adjustment processes of market economies for these two periods: primarily price adjustments before 1914 and primarily quantity adjustments after 1945. Based on data until 1965 one could have expected that the growth cycle had become obsolete (and maybe also the business cycle as it was claimed in the late 1960s). Yet, extended by the data shown in Figure 10.1, it is now obvious that nothing of this sort took place in the UK economy.

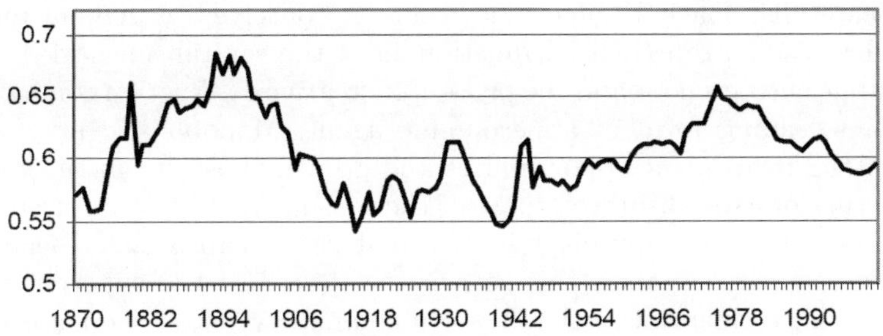

Fig. 10.1: Labor's income share, G8[1]

In fact, we see in Figure 10.1 two periods of excessive overemployment (in the language of the theory of the NAIRU) which were followed by periods of dramatic underemployment, both started by periods of the more or less pronounced occurrence of stagflation.

Generating order and economic viability in market economies by large swings in the unemployment rate (mass unemployment with human degradation of part of the families that form the society), as described and analyzed in detail in Marx (1954, Ch. 23), is one way to make capitalism work, but it must surely be critically reflected with respect to its social consequences (social segmentation or even social class clashes). Such a reproduction mechanism is not compatible with an educated and democratic society in the long-run, as we shall describe it in this chapter, which is supposed to provide equal opportunities to all of its citizens.

This situation must therefore be contrasted with an alternative social structure of accumulation that allows combining the situation of a highly competitive market economy with a human rights bill that includes the right (and the obligation) to work, and to get income from this work that at the least supports basic needs and basic happiness.

Criticizing existing Eastern state socialism that existed at the time from the viewpoint of immaturity, Schumpeter (1942) developed a concept of socialism for countries in the state of maturity that can be characterized as competitive socialism built on foundations erected unconsciously through the big enterprises created by the Rockefellers, the Vanderbilts and other famous dynasties in the Western industrialized countries. In Part II of his book, Schumpeter discusses the question of whether this type of socialism can work, what the corresponding socialist blueprints should look like and to what extent they are superior to the capitalist mark II blueprints that he conceived as having made obsolete the entrepreneurial functioning of the capitalism mark I, the dynamic entrepreneur and the process of creative destruction conducted by this leading form of an economic agent. Monopolistic practices, vanishing investment opportunities and growing hostility in the social structure of capitalism were part of the reasons that characterized the decomposition of capitalism in his analysis of capitalism, socialism and democracy. Against this scenery he described the superiority of the socialist blueprint of the Western competitive type, the transition to this form of social structure of accumulation and the comparative efficiency of such economies. In a separate chapter he discusses the human element in this type of economy, the problem of work organization and the integration of bourgeois forms of management under capitalism into this type of socialism and the incentive problems this creates for the behavior of these economic agents.

The central message of Schumpeter's (1942) work, *Capitalism, Socialism and Democracy*, is that socialism is created out of Western capitalist economies, and not on the basis of the (now past) Eastern type of socialism (which he characterized as 'the case of premature adoption of the principle of socialism', p.223). Instead, socialism had to be competitively organized through large production units and their efficient – though bureaucratic – management, a form of management that is developed out of the principles used under capitalism in the efficient conduct of large (internationally oriented) enterprises. Schumpeter viewed his type of socialism as culturally indeterminate, but then discusses extensively the possibility of democracy under socialism, organized as dynamic competition for political leadership under majority voting, leading to specific rules for a strong government. It is one of the great contributions of Schumpeter's (1942) book to not only have initiated a new concept of socialism, but also of having established a new type of democracy theory and its principles under a socialist type of accumulation structure.

After World War II the discussion of how to incorporate welfare principles in the conduct of existing capitalist economies has, however, become more or less the focus of interest, formulated as 'social market economy' by Ludwig Erhard in Germany in particular. The rise of the welfare state was thus the central topic, at least in European market economies, by which they responded to the strengthened influence of the Eastern socialist economies on world politics and on the evolution of socialism in various parts of the world. Types of welfare states were, for example, discussed in detail in Esping-Anderson's (1990) *The Three Worlds of Welfare Capitalism* among others. But Kalecki (1943) had already pointed to limitations in the evolution of the welfare state and its full employment concept in his essay on the 'Political aspects of full employment'. Deregulation principles and the fall of the welfare indeed took place in Western market economies after the stagflationary period of the 1970s in a more or less intensive way, with the gradual fall of the welfare state often being associated with an insufficient recovery from the inflationary episodes and their implication for unemployment after World War II.

Yet, labor market deregulation theories and policy proposals have meanwhile also created a situation where questions are raised concerning the social consequences of such policies when they are conducted as a 'cold turkey' strategies as they are often suggested by neoclassical mainstream economists. Social degradation, social segmentation processes and the progressive evolution of social conflicts based on them may indeed be incompatible with the proper conduct of democracy in the Western type of economies where labor market deregulation processes and the cutback of the welfare state occurred to a significant degree – at least in the longer-run. 'Workfare' has therefore become one of the keywords that attempts to combine efficient labor market performance with welfare principles; see for example Vis (2007) on 'States of welfare or states of workfare? Welfare state restructuring in 16 capitalist democracies, 1985–2002'.

In this chapter we will, however, favor another concept that attempts to overcome the deficiencies of the purely economically oriented process of labor market deregulations, the concept of flexicurity capitalism (in place of the Schumpeterian concept of competitive socialism, to which it is in fact not related in the literature and in the current numerous political discussions of flexicurity principles); see for example the discussion 'Towards Common Principles of Flexicurity – Council Conclusions' conducted by the Council (Employment, Social Policy, Health and Consumer Affairs) of the European Union.

The Danish flexicurity discussion may provide a typical example on the way to such an alternative; see for example the newsletter: 'Future Watch, October 2006: Flexicurity – Denmark-Style' of the Center for Strategic and International Studies (CSIS). However, the discussions held so far lack rigorous and formal model building of the principles, the economic structure and the dynamics of flexicurity capitalism. To build a model of the reproduction schemes of this future type of an economy needs a presentation of its system of national accounts and the behavior of economic agents within such a system. Moreover, the adjustment processes on the market for labor and for goods as well as the functioning of financial markets in such an economy need detailed investigation. Analysis of this type is surely at best in its state of infancy. The present chapter intends to contribute to such an analysis and does so against the background of the models of capitalism we have developed in this book, in particular concerning Marx's general law of capitalist accumulation. In modeling our future in this way we hope to show that there is a variety of capitalism that not only pays respect to human rights, in particular UN article 23,[2] but that is compatible with the evolution of democracy in the long-run.

By contrast, a laissez-faire capitalistic society that ruins family structures to a considerable degree (through alienated work, degrading unemployment and education- and value-decomposing visual media) cannot be made compatible with a democratic society in the long-run, since it produces conflicts that may range from social segmentation to class conflicts, racial clashes and more. We argue in this chapter that stable balanced reproduction is possible under a social regime of flexicurity capitalism that is in addition backed by reflected educational principles concerning skill formation, equal opportunities and citizenship education in a democratic society.

The abstract vision of a new reproduction scheme of capitalism as it is formulated in this chapter can be compared – as already indicated in part – with the work of Quesnay, Marx, Schumpeter and Keynes. It may be considered as radical and fundamental (but also as infeasible) as Quesnay's design of the *Tableau Économique* for the French economy, an ideal system where the productive sector was at the center of interest and all taxes were paid out of rent (by the landlords). It may be compared with Marx's reproduction schemes, in *Capital* Volume II, for a capitalist economy of his times (not considered feasible under capitalism by him). It may also be compared to Schumpeter's vision in his work *Capitalism, Socialism and Democracy*, where he claimed that socialism would be the consequence of Western type capitalism (as created by the Rockefellers and other industrial dynasties) and not the result of the Eastern socialism that existed at his time. It may finally also be compared with the Social Philosophy of Keynes' *General Theory* and his discussion of the means by which the trade cycle of conventional Western capitalism might be tamed. All these aspects may play a role in the understanding and the appraisal of the model of flexicurity capitalism that is designed in this chapter.

In Section 10.2 we consider the accounts of such an economy with particular emphasis on the distinction between skilled and high–skilled workers both in the private and the public sector. Section 10.3 considers the stability of such an economy, where the wage dynamics are determined by high-skilled workers according to a Blanchard and Katz type Phillips curve and where labor intensity growth is determined by realized profits. Section 10.4 considers stylized presentations of the schooling system for Finland as an existing example as well as our hypothetical flexicurity model. In section 10.5 we discuss the role of nominal credits in such an economy. The flexicurity system is here extended to a treatment of nominal financial assets and resulting Keynesian business cycle fluctuations. Section 10.6 concludes the chapter.

10.2 Skill Differentiated Labor Markets in Models of Flexicurity Growth

The concept of 'flexicurity' attempts to find a balance between flexibility for employers (and employees) and security for employees.

> The Commission's 1997 Green Paper on 'Partnership for a new organization of work' stressed the importance of both flexibility and security to competitiveness and the modernization of work organization. The idea also features prominently in the 'adaptability pillar' of the EU employment guidelines, where 'the social partners are invited to negotiate at all appropriate levels agreements to modernise the organization of work, including flexible working arrangements, with the aim of making undertakings productive and competitive and achieving the required balance between flexibility and security.' This 'balance' is also consistently referred to in the Commission's Social Policy Agenda 2000–2005. (COM (2000) 379 final, Brussels, 28 June 2000)[3]

We now design, as a rigorous modeling proposal for the flexicurity debate in Europe and as an alternative to the Goodwin growth cycle representation of capitalism, a model of economic growth that rests in place of overaccumulation (in the prosperity phase) and mass unemployment (in the stagnant phase) on a second labor market, which through its institutional setup guarantees full employment in its interaction with the first labor market, the employment in the industrial sector of the economy, which is modeled as highly flexible and competitive. This model of flexicurity capitalism extends the approach of Flaschel, Greiner, Luchtenberg and Nell (2008), towards a treatment of heterogeneous skills and the skill formation processes this requires in an advanced macroeconomy.

In the basic framework we are considering an economy where the workforce (and all of its components) are growing with a given natural rate n. We denote the sector of firms of the economy as sector 1. The account of that sector is identical to that presented in Section 8.2 so that we do not repeat it here but refer to that chapter. Instead, we next consider the skilled and high-skilled household sectors.

Skilled and high-skilled household sectors are composed of two types of workers, one working in the private sector and the remaining part in the public sector of the economy. The total number of high-skilled workers is $L_a^w = \alpha_s t_a L_o$ and that of skilled workers is given by: $L_b^w = (1-\alpha_s)t_b L_o$. We are assuming here a given population L with constant deterministic age structure $L = tL_o$, where T is the given lifetime of an individual household and where L_o denotes the number of people of a certain year of age. This number is assumed as constant for all vintages between 0 and T. We moreover assume here that the work life of skilled workers is t_b years and that of high-skilled ones $t_a(< t_b)$ years. We finally have assumed here that there is a given ratio α_s of students[4] having just finished their (comprehensive and all day) schooling years who are (by exit or entry exams) qualified to enter the phase of higher education (leading to high-skilled degrees at 'universities' and other tertiary education institutions). Given the constant vintage structure within the population we thus have a workforce $L_b^w = (1-\alpha_s)t_b L_o$ of skilled workers in the economy (who start their working life directly after (primary and secondary) schooling, while $L_a^w = \alpha_s t_a L_o$ is the number of high-skilled workers of the considered model economy. Year-in year-out the economy has therefore a given amount of school students L_s, university students L_u, high-skilled workers L_a^w, skilled workers L_b^w and retired workers L_r (contributing work according to their willingness and capability) for which it must organize education and work in the primary and the secondary labor markets (including the government activities as an employer of first resort).

Table 10.1: Households 1 and 2: income account (households A, B)

Households 1: high-skilled (a) and skilled (b) workers in primary labor markets

Uses	Resources
$C_1 = c_1(1-\tau_1)(\omega_{1a}L_{1a}^d + \omega_{1b}L_{1b}^d)$	
$T = \tau_1(\omega_{1a}L_{1a}^d + \omega_{1b}L_{1b}^d)$	
$\omega_{2a}L_{3a}^w,\ L_{3a}^w = L_a^w - (L_{1a}^w + L_{2a}^w)$	
$\omega_{2b}L_{3b}^w,\ L_{3b}^w = L_b^w - (L_{1b}^w + L_{2b}^w)$	
$\omega_{2b}L_r, L_r = t_r L_o$	
S_1	$\omega_{1a}L_{1a}^d + \omega_{1b}L_{1b}^d$
$Y_1^w = \omega_{1a}L_{1a}^d + \omega_{1b}L_{1b}^d$	Y_1^w

Households 2: Secondary high-skilled (a) and skilled (b) workers

Uses	Resources
C_{2a}	$\omega_{2a}(L_{2a}^w + L_{3a}^w) = Y_{2a}^w$,
	$\omega_{2a} = \alpha_{2a}\omega_{1a}$
C_{2b}	$\omega_{2b}(L_{2b}^w + L_{3b}^w) = Y_{2b}^w$,
	$\omega_{2b} = \alpha_{2b}\omega_{1b}$
$Y_2^w = Y_{2a}^w + Y_{2b}^w$	$Y_2^w = Y_{2a}^w + Y_{2b}^w$

Both households of type 1 are taxed at the same tax rate τ_1 and consume with the same marginal propensity to consume c_1 goods of amount C_1. They pay (all) income taxes T and they pay in addition – via further transfers – all workers' income in the labor markets that is not coming from firms and from government tax revenues (which is equivalent to an unemployment insurance and therefore indexed with an index 3). Moreover, they pay the pensions of the retired households ($\omega_{2b}L_r$) and accumulate their remaining income S_1 in the form of company pensions into a fund R that is administrated by firms (with inflow S_1, see the sector of households and with outflow $\delta_1 R$). Wage rates are determined by wage negotiations of high-skilled workers in the industrial sector, while all other real wages are constant fractions of these negotiated wages and are uniform for all skilled workers in the government sector and for retired persons (who, however, receive extra company pension payments according to their accumulated contributions to the work, their occupation time in the primary sector).

The transfers $\omega_{2a}(L_a^w - (L_{1a}^w + L_{2a}^w))$ and $\omega_{2b}(L_b^w - (L_{1b}^w + L_{2b}^w))$ can be considered as solidarity payments, since workers from the primary labor markets who lose their job will automatically be employed in the second labor market where full employment is guaranteed by the government (as employer of first resort). We consider this employment as skill preserving, since it can be viewed as ordinary office or handicraft work (subject only to learning by doing when such workers return to the first labor market).

The secondary sector of households is here modeled in the simplest way that is available. Households employed in the secondary labor markets, that is, $L_{2a}^w + L_{3a}^w, L_{2b}^w + L_{3b}^w$, pay no taxes and totally consume their income. We thus have classical saving habits in this household sector, while households of type 1 may have positive or negative savings S_1 as residual from their income and expenditures. We assume as the law of motion for pension funds R:

$$\dot{R} = S_1 - \delta_1 R$$

where δ_1 is the rate by which these funds are depreciated through company pension payments to the 'officially retired' workers L_r assumed to be a constant fraction of the 'active' workforce L^w. These worker households are added here as not really inactive, but offer work according to their still existing capabilities and willingness that can be considered as an addition to the supply of work already organized by the government, $L_{2a}^w + L_{3a}^w + L_{2b}^w + L_{3b}^w$, that is the working potential of the officially retired persons remains an active and valuable contribution to the working hours that are supplied by the members of the society. It is obvious that the proper allocation of the work hours under the control of the government needs thorough reflection from the microeconomic and the social point of view which, however, cannot be a topic in a chapter on the macroeconomics of such an economy.

Table 10.2: Retired households: income account

Uses	Resources
C_r	$\omega_{2b}L_r + \delta_1 R, L_r = t_r L_o$
Y^r	Y^r

The income account of the retired households, shown in Table 10.2, shows that they receive pension payments as if they worked in the secondary skilled segment of the economy and they get in addition individual transfer income (company pensions) from the accumulated funds R in proportion to the time (and type as which) they have been active in the first labor market as portion of $\delta_1 R$ by which the pension funds R are reduced in each period.

There is finally the government sector which is also formulated in a very simple way:

Table 10.3: The government: income account – fiscal authority/employer of first resort

Uses	Resources
$G = \alpha_g T$	$T = \tau_1(\omega_{1a}L^d_{1a} + \omega_{1b}L^d_{1b})$
$\omega_{2a}L^w_{2a} = \alpha_a T$	
$\omega_{2b}L^w_{2b} = ((1-\alpha_g) - \alpha_a)T$	
$\omega_{2a}L^w_{3a}, L^w_{3a} = L^w_a - (L^w_{1a} + L^w_{2a})$	$\omega_{2a}L^w_{3a}$
$\omega_{2b}L^w_{3b}, L^w_{3b} = L^w_b - (L^w_{1b} + L^w_{2b})$	$\omega_{2a}L^w_{3a}$
$\omega_{2b}L^w_r$	$\omega_{2b}L^w_r$
Y^g	Y^g

The government receives income taxes, the solidarity payments (employment benefits) for the secondary labor markets paid by workers in the primary labor markets and old-age pension payments. It uses the taxes to finance government goods demand G and the surplus of taxes over these government expenditures to actively employ both skilled and high-skilled workers in the government sector. In addition it employs the workers receiving 'unemployment benefits' and it in fact also employs the 'retired' persons to the extent they can still contribute to the various employment activities. We therefore have that the total labor force in the secondary labor markets is employed through the government which is organized by government in the way it does this in the administration of the state in all modern market economies.

We assume that real wages in the public sector are limited by the following conditions

$$\omega_{2a} \geq \bar{\omega}_{2a}, \quad \omega_{2b} \geq \bar{\omega}_{2b},$$

where $\bar{\omega}_{2a}, \bar{\omega}_{2b}$ are the levels of real wages where the expressions L^w_{3a}, L^w_{3b} are zero, that is where the planned employment in the private and the public sector are just sufficient to clear the labor market. This condition therefore provides a lower bound for public real wages which prevents supply constraints from the side of the labor market in this model of flexicurity capitalism.

In sum we get that workers are employed either in the primary labor market and if not there then by the government sector concerning public administration, infrastructure services, educational services or other public services (in addition there is potential labor supply L_r from the retired households, which due to the long life expectancy in modern societies can remain effective suppliers of specific work over a considerable span of time). In this way the whole workforce is always fully employed in this model of social growth (and the retired persons according to their capabilities and willingness) and thus does not suffer from human degradation in particular. Of course, there are a variety of issues concerning state organized work that point to problems in the organization of such work, but all such problems also exist in all actual industrialized market economies in one way or another. We thus have a Classical growth model where full employment is not assumed, but actively constructed and where – due to the assumed expenditure structure – Say's law holds true, that is the capital stock of firms is also always fully utilized, since all savings are additions to the pension fund in terms of commodities and since all profits are invested. For the inclusion of debt financed investment (which is excluded here) see Flaschel, Greiner, Luchtenberg and Nell (2008).

10.3 Dynamics: Stable and Sustainable Balanced Reproduction

Based on Flaschel, Greiner, Luchtenberg and Nell (2008) we have in this model type a real wage Phillips curve as it was described here in the introductory section which can be represented in stylized form as follows ($G^1(1) = 0, G^2(0) = 0$):[5]

$$\hat{v}_{1a} = G^1\left(\frac{v_{1a}}{v^o_{1a}}\right) + G^2\left(\frac{y^p}{l^w_{1a}} - \bar{u}_w\right) = \tilde{G}^1(v_{1a}) + \tilde{G}^2(l^w_{1a}), \quad (10.1)$$
$$\tilde{G}^{1'}, \tilde{G}^{2'} < 0, \; v_{1a} = \frac{\omega_{1a}}{z}$$

The first term on the right-hand side represents the Blanchard and Katz (1999) real wage error correction term, while the second one derives from the utilization rate $u_w = L^d_{1a}/L^w_{1a} = l^d_{1a}/l^w_{1a}$ of the workforce employed by firms expressed in per unit of capital form (see the next law of motion) where l^d_{1a} is here assumed a given magnitude due to fixed proportions in production and due to full capacity growth. The assumption $\tilde{G}^{2'} < 0$ thus simply states that real wage dynamics depends positively on the utilization rate of the high-skilled workers employed by firms. We stress again that all other types of work exhibit fixed wage differentials with respect to the high-skilled workers of the primary labor market. This allows us to consider only their real wage in the dynamical investigations that follow below – in place of the full array of real wages represented by: $0 < \omega_{2b} < \omega_{2a} < \omega_{1b} < \omega_{1a} < z$. The growth rate of the high-skilled workforce of firms (the recruitment of new high-skilled workers), $\hat{L}^w_{1a}$, also depends positively on the rate of capacity utilization $u_w = l^d/l^w_{1a}$, more precisely: the above shown utilization gap, as suggested by Okun's law, and thus also negatively on its own level. Moreover, since the second state variable of the model $/l^w_{1a}$ is to be defined by zL^w_{1a}/K we get a negative effect from the rate of profit on the growth rate of this state variable (through the investment behavior of firms) and thus a positive effect of real wages in the second law of notion of the economy which in general terms therefore reads:

$$\hat{l}^w_{1a} = -\hat{K} + \hat{z} + \hat{L}^w_{1a} = H^1(v_{1a}) + H^2(l^w_1), \quad (10.2)$$
$$H^{1'} > 0, H^{2'} < 0, \quad l^w_{1a} = zL^w_{1a}/K.$$

We assume that the steady state value of v^o_{1a} is given (by social compromise) in such a way that we get for the rate of profit of firms in the steady state the equation:

$$\hat{K} = \rho^o = y^p - \delta - v^o_{1a} l^{wo}_{1a} - v^o_{1b} l^{wo}_{1b} = y^p - \delta - v^o_{1a} l^{wo}_{1a} - \alpha_{1b} v^o_{1a} l^{wo}_{1b} = \hat{z} = \bar{m}$$

with $l^{wo}_{1a} = l^{wo}_{1b} = y^p/\bar{u}^w$. Under this assumption we have that the laws of motion (10.1), (10.3) indeed exhibit the values v^o_{1a}, l^{wo}_{1a} as their in general unique interior steady state position. Moreover, all ratios of the type zL/K are then constant in the steady state, since all possible l values that can be considered here are constant in time.[6]

The 2D dynamics (10.1), (10.3) allow for the application of the following Liapunov function to be used in the stability proof that follows:

$$V(v_{1a}, l_{1a}^w) = \int_{v_{1a}^o}^{v_{1a}} H^1(\tilde{v}_{1a})/\tilde{v}_{1a} d\tilde{v}_{1a} + \int_{l_{1a}^{wo}}^{l_{1a}^w} -\tilde{G}^2(\tilde{l}_{1a}^w)/\tilde{l}_{1a}^w d\tilde{l}_{1a}^w.$$

This function describes by its graph a 3D sink with the steady state of the economy as its lowest point, since the above integrates two functions that are negative to the left of the steady state values and positive to their right. For the first derivative of the Liapunov function along the trajectories of the considered dynamical system we moreover get:

$$\begin{aligned}
\dot{V} &= dV(v_{1a}(t), l_{1a}^w)/dt = \left(H^1(v_{1a})/v_{1a}\right)\dot{v}_{1a} - \left(\tilde{G}^2(l_{1a}^w)/l_{1a}^w\right)\dot{l}_{1a}^w \\
&= H^1(v_{1a})\hat{v}_{1a} - \tilde{G}^2(l_{1a}^w)\hat{l}_{1a}^w \\
&= H^1(v_{1a})(\tilde{G}^1(v_{1a}) + \tilde{G}^2(l_{1a}^w)) - \tilde{G}^2(l_{1a}^w)(H^1(v_{1a}) + H^2(l_{1a}^w)) \\
&= H^1(v_{1a})\tilde{G}^1(v_{1a}) - \tilde{G}^2(l_{1a}^w)H^2(l_{1a}^w) \\
&= -H^1(v_{1a})(-\tilde{G}^1(v_{1a})) - (-\tilde{G}^2(l_{1a}^w))(-H^2(l_{1a}^w)) \\
&\leq 0 \qquad [= 0 \quad \text{if and only if} \quad v_{1a} = v_{1a}^o, l_{1a}^w = l_{1a}^{wo}],
\end{aligned}$$

since the multiplied functions have the same sign to the right and to the left of their steady state values and thus lead to positive products with a minus sign in front of them (up to the situation where the economy is already sitting in the steady state). We thus have proved that there holds:

Proposition 1: *The interior steady state of the dynamics (10.1), (10.3) is a global sink of the function V, defined on the positive orthant of the phase space, and is attracting in this domain, since the function V is strictly decreasing along the trajectories of the dynamics in the positive orthant of the phase space, that is its economic part.*

There is a further law of motion in the background of the model that needs to be considered in order to provide a complete statement on the viability of the considered model of flexicurity capitalism. This law of motion describes the evolution of the pension fund per unit of the capital stock $\eta = \frac{R}{K}$ and is obtained from the defining equation $\dot{R} = S_1 - \delta_1 R$ as follows:

$$\hat{\eta} = \hat{R} - \hat{K} = \frac{\dot{R}}{K}\frac{K}{R} - \rho = \frac{S_1 - \delta_1 R}{K}/\eta - \rho, \text{ i.e.:}$$

$$\dot{\eta} = \frac{S_1}{K} - (\delta_1 + \rho)\eta = s_1 - (\delta_1 + \rho)\eta,$$

with savings of households of type 1 and profits of firms per unit of capital being given by:[7]

$$\begin{aligned} s_1 &= (1 - c_1)(1 - \tau_1)(v_{1a} + v_{1b})y^p - v_{2b}l_r \\ &\quad - [v_{2a}l_a^w - (v_{1a} + v_{2a}\alpha_a\tau_1(v_{1a} + v_{1b}))y^p] \\ &\quad - [v_{2b}l_b^w - (v_{1b} + v_{2b}((1 - \alpha_g) - \alpha_a)\tau_1(v_{1a} + v_{1b}))y^p], \\ \rho &= y^p[1 - (v_{1a} + v_{2a})] - \delta. \end{aligned}$$

For the ratio of savings to GDP $\theta_1 = S_1/Y^p = s_1/y^p$ we get in the steady state of the economy the expression:

$$\begin{aligned} \theta_1^o &= (1 - c_1)(1 - \tau_1)(v_{1a}^o + v_{1b}^o) - v_{2b}^o y_r^o \\ &\quad - [v_{2a}^o y_a^{wo} - (v_{1a}^o + v_{2a}^o\alpha_a\tau_1(v_{1a}^o + v_{1b}^o))] \\ &\quad - [v_{2b}^o y_b^{wo} - (v_{1b}^o + v_{2b}^o((1 - \alpha_g) - \alpha_a)\tau_1(v_{1a}^o + v_{1b}^o))], \end{aligned}$$

with $y_r = l_r/y^p = zL^r/Y^p, y_a^w = zL^w/Y^p, y_b^w = zL_b^w/Y^p$. For $v_{2a}^o = \bar{v}_{2a}, v_{2b}^o = \bar{v}_{2b}$, that is the case where wages in the government sector are clearing the labor market without any need for employment of first resort, this gives:

$$\theta_1^o = (1 - c_1)(1 - \tau_1)(v_{1a}^o + v_{1b}^o) - \bar{v}_{2b}l_r^o,$$

that is, this ratio is positive if $L_r/(Y^p/z) = L_r/L_{1a}^d$ is sufficiently small. We therefore need a condition that limits the ratio $L_r/L = t_r L_o/L = t_r/t$ from above in combination with conditions that limit (from above) the real wages $\omega_{2a}^o \geq \bar{\omega}_{2a}, \omega_{2b}^o \geq \bar{\omega}_{2b}$ paid in the government sector in order to get a positive ratio θ_1^o. This shows that such upper limits on wages in the public labor markets as well as in base pension payments are needed and provide sufficient conditions for a positive savings ratio with respect to GDP Y^p. If this is given, we will have a positive steady state value for company pension funds per unit of capital $\eta^o = s_1^o/(\delta_1 + \bar{m})$ and also a positive value for the percentage of company pension payments as a fraction of base pension payments γ_1^o, which is given by:

$$\gamma_1^o = \theta_1^o/\sigma_r \leq (1 - c_1)(1 - \tau_1)\frac{v_{1a}^o + v_{1b}^o}{v_{2b}^o}\frac{y^p}{y_r} - 1,$$

where $\sigma_r = \omega_{2b}^o L_r / Y^p$ is the share of base pension payments in GDP. The establishment of a desired ratio between company pension payments and base pension payments therefore demands (besides a viable ratio t_r concerning the age structure of the economy) the choice of appropriate real wages in the public sector and it is in any case limited from above by the expression on the right-hand side in the above equation.

10.4 Educational Systems: Basic Structures and Implications

In this section we extend the flexicurity model towards the integration of an educational sector. We assume as in the preceding sections that there are only two types of workers, skilled (b) and high-skilled (a) ones. We stress that we assume a stationary population $L = tL_o$ in this and the next section, where L_o is the stationary number of people of age $\tau, \tau = 1, \cdots, t$, with t denoting the given lifespan of each individual agent of the economy. There are $L_r = t_r L_o$ retired people in each given year, $L_s = t_s L_o$ students on the primary and secondary education level, $L_u = \alpha_g t_u L_o$ students on the tertiary education level, $L_b = t_b L_o$ skilled workers and $L_a = t_a L_o$ high-skilled workers (and $L_c = t_c L_o$ children in the background of the model). The natural rate of the preceding sections is thus set equal to 0 here for reasons of simplicity. The t_x coefficients express the number of years an agent will be part of this population group.[8] Finally, it is assumed that the current system allows a fraction α_s of $t_s L_o$ to go to university to become high-skilled workers, while the remainder enters the workforce as a member of L_b^w after having finished school with a final certificate. To keep the model simple, we abstain from vocational schools, apprenticeships or dual systems.

Before we come to a graphical representation and analysis of such a stylized educational system, we provide in Figure 10.2 a brief representation of an existing example: the Finnish educational structure as it is provided by the National Board of Education in Finland.

The distinguishing factors of this school systems are:

1) a comprehensive compulsory school for all students with no differentiation between good learners and those with learning difficulties,
2) two ways to finish secondary school, both of which can lead to a higher qualification (to enter universities or polytechnics),

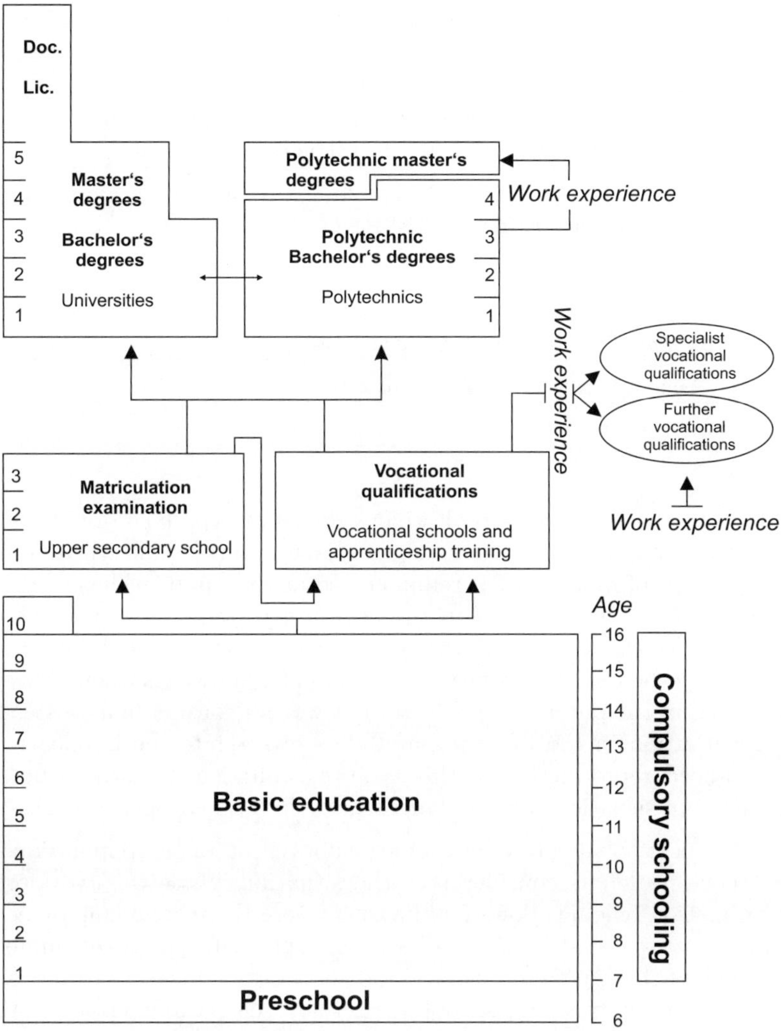

Fig. 10.2: The education system of Finland: stylized representation[9]

3) further details which are not seen in this figure such as the renouncement of grading until the last two years of basic education.

For our purposes, however, we use the somewhat simplified structure for an educational system underlying our model of flexicurity capitalism, as shown in Table 10.4 below.

Table 10.4: Education in the flexicurity model: baseline case of a stationary population

Retired People $t_r L_o$: base pensions and company pensions (labor market contribution acc. to willingness and capability)				
Occup. 1b active	Occup. 2b (partly EFR)	Occup. 2b (EFR)	Occup. 2a	Occup. 1a
			Tertiary Education (at Universities)	
Secondary School Education: $t_s L_0$ (aggregated)				
Primary School Education: $t_s L_0$ (aggregated)				
Pre-School (not modeled)				

Note with respect to this table that workers of type b can only be in one of two situations as far as their salary group is concerned, since employment of first resort is remunerated at the same level as workers of type b actively employed in the government sector. For workers of type a, however, this implies that they can be in one of three states concerning their salaries, since they are paid higher wages when actively employed in the public sector. Note that we will consider only a steady state situation in the following and thus investigate the implications of balanced reproduction in this type of capitalism (shown to be an attractor of situations of unbalanced growth in an earlier section).

With respect to the above stationary subdivision of the population of the economy let us consider now the situation where this workforce reproduction scheme allows for the case where there is no employment of first resort needed for the workforce of type a. If $\alpha_s L_o$ is the number of students that go from primary and secondary education to tertiary education after finishing school we get for the parameter α_s in the considered situation on the one hand the definitional relationship:

$$L_a^w = \alpha_s t_a L_o, \quad L_b^w = (1-\alpha_s) t_b L_o.$$

On the other hand we have as active employment rules for workers of type 1:

$$L_{1a}^w = \frac{Y^p}{z}, \quad L_{2a}^w = \alpha_h T/\omega_{2a} = \alpha_h \tau_h \left(\frac{\omega_{1a}}{\omega_{2a}} L_{1a}^w + \frac{\omega_{1b}}{\omega_{2a}} L_{1b}^w \right).$$

The equilibrium condition $L_a^w = L_{1a}^w + L_{2a}^w$ then implies

$$\alpha_s t_a L_o = \frac{Y^p}{z}\left(1 + \alpha_h \tau_h \left(\frac{\omega_{1a}}{\omega_{2a}} + \frac{\omega_{1b}}{\omega_{2a}}\right)\right)$$

which in turn gives:[10]

$$\alpha_s = 1 + \alpha_h \tau_h \left(\frac{\omega_{1a}}{\omega_{2a}} + \frac{\omega_{1b}}{\omega_{2a}}\right) \frac{L_{1a}^d}{t_a L_o}$$

This ratio must be applied for the access to universities if the reproduction of high-skilled workers is such that no first resort employment is necessary for them. A numerical example may help to understand this condition in more detail. Since workers employed in the industrial sector pay all taxes we may assume the following crude estimates for the expressions that determine the equilibrium α_s:

$$\alpha_h = 1/3, \quad \tau_h = 0.5, \quad \frac{\omega_{1a}}{\omega_{2a}} = 4, \quad \frac{\omega_{1b}}{\omega_{2a}} = 2, \quad \frac{L_{1a}^d}{t_a L_o} = 0.5.$$

This gives for α_s the value $\alpha_s = 0.5$, a value that coincides with what is suggested by studies of the OECD. The above formula for the university access ratio α_s clearly shows the possibilities by which this ratio may be increased (if desirable).

Even though we divide the working population into two groups – skilled and high-skilled workers – it should be taken into consideration that skilled workers have finished their schooltime on the same level as high-skilled ones, only with lesser results in their final examinations which are equal to 'Abitur' in Germany, 'Baccalaureate' in France or 'A levels' in Great Britain. Thus it is guaranteed that the workforce as a whole is well educated and trained far above basic skills. To gain such high qualifications might be regarded as an exaggerated aim, but examples, especially from the Scandinavian countries, show that a strict concept of 'demand and support' will be able to get such results in the school population.

In this section, we will first discuss the conditions of a suitable educational system (pre-school and school, yet with an emphasis on school education). To gain the described results demands a strict support of the rules of 'equal opportunities' in order to eliminate all hindrances for children to participate in an education that fits their abilities and allows them to meet the requirements of the schools. Furthermore we will discuss the competitive way in which students in their final exams gain university access or not. This concludes the relationship of equal opportunities and competition in a more general aspect.

Secondly, we will deal with the demand of lifelong learning assuming that part of all the peoples' leisure time is used for keeping their skills up to date as well as accepting skills enhancements offered by their employers. A generally accepted necessity of lifelong learning will allow for a continuous high skill level in all sectors where skilled or high-skilled workers are doing their job, but it holds true in a similar way for all pensioners who still feel fit to take an active part in the workforce.

We will finally deepen our reflections on education by discussing the role of equal opportunities in its close relationship to human rights which are strongly related to democracy. This leads to the discussion of democracy and citizenship education as well as human rights education. It should be clarified that we can here only outline these questions which will be discussed in more detail in future work.

The School System

To become – and be – a member of the workforce demands great engagement even if employment is guaranteed, although the industrial sector is free to hire and fire, since the employer of first resort will take over the fired workers, both skilled and high skilled persons. All workers owe their education and welfare expenses to the taxpayers, the industrial workers in this model type. Thus, the system is extremely supportive by giving work to all, but it is also highly demanding by expecting full commitment by everyone due to the fact that it depends on the mutual giving and taking in this society. This demands a high consensus within the society with regard to the necessity of work and the working conditions. It is the task of education to provide students in (pre)schools not only with the necessary skills to become adequate workers in their later professions and jobs but also to help them to understand this system and to integrate themselves into it. This kind of integration is not to be misunderstood as a simple adaption but it concludes – as does socialization – the development of an independent, mature and responsible personality which is part of the aim of education as described in this chapter. A positive view on work is a necessity in a society where all persons are assumed to find work, but are also obliged to engage in their work, even after their retirement. A contradicting attitude towards work in the public and media discourse where consumption and leisure time are often more favored than work, is not compatible with the demands of our model. Based on these underlying assumptions, skills are here understood in a broad sense which transcends intellectual or technical competencies, but include work attitudes, teamwork etc.

As we have made clear above, all students will be led to leave school on the level of 'Abitur'. This demands a good education from the very beginning. Therefore, in our society 'school' starts in an early stage, also due to the fact that the mother will normally return to work two years after the birth of the child. Our educational system – named school system for reasons of simplicity – begins for children at the age of 2, though nursery schools may be available for younger children if parents prefer so. All forms of schooling are thought to be all-day institutions though families may have a choice of lesser schooling until the child is 3 years old. In nursery schools children are cared for by trained personnel. Even if there is no formal training, they already learn first – mainly social – skills which include first behavior rules in a community.

Further skills that are learnt in this age are linguistic and communicative ones. This happens in families, too, but in an educational setting as in a nursery school more support will be given by guiding the children. As in kindergarten, children also learn at the age of 2 to use materials and thus train their fine motor skills. They are also trained to use their bodies and exercise their movements. This demands caretakers with a good training at university level. This also holds true for the following kindergarten period which should last for three years. Skills which are already trained in a first approach in the nursery schools will now be deepened in a more and more systematic way though, of course, the stages of development of a child have to be kept in mind as well as the necessity of formal and especially informal play. When the last kindergarten year is either transferred to primary schools or organized together with them, it is possible to allow for a gradual transition into school.

Following the Scandinavian role model of schooling, all children will be together in a general school at least until grade 8 or 9 when they are about 15 or 16 years old (see, for example, Ministry of Education and Science of Sweden 2004). Any earlier division into different school types would lead to a selection before all main abilities are developed so that young people would be bereaved of the chance to evolve into the skilled person that they are. A longer period of learning together will furthermore help them to develop social skills. Finally, a selection before or just when they have reached puberty would probably intensify the general problems of that time. When students have to opt for different types of secondary or high school thereafter they can be aware that all types will lead them to a matriculation certificate though with different focuses (either more academic or more technical) and a different length of schooling (between two and four years depending on the preferences of a student) so that they are able to plan their secondary school time with the help of their teachers, following their individual abilities and interests.

This school system needs to bring to light all abilities and interests a child may have, since otherwise the ambitious aim of a final certificate for all cannot be reached. This means that the school education works in a way such that educational support for the differently talented students obeys the principle of equal opportunities. We have a double task resulting from the principles of equal opportunities where each child will be given the optimal support. The one task is to eliminate social or structural hindrances such as family income, level of education of the parents, social stratum, migration background etc. In our system, these forms of disadvantages should become less important when all – or at least most – parents will be skilled or high-skilled persons with an adequate income. Yet, disadvantages – which are often connected with discrimination – may remain, due, for example, to the social, regional or political background of a family. Here, it is an important task of all forms of schooling to overcome these disadvantages by giving the necessary support.

While this is also a task to be fulfilled by the state and the society, it is the domain of schools and education to find the special abilities of a child and support them as the second task. Education has to improve its didactic and methods, so that each child can be supported in his/her special competencies, and furthermore that each child can be supported individually so that he/she will be able to pass a successful school career. This strong focus on individual support in relationship with the common aim of reaching the final certificate demands not only a well-equipped school with regard to teaching personnel, further personnel such as social workers, psychologists, librarians, medical helpers and close relationships with professionals from outside such as sport trainers, artists etc., but it also demands a well-equipped school with attractive rooms and interiors. Special support will also be given for students with disabilities within integrative classes.[11] Equal opportunities are thus an aim in the school system but also the way in which the ambitious aim of a final certificate for all can be reached.

It has to be asked how the end of school, when only those with the best results will be allowed to go to university, fits into this approach, even if this could be about 50 percent. This is surely a more general question of whether equal opportunities are compatible with competition, and if so, in which way. Competition is part of school life and in most cases it is a planned part of education, for example in those sports where a winner will naturally be declared at the end, such as sprinting or high jumping, where students are not equally quick. In schools where individual abilities are detected and supported, competition in this sense will do no harm since students learn that they have different abilities which makes them winners in different disciplines, yet education has to make sure that there are no obvious losers.

This attitude is supported when students are not ranked within their class but measured by their individual progress. Then there will be a winner after the 100m sprinting, but each child will learn about his or her individual successes or be supported to further improve him/herself, since all children will take part in sports even if their main abilities are, for example, in music. The competition at the end of the school time is of a different character, since it is a competition due to the fact that there are not enough university places and subsequent job opportunities for all – following the idea that the society needs only a certain amount of high-skilled persons with university degrees.

Tertiary Education, Lifelong Learning and Equal Opportunities

This is not the place to discuss the question whether a society and workforce can be imagined where all persons may go to university mainly to complete their personal education, though the division into skilled and high-skilled positions will not be abandoned. The graded high school where students attend different types of either mainly academic or mainly technical education will already lead to a kind of preliminary decision between those who want to go to university and those who will enter only the skilled workforce after receiving their certificate. It will certainly be a task of school education to prepare students to such situations of competition and the possibility of not gaining the wanted position. This has to be compensated by developing individual abilities and skills, some of which may be more valid for leisure time, for example playing an instrument without reaching the top level for orchestra music.

The selection for university will be based on school results in the final certificate, though entry exams are also an option. According to recent results by OECD, there exist realistic expectations of about 50 percent students going to university (see OECD 2007). About half of the students with the final certificate can thus be supposed to become high-skilled workers in our model. This is not the place to go into the details of university education and the distribution of students to different studies, but concluding this discussion of the school system we want to stress the necessity of an education that allows for individual development and support under the principles of equal opportunities.

Students who finish school with the final certificate and enter the workforce as well as those who do so after having finished university are already well trained in organizing their learning processes, since one of the principles of teaching will be to teach students how to adopt learning competencies, that is, how to learn to organize a learning program, how to work together with others and to learn how to find out about special skills as well as about weak points. The aim is to lead students to an independent learning style that fits best for the individual learner. Learning portfolios may be a recommendable way to keep records of this learning process. It can be assumed that young adults will be able to continue with this procedure as well as to continue documenting it.

The European Union had already declared the year 1996 as the European year of lifelong learning and passed a resolution on 'Lifelong Learning' in 2002 (Council 2002). It is here stressed that learning starts in the pre-school age and lasts until post-retirement. Furthermore, it is relevant here that the resolution refers not only to all kinds of learning, including the entire spectrum of formal, non-formal and informal learning, and that the aim of learning is not restricted to skills and competencies with regard to later employment. Instead it is regarded as important within a personal, civic or social perspective as well. While school education and thus learning in schools follows a common curriculum where the highest possible grade of individualization and interest-dependence is guaranteed though a general curriculum remains to be followed, lifelong learning after school and university is far more guided by individual interests and the needs of a person, though there will also be on-the-job training in most professions, since skills and knowledge have to be updated on a regular basis.

The idea of lifelong learning adds to the concept of equal opportunities, since the personal access to knowledge and competencies is increased by the possibilities of learning independently of age or position. Therefore it is necessary that the educational system offers a variety of learning procedures after school and university, such as adult education centers but also the possibility of access to arts, museums, nature and its learning opportunities. Mobility will add to lifelong learning of languages and cultures, but also of professional skills. Lifelong learning includes all forms of social learning and is also highly important for political learning.

Political learning plays an important role in education, especially in a model where the state has a major role as employer and provider of social services. Political learning, which is often referred to as citizenship education, is of high relevance in a system that depends on the individual skills and knowledge of its workforce but at the same time demands a high amount of social commitment and acceptance of different work places though no unemployment. Furthermore, the principles of equal opportunities on which we have commented above are integrated in political concepts such as human rights so that the necessity of political learning is again underlined. Political learning will be part of school education as well as of lifelong learning. Human rights education provides all the necessary content and skills to cope in a democratic society, especially since human rights and democracy are inseparably interconnected. Thus, democracy as the underlying state model as well as equal opportunities as the adequate principle for social justice can be deduced from human rights. Democracy education, citizenship education and human rights education are well-established and partly overlapping forms of education which provide not only an introduction into the necessary knowledge of political structures, but prepare furthermore for different kinds of participation in democratic procedures. Additionally they intend to increase media competence to allow students as well as adult learners to understand actual political decision–making processes.

10.5 Flexicurity and the Keynesian Trade Cycle Challenge

So far the economy was purely supply driven one, with growth of the capital stock driven by net profits and credit from pension funds (see Section 8.6) such that Say's law remained true, that is aggregate demand has always been equal to potential output due to the expenditure behavior of households, the government and the firms. In this section we now briefly sketch a situation where capacity utilization problems as well as stability problems may arise within the flexicurity variant of a capitalistic economy. We modify the baseline credit model of Section 8.6 in a minimal way in order to obtain such results. In place of its pension funds as well as the credits they give to firms we now consider the situation where firms finance their investment plans through their profits and through the issuing of corporate paper bonds.

We assume these bonds to be of the fixprice variety and we also keep the rate of interest that is paid on these bonds fixed for simplicity.

Despite this simple change we will now get the situation that actual goods market equilibrium will depart from potential output (here reinterpreted by a normal rate of capacity utilization of potential output) and may now fluctuate around the assumed normal capacity output. We therefore have the first real problem – here on the macrolevel – the flexicurity society has to cope with, namely the possibility of recessions or even depressions when aggregate demand is behaving accordingly, but also the possible situation of an overheated economy. Clearly, there is now a need for economic policy, that is fiscal, monetary or even income distribution policy, in order to avoid large swings in economic activity and thus large imbalances between the industrial and the public labor markets. However, this section will only provide the basics for such an analysis and leaves policy consideration for future research.[12]

Table 10.5: Firms: production and income account

Uses	Resources
δK	δK
$\omega_1 L_1^d, L_1^d = Y/z$	$C_1 + C_2 + C_r$
	G
rB/p	$I = i_\rho(\rho - \rho_o)K - i_b(\frac{B}{p} - (\frac{B}{p})_o) + \bar{a}K$
$\Pi(=Y^f)$	$[I = \Pi + \dot{B}^s/p]$
$\delta_1 R + \dot{R}$	S_1
Y	Y

The amount of corporate bonds that firms are now assumed to have issued in the past is denoted by B and their price is 1 in nominal units. Firms thus have to pay rB as interest at the current point in time and they intend to use their real profits net of interest rate payments and in addition the issue $\dot{B}^s/p$ to finance their rate of investment $I/K = i_\rho(\rho - \rho_o) - i_b(\frac{B}{pK} - (\frac{B}{pK})_o) + \bar{a}$. This rate of investment is assumed to depend positively on excess profitability compared to the steady state rate of profit and negatively on the deviation of their debt from its steady state level.

Households of type 1 behave as was assumed so far, but now attempt to channel their real savings into corporate bond holdings as shown below. They will be able to exactly satisfy their demand for new bonds when there is goods market equilibrium prevailing ($I = S$), since only firms and these households act on this market, while all other economic units just spend what they get (with balanced transfer payments organized by the government). The real return from savings in corporate bonds rB/p, at each moment in time, will be added below to the base rent payments of retired households, who receive these benefits in proportion to the bonds they have allocated during their work life in the private sector of the economy. The bonds allocated in this way thus only generate a return when their holders are retired and then – as in the pension fund scheme of Section 8.6 – at the then prevailing market rate of interest (which is here a given rate still). The pension fund model is therefore here only reformulated in terms of nominal paper holdings (coupons) and thus no longer based on the storage of physical magnitudes. Hence, corporate bonds are here not only of a fixprice variety, but also provide their return only after retirement. This is shown in the income account of retired persons below. The income account of the workers in the second labor market is unchanged and therefore not shown here again.

Table 10.6: Household 1 (primary labor market): income account

Households 1:

Uses	Resources
$C_1 = c_{h1}(1-\tau_h)\omega_1 L_1^d$	
$\omega_2 L_{2h}^w = c_{h2}(1-\tau_h)\omega_1 L_1^d$	
$T = \tau_h \omega_1 L_1^d$	
$\omega_2(L-(L_1^w + L_{2h}^w + L_{2g}^w))$	
$\omega_2 L^r, L^r = \alpha_r L$	
$S_1[= \dot{B}^d/p]$	$\omega_1 L_1^d$
$Y_1^w = \omega_1 L_1^d$	$Y_1^w = \omega_1 L_1^d$

Table 10.7: Retired households: income account

Retired Households:

Uses	Resources
C_r	$\omega_2 L^r + rB/p, L^r = \alpha_r L$
Y^r	Y^r

The government income account (not shown) is also kept unchanged and in particular balanced in the way used in the preceding model types. The modifications of the model of Section 8.6 are therefore of a minimal kind, largely concerning a different type of investment behavior of firms and a new type of organizing the formerly assumed company pension funds.

However, the assumed flexicurity system becomes now of real importance, since we here will get demand-determined (Keynesian) business cycle fluctuations in the dynamics implied by the model, whereas firms did not face capacity under- or over-utilization problems in the earlier model types. Keynesian IS equilibrium determination has to be considered now and gives rise to the following equation for the effective output per unit of capital (characterizing goods market equilibrium):[13]

$$\begin{aligned} Y/K &= y \\ &= C_1/K + C_2/K + C_r/K + \delta + I/K + G/K \\ &= c_h(1-\tau_h)\omega_1 \frac{y}{z} + \alpha_\omega \omega_1 (\bar{l} - l_1^w) + \alpha_\omega \alpha_r \omega_1 \bar{l} + rb + \\ &\quad \delta + i_\rho(\rho - \rho_o) - i_b(b - b_o) + \bar{a} + \alpha_g \tau_h \omega_1 y/z \\ \rho &= y - (1 + \alpha_f \alpha_\omega)\omega_1 y/z - \delta - rb, \qquad b = B/(pK), \end{aligned}$$

which, taken together, gives:

$$\begin{aligned} y &= \frac{1}{1 - [c_h(1-\tau_h) + \alpha_g \tau_h - i_\rho(1 + \alpha_f \alpha_\omega)]\omega_1/z - i_\rho} \cdot \\ &\quad \Big(\alpha_\omega \omega_1 (\bar{l} - l_1^w) + \alpha_\omega \alpha_r \omega_1 \bar{l} + (rb + \delta)(1 - i_\rho) \\ &\quad - i_\rho \rho_o - i_b(b - b_o) + \bar{a}\Big) \\ &= y(l_1^w, \omega_1, b, \ldots). \end{aligned}$$

Note that we have modified the investment function in this section to $i(\cdot) = i_\rho(\rho - \rho_o) - i_b(b - b_o) + \bar{a}$. Note also that we have again assumed that natural growth n is always adjusted to the growth rate of the capital stock $\hat{K}$. We also assume that the denominator in the above fraction is positive and now get the important result that output per unit of capital is no longer equal to its potential value, but now depending on the marginal propensity to spend as well as on other parameters of the model. This is due to the new situation that firms use corporate bonds to finance their excess investment (exceeding their profits) or buy back such bonds in the opposite case and that households of type 1 buy such bonds from their savings (and thus do not buy goods in this amount any more to increase the pension fund). We thus have independent real investment and real savings decisions which – when coordinated by the achievement of goods market equilibrium as shown above – lead to a supply of new corporate bonds that is exactly equal to the demand for such bonds at this level of output and income. This simply follows from the fact that only firms and households of type 1 are saving, while all other budgets are balanced. Households of type 1 thus just have to accept the amount of the fixed price bonds offered by firms and are thereby accumulating these bonds (whose interest rate payments are paid out to retired people according to the percentage they have achieved when retiring).

Assuming the accumulation of corporate bonds in the place of real commodities and an investment function that is independent from these savings conditions thus implies that the economy is subject to Keynesian demand rationing processes (at least close to its steady state). These demand problems are here derived on the assumption of IS equilibrium and thus represented in static terms in place of a dynamic multiplier approach that can also be augmented further by means of Metzlerian inventory adjustment processes. We stress once again that the possibility for full capacity output is here prevented through the Keynesian type of underconsumption assumed as characterizing the household type 1 sector, and the fact that there is then only one income level that allows savings in bonds to become equal to bond financed investment in this simple credit market that is characterizing this modification of the flexicurity model, due to the now existing effective demand schedule $y(l_1^w, \omega_1, b, \dots)$. We assume that the parameters are chosen such that we get for the partial derivatives of the effective demand function y :

$$y_{l_1^w}(l_1^w, \omega_1, b, \dots) < 0, \quad y_{\omega_1}(l_1^w, \omega_1, b, \dots) > 0, \quad y_b(l_1^w, \omega_1, b, \dots) < 0$$

holds true. This is fulfilled, for example, if the expression in the denominator of the effective demand function is negative and if the parameter i_b is chosen sufficiently large. Effective demand is then wage led and flexible wages therefore dangerous for the considered economy.

As now significantly interacting laws of motion we have in the considered case:

$$\begin{aligned}
\hat{l}_1^w &= H\left(\frac{y}{zl_1^w} - \bar{u}_w\right), \quad H' > 0, \\
\hat{\omega}_1 &= G^1\left(\frac{\omega_1}{\bar{\omega}_1}\right) + G^2\left(\frac{y}{l_1^w} - \bar{u}_w\right), \quad G^{1'}, G^{2'} < 0, \\
\dot{b} &= (1-b)(i_\rho(\rho - \rho_o) - i_b(b - b_o) + \bar{a}) - \rho - \hat{p}b,
\end{aligned}$$

$$\hat{p} = \kappa \left[\beta_{py} \left(\frac{y}{y^p} - \bar{u}_c \right) + \beta_{p\omega} \ln \left(\frac{\omega_1}{\omega_1^o} \right) + \kappa_p \left(\beta_{wu} \left(\frac{y}{z l_1^w} - 1 \right) \right. \right.$$
$$\left. \left. - \beta_{w\omega} \ln \left(\frac{\omega_1}{\omega_1^o} \right) \right) \right] + \pi^c$$

where $\hat{p}$ has to be inserted into the other equation (where necessary) in order to arrive at an autonomous system of four ordinary differential equations. This particular formulation of the debt financing of firms thus makes the model considerably more advanced from the mathematical as well as from an economic point of view. We note that there is not yet an interest rate policy rule involved in these dynamics, but that the assumption of an interest rate peg is maintained still: $r = const.$

Since the model is formulated partly in nominal terms we have to consider now the price inflation rate explicitly. We do this on the basis of a wage–price spiral mechanism as it has been formulated in Flaschel, Greiner, Luchtenberg and Nell (2008) with respect to the industrial sector of the economy:

$$\hat{w} = \beta_{wu}(\frac{y}{z l_1^w} - \bar{u}_w) - \beta_{w\omega} \ln(\frac{\omega}{\omega^o}) + \kappa_w \hat{p} + (1 - \kappa_w)\pi^c$$
$$\hat{p} = \beta_{py}(\frac{y}{y^p} - \bar{u}_c) + \beta_{p\omega} \ln(\frac{\omega}{\omega^o}) + \kappa_p \hat{w} + (1 - \kappa_p)\pi^c$$

In these equations, $\hat{w}$, $\hat{p}$ denote the growth rates of nominal wages w and the price level p (their inflation rates) and π^c a medium-term inflation-climate expression which, however, is of no relevance in the following due to our neglect of real interest rate effects on the demand side of the model (and thus set equal to zero). We denote again by $\bar{u}_w$ the normal ratio of utilization of the workforce within firms and now by $\bar{u}_c$ the corresponding concerning the utilization of the capital stock. Deviations from these normal ratios measure the demand pressure on the labor and the goods market respectively. In the wage Phillips curve C as well as the price Phillips curve we in addition employ a real wage error correction term $\ln(\omega/\omega_0)$ as in Blanchard and Katz (1999), see Flaschel and Krolzig (2006) for details, and as a cost pressure term a weighted average of short-term (perfectly anticipated) wage or price inflation $\hat{w}, \hat{p}$, respectively and the medium-term inflation climate π^c in which the economy is operating.

The above structural equations of a wage–price spiral read in reduced form as follows:

$$\hat{w} = \kappa \left[\beta_{wu} \left(\frac{y}{zl_1^w} - \bar{u}_w \right) - \beta_{w\omega} \ln \left(\frac{\omega_1}{\omega_1^o} \right) + \kappa_w \left(\beta_{py} \left(\frac{y}{y^p} - \bar{u}_c \right) + \beta_{p\omega} \ln \left(\frac{\omega_1}{\omega_1^o} \right) \right) \right] + \pi^c,$$

$$\hat{p} = \kappa \left[\beta_{py} \left(\frac{y}{y^p} - \bar{u}_c \right) + \beta_{p\omega} \ln \left(\frac{\omega_1}{\omega_1^o} \right) + \kappa_p \left(\beta_{wu} \left(\frac{y}{zl_1^w} - \bar{u}_w \right) - \beta_{w\omega} \ln \left(\frac{\omega_1}{\omega_1^o} \right) \right) \right] + \pi^c,$$

which give the above equation for the price inflation rate and also the above real dynamics when the price equation is deducted from the wage equation.

Note that our model only considers the utilization rate of insiders (within firms) in the wage dynamics, since the markets for labor are always cleared in flexicurity capitalism. We thus now use the output–capital ratio $y = Y/K$ to measure the output gap in the price inflation PC and the deviation of the real wage $\omega = w/p$ from the steady state real wage ω^o as an error correction expression also in the price PC. Cost pressure in this price PC is formulated as a weighted average of short-term (perfectly anticipated) wage inflation and our concept of an inflationary climate π^c, see Flaschel and Krolzig (2006) for details. In this price Phillips curve we have three elements of cost pressure interacting with each other, a medium-term one (the inflationary climate) and two short–term ones, basically the level of real unit wage labor costs (a Blanchard and Katz (1999) error correction term) and the current rate of wage inflation, which taken by itself would represent a constant markup pricing rule. This basic rule is, however, modified by these other cost-pressure terms and in particular also made dependent on the state of the business cycle by way of the demand pressure term $y/y^p - \bar{u}_c$ in the market for goods.

The laws of motion describe again (in this order) our formulation of Okun's law, the real wage dynamics as it applies in a Keynesian environment (see Section 10.3), the debt dynamics of firms and a simple regressive expectations scheme concerning the inflationary climate surrounding the wage–price spiral where it is assumed (and in fact also taking place) that inflation converges back to a constant price level. There is therefore not yet an inflation accelerator present in the formulation of the dynamics of the four state variables of the model.

Nevertheless, price level inflation is now explicitly taken account of, indeed for the first time in this chapter.

Steady state and stability analysis is no longer straightforward in this Keynesian variant of flexicurity capitalism. With respect to steady state positions we have to solve now a simultaneous equation system in the variables ω_1, ρ, b. Due to the structure of the effective demand function we have moreover no longer zero entries in the Jacobian of the dynamics at the steady state of the first three state variables (the last law of motion is a completely trivial one). As an economic mechanism we can identify a real wage channel as in the Kaleckian dynamics of Flaschel, Franke and Semmler (2008) (working here in a wage-led environment by assumption). There is furthermore the dynamic of the debt to capital ratio of firms. These feedback channels can be tamed through appropriate assumptions, but are even then working in an environment that gives no straightforward economically plausible stability assertions, due to the strong interactions present in the dynamics. We therefore have to leave the stability analysis here for future research.

The conclusion of this section therefore is that effective demand problems can make flexicurity capitalism significantly more difficult to analyze (and to handle) and therefore demand a treatment of much more depth – including inflation and interest rate policy rules, government deficits and fiscal policy rules, etc. – than was possible in this short section. Moreover, credit relationships may be looked for that can avoid the increase in complexity of the dynamics of this section.

10.6 Conclusions and Outlook

Starting from the problematic features and the social consequences of the reserve army dynamics characterizing the evolution of the labor markets of many contemporaneous developed capitalist economies, this chapter tried to demonstrate that a combination of ideas of Marx, Keynes and Schumpeter on the future of capitalism can provide an alternative to the ruthless form of competition that is currently ruling the world (in developed as well as developing countries). In place of the multilayered degradation of a significant proportion of the population also of democratically governed societies we designed economic reproduction schemes (including education and skill formation) of a competitive form of capitalism that combines flexicurity of a very high degree with security of income as well as employment for the workforce.

Schumpeter's investigation of the workability of a competitive type of socialism is thereby carried one step further towards a social vision which preserves to a greater extent the advantages of the existing capitalist forms of production and circulation, but which nevertheless creates a social structure of accumulation which in its essence is liberated from the human degradation we can even observe in leading industrialized countries in the world economy.

The essential ingredients along the progress path towards such a social structure are not only a basic income guarantee of the workfare type (which includes the obligation to work), but also a reorganization of the labor market towards an employer of first (not last) resort who organizes in a decentralized way the work for all people not employed within privately run industries, but also the work of officially retired persons who are still willing to offer their human capital on the labor markets of the economy. The workability of the designed reproduction scheme of flexicurity type of course depends – in the same way as many other actual organizational problems – on detailed microeconomic analyses of the labor relations within large, medium-sized and small business firms as well as in the public sector. Yet, economic incentives need to be coupled with an educational system that not only creates the basis for skill formation, but also provides the proper foundations for citizenship education in a democratic society, where citizens essentially approve the high degree of flexibility in the industrial part of the economy (and not only there) on the basis of the security aspects of the flexicurity concept and the equal opportunity principles during primary and secondary education.

The main support for the need of an evolution towards such a flexicurity society in our view comes from the fact that the currently existing alternative reproduction schemes of capitalism do not provide a social structure of accumulation that is compatible with an educated and democratic society in the longer run, since their recurring situations of mass unemployment undermine social cohesion in many ways in such societies (if this cohesion existed in them at all), leading to social segmentation, social class clashes and more. The evolution in the Nordic states of the European Union provide examples of how such a development towards socially accepted flexicurity based on a modern schooling system may be approached. We close the chapter, however, with the observation that it does not yet say much on how the modeled situation can in fact be reached in actual economies, at current primarily in the Nordic countries.

We here simply assume that the individual experience with progress in educational systems (towards equal opportunities in particular), with the need for flexibility as well as security during the working life and with democratic institutions on all levels of the society will implement ratchet effects in individual and social choice mechanisms which prevent a return to the Marxian reserve army mechanism as it has been and continues to be investigated in the many contributions to the original Goodwin growth cycle model in view of what happens in actual capitalist economies.

We have started, in Chapter 1 of this book, from a very basic model of a capitalist economy which on the one hand used microfoundations (in a very simple manner) as a relevant modeling tool, but which stressed on the other hand the need to have at least two agents (capitalist and workers) if the model is really meant to represent a capitalistic society. The model therefore rejected the representative agent approach of mainstream macroeconomics, where the conflict between labor and capital is integrated into a single 'soul'. In the chosen continuous time framework we moreover argued, as in Flaschel, Groh, Proaño and Semmler (2008, ch.1), that the assumption of permanent market clearing (at any 'micro-second') is not an appropriate hypothesis to characterize the working of (at least) the real markets of the economy.

We therefore used an expectations-augmented wage Phillips curve (with model-consistent expectations) as an adjustment process on the market for labor (but left out Keynesian demand problems on the market for goods to keep the model simple). The implied differentiated saving habits of workers and capitalists led in this model to a law of motion for the distribution of the capital stock between workers and pure capitalists, so that in particular the savings of workers out of wage income and profit income did not rule out the existence of pure capitalists in the steady state.

The limiting extremely Classical situation where workers do not save and where capitalists do not consume, and where therefore the latter own the whole capital stock of the economy, may be considered an approximation of the situation before World War I, and be characterized as constituting capitalism mark I, while the above case with differentiated saving habits may be called capitalism mark II.[14] Both types of capitalism can be characterized by and large as being dissent-driven. For the latter type this dissent may be exemplified by the rise and the subsequent fall of the welfare state in most Western capitalist economies (corresponding to a certain degree to the rise and the fall of Eastern socialism).

In the present chapter, by contrast, we have attempted to formulate a model of capitalism mark III, where essentially consent (on macroeconomic issues) between the management of firms and the workers is one of the pillars of the economy and the considered society, while Chapters 8 and 9 considered the working of capitalism mark II.[15] It may well be that capitalism mark III may be difficult to reach in the globalized world we are now living in. But there are – for example in the Nordic Countries of Europe – elements of a progress path towards flexicurity capitalism already visible and the debate on such transformational processes is a lively one in the European Union at present. It is the hope of the authors of this book that it can contribute to such a debate, by showing that aspects of Marx's, Keynes's and Schumpeter's work can be successfully combined to model and understand the current situation of world capitalism and its future evolution. Such an MKS system – as called by Richard Goodwin – in our view provides a proper synthesis for the analysis of the macrodynamics of capitalism, a synthesis of very differing research profiles that at first sight seems to be impossible, but which indeed unifies complementary approaches to the understanding of capitalism.

Notes

[1] Taken from Groth and Madsen 2007, p. 4

[2] See United Nations (1998, article 23): Universal Declaration of Human Rights, 1948 (http://www.un.org/Overview/rights.html)

[3] http://www.eurofound.europa.eu/areas/industrialrelations/dictionary/definitions/FLEXICURITY.htm

[4] The determination of which will be discussed later on.

[5] See Flaschel, Greiner, Luchtenberg and Nell (2008) for the details of the derivation of this real wage (or better wage share) Phillips curve and note that this equation implicitly assumes that v_{1a}^o describes the situation where capital stock growth is equal to natural growth n.

[6] The reader is referred to Flaschel, Greiner, Luchtenberg and Nell (2008) for details.

[7] $l_a^w = zL_a^w/K, l_r = zL_r/K, s_1 = S_1/K$.

[8] With respect to concrete numbers one therefore could, for example, assume $t_c = 6, t_s = 12, t_u = 5, t_b = 47, t_a = 42, t_r = 15$.

We stress here that the considered age structure is still a very stylized one in view of what is shown in Figure 10.2.

[9] Source: http://www.edu.fi/english/SubPage.asp?path=500,4699

[10] The ratio $\frac{L_{1a}^{d}}{t_a L_o}$ compares employment in the first sector (of high-skilled workers) with the common core employment of all workers.

[11] See Muñoz (2006) for details

[12] To simplify the expressions for Keynesian effective demand, we here only consider three labor markets, a private and a public one, and the one organized by the employer of first resort. The framework used is thus one of Chapter 8.

[13] Standard Keynesian assumptions will again ensure that $y^o > 0$ holds true.

[14] This is not identical to the way these terms are used to characterize the evolution of Schumpeter's theory of capitalism which was focused on the figure of the dynamic entrepreneur.

[15] Without studying the consequences of the savings of workers, however, as in Chapter 1

11. Leashing Capitalism: Monetary–Fiscal Policy Measures and Labor Market Reforms

11.1 Introduction

In this chapter we extend the Tobin type stock–flow interaction of the financial markets with the real markets of Chapter 1 towards an integration of the flexicurity principles and labor market reforms considered in Chapters 8–10.

The literature on the interaction of stocks and flows on the macro level is to a certain degree still in its infancy. Surely Tobin's work (see in particular Tobin 1980, 1982) has pushed this topic a decisive step forward, but the analytical treatment (not to speak of an empirical analysis) of a full interaction of the real and the financial side of the macroeconomy is by and large missing. There are works by Godley and Lavoie, see in particular the work by Godley (1999), Godley and Lavoie (2007), Franke and Semmler (1999), by Foley and Taylor (2006), and by Zezza and Dos Santos (2006) which attempt to improve the situation, but the dominant tradition – in particular in mainstream economics – is the use of return parity conditions (up to the money market) in order to study the interaction of the financial with the real markets.

We have shown in Chapter 1 how an integration of the Tobin macroeconomic portfolio approach with the Keynes–Metzler–Goodwin model of business and distributive cycles can be performed and analyzed, in particular with respect to the ways monetary and fiscal policy can stabilize such an economy (where a variety of destabilizing feedback channels are present in the private sector). We now extend these policy interventions to the labor market by integrating into the KMGT approach the type of labor market policies that are proposed by the 'flexicurity' concept.

This forms the foundations for a new social structure of capital accumulation where not only financial instabilities and the business cycle but also the wage–price spiral can be tamed to a certain degree, and this in the presence of full employment, based on the principles of an employer of first resort. It goes without saying that this is just the beginning of the study of monetary, fiscal and labor market measures aimed at providing a stable full-employment environment in a competitive capitalist economy where not only free hiring and firing of labor are present, but also in production processes of creative destruction based on the Schumpeterian trilogy of invention, innovation and diffusion of new products and new production techniques.

11.2 Interacting Real–Financial Disequilibrium Adjustment Processes

The goal of this chapter is to present a Keynesian macrodynamic model of a growing monetary economy, that builds on the analysis of the working KMG model of Chiarella and Flaschel (2000a) and Chiarella, Flaschel and Franke (2005) and that explains the real–financial interaction in Keynesian dynamics in a more satisfactory way than in the working KMG model from which it has been derived. In this latter model type, asset markets influence the real dynamics only in a very traditional way, by means of an LM curve, representing a stable relationship between the nominal rate of interest, the output–capital ratio and real balances per unit of capital, or in a less traditional way by means of a Taylor interest rate rule. Neither bond dynamics nor the evolution of the stock of equities could there influence the interest rate and the real part of the economy due to the lack of wealth and interest income effects on aggregate demand. The present chapter will now introduce a portfolio theory of asset market behavior in place of a single LM curve and will thereby improve the representation of asset market dynamics considerably, though wealth and interest income effects will still be ignored. Nevertheless bond and equity stock dynamics now feeds back into the real part of the economy, yet still by a single route namely through Tobin's average q as one important argument in the investment behavior of firms.

Our KMG approach to macrodynamics investigates the interaction of all important markets of the macroeconomy (for labor, goods, money, bonds and equities) still in a non-stochastic environment without explicit utility maximization of households and profit maximization of firms. Households' behavioral equations are in the tradition of the

Kaldorian approach (Kaldor 1940) with differentiated saving habits (that can be derived by optimizing a Cobb–Douglas utility function of workers or capitalists). This allows us to leave the model sufficiently simple in order to concentrate on the description and analysis of asset market dynamics. Combining a full disequilibrium approach in the real part of the economy with a general equilibrium approach in the financial part gave rise to various considerations of the dynamics which then drives the economy. The model therefore presents an integrated approach to macrodynamics that accounts for all budget constraints of all types of agents in the economy, exhibits a uniquely determined steady state solution surrounded by a variety of interesting propagation or the feedback mechanisms existing in the economy. Now also disequilibrium adjustment rules in the financial part of the model are taken into consideration.

The main properties of this approach should be presented briefly. The economy consists of various private agents: workers, asset holders and firms. The public sector consists of the government and the central bank. Concerning the goods market, there exists a production good exclusively produced by firms that can be, on the one hand, consumed by the workers, asset holders or the government, and on the other hand invested as business fixed capital or used for inventory investment by firms. Firms do not have perfect foresight with respect to the demand for goods and do not adjust their output instantaneously towards the level of aggregate demand. Hence, in order to be able to satisfy actual and future demands, they have to hold stocks of inventories of produced goods. The adjustment policy for reaching a desired stock of inventories is modeled in a Metzlerian way (Metzler 1941).

The labor market is assumed to take place under a Keynesian regime in the sense that any demand can be satisfied by an always positive excess supply of labor at the actual wage rate. Goodwin's (1967) contribution to the model is the study of the dynamic interaction of employment and the real wage rate.

We want to model a monetary economy with various financial assets in order to investigate their interaction with the real parts, namely goods market and labor market. There are various assets: money and short-term bonds issued by the government, and equities issued by firms in order to finance investments. All these financial assets are exclusively held by the asset holders.

In Section 11.3 we develop the extensive form of the model and give a detailed explanation of its structure. In Section 11.4 the intensive form of the dynamics is derived in order to allow for steady state considerations on the basis of eight autonomous laws of motion that, as will be shown, indeed exhibit a unique point of rest or steady state. The stability features of the full 8D dynamical system are also briefly characterized in this section by way of a sequence of subsystems of increasing dimension. Policy issues are studied in Section 11.5 where we consider monetary policy, fiscal policy and labor market policy. Section 11.6 briefly shows how Schumpeterian elements such as innovation and creative destruction can be integrated into our framework. Section 11.7 provides an outlook on 'Social Capitalism', a notion that we consider as a next step in the completion of the design of capitalist flexicurity economies.

11.3 Portfolio Choice and Asset Accumulation within the KMG Framework

In this section we provide the extensive or structural form of a Tobin type portfolio (KMGT) model of the KMG variety, exhibiting a portfolio adjustment block in place of a simple LM (Taylor) theory of the short-run rate of interest and the simple dynamic adjustment equations for the prices of the other assets as considered in Chiarella, Flaschel, Groh and Semmler (2000) . We split the model into appropriate modules which primarily concern the sectors of the economy, namely households, firms and the government (fiscal and monetary authority), but also represent the wage–price interaction and the dynamics of the asset markets.

11.3.1 Firms

In order to model a flexicurity economy based on the KMGT approach to business cycles and growth we consider first the sector of private firms and through them the first labor market of the economy where free hiring and firing is assumed in the strict sense that firms are always on their labor demand schedule regarding the workforce they employ. The first labor market is later on augmented by a second labor market – within the public sector – where all workers not employed in the first labor market find meaningful employment. Workers working in these two markets are indexed by 1,2 respectively.

We consider the behavior of firms by means of two submodules. The first describes the production frameworks and their investment in business fixed capital and the second introduces the Metzlerian approach of inventory cycles concerning expected sales, actual sales and the output of firms.

Firms: production and investment

$$r^e = (pY^e - wL_1^d - p\delta_k K)/(pK), \quad (11.1)$$
$$Y^p = y^p K, \quad (11.2)$$
$$u = Y/Y^p, \quad (11.3)$$
$$L_1^d = Y/z, \quad (11.4)$$
$$e_1 = L_1^d/L = Y/(zL), \quad (11.5)$$
$$q = p_e E/(pK), \quad (11.6)$$
$$I = i_q(q-1)K + i_u(u-\bar{u})K + nK, \quad (11.7)$$
$$\hat{K} = I/K, \quad (11.8)$$
$$p_e\dot{E} = pI + p(\dot{N} - \mathcal{I}). \quad (11.9)$$

Firms are assumed to pay out dividends according to expected profits (expected sales net of depreciation and minus the wage sum), see the above module of the asset-owning households. The rate of expected profits r^e is expected real profits per unit of capital as stated in equation (11.1). For producing output firms utilize a production technology that transforms demanded labor L_1^d combined with business fixed capital K into output. For convenience we assume that the production takes place by a fixed proportion technology.[1] According to (11.2) potential output Y^p is therefore given in each moment of time by the fixed coefficient y^p times the existing stock of physical capital. Accordingly, the utilization of productive capacities is given by the ratio u of actual production Y and the potential output Y^p. The fixed proportions in production also give rise to a constant output–labor coefficient z, by means of which we can deduce labor demand from goods market determined output as in equation (11.4). The ratio L_1^d/L thus defines the rate of employment of the model concerning the first labor market, that is the portion of workers that are working in this market.

The economic behavior of firms also comprises the investment decision into business fixed capital, which is determined independently from households savings decision. We here model investment decisions per unit of capital as a function of the deviation of Tobin's q (see Tobin 1969) from its long-run value 1, and the deviation of actual capacity utilization from a normal rate of capital utilization, and add an exogenously given trend term, here given by the natural growth rate n in order to allow this rate to determine the growth path of the economy in the usual way.[2] We employ here Tobin's average q which is defined in equation (11.6). It is the ratio of the nominal value of equities and the reproduction costs for the existing stock of capital. Investment in business fixed capital is enforced when q exceeds one, and is to be reduced when q is smaller than one. This influence is represented by the term $i_q(q-1)$ in equation (11.7). The term $i_u(u-\bar{u})$ models the component of investment which is due to the deviation of the utilization rate of physical capital from its non-accelerating inflation value $\bar{u}$. The last component, nK, takes account of the natural growth rate n which is necessary for steady state analysis if natural growth is considered as exogenously given. Equation (11.9) is the budget constraint of the firms. Investment in business fixed capital and unintended changes in the inventory stock $p(\dot{N}-\mathcal{I})$ must be financed by issuing equities, since equities are the only financial instrument of firms in this chapter. Capital stock growth finally is given by net investment per unit of capital I/K in this demand-determined modeling of the short-run equilibrium position of the economy.

Next we model the inventory dynamics in the model following Metzler (1941) and Franke (1996). This approach is a very useful concept for describing the goods market disequilibrium dynamics with all of its implications.

Firms: output adjustment

$$N^d = \alpha_{n^d} Y^e, \tag{11.10}$$
$$\mathcal{I} = nN^d + \beta_n (N^d - N), \tag{11.11}$$
$$Y = Y^e + \mathcal{I}, \tag{11.12}$$
$$Y^d = C + I + \delta_k K + G, \tag{11.13}$$
$$\dot{Y}^e = nY^e + \beta_{y^e}(Y^d - Y^e), \tag{11.14}$$
$$\dot{N} = Y - Y^d, \tag{11.15}$$
$$S_f = Y - Y^e = \mathcal{I}, \tag{11.16}$$

where $\alpha_{n^d}, \beta_n, \beta_{y^e} \geq 0$.

As stated in equation (11.10), the desired stock of physical inventories is denoted by N^d and is assumed to be a fixed proportion of the expected sales. The planned investments $\mathcal{I}$ in inventories follow a sluggish adjustment process towards the desired stock N^d according to equation (11.11). Taking account of this additional demand for goods we write the production Y to be set equal to the expected sales of firms plus $\mathcal{I}$ in equation (11.12). For explaining the expectation formation for good demand, we need the actual total demand for goods which is given by consumption (of private households and the government) and gross investment by firms (11.13). By knowing the actual demand Y^d, which is always served, the dynamics of expected sales is given in equation (11.14). It models these expectations to be the outcome of an error correction process, that incorporates also the natural growth rate n in order to take account of the fact that this process operates in a growing economy. The adjustment of sales expectations is driven by the prediction error $(Y^d - Y^e)$, with an adjustment speed that is given by β_{y^e}. Actual changes in the stock of inventories are given by the deviation of production from goods demanded (11.15). The savings of the firms S_f is as usual defined by income minus consumption. Because firms are assumed to not consume anything, their income equals their savings and is given by the excess of production over expected sales, $Y - Y^e$. According to the production account shown below, the gross accounting profit of firms finally is $r^e pK + p\mathcal{I} = pC + pI + p\delta_k K + p\dot{N} + pG$. Plugging in the definition of r^e from equation (11.1), we compute that $pY^e + p\mathcal{I} = pY^d + p\dot{N}$ or equivalently $p(Y - Y^e) = \mathcal{I}$ as stated in equation (11.16).

We summarize the sector of private firms through its production and income account:[3]

Table 11.1: Firms: sales and income account

Uses	Resources
$\delta_k pK$	$\delta_k pK$
$w_1 L_1^d, \quad L_1^d = Y/z$	$pC_1 + pC_2 + pC_r$
–	pG
Π	pI
$\delta_p P_1 + \dot{P}_1$	pS_1
$pY^d(+\delta_p P_1 + \dot{P}_1)$	$pY^d(+pS_1)$

Note with respect to this account that employment is based on actual production Y and actual profits Π on actual sales Y^d. They differ therefore from expected profits Y^e as introduced above by the windfall profits or losses $Y^d - Y^e$ related with them (based on the assumption that expected profits are the basis of the dividend payments of firms). Note also that demand is always served (if needed out of the actual inventory holdings of firms). Note finally that we have added a new item to this account, describing the accumulation of company pension funds P_1 by means of the savings pS_1 of households working in the first labor market. These savings augment company pension funds, though this extension is reduced again through the current payment of company pensions $\delta_p P_1$ to the retired workers that have worked (for some time) in the private sector of the economy. A next step would be here to assume that firms get loans out of these pension funds P_1 at the loan rate i_l, see Flaschel, Greiner, Luchtenberg and Nell (2008) for details. Moreover, commercial banks may be added as depository institutions paying interest on saving deposits and receiving interest on their loans. Such an extension will be considered briefly at the end of this chapter.

11.3.2 Worker Households

As discussed in the introduction we disaggregate the sector of households into worker households and asset-holder households. We begin with the description of worker households.

The households sector of our model is composed of worker households working in the first labor market and the remaining ones that are all working in the second labor market, as well as retired households (who can work in the government sector on a voluntary basis). From now on we will use real magnitudes in order to describe the budget behavior of the agents of the economy and will refer to the price level p only in certain cases. We denote real wages by ω in distinction from money wages w.

Table 11.2: Households 1 and 2 (primary and secondary labor market): income account

Worker Households 1:

Uses	Resources
$C_1 = c_1(1-\tau_1)\omega_1 L_1^d$	
$T = \tau_1 \omega_1 L_1^d$	
$\omega_2(L - (L_1^d + L_g^d))$	
$\omega_2 L^r, L^r = \alpha_r L$	
S_1	$\omega_1 L_1^d$
$Y_1 = \omega_1 L_1^d$	$Y_1 = \omega_1 L_1^d$

Worker Households 2:

Uses	Resources
C_2	$\omega_2 L_2, L_2 = L - L_1^d, \quad \omega_2 = \alpha_\omega \omega_1$
Y_2	Y_2

Households of type 1 consume manufacturing goods of amount C_1. They pay all income taxes T and they pay in addition – via further tax transfers – all workers' income in the labor market that is not coming from firms and government (which is equivalent to an unemployment insurance). Moreover, they pay the base pensions of the retired households ($\omega_2 L^r$) and accumulate their remaining income pS_1 in the form of a company pension (that is administrated by asset holders) into a fund P_1, with inflow pS_1, see the sector of households, and with outflow $\delta_p P_1$.

The transfer $\omega_2(L - (L_1^w + L_g^w))$ can be considered as solidarity payments, since workers from the first labor market who lose their job will automatically be employed in the second labor market where full employment is guaranteed by the government (as employer of first resort). We consider this employment as skill preserving, since it can be viewed as ordinary office or handicraft work (subject only to learning by doing when such workers return to the first labor market, that is employment in the production process of firms).

The second sector of households is here modeled in the simplest way that is available: households actively employed in the second labor market, that is L_g, as well as those employed under the principles of an employer of first resort (EFR) pay no taxes (or are considered on a net income basis) and totally consume their income. We have thus Classical saving habits in this household sector, while households of type 1 may have positive or negative savings S_1 as residual from their net income and expenditures. We here assume that they can accumulate these savings (or dissave in case of a negative S_1) from the stock P_1 they have accumulated in the past.

We have a consistent distribution of the funds R that are accumulated by households of type 1 on the basis of their savings S_1, according to the stock–flow relationship:

$$\dot{P}_1 = pS_1 - \delta_p P_1$$

where δ_p is the rate by which these funds are depreciated through company pension payments to the 'officially retired' workers L^r assumed to be a constant fraction of the 'active' workforce $L^r = \alpha_r L$. These worker households are added here as not really inactive, but offer work according to their still existing capabilities that can be considered as an addition to the supply of work organized by the government $L - L_1^d$, that is the working potential of the officially retired persons remains an active and valuable contribution of the work hours that are supplied by the members of the society. It is obvious that the proper allocation of the work hours under the control of the government needs thorough reflection from the microeconomic and the social point of view which, however, cannot be a topic in a chapter on the macroeconomics of such an economy.

As the income account of the retired households (see Table 11.3) indicates, they receive pension payments as if they worked in the second labor market and they get in addition individual transfer income (company pensions) from the accumulated funds P_1 in proportion to the time they have been active in the first labor market and as an aggregate household group of the total amount $\delta_p P_1$ by which the pension funds P_1 are reduced in each period.

Table 11.3: Retired households: income account

Uses	Resources
C_r	$\omega_2 L_r + \delta_p P_1/p, L_r = \alpha_r L$
Y_r	Y_r

We next come to the sector of pure asset holders which we – following the model used in Chapter 1 – still keep completely separated from the sector of worker households. Of course both groups should show some or even significant overlap in an extended version of the model, but are here still presented separately from each other in order to keep the initial treatment of a flexicurity KMGT model a simple one.

The modeling of the asset holders' income, consumption and wealth is described by the following set of equations:

Asset-holder households

$$r^e = (Y^e - \delta_k K - \omega_1 L_1^d)/K, \tag{11.17}$$

$$C_c = (1 - s_c)[r^e K + iB/p - T_c], \quad 0 < s_c < 1, \tag{11.18}$$

$$S_c = s_c[r^e K + iB/p - T_c], \tag{11.19}$$

$$= (\dot{M} + \dot{B} + p_e \dot{E})/p, \tag{11.20}$$

$$W_c = (M + B + p_e E)/p, \quad W_c^n = pW_c. \tag{11.21}$$

The first equation (11.17) of this module of the model defines the expected rate of return on real capital r^e to be the ratio of the currently expected real cash flow and the real stock of business fixed capital K. The expected cash flow is given by expected real revenues from sales Y^e diminished by real depreciation of capital $\delta_k K$ and the real wage sum ωL^d. We assume that firms pay out all expected cash flow in form of dividends to the asset holders. These dividend payments are one source of income for asset holders. The second source is given by real interest payments on short-term bonds (iB/p) where i is the nominal interest rate and B the stock of such bonds. Summing up these types of interest incomes, and taking account of lump sum taxes T_c in the case of asset holders (for reasons of simplicity), we get the disposable income of asset holders within the square brackets of equation (11.18), which together with a postulated fixed propensity to consume $(1 - s_c)$ out of this income gives us the real consumption of asset holders.

Real savings of pure asset owners is real disposable income minus their consumption as exposed in equation (11.19). They can allocate it in the form of money $\dot{M}$, or buy other financial assets, namely short-term bonds $\dot{B}$ or equities $\dot{E}$ at the price p_e, the only financial instruments that we allow for in the present reformulation of KMG growth. Hence, savings of asset holders must be distributed to these assets as stated in equation (11.20). Real wealth of pure asset holders is defined on this basis in equation (11.21) as the sum of the real cash balance, real short-term bond holdings and real equity holdings of asset holders. Note that the short-term bonds are assumed to be fixed price bonds with a price of one, $p_b = 1$, and a flexible interest rate i.

We now describe the demand equations of asset-owning households for financial assets following Tobin's general equilibrium approach Tobin (1969):

$$M^d = f_m(i, r_e^e)W_c^n, \tag{11.22}$$
$$B^d = f_b(i, r_e^e)W_c^n, \tag{11.23}$$
$$p_e E^d = f_e(i, r_e^e)W_c^n, \tag{11.24}$$
$$W_c^n = M^d + B^d + p_e E^d. \tag{11.25}$$

The demand for money balances of asset holders M^d is determined by a function $f_m(i, r_e^e)$ which depends on the interest rate on short-run bonds i and the expected rate of return on equities r_e^e. The value of this function times the nominal wealth W^n gives the nominal demand for money M^d, namely f_m describes the portion of nominal wealth that is allocated to pure money holdings. Note that this formulation of money demand is not based on a transaction motive, since the holding of transaction balances is the job of firms in the present chapter. We also do not assume that the financial assets of the economy are perfect substitutes, but indeed assume that financial assets are imperfect substitutes by the approach that underlies the above block of equations. But what is the motive for asset holders to hold a fraction of their wealth in the form of money, when there is a riskless interest-bearing asset? In our view it is reasonable to employ a speculative motive: asset holders want to hold money in order to be able to buy other assets or goods with zero or very low transaction costs. This of course assumes that there are (implicitly given) transaction costs when fixed price bonds are turned into money.

The nominal demand for bonds is determined by $f_b(i, r_e^e)$ and the nominal demand for equities by $f_e(i, r_e^e)$, which again describe the fractions that are allocated to these forms of financial wealth. From equation (11.21) we know that actual nominal wealth equals the stocks of financial assets held by the asset holders. We assume, as is usual in portfolio approaches, that the asset holders buy assets where demand equals in sum their nominal wealth, as stated in equation (11.21). In other words, they just reallocate their wealth in view of new information on the rates of returns on their assets and thus take care of their wealth constraint.

What is left to model in the households sector is the expected rate of return on equities r_e^e which consists of real dividends per equity $(r^e pK/p_e E)$, and expected capital gains, π_e, the latter being nothing other than the expected growth rate of equity prices.

$$r_e^e = \frac{r^e pK}{p_e E} + \pi_e \tag{11.26}$$

In order to complete the modeling of asset-holders' behavior we thus have to describe the evolution of π_e. We here assume that there are two types of asset holders, which differ with respect to their expectation formation of equity prices.

There are chartists who in principle employ an adaptive expectations mechanism:

$$\dot{\pi}_{ec} = \beta_{\pi_{ec}}(\hat{p}_e - \pi_{ec}), \tag{11.27}$$

where $\beta_{\pi_{ec}}$ is the adjustment speed towards the actual growth rate of equity prices. The other asset holders, the fundamentalists, employ a forward looking expectations formation mechanism:

$$\dot{\pi}_{ef} = \beta_{\pi_{ef}}(\bar{\eta} - \pi_{ef}), \tag{11.28}$$

where $\bar{\eta}$ is the fundamentalists' expected long-run inflation rate of share prices. Assuming that the aggregate expected inflation rate is a weighted average of the two expected inflation rates, where the weights are determined according to the sizes of the groups, we postulate

$$\pi_e = \alpha_{\pi_{ec}}\pi_{ec} + (1 - \alpha_{\pi_{ec}})\pi_{ef}. \tag{11.29}$$

Here $\alpha_{\pi_{ec}} \in (0,1)$ is the ratio of chartists to all asset holders.

11.3.3 Fiscal and Monetary Authorities

The traditional formulation of the role of the government in this chapter is to provide the economy with public (unproductive) services within the limits of its budget constraint. Public purchases (and interest payments) are financed through taxes, through newly printed money, or newly issued fixed-price bonds ($p_b = 1$). The budget constraint gives rise to some repercussion effects between the public and the private sector.

$$T = \tau_1\omega_1 L_1^d + T_c, \tag{11.30}$$
$$T_c = t_c K + iB/p, \qquad t_c = \text{const.} \tag{11.31}$$
$$G = \alpha_g gK, \qquad \alpha_g \in (0,1) \tag{11.32}$$
$$L_g^d = (1-\alpha_g)gK, \qquad g = \text{const.} \tag{11.33}$$
$$S_g = T - iB/p - gK, \tag{11.34}$$
$$\dot{M} = \mu M = \dot{B}_c, \tag{11.35}$$
$$\dot{B} = pgK + iB - pT - \dot{M}. \tag{11.36}$$

We model the tax income consisting of taxes on wage income and lump sum taxes on capital income T_c. The latter is assumed for reasons of analytical simplicity solely (for the time being) in a way that makes aggregate demand independent of the interest payments of the government, which in particular simplifies steady state calculations significantly, adding to our simplification of not including wealth effects on consumption into our model.[4]

For the real purchases of the government for providing governmental goods and services we assume, again as in Sargent (1987), that they are a fixed proportion g of real capital, which taken together allows representing fiscal policy by means of simple parameters on the intensive form level of the model and in the steady state considerations to be discussed later on. The real savings of the government, which is a deficit if it has a negative sign, is defined in equation (11.34) by real taxes minus real interest payments minus real public services. Again for reasons of simplicity the growth rate of money is given by a constant μ. Equation (11.35) is the monetary policy rule of the central bank and money is assumed to enter the economy via open market operations of the central bank, which buys short-term bonds from the asset holders when issuing new money. Then the changes in the short-term bonds supplied by the government are given residually in equation (11.36), which is the budget constraint of the governmental sector. This representation of the behavior of the monetary and the fiscal authority clearly shows that the treatment of policy questions is not yet a central part of the chapter. In a flexicurity economy the government has also to manage the work and income of the EFR workers as well as that of retired persons as is shown in the table below:

Table 11.4: The government: fiscal authority – employer of first resort

Uses	Resources
$G = \alpha_g gK$	$T = \tau_1 \omega_1 L_1^d + t_c K$
$\omega_2 L_g^d = (1-\alpha_g) gK$	
$\omega_2(L - (L_1^d + L_g^d))$	$\omega_2(L - (L_1^d + L_g^d))$
$\omega_2 L_r$	$\omega_2 L_r$
S_g	
Y_g	Y_g

11.3.4 Wage–Price Interaction

We now turn to the last module of our model which is the wage–price sector which is based on the Rose approach (Rose, 1990) of two short-run Phillips curves, 1) the wage Phillips curve and 2) the price Phillips curve. Note – in contrast to what was assumed in Chapter 1 in this regard – that money wages are negotiated in the first labor market solely, while wages of workers of type 2 (and base pension payments) are just a constant fraction of these negotiated wages.

$$\hat{w}_1 = \beta_w(e_1 - \bar{e}_1) + \kappa_w \hat{p} + (1-\kappa_w)\pi^c, \tag{11.37}$$

$$\hat{p} = \beta_p(u - \bar{u}) + \kappa_p \hat{w}_1 + (1-\kappa_p)\pi^c, \tag{11.38}$$

$$\dot{\pi^c} = \beta_{\pi^c}(\alpha_{\pi^c}\hat{p} + (1-\alpha_{\pi^c})(\mu - n) - \pi^c), \tag{11.39}$$

where $\beta_w, \beta_p, \beta_{\pi^c} \geq 0$, $0 \leq \alpha_{\pi^c} \leq 1$ and $0 \leq \kappa_w, \kappa_p \leq 1$. This approach makes use of the assumption that relative changes in money wages are influenced by demand pressure in the market for labor and price inflation (cost-pressure) terms and that price inflation in turn depends on demand pressure in the market for goods and on money wage (cost-pressure) terms. Wage inflation therefore is described in equation (11.37) on the one hand by means of a demand pull term $\beta_w(e - \bar{e})$, which tells us that relative changes in wages depends positively on the gap between actual employment e and its NAIRU value $\bar{e}$. On the other hand, the cost push elements in wage inflation are the weighted average of short-run (perfectly anticipated) price inflation $\hat{p}$ and medium-run expected overall inflation π^c, where the weights are given by κ_w and $1 - \kappa_w$. The price Phillips curve is quite similar, it displays a demand pull and a cost push component, too. The demand pull term is given by the gap between capital utilization and its NAIRU value, $(u - \bar{u})$, and the cost push element is the κ_p and $1 - \kappa_p$ weighted average of short-run wage inflation $\hat{w}$ and expected medium-run overall inflation π^c.

What is left to model is the expected medium-run inflation rate π^c. We postulate in equation (11.39) that changes in expected medium-run inflation are due to an adjustment process towards a weighted average of the current inflation rate and steady state inflation. Thus we introduce here a simple kind of forward looking expectations into the economy. This adjustment is driven by an adjustment velocity β_{π^c}.

It is obvious from this description of the model that it is, on the one hand, already a very general description of macroeconomic dynamics. On the other hand, it is still dependent on some very special assumptions, in particular with respect to financial markets and the government sector. This can be justified at the present stage of analysis by observing that many of its simplifying assumptions are indeed typical for macrodynamic models, which attempt to provide a complete description of a closed monetary economy with labor, goods markets and three markets for financial assets (see in particular the model of Keynesian dynamics of Sargent (1987)).

11.3.5 Capital Markets: Gross Substitutes and Stability

The Stable Core Dynamics on the Financial Markets

We have not yet discussed the determination of the nominal rate of interest i and the price of equities p_e and thus have not yet formulated how capital markets are organized. Following Tobin's (1969) portfolio approach, and also Franke and Semmler (1999), we here for the time being consider that the following equilibrium conditions (11.40)–(11.42) always hold (with ρ the rate of profit of firms) and thus determine the above two prices for bonds and equities as statically endogenous variables of the model.

$$M = M^d = f_m(i, r_e^e)W_c^n, \; W_c^n = M + B + p_e E, \tag{11.40}$$
$$B = B^d = f_b(i, r_e^e)W_c^n, \tag{11.41}$$
$$p_e E = p_e E^d = f_e(i, r_e^e)W_c^n, \tag{11.42}$$
$$r_e^e = \frac{pY^e - wL_1^d - p\delta_k K}{p_e E} + \pi_e^e = \frac{\rho}{q} + \pi_e^e.$$

Note here that all asset supplies are given magnitudes at each moment in time and recall from (11.26) that r_e^e is given by $\frac{r_k^e pK}{p_e E} + \pi_e$ and thus varies at each point in time here solely due to variations in the share price p_e. Our model thus supports the view that the secondary market is the market where the prices or interest rates for the financial assets are determined such that these markets are cleared at all moments in time. This implies that newly issued assets do not impact significantly on these prices.

The trade between the asset holders induces a process that makes asset prices fall or rise in order to equilibrate demands and supplies. In the short-run (in continuous time) the structure of wealth of asset holders W_c^n is, disregarding changes in the share price p_e, given to them and for the model. This implies that the functions $f_m(\cdot)$, $f_b(\cdot)$ and $f_e(\cdot)$, introduced in equations (11.22) to (11.24) must satisfy the well known conditions

$$f_m(i, r_e^e) + f_b(i, r_e^e) + f_e(i, r_e^e) = 1, \tag{11.43}$$
$$\frac{\partial f_m(i, r_e^e)}{\partial z} + \frac{\partial f_b(i, r_e^e)}{\partial z} + \frac{\partial f_e(i, r_e^e)}{\partial z} = 0, \quad \forall\, z \in \{i, r_e^e\}. \tag{11.44}$$

These conditions guarantee that the number of independent equations is equal to the number of statically endogenous variables (i, p_e) that the asset markets are assumed to determine at each moment in time.

We postulate that the financial assets display the following specific choice of the gross substitution condition

$$\begin{aligned} f_{b1} &= \frac{\partial f_b(i, r_e^e)}{\partial i} > 0, \quad f_{m1} = \frac{\partial f_m(i, r_e^e)}{\partial i} < 0, \\ f_{e1} &= \frac{\partial f_e(i, r_e^e)}{\partial i} = 0, \\ f_{e2} &= \frac{\partial f_e(i, r_e^e)}{\partial r_e^e} > 0, \end{aligned} \tag{11.45}$$
$$f_{m2} = \frac{\partial f_m(i, r_e^e)}{\partial r_e^e} = f_{b2} = \frac{\partial f_b(i, r_e^e)}{\partial r_e^e} < 0, \tag{11.46}$$

which basically considers $M_2 = M+B$ and E as gross substitutes, while the rate of interest only determines the allocation of M_2 between money and government bonds $M_2 = M(i) + B(i)$. This implies that open market operations between money and bonds represent an ineffective monetary policy measure, since they do not impact the real markets, but only influence the cash management process of asset holders.

In contrast to Chapter 1 we now also employ a disequilibrium approach in the financial part of the model where we consider the relative excess demand functions

$$\frac{f_e(r_e^e)W_c^n - p_eE}{p_eE}, \qquad \frac{f_b(i, r_e^e)W_c^n - B}{B}$$

as giving rise to (smaller) actual changes (flows) in the corresponding asset. These changes in turn influence stock price inflation in a positive way and the growth rate of the nominal rate of interest in a negative way (just as in the hypothetical ultra short-run asset price dynamics we have considered in Chapter 1. Note, however, that these laws of motion now relate percentages of market disequilibrium with percentages in stock price and interest rate changes and are therefore now more coherently formulated from the viewpoint of dimensional analysis. The impact of stock imbalances on stock prices and interest rates are represented by single parameters β_e, β_b below.

Assuming that bonds and equities (and money) as well as all real variables are temporarily given magnitudes and assuming that the above form of gross substitutes conditions are holding, we get the following proposition for the stability of the asset markets:

Theorem 1 Stable Financial Markets Interaction
Assume that capital gain expectations are static. Then: the dynamics for asset prices p_e and the rate of return i on short-term bonds

$$\hat{p}_e = \beta_e\left(\frac{f_e(r_e^e)W_c^n}{(p_eE)} - 1\right), \quad i.e.,$$

$$\dot{p}_eE = \beta_e(f_e(r_e^e)W_c^n - p_eE) \tag{11.47}$$

$$\hat{i} = -\beta_b\left(\frac{f_b(i, r_e^e)W_c^n - B}{B}\right), \tag{11.48}$$

$$with\ r_e^e = \frac{pY^e - wL_1^d - p\delta_kK}{p_eE} + \bar{\pi}_e^e$$

converge to the current equilibrium state of the asset markets for all adjustment speeds β_e, β_b *of stock prices* p_e *and interest rates* i.

Proof: The first law of motion is only dependent on the stock price p_e and this in a negative way, since there holds

$$\frac{d\hat{p}_e}{dp_e} = \beta_e f_e'(\cdot)\frac{dr_e^e}{dp_e}W_c^n + (f_e(\cdot) - 1)E < 0, \quad f_e(\cdot) < 1.$$

Such a negative relationship more obviously also holds for the second law of motion if only interest rate adjustments are considered and is also convergent if the share price is adjusting according to the first law of motion (since the resulting 2D Jacobian is then characterized by $J_{12} < 0, J_{21} = 0$).

We thus get the result that the adjustment processeson the financial market are stable as long as expectations do not disturb them too much. This provides a fairly tranquil starting point for the discussion of the accelerating processes in expectations that may destabilize the functioning of the financial sector of our economy.

11.4 The Model in Intensive Form

In this section we derive the intensive form of the model, namely we will express all stock and flow variables in the laws of motion to be derived, and also in the needed algebraic equations, per unit of capital. We thus divide nominal stock and flow variables by the nominal value of the capital stock pK and all real ones by K, the real capital stock. This allows the determination of a (unique) steady state solution as the interior point of rest in the economic state space of the model.

We begin with the intensive form of some necessary definitions or identities, and also behavioral equations, needed for representing the dynamic system in a sufficiently comprehensible form. These algebraic equations are given as follows:

$$\begin{aligned}
y &= \frac{Y}{K} = (1 + \alpha_{n^d}(n + \beta_n))y^e - \beta_n \nu, \\
l_1^d &= L_1^d/K = y/z, \\
e_1 &= l_1^d/l, \\
u &= y/y^p, \\
r^e &= y^e - \delta_k - \omega_1 l_1^d,
\end{aligned}$$

$$
\begin{aligned}
c(\cdot) &= \frac{C}{K} = (1-(\tau_1+\alpha_\omega))\omega_1\frac{y}{z} + \alpha_\omega\omega_1(1+\alpha_r)l + \delta_p p_1 \\
&\quad +(1-s_c)(y^e - \delta_k - \omega_1 l_1^d - t_c), \\
i(\cdot) &= \frac{I}{K} = i_q(q-1) + i_u(u-\bar{u}) + n, \\
y^d &= \frac{Y^d}{K} = c(\cdot) + i(\cdot) + \delta_k + \alpha_g g, \\
q &= (p_e E)/pK, \\
r_e^e &= r^e/q + \pi_e, \\
\pi_e &= \alpha_{\pi_e}\pi_{ec} + (1-\alpha_{\pi_e})\pi_{ef}.
\end{aligned}
$$

The above equations describe output and employment per unit of capital, the rate of utilization of the existing stock of labor and capital, the expected rate of profit, consumption, investment and aggregate demand per unit of capital, Tobin's average q, and the expected rate of return on equities (including expected capital gains π_e).

Now we translate the laws of motion of the dynamically endogenous variables into capital-intensive form. The law of motions for the nominal wages and price level stated in equations (11.37) and (11.38) are interacting instantaneously and thus depend on each other. Solving these two linear equations for $\hat{w}$ and $\hat{p}$ gives

$$\hat{w}_1 = \kappa\left(\beta_w(e_1-\bar{e}_1) + \kappa_w\beta_p(u-\bar{u})\right) + \pi^c, \tag{11.49}$$

and

$$\hat{p} = \kappa\left(\beta_p(u-\bar{u}) + \kappa_p\beta_w(e_1-\bar{e}_1)\right) + \pi^c, \tag{11.50}$$

with $\kappa = (1-\kappa_w\kappa_p)^{-1}$. From these two inflation rates one can compute the growth law of real wages $\omega_1 = w_1/p$ by means of the definitional relationship $\hat{\omega}_1 = \hat{w}_1 - \hat{p}$. This gives us

$$\hat{\omega}_1 = \kappa[(1-\kappa_p)\beta_w(e_1-\bar{e}_1) + (\kappa_w - 1)\beta_p(u-\bar{u})]. \tag{11.51}$$

The next set of equations explains the dynamic laws of the expected rate of inflation, the labor capital ratio,the expected sales, and the stock of inventories in intensive form:

$$
\begin{aligned}
\dot{\pi^c} &= \alpha_{\pi^c}\beta_{\pi^c}\kappa\big(\beta_p(u-\bar{u}) + \kappa_p\beta_w(e_1-\bar{e}_1)\big) + \\
&\quad (1-\alpha_{\pi^c})\beta_{\pi^c}(\mu - n - \pi^c), && (11.52) \\
\hat{l} &= n - i(\cdot) = -i_q(q-1) - i_u(u-\bar{u}), && (11.53) \\
\dot{y}^e &= \beta_{y^e}(y^d - y^e) + (n - i(\cdot))y^e, && (11.54) \\
\dot{\nu} &= y - y^d - i(\cdot)\nu. && (11.55)
\end{aligned}
$$

Equation (11.52) is almost the same as in the extensive modeling, but here the term $\hat{p} - \pi^c$ is substituted according to equation (11.50). Equation (11.53), the law of motion of relative factor endowment, is given by the (negative) of the investment function as far as its dependence on asset markets and the state of the business cycle are concerned. Equation (11.54) is obtained by way of the time derivative of y^e as follows:

$$\begin{aligned}\dot{y}^e &= \frac{d(Y^e/K)}{dt} = \frac{\dot{Y}^e K - Y^e \dot{K}}{K^2} \\ &= \frac{\dot{Y}^e}{K} - y^e i(\cdot) = \beta_{y^e}(y^d - y^e) + y^e(n - i(\cdot)).\end{aligned}$$

In essentially the same way one gets equation (11.55). The laws of motion governing the expectations about the equity prices are not changed by the intensive form modeling and thus again read as follows:

$$\dot{\pi}_{ef} = \beta_{\pi_{ef}}(\bar{\eta} - \pi_{ef}), \tag{11.56}$$

$$\dot{\pi}_{ec} = \beta_{\pi_{ec}}(\hat{p}_e - \pi_{ec}). \tag{11.57}$$

In the following laws of motion for Tobin's q and the nominal rate of interest only the value of aggregate capital gains expectations is needed (in the definition of the expected rate of return on equities).

$$\hat{q} = \beta_e(f_e(i, r_e^e)(m + b + q)/q - 1) - \hat{E} - (\hat{p} + \hat{K}), \tag{11.58}$$

$$\hat{i} = -\beta_b(f_b(i, r_e^e)(m + b + q)/b - 1) - \hat{E} - (\hat{p} + \hat{K}), \tag{11.59}$$

where $\hat{E}$ is given by the budget equation of firms as follows:

$$\hat{E} = \frac{p_e \dot{E}}{p_e E} = \frac{I + \dot{N} - \mathcal{I}}{K}/q = \frac{i(\cdot) + y^e - y^d}{q}.$$

Finally, the laws of motion for real balances and real bonds and pension funds per unit of capital have to be derived. Based on the knowledge of the laws of motion for inflation $\hat{p}$ and investment $i(\cdot)$ we can derive the differential equation for bonds per unit of capital shown in equation (11.60) from the following expression:

$$\dot{b} = \frac{d(B/pK)}{dt} = \frac{\dot{B}}{pK} - b(\hat{p} + i(\cdot)),$$

where $\dot{B}$ is given by equation (11.36). The same idea is used for the changes in the money supply. We thus get the following two differential equations:

$$\dot{b} = g - t_c - \tau_1 \omega_1 l_1^d - \mu m$$
$$- b\left(\kappa[\beta_p(u - \bar{u}) + \kappa_p \beta_w(e_1 - \bar{e}_1)] + \pi^c + i(\cdot)\right), \tag{11.60}$$
$$\dot{m} = m\mu - m(\kappa[\beta_p(u - \bar{u}) + \kappa_p \beta_w(e_1 - \bar{e}_1)] + \pi^c + i(\cdot)). \tag{11.61}$$

For $p_1 = \frac{P_1}{pK}$ we finally get in a similar way:

$$\dot{p}_1 = (1 - c_1 - \alpha_\omega)\omega_1 y/z - \alpha_\omega \omega_1(1 + \alpha_r)l -$$
$$(1 - \alpha_g)g - \delta_p - (\hat{p} + \hat{K})p_1. \tag{11.62}$$

According to the above, the dynamics in extensive form can therefore be reduced to nine (eight) differential equations, where, however, the law of motion for share prices has not been determined yet, or to seven differential and one integral equation which is easier to handle than the alternative representation, since there is no law of motion for the development of future share prices to be calculated then. Note with respect to these dynamics that economic policy (fiscal and monetary) is still represented in very simple terms here, since money supply is growing with a given rate and since government expenditures and taxes on capital income net of interest payments per unit of capital are given parameters. This makes the dynamics of the government budget constraint (see the law of motion for bonds per unit of capital b) a very trivial one, as in Sargent (1987, ch.5), and thus reserves the problems associated with these dynamics in the literature a matter for future research. The advantage is that fiscal policy can be discussed in very simple way here by means of three parameters solely.

Comparing the present dynamics with those of the working KMG model of Chiarella and Flaschel (2000a) and Chiarella, Flaschel, Groh and Semmler (2000) shows that there are now two variables from the financial sector that feed back to the real dynamics in this extended system, the bond to capital ratio b representing the evolution of government debt and Tobin's average q. The first (dynamic) variable, however, only influences the real dynamics since it is one of the factors that influences the statically endogenous variable q which in turn enters the investment function as a measure of the firms' performance. Government bonds do not influence the economy in other ways, since there are no wealth effects in consumption yet and since the interest income channel to consumption has been suppressed by the assumption on tax collection concerning capital income. In addition, the interest rate channel of the earlier KMG approaches, where the real rate of interest as compared to the real profit rate entered the investment function, is now absent from this function. The nominal interest rate as determined by portfolio equilibrium thus does not matter in the present formulation of the model, where Tobin's q in the place of this interest rate now provides the channel by which investment behavior is reacting to the results brought about by the financial markets.

The present dynamics no longer has laws of motion that are left implicit in its discussion (the bond and the share price dynamics of the working KMG models cited above), but is now a completely formulated dynamics, yet still one where the real financial interaction is represented in basic terms. Price inflation (via real balances and real bonds) and the expected rate of profit (via the dividend rate of return) influence the behavior of asset markets via laws of motion for them, while the reaction of asset markets feeds back into the real part of the economy instantaneously through the change in Tobin's q that is caused by them (and the dynamics of expected capital gains).

Steady State Considerations

In this subsection we assert the existence of a steady state in the modeled economy. We here stress that this can be done independently of the knowledge on the comparative statics of the asset market equilibrium system, since Tobin's q is given by 1 in the steady state via the real part of the model and since the portfolio equilibrium equations can be uniquely solved in conjunction with the government budget constraint for the three variables i, m, b which they then determine.

Theorem 2 *We consider the special case $\delta_p = 0, \alpha_\omega = 0, \beta_e = \beta_b = \infty$, that is where we abstract from pension funds and the second labor market and where financial markets are in equilibrium at each moment in time. Assume moreover $s_c > \tau_w$ and $s_c r_o^e > n+g-t_c$. Assume finally that the parameter ϕ defined below has a positive numerator, that is the government runs a primary deficit in the steady state. The dynamic system given by equations (11.51) to (11.61) possesses a unique interior steady state solution $(\omega_o, l_o, m_o > 0)$, with equilibrium on the asset markets, if the fundamentalists' long-run reference rate of equity price inflation equals the steady state inflation rate of goods prices*

$$\bar{\eta} = \hat{p}_o,$$

and if

$$\lim_{i\to 0}(f_m(i, r_{e0} + \pi_{eo} + f_b(i, r_{e0} + \pi_{eo}) < \bar{\phi}$$
$$\text{and} \quad \lim_{i\to \infty}(f_m(i, r_{e0} + \pi_{eo} + f_b(i, r_{e0} + \pi_{eo}) > \bar{\phi}$$

holds true with respect to $\bar{\phi} = \frac{g-t_c-\tau_w\omega_{1o}l_{1o}^d}{g-t_c-\tau_w\omega_{1o}l_{1o}^d+\mu}$.

Proof: See Asada, Chiarella, Flaschel and Franke (2010), also with respect to explicit expressions for the steady state values of the economy.

Returning to the initially considered situation with an augmented consumption function of workers (that also depends on company pension funds per unit of capital) and with disequilibrium adjustment processes on the financial markets does not in our view alter the dynamics in significant ways, so that we expect that the existence and stability of their steady state is basically of the same kind as we have considered it for the baseline KMGT model of the Chapter 1. We therefore expect that the philosophy of the feedback channel investigations and the policy theorems that were based on them in this chapter also applies to the present situation of a flexicurity economy of the Keynesian KMGT type. Some of these policy theorems are, however, now briefly reconsidered in this extended framework in the next section, now including labor market policies as they suggest themselves in the context of flexicurity.

11.5 Economic Policy

In this section we analyze the effects of specific monetary policies, fiscal policies and labor market policies with respect to the dynamics of our model. We here provide – based on the model of this chapter – some foundations for a new social structure of capital accumulation where not only financial instabilities and the business cycle, but also the wage–price spiral, can be tamed to a certain degree in the presence of full employment guaranteed by the government as an employer of first resort. However, this is just the beginning of the study of monetary, fiscal and labor market measures aimed at providing a stable full-employment scenario in a competitive capitalist economy where not only free hiring and firing of labor, but also creative destruction through Schumpeterian processes of invention, innovation and diffusion are present.

11.5.1 Monetary Policy

We first consider monetary policy which as the model is designed can only influence real activity if it can have an impact on Tobin's q. This immediately implies that open market operation in the assets M and

B are completely ineffective, since they only change the composition of $M+B$, but not its level, and thus do not have an impact on the stock market. As argued in Chapter 1, open market policies must therefore operate on the stock market, and this specifically by selling equities in the boom and by purchasing them in the bust through corresponding changes in the money supply. This reduces the positive dependence of economic activity on Tobin's q and thus weakens the positive feedback loop between the stock market and economic activity.

We concentrate in this subsection, however, on the asset markets themselves and recapitulate their dynamics as follows:

$$\begin{aligned}
\dot{p}_e &= \beta_e(f_e(r_e^e)W_c^n/E - p_e), \quad r_e^e = \frac{pY^e - wL_1^d - p\delta_k K}{p_e E} + \alpha_{\pi_e}\pi_{ec}, \\
\dot{i} &= -\beta_b(f_b(i, r_e^e)W_c^n/B - 1)i, \quad W_c^n = M + B + p_e E, \\
\dot{\pi}_{ec} &= \beta_{\pi_{ec}}(\hat{p}_e - \pi_{ec}).
\end{aligned}$$

We ignore here the expectation formation of fundamentalists, since they enlarge the Jacobian J of the dynamics of the asset markets only by a negative term in the trace of J and are thus completely neutral with respect to the stability features of the dynamics.

For the sign structure of the matrix J one easily gets:

$$\begin{pmatrix} - & 0 & + \\ - & - & + \\ - & 0 & \pm \end{pmatrix}.$$

This implies a stable matrix J if $\pm$ is in fact negative and the adaptive expectations mechanism therefore sufficiently slow, since the Routh–Hurwitz conditions are then easily obtained.[5] Choosing the parameter $\beta_{\pi_{ec}}$ sufficiently large will, however, make the trace positive and thus destroy the stable adjustment process on the asset markets (since det J is always negative). Chartists' expectation formations – if sufficiently fast – are thus making the financial markets unstable in their reaction patterns and this is in fact the only destabilizing mechanism on these markets in their present formulation.

We therefore now introduce a Tobin type taxation parameter, τ_e, but one that is applied to capital gains and not to financial transactions per se.[6] This modifies the above dynamics as follows:

$$\dot{p}_e = \beta_e(f_e(r_e^e)W_c^n/E - p_e), \quad r_e^e = \frac{pY^e - wL_1^d - p\delta_k K}{p_e E} + \alpha_{\pi_e}\pi_{ec},$$
$$\dot{\pi}_{ec} = \beta_{\pi_{ec}}((1-\tau_e)\hat{p}_e - \pi_{ec}),$$
$$\dot{i} = -\beta_b(f_b(i, r_e^e)W_c^n/B - 1)i, \quad W_c^n = M + B + p_e E.$$

It is obvious that 100 percent capital gain taxation will make the financial system stable again. It is, however, equally obvious that the following sufficient condition for stability holds, since $J_{33} < 0$ holds true in this case:

$$\tau_e \geq \max\left\{0, 1 - \frac{1}{\alpha_{\pi_e}\beta_e f_e'(\cdot)W_c^n/E}\right\}$$

We get that the Tobin tax must be the higher the higher the portion of chartists in the financial markets, the faster stock prices are adjusting and the more elastic the stock demand function is with respect to the rate of return on equities.

This sufficient condition can, however, be easily replaced by one that is sufficient and necessary if one observes that the first two of the above rearranged laws of motion are independent from the last one (the eigenvalue of which is simply given by $J_{33} < 0$). The condition $J_{11} + J_{22} = 0$ therefore separates stability from instability (since the determinant of the 2D subsystem is positive) which gives:

$$\begin{aligned}\tau_e^H =& 1 - \frac{-\beta_e[f_e'(\cdot)\frac{\partial r_e^e}{\partial p_e}\frac{W_c^n}{E} + f_e(\cdot) - 1] + \beta_{\pi_{ec}}}{\alpha_{\pi_e}\beta_{\pi_{ec}}\beta_e f_e'(\cdot)} \\ =& 1 - \frac{[f_e'(\cdot)\frac{\rho}{q}\frac{W_c^n}{p_e E} + 1 - f_e(\cdot)]/\beta_{\pi_{ec}} + 1/\beta_e}{\alpha_{\pi_e} f_e'(\cdot)},\end{aligned}$$

as a Hopf bifurcation parameter value (at the steady state of the dynamics).[7] In addition to the above we thus here also see that a lowering of the parameter $\beta_{\pi_{ec}}$ is stabilizing the economy.

Summing up, monetary policy is here primarily concerned with regulating the stock market which when exercised with sufficient strength should weaken the positive feedback channel between capital gains, expected capital gains and economic activity to a sufficient degree. We refer the reader here back to Chapter 1 as far as the handling of funds generated by the Tobin tax is concerned.

11.5.2 Fiscal Policy

Concerning fiscal policy, we can state that Theorem 1 of Chapter 1 remains applicable if the special situation considered at the end of the preceding section – which formally seen leads us back to the model of Chapter 1 – is adopted. It formulates how fiscal policy should be designed in order to create damped oscillations around the balanced growth path of the economy (if they are not yet present).

$$\begin{aligned}\dot{m} =& \mu m - [\kappa[\beta_p(u-\bar{u}) + \kappa_p\beta_w(e_1-\bar{e}_1)] + \pi_o^c + i(\cdot)]m,\\ \dot{b} =& g - t_c - \tau_1\omega_{1o}l_1^d - \mu m - \\ & [\kappa[\beta_p(u-\bar{u}) + \kappa_p\beta_w(e_1-\bar{e}_1)] + \pi_o^c + i(\cdot)]\, b,\\ \dot{y}^e =& \beta_{y^e}(y^d - y^e) + (n - i(\cdot))y^e,\end{aligned}$$

with

$$\begin{aligned}y^d =& c(\cdot) + i(\cdot) + \delta_k + \alpha_g g,\\ c(\cdot) =& (1-(\tau_1+\alpha_\omega))\omega_{1o}y/z + \alpha_\omega\omega_{1o}(1+\alpha_r)l_o + \delta_p p_{1o},\\ i(\cdot) =& i_q(q(m,b)-1) + i_u(u-\bar{u}) + n, \quad u = y/y^p,\\ y =& (1+\alpha_{n^d}(n+\beta_n))y^e - \beta_n\nu_o.\end{aligned}$$

We here consider the case $s_c = 1$. Note that we have fixed several magnitudes to their steady state values in the above partial reconsideration of our dynamical model. Note also that the link $q(m,b)$ to the financial markets is considered as sufficiently weak in the interaction of these three laws of motion for real balances, real government debt and expected sales per unit of capital (due to the working of monetary policy).

Theorem 3 *Assume an independent fiscal authority responsible for the control of business fluctuations which implements the following two rules for its activity-oriented expenditures and their financing:*

$$g^u = -g_u(u-\bar{u}), \quad t^u = g_u(u-\bar{u})$$

We assume that the tributes t^u are paid by asset holders. The expenditure rule augments the aggregate demand function by g^u without impacting the other laws of motion. Then: an anti-cyclical policy g^u that is chosen in a sufficiently active way can enforce damped oscillations in the subdynamics m, b, y^e, if β_{y^e} is sufficiently large.

This theorem therefore provides conditions under which the Harrodian quantity dynamics on the goods market and their interaction with the evolution of real balances and real government debt can be tamed by fiscal policy.

11.5.3 Labor Market Policy

Here, we already have a flexicurity system in operation and only want to study in addition to the normal working of the wage–price dynamics in its KMGT-setup possibilities that make the wage–price dynamics even less prone to accelerating forces. We do this by isolating the dynamics of real wages of workers in the first labor market in their interaction with the goods market dynamics. We assume for reasons of simplicity that $s_c = 1$ holds and that capacity utilization of firms is measured by $u = y^e/y^p$, namely by the proportion of expected sales in potential output. Moreover we fix some magnitudes at their steady state values, since they are not of central importance in the investigation of the positive feedback chain that can exist between capacity utilization and real wages. This gives us the following subdynamics of the flexicurity KMGT model.

$$\begin{aligned}\hat{\omega}_1 =& \kappa[(1-\kappa_p)\beta_w(e_1(y^e/y^p)-\bar{e}_1)+(\kappa_w-1)\beta_p(y^e/y^p-\bar{u})], \quad e_1^{'}>0,\\ \hat{y}^e =& \beta_{y^e}(y^d/y^e-1)+(n-i(\cdot))_o,\end{aligned}$$

with

$$\begin{aligned}y^d =& c(\cdot)+i(\cdot)+\delta_k+\alpha_g g,\\ c(\cdot) =& (1-(\tau_1+\alpha_\omega))\omega_1 y/z+\alpha_\omega\omega_1(1+\alpha_r)l_o+\delta_p p_{1o},\\ i(\cdot) =& i_q(q_o-1)+i_u(y^e/y^p-\bar{u})+n,\\ y =& (1+\alpha_{n^d}(n+\beta_n))y^e-\beta_n\nu_o.\end{aligned}$$

Note that we have assumed here that the employment rate e_1 depends positively on the rate of capacity utilization which is a simple form of Okun's law, relating utilization of machinery with the recruitment of new workers. We assume moreover that the propensity to consume and invest parameters are such that we get the usual Keynesian stability condition: $Y^d_{y^e} < 1$, an overall marginal propensity to spend less than one. Otherwise the fiscal policy considered in the preceding subsection must be chosen such that this condition is fulfilled.

Inserting the static equations into the dynamics gives a 2D system in the two state variables ω_1, y^e, the Jacobian of which is characterized by:

$$\begin{pmatrix} J_{11} & J_{12} \\ J_{21} & J_{22} \end{pmatrix} + \begin{pmatrix} 0 & \pm \\ + & - \end{pmatrix}.$$

Aggregate demand is wage-led in our KMGT model, namely it depends positively on the real wage, since investment is only dependent on Tobin's q which only indirectly depends on the real wage of the workers employed by firms. Therefore, the following condition is necessary and sufficient for asymptotic stability:

$$(1 - \kappa_p)\beta_w e_1^{'} + (\kappa_w - 1)\beta_p < 0.$$

This condition is fulfilled if there is agreement between capital and labor so that nominal wages are adjusted sufficiently sluggishly. This condition will be fulfilled for a value of κ_p sufficiently close to one. The stability condition is also further enforced if the recruitment policy of firms is sufficiently sluggish, meaning that overtime or undertime work is used in the first instance to cope with the business cycle. In a wage-led economy there is therefore the need for cooperation between capital and labor that guarantees that real wages react negatively (in a countercyclical way) to changes in economic activity in order to avoid an accelerating wage–price spiral. Shared insight into this wage–price spiral dynamics is therefore essential to at least limit it in the overall dynamics to a sufficient degree.

It may also be a possibility to agree on a 'scala mobile' mechanism where wages are automatically adjusted to price inflation ($\beta_w = 0, \kappa_w = 1$), since this removes all demand pressure terms from real wage adjustment. Such real wage adjustments may be necessary from time to time (if labor productivity is changing). Real wages should of course also fulfill then the minimum and maximum consideration we have conducted in Chapter 2. All this implies that there is a need for proper wage management in the flexicurity version of the KMGT growth dynamics in order to avoid real wage dynamics that may question the stability of the overall dynamics.

11.5.4 A Summing Up

The considered policies suggest that monetary policy should be concentrated in specific ways on financial markets in order to reduce their volatility, that fiscal policy (demand management) should be implemented in an anticyclical Keynesian way in order to reduce business fluctuations (and therewith inflationary pressure) and that labor market policies (wage management) should be used in addition to that, in order to avoid inflationary spirals and the Marxian distributive cycle. This is a significant rearrangement in the assignment of monetary, fiscal and labor market policies characterizing the proper starting point for a discussion of the choice of policy measures in the flexicurity KMGT model of this chapter.

11.6 Credit and Schumpeterian Processes of Creative Destruction

In this section we briefly introduce credit to firms into our KMGT flexicurity model as the basis for a discussion of Schumpeterian innovation processes and the creative capital destruction they imply. Pension funds now again give loans to firms which are used for real capital formation instead of remaining largely idle. The productive use of part of the pension fund P_1 is here assumed to be rewarded at the constant interest rate r applied to the debt level D accumulated by the firms in the private sector of the economy.

Pension funds thus act as quasi commercial banks who give credit to firms out of their funds and thus allow firms to invest beyond their equity issue $p_e\dot{E}$ – which is now simplified and assumed to finance capital expansion npK solely. This implies for the issue of new equities the simple rule: $\hat{E} = n/q$. This rule is in line with what equity owners might consider an admissible equity issuing rule, concerning the protection of their share values. Note that profits are again paid out as dividends so that the variable component in the rate of investment must be financed by loans exclusively.

Table 11.5: Firms: production and income account

Uses	Resources
$\delta_k K$	$\delta_k K$
$\omega_1 L_1^d$	$C_1 + C_2 + C_r$
–	G
rD	–
Π	I
Y^p	Y^p

With the accounts, see Table 11.5–Table 11.10, we only provide the changes that are now made to the KMGT flexicurity model. The behavior and financing of gross investment is shown in Table 11.6.

We now assume the extended functional relationship as the investment behavior of firms:

Table 11.6: Firms: investment and credit

Uses	Resources
$\delta_k K$	$\delta_k K$
$I = (i_q(\cdot) + i_u(\cdot) - i_d(d - d_o) + n)K$	$npK = p_e E$
	$\dot{D} = pI - npK$
I^g	I^g

$$I/K = i_q(q-1) + i_u(u - \bar{u}) - i_d(d - d_o) + n, d = D/pK.$$

This investment schedule states that investment plans now in addition depend negatively on the deviation of the debt to capital ratio from its steady state value. The exogenous trend term in investment is again n, the natural rate of growth of the economy.

Table 11.7: Firms' net worth

Assets	Liabilities
pK	D
	$p_e E$
	Real Net Worth
pK	pK

In the management of pension funds we assume that a portion sP_1 of them is held as minimum reserves and that a larger portion of them has been given as credit D to firms. The remaining amount are idle reserves X, not yet allocated to any interest bearing activity.

Table 11.8: Pension funds and credit (stocks)

Assets	Liabilities
P_1	sP_1 reserves
	D
	X excess reserves
P_1	P_1

Pension funds receive the savings of households of type 1 (the other households do not save) and they receive the interest payments of firms. They allocate this into required reserve increases, payments to pensioners, new credit demand of firms and the rest as an addition or substraction to their idle reserves.

Table 11.9: Pension funds and credit (flows)

Resources	Uses
pS_1	$s\dot{P}_1$
rD	$\delta P_1 + rD$
	$\dot{D} = I - npK$
	$\dot{X}$
$pS_1 + rD$	$pS_1 + rD$

The above representation of the flows of funds in the pension funds system implies for the time derivative of accumulated funds P_1 the relationship

$$\dot{P}_1 = pS_1 - \delta P_1 - rD.$$

This is also mirrored by the income account of retired households.

Table 11.10: Retired households: income account

Uses	Resources
C_r	$\omega_2 L_r + \delta_p P_1 + rD$
Y^r	Y^r

After having considered the macroeconomic problems a flexicurity KMGT economy might face in the preceding section, we now come to a brief discussion of the microeconomic problems it has been constructed for as a solution, namely the socially acceptable handling of exit and entry problems with respect to real capital as well as the employment of labor.

The most remarkable feature of existing capitalism is definitely its ability to revolutionize the technological foundations and the product and production frame of market economies. The first in depth treatment of this fundamental tendency was given in Marx's (1954) *Capital* based on what he called the law of value. Schumpeter knew Marx's work very well, but developed his own vision of the microdynamics of capitalism which in place of some questionable monotonic tendencies asserted by Marx, with the exception of the secular law of increasing labor productivity, led him to the consideration of long waves in his work on business cycles (see Schumpeter 1939). Marx, of course, had not lived long enough to become aware of long-phased cyclical changes in the economic and social structure of capitalist economies, but was nevertheless able, on the basis of his value theory, to discuss the secular tendencies of the concentration and centralization of capital and this even on a globalized scale.

Schumpeter's (1934) *The Theory of Economic Development* started from a quite different theoretical apparatus as compared to the classical theory of labor values and production prices, namely from the Walrasian concept of a perfectly (non-)competitive market economy which for him described the circular flow of economic life in given circumstances. To this he then added economic development and credit and most fundamentally the dynamic character of the entrepreneur who is initiating spontaneous and discontinuous changes which forever alter and displace the previously existing equilibrium state.

> These spontaneous and discontinuous changes in the channel of the circular flow and these disturbances in the center of equilibrium appear in the sphere of industrial and commercial life, not in the sphere of the wants of the consumer of final products. (Schumpeter 1934, p.65)

Concerning today's Walrasian theory of general equilibrium where production is but an appendix to consumption theory, this is a totally different perspective and this may also give one of the reasons why Schumpeter (1942) later on used the theory of monopolistic competition as the starting point of his analysis of the dynamics of capitalism. Defining development as driven by the spontaneous action of the dynamic entrepreneur Schumpeter (1934, p.66) then classifies the possibilities for such actions as follows:

> Development in our sense is then defined by the carrying out of new combinations. This concept covers the following five cases: (1) The introduction of a new good – that is one with which consumers are not yet familiar – or of a new quality of a good. (2) The introduction of a new method of production, that is one not yet tested by experience in the branch of manufacture concerned, which need by no means be founded upon a discovery scientifically new, and can also exist in a new way of handling a commodity commercially. (3) The opening of a new market, that is a market into which the particular branch of manufacture of the country in question has not previously entered, whether or not this market has existed before. (4) The conquest of a new source of supply of raw materials or half-manufactured goods, again irrespective of whether this source already exists or whether it has first to be created. (5) The carrying out of the new organization of any industry, like the creation of a monopoly position (for example through trustification) or the breaking up of a monopoly position.

To realize these various activities the role of credit is essential, since it allows starting such projects with a significant degree of innovation, often created by new ideas of new entrants in certain markets. Credit helps to redirect labor and capital from old combinations to definitely new ones through process or product innovation and more; see the above list given by Schumpeter. It is therefore not just the use of idle resources of the economy, but the redirection of the employed resources towards new projects and the extra profits they can generate in comparison to their competitors. A typical example here is the railroadization discussed at length in Schumpeter (1939).

The innovative character of the Schumpeterian entrepreneurs thus alters the way the economy has been functioning so far and this the more rapidly the larger the scale on which such entrepreneurs enter the scene. Of course there are subsequent processes of the diffusion of the newly created technology or products which in the course of time reduce extra profits when these new projects have become a routinized economic activity. Yet processes of innovation and diffusion may cluster in historical time and may thus lead to the long-phased evolution of social structures of accumulation as they are described historically in Schumpeter (1939) as three Kondratieff waves (superimposed by shorter cycles in addition).

It is not our intention here to go into the details of Schumpeter's analysis of the forces that drive the evolution of capitalist economies. We refer the reader instead to the paper by Swedberg (1991) on Schumpeter's work and biography and to a voluminous edition on Schumpeter and Neo-Schumpeterian Economics edited by Hanusch and Pyka (2007). Our interest instead is to go on from Schumpeter's analysis of capitalism to his analysis of competitive socialism and the implications it may have for the model of flexicurity capitalism that is the subject of this chapter.

Questioning the viability of (at his time) existing (and now past) Eastern state socialism from the viewpoint of immaturity, Schumpeter (1942) developed a concept of socialism for Western countries in the state of maturity characterized as a type of competitive socialism built on foundations erected unconsciously through the big enterprises created by the Rockefellers, the Vanderbilts and other famous dynasties in the Western industrialized countries. Schumpeter discusses the question of whether this type of socialism can work, what the corresponding socialist blueprints should look like and to what extent they are superior to the capitalist mark II blueprints (of the mega-corporations) that he conceived as having made obsolescent the entrepreneurial functioning of his view of capitalism mark I, the dynamic entrepreneur and the process of creative destruction which is conducted by this leading form of an economic agent.

Monopolistic practices, vanishing investment opportunities and growing hostility in the social structure of capitalism were part of the reasons that in Schumpeter's view characterized the decomposition of capitalism as he investigated it in 1942. Against this scenery he described the superiority of the socialist blueprint of the Western competitive type, the transition to this form of social structure of accumulation and the comparative efficiency of such economies. In a separate chapter he discusses the human element in this type of economy, the problem of work organization and the integration of bourgeois forms of management under capitalism into this type of socialism including the incentive problems concerning the behavior of these economic agents.

A typical statement with respect to the latter situation is:

> It is not difficult however to insert the stock of bourgeois extraction into its proper place within that machine and to reshape its habits of work. ... Rational treatments of the ex-bourgeois elements with a view to securing a maximum performance from them will then not require anything that is not just as necessary in the case of managerial personnel of any other extraction. (Schumpeter 1942, p.65)

It may appear from today's perspective that his focused and provocative discussion of these points in Section III of the chapter 'The Human Element' can be questioned to a certain degree. However, the managerial element in existing Western capitalism has become more and more the focus of public debate ranging from the salaries to the ethics the (top) managerial personal should receive and adopt, respectively. Actual discussions on the behavior of industrial management therefore are already preparing the ground for a situation where these persons may be attributed an appropriate level of exclusiveness, that may completely suffice to motivate their efforts to a sufficient degree with a problem-adequate perspective. We do not, however, claim here that such short characterizations suffice as considerations of the issue. On the contrary, detailed microeconomic and other investigations are absolutely necessary to deal with such issues, yet these issues have to be dealt with in actual capitalist management problems anyway. The important point in Schumpeter's arguments is that Western capitalism may transform itself automatically into some kind of competitive socialism on the basis of Western management principles. Such a statement can also be applied to the evolution of the Nordic European countries which may be on a progress path towards a kind of social structure of accumulation we have modelled as flexicurity capitalism in this chapter.

With respect to the workforce of firms in capitalism as well as in his type of socialism, Schumpeter (1942, p.213) states:

> Second, closely allied to the necessity of incessant training of the normal is the necessity of dealing with the subnormal performer. This term does not refer to isolated pathological cases, but to a broad fringe of perhaps 25 % of the population. So far as subnormal performance is due to moral or volitional defects, it is perfectly unrealistic to expect that it will vanish with capitalism. The great problem and the great enemy of humanity, the subnormal, will be as much with us as he is now. He can hardly be dealt with by unaided group discipline alone – although of course the machinery of authoritarian discipline can be so constructed as to work, partly at least, through the group of which the subnormal is an element.

In view of our discussion of the working of Marx's general law of accumulation under today's conditions in Western type economies, see Part I, we would however point here to the fact that capitalism itself is in part responsible for the existence of the subnormal element as characterized in the above quote from Schumpeter's work. Mass unemployment, and its consequences for family life much beyond the current status on the labor market – alienation from human types of work organization, degradation of part of the workforce as the unskilled element in an otherwise flourishing economy, the rise and the fall of the welfare state and the latter's consequences for basic income needs, sufficient health care, sufficient care for the children and the elderly and adequate schooling systems – are just some of the reasons why the 'subnormal' element in the population is a persistent fact of life. In this respect, we would claim that the social acceptance of a system of flexicurity – as we have implanted it in this chapter into the KMGT framework – would be one way to eliminate the 'subnormal' segment from the population gradually, but maybe not totally.

We therefore assert here that a system of flexicurity capitalism, based on the principles we have modelled in this chapter, would progressively tend towards social acceptance and social learning processes that put it on a progress path towards viable economic reproduction, sufficient income and care for everybody and – if security is well developed to cope with flexibility of a Schumpeterian kind (creative destruction) –

that leads it into a situation where it can compete with societies that are subject to the Marxian reserve army mechanism and the ruthless capitalism that is related with it.

The central message of Schumpeter's (1942) work, *Capitalism, Socialism and Democracy* – that socialism is created out of Western capitalist economies, and not on the basis of (the now past) Eastern type of socialism – can thus be carried over to the current debate on the possibility of flexicurity capitalism. Also this form of socio-economic reproduction may be organized through large production units and their efficient – though bureaucratic – management; a form of management that is to be developed out of the principles used under capitalism in the efficient conduct of large (internationally oriented) enterprises. Equally well, as we currently experience in the service sector (both for industrial production as well as for private consumption), there may be sufficient room for the dynamic entrepreneur of the Schumpeterian type, in particular through the flexible entry and exit conditions the flexicurity variant of capitalism may allow for.

It is certainly true that contemporaneous capitalism (often of the ruthless type, but in certain countries also of a socially acceptable kind) is not likely to be forced into a defensive position, at least regarding its performance on the goods and on the labor markets (though the current operation of financial markets may produce extremely undesirable results). Yet, the consciousness that ruthless, unrestricted capitalism is producing significant negative external social and environmental effects is increasing throughout the world economy and this gives the hope that an alternative form of capitalism – based on flexicurity principles – may be superior in its socio-economic performance, at least when approached in the state of maturity as was already considered a necessity in Schumpeter's vision of a democratic society based on competitive socialism.

To a certain degree this alternative variety of capitalism is also of a ruthless type, if Schumpeterian creative destruction processes are allowed for, but as in any democratic society there are of course more or less close limits to the choice of techniques (for example in bio-genetics) and the choice of products (for example in war-games); limits that are to be set by the elected political leadership of each country.

Marx viewed the general law of capital accumulation and its perpetual reserve army mechanism as the element that not only allowed, but was also needed for the reproduction of capitalism. Schumpeter considered changes towards a competitive socialism as a possible alternative to the form of capitalism of his times. We think that there is a chance for an alternative to current forms of ruthless capitalism that not only adopts some welfare principles, but that is founded on a coherently based socio-economic structure that is socially accepted, but that is flexible enough to quickly adjust to the changing world market conditions. The foundations are social acceptance in an educated democratic society. The problems are given by the mastering of Keynesian types of business fluctuations and Schumpeterian types of creative process and product revolutions and – of course – of the control of financial markets such that the real activities of an economy do not just become the side-product of a casino as was already observed in Keynes's (1936) *General Theory*.

There are of course many micro problems to be solved on the way towards a proper working model of the Schumpeterian process of creative destruction in the flexicurity economy; problems that have been only touched upon in our presentations of a very simple model of flexicurity capitalism. There are also many macro problems to be solved on the way, since Keynesian effective demand constraints may lead to unwanted fluctuations in the industrial sector of the economy, caused by malfunctions in the financial sector of the economy in particular. It is far from clear at the present stage of our investigation whether these micro and macro problems can indeed all be coped with on the way to a well-educated democratic society which provides income and employment guarantees (and therewith interrelated obligations), but no job guarantees, but also significant job discontinuities coupled with a process of lifelong learning.

In this section we have briefly discussed a way in which nominal credit can be introduced into KMGT growth based on flexicurity type labor market institutions, and against this background a route that leads from Schumpeterian creative destruction via his vision of a competitive type of socialism to the current debate on flexicurity capitalism. This is a scenario that needs more thorough investigation, but that must be left for future research here.

11.7 The Road Ahead: Social Capitalism

There is a long tradition in economic thinking that suggests the cleansing effects of (great) depressions as the main mechanism to generate a new long-lasting boom period with new institutions, strong growth and higher employment. The late Robert Heilbroner, a student of Joseph Schumpeter and an eminent economist himself, teaching at the Graduate Faculty of the New School for Social Research, used to cite remarks that Schumpeter made in his lectures: 'A recession is like a cold dush'. Of course the word 'dush' was wrongly translated by Schumpeter from the German word 'Dusche' and actually he meant '...a cold shower'. But this expresses what many market economists and in particular Schumpeterians believe: significant busts have cleansing effects in removing disproportions in industrial development, in income distribution (where labor has become too self-confident and demanding), imbalances in the number of firms in an industry, imbalances in the relationship between real and financial development and imbalances in international economic relationships, such as the trade account. Moreover, significant institutional change may come about in the attempt to solve the contradictions in the observed crisis of the financial–industrial structure of the economy.

Indeed, this notion of the 'cleansing effect of busts' has been known since the 19th century in business cycle theory and is also not far from how Karl Marx viewed the dynamics of capitalist economies which correct themselves through large swings in unemployment and through economic crises, in particular through long-phased distributive cycles. The current worldwide crisis in the financial–industrial structure is of such a great significance that the chance is given, at least for some countries, to reshape their socio-economic structure to such an extent that the deregulations in labor markets (atypical or low income work and their consequences for the life-course perspectives of households), systemic instabilities in financial markets (where a casino type of behavior has become established) and the deformations in the political system of a country can all (attempt to) be replaced by a coherent new social structure of capital accumulation, an encompassing structure one might briefly call 'Social Capitalism'.

Looking at the current worldwide crisis, it seems that the opportunity to create a progress path towards such a socio-economic structure is given now, which is much more promising than the standard IMF policies that attempt to put certain countries just back on the track – a track without much innovative potential that, therefore, does not really solve the societal problems of the countries concerned. Social capitalism by contrast embeds Schumpeterian creative destruction into a regulated river bed of Schumpeterian process and product innovations, embedded in a social surrounding that allows for proper life-course perspectives of the households of the society, is based on citizenship education, skill formation and processes of lifelong learning, and is conducted by educated and responsibly behaving elites (elected executive persons in the economic, social and political structure of the considered society). This social capitalism project is certainly a very ambitious one, some might say an utopian one, but we view a progress path to such a society as inevitable, since the alternative of sticking to the current financial–capitalist mode of production will only lead the world into further economic, financial, ecological and political crises (and to the dissolution of the current form of Western democracies) in the longer run. There is thus an urgent need for radical change, encompassing all types of capital (real, financial, human, social and cultural) and the possibility of such far-reaching change is within reach when the current crises of capitalism and the political climate this has generated is grasped as a 'cleansing' opportunity.

In this book we have described the progress from welfare states of Christian- or social-democratic type towards flexicurity economies. In closing this project we feel, however, that there is a need to go beyond this largely economically-oriented understanding of flexicurity systems towards a societal structure we would now characterize as 'Social Capitalism'. This structure is built around an economy characterized by Schumpeterian creative destruction and has eliminated the Marxian reserve army mechanism, still conceived by many to be needed for maintaining economic and social stability through the threat of unemployment. By contrast; we believe that insight into the working of this mechanism under past and current capitalism can establish a cooperative regime between the elites that control the private enterprises and the representatives of the employees that overcomes the role of unemployment as a disciplining device in the establishment of social capitalism. Moreover, such a new social structure of capital accumulation can be based on the parties in the middle of the political spectrum, like Christian- and social-democrats and, thus, allows us to overcome in the further evolution of Western type capitalist societies the extreme views of the neo-liberals (laisser faire) as well as of the new left socialists, who believe that societies that do not internalize the productive forces of capitalism, and which are subject to some sort of social 'planification' in all of its sectors, are a realistic alternative and the better possibility for organizing a democratic society.

We, however, support the view that modern societies will continue to be mixed ones, where the planning experience of small, medium-sized and large capitalistic firms is operating in a strictly competitive private sector, surrounded by a public sector which is built on the following three pillars:

1. Households' life-course perspectives: Employment, income, medicare and care for the elderly.
2. The educational system: Equal opportunities, skill formation, lifelong learning and citizenship education.
3. Elected executive persons: Democratic competition for political leadership and for executive power in firms.

The central idea, therefore, is that the fertile possibilities of capitalism (its forces of production) can be embedded into a social structure of capital accumulation (its relations of production) which makes this type of social capitalism a highly productive and truly humanistic one.

Notes

[1] See Chiarella, Flaschel, Groh and Semmler (2000) for the treatment of neoclassical smooth factor substitution.

[2] This rate can be assumed to be augmented by Harrod-neutral technical change in the usual way, in which case all state variables have to be measured relative to the trend in labor productivity.

[3] C_2, C_r the consumption of workers working in the second labor market and the consumption of officially retired persons, respectively.

[4] See Sargent (1987) for another application of this assumption.

[5] All principal minors then have the correct signs and the composite Routh–Hurwitz term $a_1a_2 - a_3$ is positive, since $a_3 = \det J$ is dominated by a_1a_2.

[6] A transactions tax on both purchases and selling would presumably lower the parameter β_e and thus lead to a different dynamical system to be investigated in future research.

[7] Where $q = 1$ holds.

Some Useful Stability Theorems

1. The Concepts of Local Stability and Global Stability in a System of Differential Equations

Let $\dot{x} \equiv \frac{dx}{dt} = f(x), \quad x \in R^n$ be a system of n-dimensional differential equations that has an equilibrium point x^* such that $f(x^*) = 0$, where t is interpreted as 'time'. The equilibrium point of this system is said to be *locally asymptotically stable*, if every trajectory starting sufficiently near the equilibrium point converges to it as $t \to +\infty$. If stability is independent of the distance of the initial state from the equilibrium point, the equilibrium point is said to be *globally asymptotically stable*, or *asymptotically stable in the large* (see Gandolfo 1996, p.333).

2. Theorems that are Useful for the Stability Analysis of a System of Linear Differential Equations or the Local Stability Analysis of a System of Nonlinear Differential Equations

Theorem A.1 (Local Stability/Instability Theorem, see Gandolfo 1996, pp.360–362)

Let $\dot{x}_i = f_i(x)$, $x = [x_1, x_2, \cdots, x_n] \in R^n \mid (i = 1, 2, \cdots, n)$ be an n-dimensional system of differential equations that has an equilibrium point $x^* = [x_1^*, x_2^*, \cdots, x_n^*]$ such that $f(x^*) = 0$. Suppose that the functions f_i have continuous first-order partial derivatives, and consider the Jacobian matrix evaluated *at the equilibrium point* x^*

$$J = \begin{bmatrix} f_{11} & f_{12} & \cdots & f_{1n} \\ f_{21} & f_{22} & \cdots & f_{2n} \\ \vdots & \vdots & \ddots & \vdots \\ f_{n1} & f_{n2} & \cdots & f_{nn} \end{bmatrix},$$

where $f_{ij} = \partial f_i/\partial x_j$ $(i, j = 1, 2, \cdots, n)$ are evaluated at the equilibrium point.

(i) The equilibrium point of this system is locally asymptotically stable if all the roots of the characteristic equation $|\lambda I - J| = 0$ have negative real parts.

(ii) The equilibrium point of this system is unstable if at least one root of the characteristic equation $|\lambda I - J| = 0$ has positive real part.

(iii) The stability of the equilibrium point cannot be determined from the properties of the Jacobian matrix if all the roots of the characteristic equation $|\lambda I - J| = 0$ have non-positive real parts but at least one root has zero real part.

Theorem A.2 (See Murata 1977, pp.14–16)

Let A be an $(n \times n)$ matrix such that

$$A = \begin{bmatrix} a_{11} & a_{12} & \cdots & a_{1n} \\ a_{21} & a_{22} & \cdots & a_{2n} \\ \vdots & \vdots & \ddots & \vdots \\ a_{n1} & a_{n2} & \cdots & a_{nn} \end{bmatrix}.$$

(i) We can express the characteristic equation $|\lambda I - A| = 0$ as

$$\begin{aligned} |\lambda I - A| =& \lambda^n + a_1\lambda^{n-1} + a_2\lambda^{n-2} + \cdots + a_r\lambda^{n-r} + \cdots + \\ & a_{n-1}\lambda + a_n = 0, \end{aligned} \tag{A.1}$$

where

$$a_1 = -(trace A) = -\sum_{i=1}^{n} a_{ii}, \quad a_2 = (-1)^2 \sum_{i<j} \begin{vmatrix} a_{ii} & a_{ij} \\ a_{ji} & a_{jj} \end{vmatrix}, \cdots,$$

$$a_r = (-1)^r \sum_{i<j<\cdots<k} \underbrace{\begin{vmatrix} a_{ii} & a_{ij} & \cdots & a_{ik} \\ a_{ji} & a_{jj} & \cdots & a_{jk} \\ \vdots & \vdots & \ddots & \vdots \\ a_{ki} & a_{kj} & \cdots & a_{kk} \end{vmatrix}}_{(r)}, \cdots, \quad a_n = (-1)^n \det A.$$

(ii) Let λ_i $(i = 1, 2, \cdots, n)$ be the roots of the characteristic equation (A.1). Then, we have

$$traceJ = \sum_{i=1}^{n} a_{ii} = \sum_{i=1}^{n} \lambda_i, \quad \det A = \prod_{i=1}^{n} \lambda_i.$$

Theorem A.3 (Routh–Hurwitz Conditions for Stable Roots in an n-dimensional System, see Murata 1977, p.92; Gandolfo 1996, pp.221–222)[8]

All of the roots of the characteristic equation (A.1) have negative real parts *if and only if* the following set of inequalities is satisfied:

$$\Delta_1 = a_1 > 0, \quad \Delta_2 = \begin{vmatrix} a_1 & a_3 \\ 1 & a_2 \end{vmatrix} > 0, \quad \Delta_3 = \begin{vmatrix} a_1 & a_3 & a_5 \\ 1 & a_2 & a_4 \\ 0 & a_1 & a_3 \end{vmatrix} > 0, \cdots,$$

$$\Delta_n = \begin{vmatrix} a_1 & a_3 & a_5 & a_7 & \cdots & 0 \\ 1 & a_2 & a_4 & a_6 & \cdots & 0 \\ 0 & a_1 & a_3 & a_5 & \cdots & 0 \\ 0 & 1 & a_2 & a_4 & \cdots & 0 \\ 0 & 0 & a_1 & a_3 & \cdots & 0 \\ \vdots & \vdots & \vdots & \vdots & \ddots & \vdots \\ 0 & 0 & 0 & 0 & \cdots & a_n \end{vmatrix} > 0.$$

The following Theorems A.4–A.6 are corollaries of Theorem A.3.

Theorem A.4 (Routh–Hurwitz Conditions for a Two-dimensional System)

All of the roots of the characteristic equation

$$\lambda^2 + a_1\lambda + a_2 = 0$$

have negative real parts *if and only if* the set of inequalities

$$a_1 > 0, \quad a_2 > 0$$

is satisfied.

Theorem A.5 (Routh–Hurwitz Conditions for a Three-dimensional System)

All of the roots of the characteristic equation

$$\lambda^3 + a_1\lambda^2 + a_2\lambda + a_3 = 0$$

have negative real parts *if and only if* the set of inequalities

$$a_1 > 0, \quad a_3 > 0, \quad a_1a_2 - a_3 > 0 \tag{A.2}$$

is satisfied.

Remark on Theorem A.5:

The inequality $a_2 > 0$ is always satisfied if the set of inequalities (A.2) is satisfied.

Theorem A.6 (Routh–Hurwitz Conditions for a Four-dimensional System)

All roots of the characteristic equation

$$\lambda^4 + a_1\lambda^3 + a_2\lambda^2 + a_3\lambda + a_4 = 0$$

have negative real parts *if and only if* the set of inequalities

$$a_1 > 0, \quad a_3 > 0, \quad a_4 > 0, \quad \Phi \equiv a_1a_2a_3 - a_1^2a_4 - a_3^2 > 0 \tag{A.3}$$

is satisfied.

Remark on Theorem A.6:

The inequality $a_2 > 0$ is always satisfied if the set of inequalities (A.3) is satisfied.

3. Theorems that are Useful for the Global Stability Analysis of a System of Nonlinear Differential equations

Theorem A.7 (Liapunov's Theorem, see Gandolfo 1996, p.410)

Let $\dot{x} = f(x), x = [x_1, x_2, \cdots, x_n] \in R^n$ be an n-dimensional system of differential equations that has the unique equilibrium point $x^* = [x_1^*, x_2^*, \cdots, x_n^*]$ such that $f(x^*) = 0$. Suppose that there exists a scalar function $V = V(x - x^*)$ with continuous first derivatives and with the following properties (1)–(5):

(1) $V \geqq 0$,

(2) $V = 0$ if and only if $x_i - x_i^* = 0$ for all $i \in \{1, 2, \cdots n\}$,

(3) $V \to +\infty$ as $\|x - x^*\| \to +\infty$,

(4) $\dot{V} = \sum_{i=1}^{n} \frac{\partial V}{\partial(x_i - x_i^*)} \dot{x}_i \leqq 0$,

(5) $\dot{V} = 0$ if and only if $x_i - x_i* = 0$ for all $i \in \{1, 2, \cdots, n\}$.

Then, the equilibrium point x^* of the above system is globally asymptotically stable.

Remark on Theorem A.7:

The function $V = V(x - x^*)$ is called the 'Liapunov function'.

Theorem A.8 (Olech's Theorem, see Olech 1963; Gandolfo 1996, pp.354–355)

Let $\dot{x}_i = f_i(x_1, x_2)(i = 1, 2)$ be a two-dimensional system of differential equations that has the unique equilibrium point (x_1^*, x_2^*) such that $f_i(x_1^*, x_2^*) = 0$ $(i = 1, 2)$. Suppose that the functions f_i have continuous first-order partial derivatives. Furthermore, suppose that the following properties (1) – (3) are satisfied:

(1) $\frac{\partial f_1}{\partial x_1} + \frac{\partial f_2}{\partial x_2} < 0$ everywhere,

(2) $(\frac{\partial f_1}{\partial x_1})(\frac{\partial f_2}{\partial x_2}) - (\frac{\partial f_1}{\partial x_2})(\frac{\partial f_2}{\partial x_1}) > 0$ everywhere,

(3) $(\frac{\partial f_1}{\partial x_1})(\frac{\partial f_2}{\partial x_2}) \neq 0$ everywhere, or alternatively, $(\frac{\partial f_1}{\partial x_2})(\frac{\partial f_2}{\partial x_1}) \neq 0$ everywhere.

Then, the equilibrium point of the above system is globally asymptotically stable.

4. Theorems that are Useful to Establish the Existence of Closed Orbits in a System of Nonlinear Differential Equations

Theorem A.9 (Poincaré–Bendixson Theorem, see Hirsch and Smale 1974, ch.11)

Let $\dot{x}_i = f_i(x_1, x_2)(i = 1, 2)$ be a two-dimensional system of differential equations with the functions f_i continuous. A nonempty compact limit set of the trajectory of this system, which contains no equilibrium point, is a closed orbit.

Theorem A.10 (Hopf Bifurcation Theorem for an n-dimensional System, see Guckenheimer and Holmes 1983, pp.151–152; Lorenz 1993, p.96 and Gandolfo 1996, p.477)[9]

Let $\dot{x} = f(x;\varepsilon), x \in R^n, \varepsilon \in R$ be an n-dimensional system of differential equations depending upon a parameter ε. Suppose that the following conditions (1)–(3) are satisfied:

(1) The system has a smooth curve of equilibria given by $f(x^*(\varepsilon);\varepsilon) = 0$.

(2) The characteristic equation $|\lambda I - Df(x^*(\varepsilon_0);\varepsilon_0)| = 0$ has a pair of purely imaginary roots $\lambda(\varepsilon_0), \bar{\lambda}(\varepsilon_0)$ and no other roots with zero real parts, where $Df(x^*(\varepsilon_0);\varepsilon_0)$ is the Jacobian matrix of the above system at $(x^*(\varepsilon_0), \varepsilon_0)$ with the parameter value ε_0.

(3) $\frac{d\{Re\lambda(\varepsilon)\}}{d\varepsilon}\Big|_{\varepsilon=\varepsilon_0} \neq 0$, where $Re\lambda(\varepsilon)$ is the real part of $\lambda(\varepsilon)$.

Then, there exists a continuous function $\varepsilon(\gamma)$ with $\varepsilon(0) = \varepsilon_0$, and for all sufficiently small values of $\gamma \neq 0$ there exists a continuous family of non-constant periodic solution $x(t,\gamma)$ for the above dynamical system, which collapses to the equilibrium point $x^*(\varepsilon_0)$ as $\gamma \to 0$. The period of the cycle is close to $2\pi/Im\lambda(\varepsilon_0)$, where $Im\lambda(\varepsilon_0)$ is the imaginary part of $\lambda(\varepsilon_0)$.

Remark on Theorem A.10:

We can replace the condition (3) in Theorem A.10 by the following weaker condition (3a) (see Alexander and York 1978).

(3a) For all ε which are near but not equal to ε_0, no characteristic root has zero real part.

The following theorem by Liu (1994) provides a convenient criterion for the occurrence of the so called ‘simple’ Hopf bifurcation in an n-dimensional system. The ‘simple’ Hopf bifurcation is defined as the Hopf bifurcation in which all the characteristic roots *except* a pair of purely imaginary ones have negative real parts.

Theorem A.11 (Liu's Theorem, see Liu 1994)

Consider the following characteristic equation with $n \geqq 3$:

$$\lambda^n + a_1\lambda^{n-1} + a_2\lambda_{n-2} + \cdots + a_{n-1}\lambda + a_n = 0.$$

This characteristic equation has a pair of purely imaginary roots and $(n-2)$ roots with negative real parts *if and only if* the following set of conditions is satisfied:

$$\Delta_i > 0 \text{ for all } i \in \{1, 2, \cdots, n-2\}, \quad \Delta_{n-1} = 0, \quad a_n > 0,$$

where $\Delta_i (i = 1, 2, \cdots, n-1)$ are Routh–Hurwitz terms defined as

$$\Delta_1 = a_1, \quad \Delta_2 = \begin{vmatrix} a_1 & a_3 \\ 1 & a_2 \end{vmatrix}, \quad \Delta_3 = \begin{vmatrix} a_1 & a_3 & a_5 \\ 1 & a_2 & a_4 \\ 0 & a_1 & a_3 \end{vmatrix}, \cdots,$$

$$\Delta_{n-1} = \begin{vmatrix} a_1 & a_3 & a_5 & a_7 & \cdots & 0 & 0 \\ 1 & a_2 & a_4 & a_6 & \cdots & 0 & 0 \\ 0 & a_1 & a_3 & a_5 & \cdots & 0 & 0 \\ 0 & 1 & a_2 & a_4 & \cdots & 0 & 0 \\ 0 & 0 & a_1 & a_3 & \cdots & 0 & 0 \\ \vdots & \vdots & \vdots & \vdots & \ddots & \vdots & \vdots \\ 0 & 0 & 0 & 0 & \cdots & a_n & 0 \\ 0 & 0 & 0 & 0 & \cdots & a_{n-1} & 0 \\ 0 & 0 & 0 & 0 & \cdots & a_{n-2} & a_n \\ 0 & 0 & 0 & 0 & \cdots & a_{n-3} & a_{n-1} \end{vmatrix}.$$

The following theorems A.12–A.14 provide us with some convenient criteria for two-dimensional, three-dimensional and four-dimensional Hopf bifurcations respectively. It is worth noting that these criteria provide us with useful information on the 'non-simple' as well as the 'simple' Hopf bifurcations.

Theorem A.12

The characteristic equation

$$\lambda^2 + a_1\lambda + a_2 = 0$$

has a pair of purely imaginary roots *if and only if* the set of conditions

$$a_1 = 0, \quad a_2 > 0$$

is satisfied. In this case, we have the explicit solution $\lambda = \pm i\sqrt{a_2}$, where $i = \sqrt{-1}$.

Proof: Obvious because we have the solution $\lambda = (-a_1 \pm \sqrt{a_1^2 - 4a_2})/2$.

Theorem A.13 (see Asada 1995; Asada and Semmler 1995)

The characteristic equation

$$\lambda^3 + a_1\lambda^2 + a_2\lambda + a_3 = 0$$

has a pair of purely imaginary roots *if and only if* the set of conditions

$$a_2 > 0, \quad a_1a_2 - a_3 = 0,$$

is satisfied. In this case, we have the explicit solution $\lambda = -a_1, \ \pm i\sqrt{a_2}$, where $i = \sqrt{-1}$.

Theorem A.14 (see Yoshida and Asada 2001; Asada and Yoshida 2003)

Consider the characteristic equation

$$\lambda^4 + a_1\lambda^3 + a_2\lambda^2 + a_3\lambda + a_4 = 0. \tag{A.4}$$

(i) The characteristic equation (A.4) has a pair of purely imaginary roots and two roots with non-zero real parts *if and only if* either of the following set of conditions (A) or (B) is satisfied:

(A) $a_1a_3 > 0, \quad a_4 \neq 0, \quad \Phi \equiv a_1a_2a_3 - a_1^2a_4 - a_3^2 = 0.$

(B) $a_1 = a_3 = 0, \quad a_4 < 0.$

(ii) The characteristic equation (A.4) has a pair of purely imaginary roots and two roots with negative real parts *if and only if* the following set of conditions (C) is satisfied:

(C) $a_1 > 0, \quad a_3 > 0, \quad a_4 > 0, \quad \Phi \equiv a_1a_2a_3 - a_1^2a_4 - a_3^2 = 0.$

Remarks on Theorem A.14:

(1) The condition $\Phi = 0$ is always satisfied if the set of conditions (B) is satisfied.

(2) The inequality $a_2 > 0$ is always satisfied if the set of conditions (C) is satisfied.

(3) We can derive Theorem A.14 (ii) from Theorem A.11 as a special case with $n = 4$, although we cannot derive Theorem A.14 (i) from Theorem A.11.

Notes

[8] See also Gantmacher (1954) for many details that can be associated with and Brock and Malliaris (1989) for a compact representation of these conditions.

[9] See also Strogatz (1994), Wiggins (1990) in this regard.

Notes

[8] See also Gantmacher (1954) for many details that can be associated with and Brock and Malliaris (1989) for a compact representation of these conditions.

[9] See also Strogatz (1994), Wiggins (1990) in this regard.

Data Sources

Data are taken from Groth and Madsen (2007):

Unemployment (Figures 3.1 and 8.1)

1899–1930: Romer, C. (1986), 'Spurious Volatility in Historical Unemployment Data', *Journal of Political Economy*, **94**, 1–37.
1931–39: Darby, M.R. (1976), 'Three and a Half Million US Employees have been Misled: Or, an Explanation of Unemployment', *Journal of Political Economy*, **84**, 1–16.
1940–2001: BEA. Tobin's q. Andrew Smithers and Stephen Wright, 2000, *Valuing Wall Street*, NY: McGraw-Hill.

Labor's Income Share (Figures 3.1, 8.1 and 10.1)

Manufacturing data are used except over the periods 1899–1918 and 1935–1959, where data for the corporate non-agricultural sector are used.
1899–1909 and 1935–1949: Martin, R.F. (1939), 'National Income in the United States: 1799–1938', National Industrial Conference Board Studies, No 241, NY.
1909–1919: Schuller, G.J. (1953), 'The Secular Trend in Income Distribution By Type, 1869–1948: A Preliminary Estimate', *Review of Economics and Statistics*, 302–324, based on King's estimates.
1919–1934: Kuznets, S. (1975), *National Income and Capital Formation 1919–1935*, NY: Arno Press.
1850–1950: Liesner, T. (1989), *One Hundred Years of Economic Statistics*, Oxford: The Economist, Table US. 6. Investment and capital stock.

References

Abreu, D. and M. Brunnermeier (2003), 'Bubbles and crashes', *Econometrica*, **71**, 173–204.

Amann, H. (1983), *Gewöhnliche Differentialgleichungen*, Berlin, New York: de Gruyter.

Alexander, J.C. and J.A. York (1978), 'Global bifurcation of periodic orbits', *American Journal of Mathematics*, **100**, 263–292.

Arrow, K.J. and M. Kurz (1970), *Public Investment, the Rate of Return, and Optimal Fiscal Policy*, Baltimore: The John Hopkins Press.

Arrowsmith, D.K. and C.M. Place (1982), *Ordinary Differential Equations*, London: Chapman and Hall.

Asada, T. (1995), 'Kaldorian dynamics in an open economy', *Journal of Economics*, **62**, 239–269.

Asada, T., Chiarella, C., Flaschel, P., Mouakil, T., Proaño, C. and W. Semmler (2010), 'Stabilizing an unstable economy: On the choice of proper policy measures', *Economics: The Open-Access, Open-Assessment E-journal*, **4**, 2010-21, http://www.economics-ejournal.org/economics/journalarticles/2010-21 (read: 7-16-2010).

Asada, T., Flaschel, P., Chiarella, C. and R. Franke (2010), *Monetary Macrodynamics*, London: Routledge.

Asada, T., Flaschel, P., Greiner, A. and C.R. Proaño (2011), 'Sustainable capitalism: Full-employment flexicurity growth with real wage rigidities', *Journal of Economic Behavior and Organization*, forthcoming.

Asada, T. and W. Semmler (1995), 'Growth and finance: an intertemporal model', *Journal of Macroeconomics*, **17**, 623–649.

Asada, T. and H. Yoshida (2003), 'Coefficient criterion for four-dimensional Hopf bifurcations: a complete mathematical characterization and applications to economic dynamics', *Chaos, Solitons & Fractals*, **18**(3), 525–536.

Barro, R.J. (1979), 'On the determination of public debt', *Journal of Political Economy*, **87**, 940–971.

Barro, R.J. and X. Sala-i-Martin (1995), *Economic Growth*, New York: McGraw-Hill.

Beauchemin, K.R. (2001), 'Growth or stagnation? The role of public education', *Journal of Development Economics*, **64**, 389–416.

Benhabib, J. and Roger E.A. Farmer (1994), 'Indeterminacy and increasing returns', *Journal of Economic Theory*, **63**(1), 19–41.

Blanchard, O. and S. Fischer (1989), *Lectures on Macroeconomics*, Cambridge, MA: The MIT Press.

Blanchard, O. and L. Katz (1999), 'Wage dynamics: Reconciling theory and evidence', *American Economic Review*, Papers and Proceedings, **89**, 69–74.

Blankenau, W.F. and N.B. Simpson (2004), 'Public education, expenditures and growth', *Journal of Development Economics*, **73**, 583–605.

Bohn, H. (1995), 'The sustainability of budget deficits in a stochastic economy', *Journal of Money, Credit and Banking*, **27**, 257–271.

Bosch, G. and T. Kalina (2007), 'Niedriglöhne in Deutschland–Zahlen, Fakten, Ursachen', in G. Bosch and C. Weinkopf (eds), *Arbeiten für wenig Geld–Niedriglohnbeschäftigung in Deutschland*, Frankfurt/Main: Campus Verlag, pp. 20–105.

Bowles, S., Gordon, D. and T.E. Weisskopf (1983), *Beyond the Waste Land*, New York: Anchor Press.

Brunnermeier, M. (2009), 'Bubbles', in S. Durlauf and L. Blume (eds), *The New Palgrave Dictionary of Economics*, 2nd edition, New York: Palgrave.

Chiarella, C. and P. Flaschel (2000a), *The Dynamics of Keynesian Monetary Growth: Macro Foundations*, Cambridge, UK: Cambridge University Press.

Chiarella, C., Flaschel, P. Groh, G. and W. Semmler (2000), *Disequilibrium, Growth and Labor Market Dynamics. Macro Perspectives*, Berlin, Heidelberg: Springer.

Corsetti, G. and N. Roubini (1996), 'Optimal government spending and taxation in endogenous growth models', NBER Working Paper 5851.

Council (2002), 'Council resolution of 27 June 2002 on lifelong learning', in *Official Journal of the European Communities C 163/1*, (http://eur-lex.europa.eu/LexUriServ/LexUriServ.do?uri=OJ:C:2002:163:0001:0003:EN:PDF)(read 11-18-2007).

Dhooge, A., Govaerts, W., Kuznetsov, Y.A., Maestrom, W. and A.M. Riet (2003), 'CL_MATCONT: A continuation toolbox in Matlab', in *Proceedings of the 2003 ACM Symposium on Applied Computing* (Melbourne, Florida, USA, March 2003), 161–166.

Domar, E.D. (1946), 'Capital expansion, rate of growth, and employment', *Econometrica*, **14**, 137–147.

Esping-Anderson, G. (1990), *The Three Worlds of Welfare Capitalism*, Cambridge, UK: Cambridge University Press.

Ewijk, Casper van (1991), *On the Dynamics of Growth and Debt*, Oxford: Oxford University Press.

Flaschel, P. (1984), 'Some stability properties of Goodwin's growth cycle model', *Zeitschrift für Nationalökonomie*, **44**, 63–69.

Flaschel, P. (2009), *The Macrodynamics of Capitalism. Elements for a Synthesis of Marx, Keynes and Schumpeter*, 2nd edition, Heidelberg: Springer Verlag.

Flaschel, P., Franke, R. and W. Semmler (1997), *Dynamic Macroeconomics: Instability, Fluctuations and Growth in Monetary Economies*, Cambridge, MA: The MIT Press.

Flaschel, P., Franke, R. and W. Semmler (2008), 'Kaleckian investment and employment cycles in postwar industrialized economies', in P. Flaschel and M. Landesmann (eds), *Mathematical Economics and the Dynamics of Capitalism*, London: Routledge, 35–65.

Flaschel, P. and A. Greiner (2008), 'Employment cycles and minimum wages: A macro view', *Structural Change and Economic Dynamics*, **20**(4), 279–287.

Flaschel, P. and A. Greiner (2011), 'Dual labor markets and the impact of minimum wages on atypical employment', *Metroeconomica*, forthcoming.

Flaschel, P. and A. Greiner (2011a), *Flexicurity Capitalism. Foundations, Problems, Perspectives*, New York: Oxford University Press.

Flaschel, P., Greiner, A. and S. Luchtenberg (2008), 'Flexicurity capitalism', in H. Gischer, P. Reichling, T. Spengler and A. Wenig (eds), *Transformation in der Ökonomie*, Wiesbaden: Gabler Edition Wissenschaft, pp. 45–66.

Flaschel, P., Greiner, A., Luchtenberg, S. and E. Nell (2008), 'Varieties of capitalism: The flexicurity model', in P. Flaschel and M. Landesmann (eds), *Mathematical Economics and the Dynamics of Capitalism*, London: Routledge, pp. 76–104.

Flaschel, P., Greiner, A. and S. Luchtenberg (2010), 'Labor Market Institutions and the Role of Elites in Flexicurity Societies', Working Paper, No. 150, Bielefeld University: Center for Empirical Macro- and Microeconomics (CEMM), *Review of Political Economy*, forthcoming.

Flaschel, P., Greiner, A., Logeay, C. and C. Proaño (2010), 'Employment Cycles, Low Income Work and the Dynamic Impact of Minimum Wages. A Macro Perspective', Working Paper, No. 149, Bielefeld University: Center for Empirical Macro- and Microeconomics (CEMM), *Journal of Evolutionary Economics*, forthcoming.

Flaschel, P. and G. Groh (1995), 'The Classical growth cycle: Reformulation, simulation and some facts', *Economic Notes*, **24**, 1995, 293–326.

Flaschel, P. and H.-M. Krolzig (2006), 'Wage–price Phillips curves and macroeconomic stability: Basic structural form, estimation and analysis', in C. Chiarella, Flaschel, P., Franke R. and W. Semmler (eds), *Quantitative and Empirical Analysis of Nonlinear Dynamic Macromodels. Contributions to Economic Analysis*, Series Editors: B. Baltagi, E. Sadka and D. Wildasin, Amsterdam: Elsevier, pp. 4–48.

Flaschel, P., Tavani, D., Taylor, L. and T. Teuber (2011), 'Estimated non-linearities and multiple equilibria in a model of distributive-demand cycles', *International Review of Applied Economics*, forthcoming.

Foley, D. and L. Taylor (2006), 'A heterodox growth and distribution model', in N. Salvadori (ed.), *Economic Growth and Distribution: On the Nature and Cause of the Wealth of Nations*, Cheltenham, UK and Northampton, MA, USA: Edward Elgar, pp. 75–99.

Franke, R. (1996), 'A Metzlerian model of inventory growth cycles', *Structural Change and Economic Dynamics*, **7**, 243–262.

Franke, R. and W. Semmler (1999), 'Bond rate, loan rate and Tobin's q in a temporary equilibrium model of the financial sector', *Metroeconomica*, **50**, 351–385.

Futagami, K., Morita, Y. and A. Shibata (1993), 'Dynamic analysis of an endogenous growth model with public capital', *Scandinavian Journal of Economics*, **95**, 607–625.

Futagami, K., Iwaisako T. and R. Ohdoi (2006), 'Debt policy rule, productive government spending, and multiple growth paths', *Macroeconomic Dynamics*, **12**(4), 445–462.

Gantmacher, F.R. (1954), *Theory of Matrices*, New York: Interscience Publishers.

Gandolfo, G. (1996), *Economic Dynamics*, Berlin: Springer-Verlag.

Ghosh, S. and I. Mourmouras (2004), 'Endogenous growth, welfare and budgetary regimes', *Journal of Macroeconomics*, **26**, 363–384.

Glomm, G. and B. Ravikumar (1992), 'Public versus private investment in human capital: Endogenous growth and income distribution', *Journal of Political Economy*, **100**, 818–834.

Godley, W. (1999), 'Money and credit in a Keynesian model of income determination', *Cambridge Journal of Economics*, **23**(2), 393–411.

Goodwin, R. (1967), 'A growth cycle', in: C.H. Feinstein (ed.), *Socialism, Capitalism and Economic Growth*, Cambridge: Cambridge University Press, pp. 54–58.

Greiner, A. (2007), 'An endogenous growth model with public capital and sustainable government debt', *Japanese Economic Review*, **58**, 345–361.

Greiner, A. (2008), 'Human capital formation, public debt and economic growth', *Journal of Macroeconomics*, **30**, 415–427.

Greiner, A. (2008a), 'Does it pay to have a balanced government budget', *Journal of Institutional and Theoretical Economics (JITE), Zeitschrift für die gesamte Staatswissenschaft*, **164**, 460–476.

Greiner, A. and P. Flaschel (2009), 'Economic growth and the employer of last resort: A simple model of flexicurity capitalism', *Research in Economics*, **63**(2), 102–113.

Greiner, A. and P. Flaschel (2009a), 'Economic policy in a growth model with human capital, heterogenous agents and unemployment', *Computational Economics*, **33**, 175–192.

Greiner, A. and P. Flaschel (2010), 'Public debt and public investment in an endogenous growth model with real wage rigidities', *Scottish Journal of Political Economy*, **57**, 68–89.

Greiner, A. and H. Hanusch (1998), 'Growth and welfare effects of fiscal policy in an endogenous growth model with public investment', *International Tax and Public Finance*, **5**, 249–261.

Greiner, A., Rubart J. and W. Semmler (2004), 'Economic growth, skill-biased technical change and wage inequality: A model and estimations for the US and Europe', *Journal of Macroeconomics*, **26**(4), 597–621.

Greiner, A. and W. Semmler (2000), 'Endogenous growth, government debt and budgetary regimes', *Journal of Macroeconomics*, **22**, 363–384.

Groth, C. and J.B. Madsen (2007), 'Medium-term fluctuations and the "great ratios" of economic growth', Working Paper, University of Copenhagen, (http://www.eea-esem.com/files/papers/EEA-ESEM/2006/2918/Medium-termFluctuations15-02-06.pdf).

Hanusch, H. and A. Pyka (2007), *The Elgar Companion to Neo-Schumpeterian Economics*, Cheltenham, UK and Northampton, MA, USA: Edward Elgar.

Harrod, R. (1939), 'An essay in dynamic economic theory', *The Economic Journal*, **49**, 14–33.

Hirsch, M. and S. Smale (1974), *Differential Equations, Dynamical Systems and Linear Algebra*, London: Academic Press.

Kalecki, M. (1943), 'Political aspects of full employment', Reprinted in M. Kalecki (ed.) (1971), *Selected Essays on the Dynamics of the Capitalist Economy*, Cambridge: Cambridge University Press.

Kaldor, N. (1940), 'A model of the trade cycle', *Economic Journal*, **50**, 78–92.

Kauermann, G., Teuber, T. and P. Flaschel (2007), 'Exploring US business cycles with bivariate loops using penalized spline regression', Working Paper, No. 148, Bielefeld University: Center for Empirical Macro- and Microeconomics (CEMM).

Keynes, J.M. (1936), *The General Theory of Employment, Interest and Money*, New York: Macmillan.

Klesse, H.-J. and O. Voss (2007), 'Fremder Leute Geld', *Wirtschaftswoche*, **51**, 78–85.

Köper, C. (2003), *Real–Financial Interaction in Contemporary Models of AS–AD Growth*, Bern: Peter Lang.

Krueger, A.B. and M. Lindahl (2001), 'Education for growth: Why and for whom?', *Journal of Economic Literature*, **39**, 1101–1136.

Levine, R. and D. Renelt (1992), 'A sensitivity analysis of cross-country growth regressions', *American Economic Review*, **82**, 942–963.

Liu, W.M. (1994), 'Criterion of Hopf bifurcations without using eigenvalues', *Journal of Mathematical Analysis and Applications*, **182**, 250–256.

Lucas, R.E. (1988), 'On the mechanics of economic development', *Journal of Monetary Economics*, **22**, 3–42.

Marx, K. (1954), *Capital. A Critique of Political Economy, Vol. I*, New York: Lawrence and Wishart.

Mas-Colell, A., Whinston, M.D. and J.R. Green (1995), *Microeconomic Theory*, New York: Oxford University Press.

Metzler, L.A. (1941), 'The nature and stability of inventory cycles', *Review of Economic Statistics*, **23**, 113–129.

Minsky, H.P. (1982), *Stabilizing an Unstable Economy*, New York: McGraw Hill.

Ministry of Education and Science of Sweden (2004), *Equity in education. Thematic review. Country analytical report*, Sweden, (http://www.oecd.org/dataoecd/30/22/38697408.pdf) (read 11-18-2007).

Muñoz, V. (2006), Report of the Special Rapporteur on the right to education. Vernor Muñoz, on his mission to Germany (13–21 February 2006) (http://www.netzwerk-bildungsfreiheit.de/pdf/Munoz_Mission_on_Germany.pdf (read 11-18-2007).

Murata, Y. (1977), *Mathematics for Stability and Optimization of Economic Systems*, New York: Academic Press.

Ni, S. and X. Wang (1994), 'Human capital and income taxation in an endogenous growth model', *Journal of Macroeconomics*, **16**, 493–507.

OECD (1994), *The OECD Jobs Study: Facts, Analysis, Strategies*, Paris.

OECD (2006), *The OECD Employment Outlook*, Paris.

OECD (2007), *Education at a Glance 2007*, (www.oecd.org/dataoecd/36/4/40701218.pdf).

Olech, C. (1963), 'On the global stability of an autonomous system in the plane', in P. Lasalle and P. Diaz (eds), *Contributions to Differential Equations*, **1**, 389–400.

Phillips, A.W. (1954), 'Stabilisation policy in a closed economy', *The Economic Journal*, **64**, 290–323.

Phillips, A.W. (1958), 'The relation between unemployment and the rate of change of money wage rates in the United Kingdom, 1861–1957', *Economica*, **25**, 283–299.

Rhein, T. and S. Stamm (2006), 'Niedriglohnbeschäftigung in Deutschland – deskriptive Befunde zur Entwicklung seit 1980 und Verteilung auf Berufe und Wirtschaftszweige', IAB- Forschungsbericht, Nr.12, Nürnberg: Institut für Arbeitsmarkt- und Berufsforschung (IAB).

Romer, Paul M. (1986), 'Increasing returns and long-run growth', *Journal of Political Economy*, **94**(5), 1002–1037.

Rose, H. (1967), 'On the non-linear theory of the employment cycle', *Review of Economic Studies*, **34**, 153–173.

Rose, H. (1990), *Macroeconomic Dynamics. A Marshallian Synthesis*, Cambridge, MA: Basil Blackwell.

Sala-i-Martin, X. (1997), 'I just ran two million regressions', *American Economic Review*, Papers and Proceedings, **87**, 178–183.

Samuelson, P. (1978), 'The canonical classical model of political economy', *Journal of Economic Literature*, **16** (4), 1415–1434.

Sargent, T. and N. Wallace (1975), ' "Rational" expectations, the optimal monetary policy instrument, and the optimal money supply rule', *Journal of Political Economy*, **83**(2), 241–254.

Schumpeter, J.A. (1934), *The Theory of Economic Development*, London: Oxford University Press.

Schumpeter, J.A. (1939), *Business Cycles*, Vols. I and II, Philadelphia: Porcupine Press.

Schumpeter, J.A. (1942), *Capitalism, Socialism and Democracy*, New York: Harper & Row.

Sinn, H.-W. (2007), 'Minimum wages stop the curse of history', Press Release of CESifo Institute for Economic Research, 29th October 2007.

Solow, R. (1956), 'A contribution to the theory of economic growth', *Quarterly Journal of Economics*, **70**, 65–94.

Solow, R. (1990), 'Goodwin's growth cycle: Reminiscence and rumination', in K. Velupillai (ed.), *Nonlinear and Multisectoral Macrodynamics*, London: Macmillan, pp. 31–41.

Sraffa, P. (1970), *The Works and Correspondence of David Ricardo, Vol. I: On the Principles of Political Economy and Taxation*, Cambridge: Cambridge University Press.

Swedberg, R. (1991), *Schumpeter. A Biography*, Princeton: Princeton University Press.

Tobin, J. (1969), 'A general equilibrium approach to monetary theory', *Journal of Money, Credit, and Banking*, **1**, 15–29.

Tobin, J. (1980), *Asset Accumulation and Economic Activity*, Oxford: Basil Blackwell.

Tobin, J. (1982), 'Money and the macroeconomic process', *Journal of Money, Credit and Banking*, **14**, 171–204.

Turnovsky, S. (2007), 'The role of factor substitution in the theory of economic growth and income distribution', *Journal of Macroeconomics*, **30**, 604–629.

Uzawa, H. (1965), 'Optimum technical change in an aggregative model of economic growth', *International Economic Review*, **6**, 18–31.

Vis, B. (2007), 'States of welfare or states of workfare? Welfare state restructuring in 16 capitalist democracies, 1985–2002', *Policy & Politics*, **35**, 105–122.

Wilthagen, T, Tros, F. and H. van Lieshout (2004), 'Towards "flexicurity"?: Balancing flexibility and security in EU member states', *European Journal of Social Security*, **6**(2), 113–136.

Wirl, Franz (1997), 'Stability and limit cycles in one-dimensional dynamic optimistaions of competitive agents with a market externallity', *Journal of Evolutionary Economics*, **7**(1), 73–89.

Wörgötter, A. (1986), 'Who's who in Goodwin's growth cycle', *Jahrbuch für Nationalökonomie und Statistik*, **201**, 222–228.

Yoshida, H. and T. Asada (2001), 'Dynamic analysis of policy lag in a Keynes–Goodwin Model : Stability, instability, cycles and chaos', Working Paper No. 21, Bielefeld University: Center for Empirical Macro- and Microeconomics (CEMM).

Zezza G. and C. Dos Santos (2004), 'The role of monetary policy in post-Keynesian stock–flow consistent macroeconomic growth models', in M. Lavoie and M. Seccarecia (eds), *Central Banking in the Modern World: Alternatives Perspectives*, Cheltenham, UK and Northampton, MA, USA: Edward Elgar.

Zhou, J. (2007), 'Danish for all? Balancing flexibility with security: The flexicurity model', IMF Working Paper No. 07/36.

Author Index

Index